Microsoft®

Internet Explorer 5
Resource Kit

Microsoft Press

PUBLISHED BY
Microsoft Press
A Division of Microsoft Corporation
One Microsoft Way
Redmond, Washington 98052-6399

Library of Congress Cataloging-in-Publication Data
Microsoft Internet Explorer 5 Resource Kit / Microsoft Corporation.
    p. cm.
  Includes index.
  ISBN 0-7356-0587-4
  1. Microsoft Windows Internet Explorer.   2. Internet (Computer network)
  3. World Wide Web (information retrieval system)   4. Browsers
(Computer programs)   I. Microsoft Corporation.
TK5105.888.M54   1998
005.7'13769--dc21

98-31160
CIP

Printed and bound in the United States of America.

1 2 3 4 5 6 7 8 9   WCWC   4 3 2 1 0 9

Distributed in Canada by ITP Nelson, a division of Thomson Canada Limited.

A CIP catalogue record for this book is available from the British Library.

Microsoft Press books are available through booksellers and distributors worldwide. For further information about international editions, contact your local Microsoft Corporation office or contact Microsoft Press International directly at fax (425) 936-7329. Visit our Web site at mspress.microsoft.com.

Macintosh, QuickTime, and TrueType are registered trademarks of Apple Computer, Inc. Intel is a registered trademark of Intel Corporation. Active Accessibility, Active Channel, Active Desktop, ActiveMovie, ActiveX, Authenticode, BackOffice, DirectAnimation, DirectShow, SirectSound, DirectX, DriveSpace, FrontPage, Hotmail, JScript, Microsoft, Microsoft Internet Explorer logo, Microsoft Press, MSDN, MS-DOS, MSN, NetMeeting, Outlook, PowerPoint, Visual Basic, Visual C++, Visual InterDev, WebBot, Win32, Windows, Windows logo, Windows NT, and Windows Start logo are either registered trademarks or trademarks of Microsoft Corporation in the United States and/or other countries. Other product and company names mentioned herein may be the trademarks of their respective owners.

The example companies, organizations, products, people, and events depicted herein are fictitious. No association with any real company, organization, product, person, or event is intended or should be inferred.

Acquisitions Editor: Juliana Aldous
Project Editor: Maureen Williams Zimmerman

Contributors

Resource Kit Lead:	Kim Parris
Book Lead:	Toni Saddler-French
Editing Lead:	Kristine Haugseth
Production Lead:	Brenda Potts
Design and Production Manager:	Crystal Nemeth
Writers:	Laura Knops Toni Saddler-French
Editors:	Susie Hunter Kristine Haugseth J.A. Deveaux
Desktop Publisher:	Pam Barrow
Indexer:	Laura Pinter
Designer:	Perry Mak
Release Manager:	Chris Overton
Technical Contributors:	Brad Aiken, Kim Akers, Nick Ball, Chris Barker, Talal Batrouny, David Beder, Eric Berman, Sarah Bowers, Quintin Burns, Larry Bynum, Frank Chang, Gordon Church, Josh Cohen, Douglas Dobbins, Jerry Drain, Micheal Dunn, Tom Edwards, Dave Fester, Robert Flaming, Juan Flowers, D.J. Franchini, Andrew Goldin, Jay Goldstein, Seetharaman Harikrishnan, Paul Harper, George Hatoun, Eric Hebenstreit, Darrin Hatakeda, Kathy Hewitt, Lotfi Herzi, Christopher Ilao, Julian Jiggins, Scott Johnson, Tim Johnson, Marilyn Johnstone, Chris Jones, Loren Kohnfelder, John Knutson, Tom Laemmel, Luanne LaLonde, Brian LaMacchia, Denise La Rue, Paul LeBlanc, Oliver Lee, Sarah Lefko, Donald Logerstedt, Andrew Mackles, Russ Madlener, Erik Mikkelson, Kevin Miller, Bradley Millington, Derek Murman, Pritvinath Obla, Kevin Otnes, Hadi Partovi, Igor Peev, Brent Ponto; Glen Richardson, Ryan Roth, Donald Rule, Andres Sanabria, Shawn Sanford, Sanjay Shenoy, Max Slade, Leighton Smith, Scott Stearns, Ray Sun, Jason Taylor, Ina Teegan, Jeff Tran, Kevin Unangst, Peter Wassmann, Linda Wells, Tom Yaryan, and Kelvin Yiu.

Contents

Welcome

This book, the Microsoft® Internet Explorer 5 Resource Kit, provides comprehensive information about planning, customizing, installing, and supporting the latest version of Internet Explorer. Material in this book has been completely rewritten since the previous version to better fit the needs of its intended audience, which is corporate administrators, Internet content providers/developers, Internet service providers, and independent software vendors. If you work in one of those roles, you'll discover that this book contains useful and compelling solutions for both deploying and customizing Internet Explorer 5 in your organization.

You can use this book as a primary source of information about Internet Explorer 5 and its installation. The technical detail, tips, strategies, and tools provided in this book make it easy and cost-efficient to customize and deploy Internet Explorer 5, both on the Internet and on the corporate intranet.

You can also read this book as a supplement to information provided in the Help systems included with Internet Explorer 5 and the Microsoft Internet Explorer Administration Kit (IEAK). You'll find a listing of other resources in this book in Appendix I, "Microsoft Internet Explorer 5 Resource Directory." For additional information specifically about Internet Explorer 5, see the material posted on the Windows Web Site at http://www.microsoft.com/windows.

About This Resource Kit

This Resource Kit details the ways that you can best customize and use Internet Explorer 5 for your needs. It covers the planning process from deciding which components and features to include to distributing Internet Explorer throughout your organization or to your customers. It describes how you can make the most of browser functionality and showcase your content. It also provides detailed coverage of installation options and outlines ways to best handle support and maintenance.

Although this technical and planning resource focuses specifically on the latest version of Internet Explorer, its coverage includes much more. It describes customization and deployment features available across platforms (Windows 16-bit and 32- bit versions as well as UNIX) and discusses ways that you can design solutions that combine various tools and integrate with different Microsoft products.

This Resource Kit contains six parts, each of which covers a specific subject area:

- **Part 1, Getting Started**—Part 1 provides an overview of Internet Explorer 5 features and functionality and gives essential background about the different customization and administration processes. It also describes how to work with different platforms as well as related tools and programs. In addition, it covers a number of topics important for maintaining security, such as digital certificates and content ratings.

- **Part 2, Preparing**—Part 2 describes how to handle deployment processes and develop installation strategies. It includes an overview of accessibility features and functionality. It also outlines how to set up and administer a pilot program before deployment.

- **Part 3, Customizing**—Part 3 focuses on the process of customizing Windows Update Setup for Internet Explorer 5 and Internet Tools. It also covers how you can use the Internet Explorer Customization wizard and other tools to create a customized browser solution. In addition, it discusses strategies for changing customization settings and describes how to use information (.inf) files to manipulate files during the download and setup processes.

- **Part 4, Installing**—Part 4 outlines the steps required to deploy an Internet Explorer 5 installation. In addition, it provides detailed information about how to use server-based and serverless processes for Internet sign-up.

- **Part 5, Maintaining and Supporting**—Part 5 covers how to change Internet Explorer 5 settings globally after installation by using automatic configuration and automatic proxy. It also describes how to keep Internet Explorer programs and settings updated by using the IEAK Profile Manager, update notification pages, and software distribution channels. In addition, it provides an overview of how to implement an ongoing training and support program.

- **Part 6, Appendixes**—Part 6 provides supplemental material relating to customizing and installing Internet Explorer 5. It lists the content of the Resource Kit CD-ROM and gives sources of additional information about Internet Explorer 5 and related Microsoft products. It also contains comprehensive checklists for preparing to use the IEAK. It supplies the following reference information: structural definition of .inf files, descriptions of files used in the setup process, country and language codes, and batch-mode file syntax and command-line switches. In addition, it covers how to set system policies and restrictions and describes troubleshooting strategies for Internet Explorer 5 installations.

Also included is a glossary with definitions for terms commonly used throughout the book.

Resource Kit Tools and Utilities

In addition to the Internet Explorer 5 Web browser, you'll find the following tools and utilities on the CD-ROM that comes with this book.

- **Microsoft Windows NT 4.0 Service Pack 4**—Includes advanced management and security features for Windows NT, as well as late-breaking updates for the Year 2000 and euro currency changes.

- **Microsoft Internet Explorer 5 Resource Kit**—Reproduces the entire contents of this Resource Kit in HTML Help format.

- **Internet Explorer Administration Kit 5 (IEAK)**—Enables administrators to create, distribute, and update customized installations of Internet Explorer 5 using tools included in the kit, such as the Internet Explorer Customization wizard, the Microsoft Connection Manager Administration Kit (CMAK), and the IEAK Profile Manager.

- **Corporate Applications Kit**—Contains sample coding applications and templates for building Web-enabled programs for Internet Explorer 5.

- **Internet Explorer 5 Deployment Guide**—Provides detailed instructions, checklists, and examples for planning, deploying, and maintaining Internet Explorer 5.

- **Additional Resources page**—Lists product resources and Web sites that are sources of additional information about Internet Explorer 5 and related Microsoft products.

Note For more detailed information about the CD-ROM contents, see Appendix A, "What's on the Resource Kit CD-ROM?"

Book Conventions

The following conventions are used in this book.

Convention	Meaning
Bold	Indicates options in the user interface—such as the **Security** tab—that you click when performing procedures. This formatting is also used for keywords, such as the **currentStyle** object, and for commands that must be typed exactly as written, such as **Mkdir** *<directory name>*.
Italic	Represents a placeholder for a value or string. For example, if a syntax statement contains *filename*, you need to replace *filename* with the name of a file.
ALL UPPERCASE	Indicates an HTML element, such as an ACTION attribute, and registry keys, such as **HKEY_LOCAL_MACHINE**.
MiXed Case	Specifies case sensitivity in API elements, such as the **assertPermission** method.
monospace	Presents example blocks of code: `<FORM NAME="PAGEID"></FORM>`
…(ellipsis)	Stands for elements that can be repeated. For the following command-line switch, 0 refers to the first installation choice, 1 refers to the second choice, 2 refers to the third choice, 3 refers to the fourth choice, and so on: **/M:[0|1|2|3...]**
" " (straight quotation marks)	Specifies quotation marks required by input values or strings in code. For an example, see the monospace convention.

P A R T   1

Getting Started

Chapter 1: What's New in Microsoft Internet Explorer 5?

This chapter provides an overview of the new and enhanced features of Microsoft Internet Explorer 5. You can use this information to help you evaluate the browser before you deploy it to your users. New and enhanced features are divided into the following areas: deploying the browser, simplifying Web tasks for the user, automating Web tasks for the user, and developing and authoring for the Web.

Chapter 2: Microsoft Internet Explorer 5 Components

Microsoft Internet Explorer 5 includes a comprehensive set of components that provide solutions for your Internet- and intranet-based communication needs. This chapter describes each of the components that comes with the Internet Explorer 5 Web browser. This product information can help you decide which components to install.

Chapter 3: Understanding Customization and Administration

This chapter describes how you can tailor Microsoft Internet Explorer 5 to fit the needs of your organization. Information in this chapter applies to corporate administrators, Internet service providers (ISPs), Internet content providers (ICPs), independent software vendors (ISVs), and developers.

The Internet Explorer Administration Kit (IEAK) provides a convenient way to alter the appearance and behavior of Internet Explorer and to customize Windows Update Setup for Internet Explorer 5 and Internet Tools. In addition, the IEAK enables corporate administrators to control many user actions, including file management, desktop behavior, and Internet usage. The IEAK also enables ISPs to develop tools and processes to sign up new customers.

Chapter 4: Working with Different Platforms

This chapter identifies the platforms on which you can install Microsoft Internet Explorer 5 and describes the deployment variations among the supported platforms. This information is particularly important if you are deploying Internet Explorer on multiple platforms.

Chapter 5: Understanding Related Tools and Programs

When you use the Internet Explorer Customization wizard to build and install custom packages of Microsoft Internet Explorer 5, you can also include other tools and programs as part of the deployment process. This chapter provides an overview of the following related tools and programs: Microsoft System Management Server (SMS), Microsoft Office 2000 Custom Installation wizard (CIW), and Microsoft Internet Information Server (IIS).

Chapter 6: Digital Certificates

Microsoft Internet Explorer 5 uses digital certificates to authenticate clients and servers on the Web and to ensure secure browser communications. Read this chapter to learn about certificates and about how to configure settings for the certificates you trust.

Chapter 7: Security Zones and Permission-Based Security for Microsoft Virtual Machine

Microsoft Internet Explorer 5 provides comprehensive management and enforcement of Internet and network security. This chapter describes two key features of security management: security zones and permission-based security for Microsoft Virtual Machine. Read this chapter to learn how these security features can help protect access to individuals and information in your organization.

Chapter 8: Content Ratings and User Privacy

Using the content-rating and user-privacy features of Microsoft Internet Explorer 5, you can create a secure environment that protects users from inappropriate Web content and ensures the privacy of their information. This chapter describes these features and explains how you can configure rating and privacy settings.

CHAPTER 1

What's New in Microsoft Internet Explorer 5?

This chapter provides an overview of the new and enhanced features of Microsoft Internet Explorer 5. You can use this information to help you evaluate the browser before you deploy it to your users.

New and enhanced features are divided into the following areas:

- **Deploying the browser**—Learn about customizing new browser and setup options by using the Internet Explorer Customization wizard. Also read about how you can deploy Internet Explorer as part of your custom Microsoft® Office package.

- **Simplifying Web tasks for the user**—Learn about the browser features and functions that can simplify the users' daily tasks and activities on the Web.

- **Automating Web tasks for the user**—Understand how new features can help you automate common Web tasks, such as installing components and searching the Internet.

- **Developing and authoring for the Web**—Learn about the new technologies and platform features for building Web-based applications.

In This Chapter

See Also

- For more information about planning your deployment of Internet Explorer, see Chapter 9, "Planning the Deployment."

- For more information about rolling out Internet Explorer to your users, see Chapter 19, "Deploying Microsoft Internet Explorer 5."

Deploying the Browser

Using the Internet Explorer Administration Kit (IEAK) 5, you can easily customize, deploy, and manage your Internet Explorer packages. The IEAK includes the Internet Explorer Customization wizard, the IEAK Profile Manager, and the Connection Manager Administration wizard (CMAK), which enable you to build and maintain custom packages of Internet Explorer 5 that are tailored to meet the needs of your users. You can easily specify user setup options and control most browser and component features.

The following sections describe new and enhanced features that streamline the process of deploying Internet Explorer 5.

Internet Explorer Customization Wizard

The Internet Explorer Customization wizard has been enhanced to provide a simpler, more organized interface for creating custom packages of Internet Explorer 5. Using the new Feature Selection screen in Stage 1 of the wizard, you can select the features that you want to customize. All other feature pages will not be shown, so you can more quickly customize only the features you want. For example, if you want to customize only the Favorites, you can select this option, and you will see only the required wizard pages and the wizard pages necessary for customizing Favorites.

The following illustration shows the Feature Selection screen.

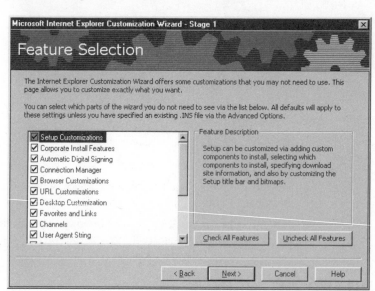

Browser Setup Options

The Internet Explorer Customization wizard includes the following new and enhanced options for setting up the browser:

- **Single-disk branding**—For systems that already have Internet Explorer 4.01 Service Pack 1 (or later) or Internet Explorer 5 installed, you can select single-disk branding as the distribution method. This option creates a single floppy disk that brands the system with custom text and logo information but does not install the browser.

- **Media production**—You can use the Internet Explorer Customization wizard to produce custom packages for Web download, CD-ROM, floppy disk, and network installations, all at the same time.

- **Preinstalled components**—Custom components can be installed before the browser is installed on users' computers. This is particularly useful for utilities that prepare the computers for the browser installation. For example, a registry-cleaning utility could be run first to ensure that no browser registry keys have been deleted.

- **Controlled user interaction**—You can select the most appropriate level of user involvement for each Internet Explorer installation:
  - Interactive installation, which allows users to customize components during installation.

- Hands-free installation, which shows only error messages and progress dialog boxes. The user does not have the option of customizing components.

- Completely silent installation, which involves no interaction and is completely hidden from users.

- **Improved Web deployment**—You can configure Web installations to choose from up to 10 download sites. If a connection problem occurs, Web installations can switch between sites and resume an interrupted download. Windows Update Setup for Internet Explorer 5 and Internet Tools can also detect whether a compatible version of an Internet Explorer component is already available on a user's computer. If the component already exists, it is not downloaded again.

- **Versioning**—The Internet Explorer Customization wizard automatically assigns a version number to every custom package of Internet Explorer. You can use the Internet Explorer Customization wizard to configure your custom packages to prevent overwriting newer browser versions. The wizard also assigns a version number to each component of Internet Explorer 5, so that an individual component can be updated.

- **Automatic install**—Using the automatic install feature, you can include components with your custom packages that won't be installed until the user requires them. For example, if Internet Explorer 5 detects that the user needs to use Microsoft Virtual Machine to perform a task, the browser automatically locates the distribution point and installs the component. This feature helps you reduce the size of your installation package by deploying only the components that your users require.

- **Automatic digital signing**—Internet Explorer 5 packages can be digitally signed for distribution. A digital signature guarantees that your custom package hasn't been changed by an unknown source.

- **Update notification page**—You can use the Internet Explorer Customization wizard to customize the update notification page, which automatically notifies your users when a new version of the browser is available. At a specified interval, the Internet Explorer home, or start, page is replaced temporarily by an update notification page when the user starts the browser. You can customize this page to include information specific to your organization, such as company news or Web links.

For more information about browser options, see Chapter 15, "Running the Internet Explorer Customization Wizard," or review the IEAK Help files.

System Policies and Restrictions

You can use the Internet Explorer Customization wizard or IEAK Profile Manager to do the following:

- Implement new and enhanced settings both by computer and by user and, if you are a corporate administrator, control computer and user privileges.

- Standardize browser settings for your user communities.

You can also configure advanced settings for components such as Microsoft NetMeeting®, Microsoft Outlook® Express, and Microsoft Chat.

You have the option to lock down certain features and functions. When features are locked down, they either don't appear, or they appear dimmed on the user's desktop. For more information about system policies and restrictions, see Appendix E, "Setting System Policies and Restrictions."

The following illustration shows the System Policies and Restrictions screen.

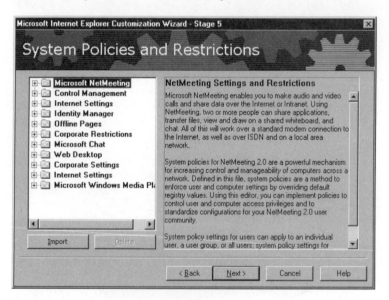

Connection Manager Administration Kit

When you create custom packages of Internet Explorer, you can use the Connection Manager Administration Kit (CMAK) to guide you through the process of customizing and configuring the Microsoft Connection Manager dialer. You can create a customized dialer to provide users with a quick and easy way to connect to the Internet or intranet.

You can use the CMAK to include custom icons, tailored help files, and special animated graphics to control the appearance of your Connection Manager dialer. The CMAK creates a self-extracting executable (.exe) file that installs the customized dialer on your users' computers. When users click the custom icon to connect to the Internet, the custom-dialer dialog box appears. For more information about the CMAK, see Chapter 14, "Customizing Connection Management and Settings."

Internet Connection Wizard

If you are an Internet service provider (ISP), you can specify that your customers use the Internet Connection wizard (ICW) to sign up and configure their computers for Internet services. You can also customize the connection and server sign-up options for your customers and create server-based solutions that exchange information with the ICW screens.

The IEAK Toolkit includes sample code for building an ICW sign-up server on different platforms. For more information about using the ICW for server-based sign-up, see Chapter 20, "Implementing the Sign-up Process."

Security Options

Internet Explorer 5 includes the following enhancements to browser security:

- **Secure transmission protocols**—Internet Explorer provides enhanced support for the following secure transmission protocols for client and server authentication:
  - Secure Sockets Layer (SSL) 2.0 (server authentication only) and SSL 3.0
  - Transport Layer Security (TLS) 1.0
  - Private Communications Technology (PCT) 1.0
- **Fortezza support**—Microsoft provides a Fortezza cryptographic service provider (CSP) plug-in for Internet Explorer 5 that supports Fortezza security technology. Users with Fortezza Crypto Cards can install the Fortezza CSP plug-in to ensure secure Internet Explorer communications based on Fortezza security standards (determined by the National Security Agency for the United States Department of Defense).
- **Certificate revocation**—Internet Explorer 5 adds support for certificate revocation, which verifies that an issuing certification authority has not revoked a certificate. This feature checks for revocation when certificate extensions are present. If the URL for the revocation information is unresponsive, Internet Explorer cancels the connection.

- **Content Advisor**—Internet Explorer 5 includes the following enhancements to the Content Advisor, which improve your ability to control the content that your users can view on the Intranet and intranet:

  - **Support for PICS rules**—The World Wide Web Consortium (W3C) standard Platform for Internet Content Selection (PICS) rules provide an architecture in which content providers can help you configure acceptable PICS settings. Users can only view content that surpasses the agreed-upon PICS criteria.

  - **List of approved and disapproved sites**—You can now create your own list of Web sites that are approved and disapproved. This capability restricts the content users can view, regardless of whether the Web sites are rated by using PICS or other ratings systems.

The following illustration shows the Content Advisor.

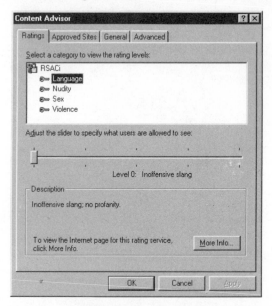

For more information about these security options, see Chapter 6, "Digital Certificates," and Chapter 8, "Content Ratings and User Privacy."

Integration with the Office 2000 Custom Installation Wizard

The Internet Explorer Customization wizard is part of the Microsoft Office 2000 Custom Installation wizard (CIW), which enables you to customize and deploy Internet Explorer and Office 2000 simultaneously. The CIW determines whether the IEAK is installed, makes the necessary changes in the registry, and then starts the Internet Explorer Customization wizard. This greatly enhances and simplifies the process of deploying and managing both productivity and Web client tools. For more information about the CIW and deploying Office 2000, see the Microsoft Office 2000 Resource Kit.

Support for Multiple Languages

Internet Explorer 5 can be deployed in more than 26 languages, and you can easily switch between languages after installation. The following language and performance features make it easier to view international content:

- **Unicode support**—Internet Explorer 5 provides improved Unicode support when you view international content. A set of conversion functions translates all current Internet character sets to Unicode. Applications can be based entirely on Unicode, freeing them from dependencies on particular Internet character sets.

- **AutoDetect language feature**—Internet Explorer 5 automatically detects the languages and code pages in which data is written. In addition, Internet Explorer determines the percentage of data that is in the detected language and the relative confidence that it has in the accuracy of the language and code-page labeling. If the language is not labeled at all or is mislabeled in the HTML code, Internet Explorer still renders it correctly.

- **Easy language switching**—With Internet Explorer 5, you can change the language of the user interface after the browser is installed just by downloading the appropriate language pack.

Support for Multiple Platforms

You can deploy Internet Explorer 5 on Windows 16-bit, Windows-32 bit, and UNIX platforms. If your organization uses several different platforms, you can deploy and maintain a separate version of Internet Explorer 5 for each platform.

Internet Explorer 5 provides a single, standards-based set of technologies for Web authoring, browsing, communication, and collaboration for all supported platforms. The HTML rendering engine for Internet Explorer on Windows and UNIX platforms was derived from the same code base, so you can be sure that content developed for one platform renders the same on all platforms.

Internet Explorer 5 has also been optimized to support each individual platform. You can take advantage of platform-specific functionality, as well as integration with platform-specific applications. For more information about supported platforms, see Chapter 4, "Working with Different Platforms."

Simplifying Web Tasks

Internet Explorer 5 can simplify the daily tasks that you perform on the Web. For example, the browser simplifies searching by helping you classify the type of information you are looking for and redirecting searches to the search engines that you specify.

The following sections describe new and enhanced features of Internet Explorer 5 that make it simple to find, organize, and use information on the Web.

Go Button

After you type a URL in the Address bar or **Run** command (on the **Start** menu), you can view the Web site by pressing ENTER or by clicking the new **Go** button. This button appears on the right side of the Address bar and **Run** command box.

If you prefer to press ENTER, you can remove the **Go** button by right-clicking it and then clearing this selection.

Home Page Object Model

You no longer need to read through extensive instructions on how to change a home page. Content providers have a new home-page object model, which enables them to programmatically reset the home page—with the user's confirmation—by using basic scripting. You can change your home page just by clicking a designated link on a content provider's Web page.

Search Assistant

The new Search Assistant helps you to quickly and easily obtain more accurate results from Internet searches. When you click the **Search** button on the Internet Explorer toolbar, the Search Assistant opens in the left side of the window. As in earlier versions of Internet Explorer, the Search Assistant provides you with the ability to search the Web using the default search engine that you specify. In addition, you can designate the type of information you are looking for, such as Web pages or mailing and e-mail addresses. Using a search engine that has been optimized to locate a specific type of information makes it easier for you to conduct a targeted search.

You have complete control of the categories that the Search Assistant displays, as well as the search engines that are used for each category. After conducting a search, you can select a different search engine and perform the same search again without retyping the search words.

The following illustration shows the Search Assistant.

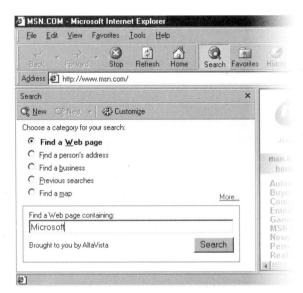

Search Highlighting

When you perform a search, the search words are highlighted automatically on any Web pages found by the search engines, so you can easily find the words on the page. For example, if you search for "Microsoft Internet technologies," this phrase is highlighted in the search results. You no longer need to use a separate search function to locate the search words on a Web page.

Helpful HTTP Error Messages

When you try to open a Web page (by clicking a link to the page or by typing a URL in the Address bar or the **Run** command box) and the page does not exist, Internet Explorer 5 replaces the standard HTTP 404 error message with a more helpful error message. The new error message provides helpful suggestions for locating the desired Web page. For example, if you type the following address— http://example.microsoft.com/link/link2.htm—in the Address bar but link2.htm does not exist, Internet Explorer provides simple instructions on how to get to the site, such as suggesting that you click the **Refresh** button on the browser toolbar. Internet Explorer also provides a link to http://example.microsoft.com/link.

You can still view the HTTP 404 error message text, which now appears at the bottom of the error message window.

Hidden Script Errors

By default, Internet Explorer does not display a dialog box that describes scripting errors. Instead, an icon in the status bar indicates when a scripting error has occurred. Because scripting errors can be resolved only by the author of the script, they are not meaningful to most users. Content developers, though, can easily enable the ability to view all scripting error messages. For more information about viewing scripting error messages, see "Developer Mode" later in this chapter.

Explorer Bar Enhancements

Explorer bars have been enhanced in the following ways:

- Explorer bars now use a white background and familiar scrollbars, which are consistent with other desktop applications.

- Explorer bars for Favorites, History, and Search are more consistent, making it easy to switch from one Explorer bar to another.

- Command buttons are now available within each Explorer bar, giving you instant access to popular commands. For example, the Explorer bar for Favorites now includes command buttons for adding and organizing Favorites.

- Explorer bars persist from one browser session to the next. When you have an Explorer bar open and then quit and restart the browser, the same Explorer bar is still open.

Add Favorites

The Add Favorite dialog box in Internet Explorer 5 has been simplified so that you can more quickly name a favorite Web site and add it to the appropriate folder in the Favorites list. A **Make available offline** check box makes it easier for you to designate content that you want to download and then read offline. You can then click the **Customize** button and specify exactly when the content should be updated and whether you want to be notified by e-mail.

When you are working offline, Internet Explorer automatically dims the options that are unavailable in Favorites and History.

The following illustration shows the Add Favorite dialog box.

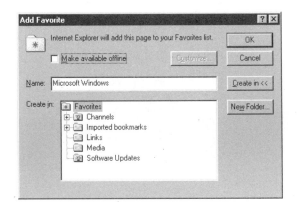

Smart Frameset Favorites

When you add a Web page that includes frames to the Favorites list, Internet Explorer now saves the frameset arrangement rather than saving the outermost frame by default (which is often not the appropriate page). Even pages with nested frames, which allow the main navigation list of contents to appear on all of a Web site's pages, link to the correct URL from the Favorites list.

Organize Favorites

Internet Explorer 5 includes a new Organize Favorites dialog box that helps you organize your Favorites list and provides additional information about the Web sites on the list. You can quickly and easily create new folders, move favorite Web sites from one folder to another, rename them, or delete them.

Also, when you select one of the links in the dialog box, the browser automatically displays the following information:

- The Web site's URL
- The last time you visited the Web site
- The number of times you have visited the Web site
- The Web site's availability offline

The following illustration shows the Organize Favorites dialog box.

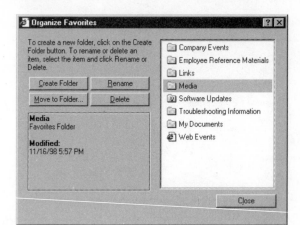

Import and Export Favorites and Cookies

Internet Explorer 5 includes a new Import/Export wizard (accessible from the **File** menu) that enables you to import and export Favorites and cookies to and from Netscape Navigator. With this capability, you can easily synchronize settings between browsers. You can also import and export Favorites and cookies to and from a file at any location you designate.

Note The Import/Export wizard is not intended for exporting Favorites between Internet Explorer 4.0 and Internet Explorer 5.

History Views

You can use the new History views to locate Web sites that you visited recently. You can view History based on the following criteria:

- By date
- By Web site
- By the most visited Web site
- By the order of Web sites visited today

Within each History view, Web sites are sorted by domain name rather than by the first portion of the URL, so you can easily identify the appropriate site. For example, the Internet Explorer Web site would be sorted under Microsoft rather than under www.microsoft.com. You also have the option of searching a History file for specific words or searching for a URL directly from the History bar.

Windows Synchronization Manager

Internet Explorer 5 introduces a new service named Windows Synchronization Manager, which provides a single location from which you can synchronize information for offline use. You can use Windows Synchronization Manager to synchronize data for any application that supports this functionality. For example, you can synchronize all relevant data, including Web pages, documents, and other publications on the Internet and intranet. You can also specify when information is synchronized and the maximum amount of hard-disk space that can be used.

Windows Synchronization Manager can manage sessions on a connection-by-connection basis. For example, if you are connected over a slower dial-up connection, you might only want to synchronize your e-mail, then wait for a higher speed connection to synchronize Web pages.

The following illustration shows the Windows Synchronization Manager.

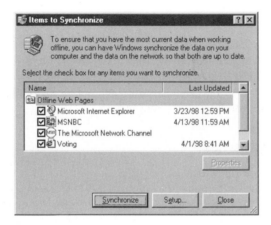

Saving Complete Web Pages

Using the **Save as** command, you can now save entire Web pages (including images) to view offline or to share with other users through e-mail. You can save the data as a Web archive in MIME HTML (MHTML) format or as a complete Web page in HTML format.

You can store complete Web pages without relying on the browser cache. For example, you might want to save some how-to information to your hard disk without worrying about whether the Web page will be updated tomorrow. Internet Explorer does not download a new version of the saved Web page when the Web site is updated.

FTP Folders

Many content providers provide FTP sites where users can download and upload files and information, avoiding the congestion of traditional Web sites. With Internet Explorer 5, the way you browse FTP folders is modeled after standard Web and file browsing. This capability provides you with a consistent view of both local and Internet data. If you have the Windows Desktop Update installed, additional information about the FTP folders, such as the folder size and the date the folder was last modified, is displayed.

Web Folders

Web Distributed Authoring and Versioning (WebDAV) is a set of standards-based extensions to HTTP that enable you to share and work with server-based HTTP Web documents. This capability is available regardless of the authoring tools, platforms, or types of Web servers or document management systems the documents are stored in.

Internet Explorer 5 supports WebDAV, enabling you to navigate to a WebDAV-compliant server, such as Microsoft Internet Information Server (IIS), and view the server as if it were a part of the local file system. You can also drag and drop files and perform other tasks, such as moving, copying, and saving files between local and remote WebDAV-compliant servers.

Per-Connection Proxy Settings

With Internet Explorer 5, you can set up multiple types of connections, each with different proxy servers, and switch automatically from one connection to another. If you need multiple Internet and intranet connections (for example, a connection to your office LAN and a connection to your personal Internet account through an Internet service provider), you no longer have to change your proxy-server settings manually each time a different connection is made. When you choose a different connection, Internet Explorer automatically uses the appropriate proxy-server settings.

Integration with Productivity Applications

Internet Explorer 5 enables you to specify default applications for e-mail, calendar, contacts, Internet dial-up, newsgroups, and HTML editing to use with the browser. When you try to perform a task that requires one of these applications, Internet Explorer automatically starts the selected application. For example, if you click the **Edit** button in Internet Explorer, the browser opens the Web page in the selected HTML editing application.

The Internet Explorer user interface and commands are also more consistent with Microsoft productivity applications, such as Microsoft Office 2000.

The following user-interface enhancements provide additional consistency between the browser and productivity applications:

- **Tools menu**—More advanced commands, such as **Internet Options**, are now available on the new Tools menu, just as they are in Office applications.

- **Toolbar appearance**—You can select smaller toolbar buttons and icons for the browser, similar to those used in Office applications.

- **Toolbar commands**—You can add popular Office commands, such as **Print**, **Cut**, **Copy**, and **Paste**, to the browser toolbar.

Integration with Web-Based Mail

You can now select Web-based e-mail providers as your default e-mail program and experience the same integrated browsing and communication features available in traditional e-mail programs, such as Microsoft Outlook and Qualcomm Eudora. When you want to compose a new message, read e-mail, send a link, or send a Web page from within Internet Explorer, the browser automatically uses the Web-based e-mail provider that you select.

Internet Explorer includes MSN™ Hotmail™ as an option for the default e-mail program, and other Web-based e-mail providers can provide the same integrated functionality.

Automating Web Tasks

Internet Explorer 5 includes new and enhanced features that automate most common browser tasks. For example, if you want, the browser can enter user names, information in forms, and even passwords automatically.

The following sections describe new and enhanced features of Internet Explorer 5 that automate common tasks and activities on the Web.

AutoCorrect

When you incorrectly type a common URL convention in the Address bar, such as the http://www. prefix or the .com suffix, the Internet Explorer AutoCorrect feature automatically resolves the error and opens the appropriate Web site. For example, if you type htpp://, Internet Explorer changes the prefix to http:// and then opens the correct Web site.

AutoComplete: Address Bar and Run Command

When you start to type a URL in the Address bar or in the **Run** command box (from the **Start** menu), the enhanced AutoComplete feature automatically displays a list of matching sites that you visited recently. You can just click the appropriate site on this list.

AutoComplete also attempts to match the partially typed URL with those in your Favorites list. For example, if you type "Mic" and "Microsoft" is one of your Favorites, the drop-down list includes a direct link to the Microsoft Web site.

The following illustration shows an AutoComplete drop-down list.

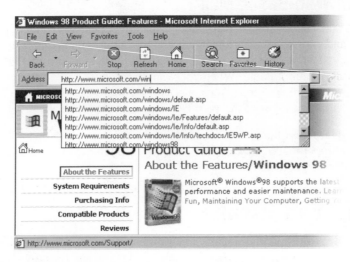

AutoComplete: Web Forms

If you repeatedly fill out forms, such as entering a name and address or typing a password, you can automate this process by using the new AutoComplete feature for Web forms (also called Intelliforms). When you start to type a value in a form field, a drop-down list displays a list of previous entries for the same field, including entries that you typed at other Web sites.

For example, every time you type a unique user name and password at a Web site login page, Internet Explorer prompts you about whether to save the entries, which are stored in the browser's encrypted personal store. If you choose to save the entries, each time you start to type your user name, Internet Explorer displays a list of available user names that have been saved. You can select the appropriate user name for that Web site, and the password is automatically inserted into the appropriate field.

If you do not want to store certain types of information, such as passwords, you can do the following:

- Highlight the entry that you want to delete in the drop-down list, and then click the DELETE key.

- On the **Content** tab (accessible by clicking **Internet Options** on the **Tools** menu), you can click **AutoComplete**, and then select or clear the options you want.

The following illustration shows the AutoComplete Settings dialog box.

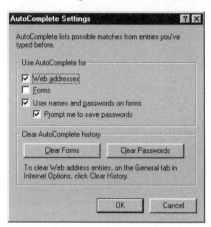

Also, content developers can use cache control to prevent Internet Explorer from storing specific information for a Web page. For more information about this feature, see "Cache Control" later in this chapter.

Automatic Search

If you type a search query directly into the Address bar, Internet Explorer displays the results for both a standard Web search and a specific recommendation on a matching site if one exists. Internet Explorer provides this recommendation when the site meets a very high probability for a match, and will automatically display the matching Web site. For example, if you type "NetMeeting" in the Address bar, the browser displays a single page that contains the standard search results plus a recommendation that the http://www.microsoft.com/netmeeting Web site is the most probable match.

The following illustration shows the search results for this example.

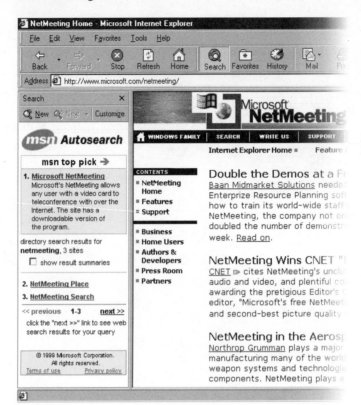

Automatic Install

You might want to install a smaller version of Internet Explorer to save space on your hard disk without giving up the functionality of a full-featured browser. With the Automatic Install feature, you can install an 8 MB browser-only version of Internet Explorer and install additional components as needed.

If you navigate to Web pages or try to view files that require an Internet Explorer component not currently installed on your computer, Internet Explorer can automatically install the component.

Automatically Detect When Offline

Internet Explorer 5 automatically detects the network status when the browser is started and on an ongoing basis and then notifies you of the status. The browser dims any items in Favorites and History that are unavailable when the browser is offline. You can easily identify the items that are available and avoid trying to connect to the Internet when a network connection is not available.

Automatic Detection and Automatic Configuration of Browser and Server Settings

When the network administrator defines the appropriate settings, the network can automatically detect and configure a browser's settings. This feature works with Dynamic Host Configuration Protocol (DHCP) servers that support the DHCPINFORM message and Domain Name System (DNS) servers.

Automatically Detect Network Connections

Internet Explorer can automatically detect the network connections that are available on your computer. If you are not already connected to the network when Internet Explorer 5 is started, the browser evaluates the available connections (for example, LAN, RAS, and ISDN) and automatically uses the highest speed connection available.

Intelligently Detect Editing Programs

Many productivity applications, such as Microsoft Office, rely on the browser as the primary means of viewing HTML content. In the past, it was difficult to switch back and forth between creating a Web document with the productivity application, viewing the document with the browser, and then editing it with the productivity application. Now, you can perform all of these functions from within the browser window.

When you view an HTML document that was created by using an application on your computer, Internet Explorer recognizes the application based on a metatag in the HTML code. The **Edit** button in Internet Explorer then automatically changes to the application icon. When you click the **Edit** button, Internet Explorer automatically opens the file in the appropriate application.

Developing and Authoring for the Web

Internet Explorer 5 offers a feature-rich platform for building Web-based applications and developing informative content for users. The browser provides enhanced support for standards-based Internet technologies and improves the ease and speed with which developers can take advantage of these technologies. Improvements to the browser programming model, such as drag-and-drop capabilities across frames and applications, further enrich the Web development platform.

The following sections describe the new and enhanced features that can help you create Web-based applications.

Enhanced Support for Dynamic HTML Standards

Enhanced support for Dynamic HTML standards provides you with a comprehensive standards-based platform for authoring interactive content. You can create content that is compatible with other browsers that also support these standards.

Internet Explorer 5 includes enhanced support for the following standards:

- HTML 4.0
- Cascading style sheets (CSS) 1.0 and CSS positioning
- Scripting and support for the Document Object Model (DOM)
- Extensible Markup Language (XML)
- Extensible Stylesheet Language (XSL)
- ECMA-262 scripting (JavaScript standard)
- HTTP

Enhanced Support for XML

XML provides you with a standard data-interchange format for building data-based applications. Internet Explorer 5 includes the following enhancements to XML support:

- Full support for the W3C XML Document Object Model (DOM) offers extensive programmatic control of XML document content, structure, and formats.
- You can embed XML in a document as data or metadata. The full XML DOM is then exposed for the element, but the elements inside the XML tag are not rendered on the page and are not included in the HTML DOM.
- You can intermix XML tags with HTML tags in a Web document. You can also apply CSS properties to these elements to control how they are displayed.
- Using native XML support, you can view XML like a regular document within the browser.
- With XSL support, you can apply style sheets to native XML documents and display the data dynamically.

Performance Improvements

With enhancements to the browser programming model, both developers and users will experience improved performance in the following areas:

- **A more efficient DHTML rendering engine**—Optimization of the DHTML rendering engine (and, in particular, the internal algorithms) has increased the performance of basic browser functions, allowing significantly faster and more efficient display of content than in earlier versions of the browser. These improvements are most noticeable when users are viewing very large documents built with Dynamic HTML and pages that include databinding technology.

- **Fixed-layout tables**—Internet Explorer 5 includes support for fixed-layout tables, which allow you to specify table-column sizes, while the content size inside the table cells does not affect the table layout. By not calculating the minimum and maximum size of each cell in the table, fixed-layout tables are progressively rendered, so the browser displays each table row as it downloads.

- **Render first for the HTTP-Expires header**—Internet Explorer 5 now supports the HTTP-Expires header on both pages and images. The browser does not automatically check the network first when an object from the cache has not yet expired. For a period before the expiration time (specified in the cache control header), Internet Explorer renders from the cache even if a newer version is available. This ability reduces network traffic and improves browser performance.

Dynamic HTML Behavior Components

Dynamic HTML behavior components are simple, lightweight components that, when applied to standard HTML elements on a page by using CSS, can enhance the element's default behavior. Additionally, behavior components separate the script from the content on a page, making it easy to reuse code across multiple pages and improving the overall manageability of the page. Just as CSS enables Web-site developers to separate the content of a page from its format, dynamic HTML behavior components extend that idea to separate scripted behaviors as well.

You can now build reusable scripts and custom XML tags that Web pages can reference. For example, you could write a script that specifies which text or pictures fly in from the right side of the page. This script can be referenced from any page simply by calling it. You can then change content without affecting the script.

For example, to build the mask-entry field by using Internet Explorer 4.0, you would have included an **INPUT** tag on the page, then added script that monitored the focus and keyboard interaction with the control. You would have needed to create the script for every page that required the new mask-entry type. Now, with the new Dynamic HTML behavior components, you can encapsulate all the script inside a component that can quickly and easily be referenced from any page, even by someone who has no knowledge of scripting.

Dynamic Properties

Instead of creating long, complicated scripts to perform relatively simple activities, you can define any property on a page as a function of any other property. This feature can be useful for pages that use CSS positioning. You can now set up very complex screen layouts that are simple to author, don't require a line of script, and respond to screen changes dynamically.

For example, the font size of a section of text can be set to 20 percent of the width of a table, and the font size will change dynamically if the page is resized without being refreshed from the Web server. As the document changes size, a recalculation engine (similar to technology used in spreadsheet applications, such as Microsoft Excel) determines a dependency and resets the property.

Full Drag-and-Drop Object Model Support

The Internet Explorer 5 object model now includes full support for drag-and-drop from Web pages to the desktop or any other application. Full control over cursors, drag initialization, and Clipboard support has also been added to the object model. You can build Web-based applications that enable users to drag content between frames and even to other applications.

Retaining Persistence

Any element on a Web page, such as a collapsible outline, can remain in its current state, even when a user leaves the page and returns later. While in the past you have been able to do this in a limited way with cookies, the new persistence technology of Internet Explorer 5 provides an XML-based method for persisting data.

You can persist form data, dynamic positions and content, styles, and script variables, which increases the speed of navigation and content authoring. For example, you can specify that a collapsible list of links within a table of contents on a page remains in the same expanded state until the user returns to the page. You can preserve documents exactly as they are displayed on the screen rather than relying on settings for a document maintained on a remote server.

Internet Explorer 5 provides a local store for retaining persistence that is protected from unauthorized cross-domain access and is not affected by the 4 KB limit imposed by cookies. Properties can be stored hierarchically by using name and value pair combinations, and you can control the storage and retrieval of this information. By allowing information to safely reside on the client computer, fewer server transactions are required.

Client Capabilities

The Internet Explorer 5 platform introduces a new feature that enables the server to request the specific capabilities of the client computer. The server creates a special HTTP request (449) that includes a script for the client computer to execute. The script queries the client computer about its system capabilities, as well as the availability of browser features. The client computer executes the script, and then sends the information back to the server. This approach is secure—the client computer executes a script that is similar to any other script the browser can run.

Client capabilities consist of information about the browsing environment, including screen resolution, screen dimensions, color depth, CPU, and connection speed. Internet Explorer 5 also detects the components installed on the system. The server is specific about the capabilities that it needs from the client computer, so only the required information is generated and transferred.

You can customize content to provide the best possible user experience based on this client information. For example, if the user has an Intel® Pentium 266 computer, you might want to provide more sophisticated content; if the user has an Intel 386 computer, you might want to provide less sophisticated content, regardless of the browser used.

Cache Control

For specific Web pages where you do not want Internet Explorer to cache content, such as the user's password, you can disable the AutoComplete feature. You would add the following tags to a Web page to prevent AutoComplete from storing information:

- pragma:no-cache
- cache-control:no-cache
- cache-control:no-store
- cache-control:private (when not using Windows NT with per user-cache)

Multiple Cascading Style Sheet (CSS) Class Support

Internet Explorer 5 includes the ability to add multiple CSS classes to an element. You simply apply a list of CSS classes to the element's class property. Any element can accept a list of CSS classes, which makes it much simpler to write script when different actions can occur for a single element. For example, by adding multiple CSS classes to an element, you can easily write the code for a picture that changes when the mouse moves over it and changes again when it is clicked.

CSS Positioning

You can use CSS positioning to gain more control over the position and layout of elements on your Web pages. You can benefit from the following enhancements to CSS positioning:

- Every HTML element can now be positioned, either absolutely or relatively.

- Elements can be placed on a page with relative positioning, but can revert to absolute positioning on the fly.

- Elements can now change from positioned to non-positioned, or vice-versa, at any time.

The currentStyle Object

Internet Explorer 5 introduces the **currentStyle** object (element.currentStyle), which exposes the current value that each element is using for all of its CSS properties (not just the ones that have been explicitly placed on that object). The **currentStyle** object represents the cascaded format and style of the object that is specified by global style sheets, inline styles, and HTML attributes.

Through the **currentStyle** object, cascaded style values of an object can be retrieved. Reading the **currentStyle** object differs from reading the **style** object, because **style** is not set inline on an object. For example, if the color property is set on a paragraph only through a linked or embedded style sheet and not inline, then *object*.currentStyle.color will return the color, whereas *object*.style.color will not return a value. If, however, you specify <P STYLE="color:'red'">, both the **currentStyle** and **style** objects will return a value of red.

The **currentStyle** object reflects the following CSS order of style precedence:

1. Inline styles
2. Style sheet rules
3. Attributes on HTML tags
4. Intrinsic definition of the HTML tag

The **currentStyle** object supports user-defined properties in style rules. It returns values that reflect the applied style settings for the page and may not reflect what is currently rendering at the time a value is retrieved. For example, an object that has "color:red; display:none" will return a currentStyle.color of red even though the object is not being rendered on the page. The **currentStyle** object, then, is not affected by the rendering constraints. Disabled style sheets also do not affect **currentStyle** objects.

Developer Mode

Internet Explorer 5 includes a Developer Mode, which enables developers and site designers to view all scripting and site error messages for debugging purposes. This option is turned off by default for most users who are simply browsing the Web. The error messages in Internet Explorer have also been improved to provide more detailed information about scripting errors, HTML structure errors, and other useful information for diagnosing application errors.

Compatibility Mode

Internet Explorer 5 has an Internet Explorer 4.0-compatibility mode. Using this special compatibility mode, you can set up a single computer to test your Web sites using the rendering capabilities of both versions of Internet Explorer.

Browserless Applications

You can create browserless (.hta) applications that are built using Internet technologies, but that do not run within the browser window. You author an .hta application by using Dynamic HTML and scripting, the same way you author Web pages for Internet Explorer 5. However, an .hta application can run in its own window, which is controlled from corner to corner, instead of running within the browser frame. The .hta applications are not subject to the security constraints imposed on Web pages; like executable (.exe) files, they can run without browser security restrictions.

An .hta application includes extensions for special behaviors and permissions that are not available to HTML pages. You can take any HTML page, set the "application/hta" MIME type, and then run it as an application. To make the HTML page into a full-featured application, you can add a few special .hta application declarations to specify the application icon, window size, window border, system menu, and other settings.

HTML-Enabled Area for User Comments

Internet Explorer 5 introduces a new intrinsic control similar to text boxes or drop-down boxes, which allows developers to insert a separate HTML-enabled area into their Web pages. Within this area, users can insert comments or any content they want.

C H A P T E R   2

Microsoft Internet Explorer 5 Components

Microsoft Internet Explorer 5 includes a comprehensive set of components that provide solutions for your Internet- and intranet-based communication needs. This chapter describes each of the components that comes with the Internet Explorer 5 Web browser. This product information can help you decide which components to install.

In This Chapter

See Also

- For more information about building custom packages of Internet Explorer components, see Chapter 15, "Running the Internet Explorer Customization Wizard."

- For more information about installing Internet Explorer components, see Chapter 19, "Deploying Microsoft Internet Explorer 5."

- For more information about system policies and restrictions for Internet Explorer components, see Appendix E, "Setting System Policies and Restrictions."

Overview

Using the Internet Explorer Setup program or the Internet Explorer Customization wizard, you can select the components you want to install with the Web browser. Internet Explorer 5 includes the following components for communication and collaboration across the Internet or local intranet:

- Microsoft Outlook® Express for e-mail and newsgroups

- Microsoft Windows Media Player for playing multimedia content

- Microsoft NetMeeting® for audio-visual conferencing and application sharing

- Microsoft FrontPage® Express for Web authoring

- Microsoft Chat for text-based communication

- Additional Microsoft and third-party components that enhance Web browser features and functionality, such as the Microsoft Offline Browsing Pack and Microsoft® DirectAnimation™

Internet Explorer components work seamlessly together, because the applications are tightly integrated and have a common menu and toolbar. Internet Explorer gives you the flexibility to implement these applications as a stand-alone communication solution or to integrate them with your existing software programs. An organization that uses Internet Explorer does not need to discard its existing applications. For example, a corporation can use its existing messaging solution together with Internet Explorer components.

If you need to move up to more advanced applications, Internet Explorer offers a scalable solution. For example, Microsoft Outlook can replace Outlook Express for those users who need a richer e-mail client. While FrontPage Express enables you to create Web pages, Microsoft FrontPage is the fuller Web-site development platform. Internet Explorer integrates with these more advanced applications just as easily as it does with its built-in components.

System policies and restrictions enable you to configure and manage Internet Explorer components easily. You can control user and computer access to components or restrict the types of component features and functionality that are available to users. For example, you can predefine values for Microsoft Chat settings, such as the default chat server, character, and chat room. For more information about system policies and restrictions, see Appendix E, "Setting System Policies and Restrictions."

Microsoft Outlook Express

E-mail has become one of the most popular and effective ways for people to communicate, both in business and in their personal lives. Until recently, most e-mail has been limited to text-only messages, with perhaps some attachments. Internet Explorer supports an entirely new type of standards-based messaging, opening the door to greater richness and detail. Outlook Express 5 supports full Hypertext Markup Language (HTML), so you can create e-mail messages that have the color and functionality of Web pages, and even send full Web pages as part of your message. You can also design your own HTML stationery or use professionally designed stationery from Microsoft Greetings Workshop to give e-mail a personal touch.

The following illustration shows the Outlook Express start page.

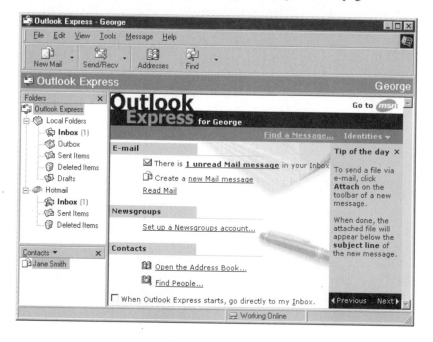

In addition, Outlook Express provides powerful mail management features, more efficient e-mail and newsgroup use, enhanced security, and full support for Internet standards and technologies. Outlook Express is flexible enough to meet the diverse e-mail needs of a variety of users—for example, users with dial-up Internet access through an Internet service provider (ISP) and users who work on a local area network (LAN) based on Internet standards, such as Simple Mail Transfer Protocol (SMTP), Post Office Protocol 3 (POP3), and Internet Mail Access Protocol 4 (IMAP4).

Microsoft Outlook Express Features

Outlook Express offers a wide range of features that make it easy for you to communicate more effectively with others, whether they are down the hall, across the city, or around the world. The following sections describe important Outlook Express features.

Setup and Migration Tools

You can get up and running easily with Outlook Express. The Internet Connection wizard guides you through each step of establishing new e-mail, news, and directory service accounts. Migration is simplified because Outlook Express automatically detects and offers the opportunity to import existing e-mail messages, message rules, e-mail account settings, news settings, and address books from Netscape Messenger, Eudora, and Internet Mail. You can import information from these products when you first start up Outlook Express or at your convenience. You can also use Outlook Express to import information from Microsoft Exchange and Microsoft Outlook (in order for Outlook Express to import messages or address books from Exchange or Outlook, you must have these applications installed on your computer).

Web Integration

As the successor to Microsoft Internet Mail and News, Outlook Express further integrates e-mail with the Web by using the Internet Explorer Web browser control. Outlook Express supports HTML as a native message format, so you can create messages in HTML and communicate using the richness of Web pages without knowing how to write HTML code. Support for MIME HTML (MHTML) enables you to send full Web pages from the Internet or intranet and insert content from existing Web pages into messages. To maintain compatibility, messages created in Outlook Express are readable by both HTML-capable and non-HTML-capable e-mail clients. Outlook Express also doubles as a newsreader, so you do not need to switch between two separate applications for e-mail and news.

Security

Internet Explorer features state-of-the-art security technology. Support for the Secure Multipurpose Internet Mail Extensions (S/MIME) standard enables you to encrypt messages, digitally sign messages, and verify senders with digital certificates. Outlook Express uses public key cryptography to facilitate the encoding and decoding of encrypted messages. Outlook Express also incorporates Internet Explorer security zones, which protect you when you access Web sites and receive e-mail with Web content. By default, Outlook Express is set to the Internet zone, but you can select a more restrictive setting to limit specific types of content, such as scripting and Java applets.

Support for Internet Standards

Outlook Express implements leading Internet messaging standards and protocols to provide e-mail services, regardless of the Internet service provider or browser. Outlook Express provides full support for the following standards and protocols:

- **POP3 and SMTP**—POP3 and SMTP are the two most commonly used protocols for sending and receiving e-mail over the Internet. Outlook Express provides full support for POP3 and SMTP, including multiple Internet e-mail accounts and distributed password authentication.

- **IMAP4**—IMAP4 is the next-generation standard for e-mail messaging. This protocol allows messages to be stored on the server so that e-mail is accessible from any computer on the network. As a result, users can have access to e-mail at both work and home. Support for IMAP4 also offers improved bandwidth use and central mail-store administration.

- **HTML Mail**—HTML Mail allows e-mail messages to be sent in standard HTML format. These messages retain their formatting, even if they are read by an e-mail client other than Outlook Express. Text and attachments can also be read by non-HTML e-mail clients.

- **MHTML**—Images embedded directly into messages by using MHTML create richer e-mail content. Recipients do not have to connect to the Internet or intranet to view the message contents.

- **S/MIME**—S/MIME helps ensure the security of e-mail and news messages by enabling users to digitally sign and encrypt messages. Digital signatures verify the authenticity and integrity of the message, and encryption protects the contents of messages from being read by anyone except their intended recipient.

- **LDAP**—LDAP provides users with a means to easily find people on the Internet through Internet white-page services, such as Bigfoot, Yahoo! People Search, and WhoWhere? Note that LDAP support applies to the Windows Address Book only.

- **NNTP**—The Network News Transfer Protocol (NNTP) enables news clients to read and post to newsgroups. This protocol also supports communication between news servers.

- **HTTP**—Hypertext Transport Protocol (HTTP) provides access to e-mail messages that have been sent to other types of Internet e-mail accounts, such as MSN Hotmail.

Identities

With the new Identity Manager, you can create multiple identities on a computer with separate e-mail accounts, passwords, contacts, and preferences. You can create a separate identity for each person who uses Outlook Express (for example, you and a co-worker may share Outlook Express on the computer). Then you can easily switch between individual identities without having to shut down your computer or cancel the Internet connection.

A new identity folder is automatically created in the Windows Address Book when you create an identity by using the Identity Manager. You can keep contacts in your main folder, as well as organize them into subfolders. If you have contacts you want to share with other people who share your computer, you can move the contacts into the Shared Contacts folder.

Note Identities exist within Windows logon profiles and are intended to be an alternative to profiles. All information within a profile is available to all users with access to that profile. Identities, though, are not secure and are not intended for environments where security between users is a concern.

Message Rules

To help you manage and prioritize your e-mail, you can use the Outlook Express Rules wizard to develop rules for your e-mail messages. You can create one or more of these e-mail rules to organize the messages that you have already received and to screen your new incoming e-mail. E-mail rules enable you to designate the types of messages, such as e-mail from a specific account or with a specific priority, that Outlook Express forwards, moves, copies, highlights, or deletes automatically.

Note Message rules do not apply to IMAP or HTTP mail (MSN Hotmail) accounts.

Newsgroup Filters

You can create filters on an individual-newsgroup basis that ignore messages based on sender, subject, date posted, or length of message. Messages matching your filter criteria are neither downloaded to your computer nor displayed in the message list. Filtered materials can also include bitmap images, writings, audio and video clips, and links to other materials that can be accessed through Internet newsgroups.

Windows Address Book

The Windows Address Book provides a convenient place to store contact information for easy retrieval by programs, such as Outlook Express. Using the address book, you can store multiple e-mail addresses, home and work addresses, and phone and fax numbers. The address book enables you to create groups of contacts, which makes it easy to send e-mail to a set of people, such as business associates, relatives, or sports groups. It also features access to Internet directory services, which you can use to look up people and businesses on the Internet. You can store individual and business Internet addresses, and link directly to them from the Address Book.

The Windows Address Book has full support for LDAP directory services, which provide access to virtual Internet white pages. Using this feature, you can easily find anyone on corporate LDAP servers or use the built-in support for Bigfoot, InfoSpace, Switchboard, Verisign, WhoWhere?, and Yahoo! People Search to locate people on the Internet. Internet Explorer also includes support for vCard, which enables you to exchange business card information with other users.

You can also use Outlook Express to create both personal and shared contacts within the Address Book. Then, you can share your Address Book with other users, and they can use your individual and group contacts for sending their own messages.

Smart Reply

Outlook Express automatically sends your replies to messages in the same format in which they were sent. For example, if you receive HTML mail, Outlook Express responds with HTML. If you receive a message in plain text, Outlook Express does not send HTML mail when replying to that message, and it remembers not to do so for future messages to that recipient.

Outlook Express also automatically sends your replies to messages using the same account that received the message. For example, users can easily separate personal and business correspondence.

Multiple E-Mail and News Server Accounts

Outlook Express enables you to access and manage multiple e-mail and news accounts from a single client. You can also send and receive mail from numerous e-mail accounts. For example, if you have e-mail accounts for home and work, you can set up Outlook Express to receive messages for both accounts and sort them into separate folders. Outlook Express keeps track of which account an incoming message is using, so when you reply to it, you can just click **Send**, and Outlook Express sends your response using the appropriate account. Or, if several people share one e-mail account, you can set up folders for each person and then automatically route incoming messages to individual folders.

Support for Roaming Users

Users may need to access their e-mail account and read messages from several different computers. Outlook Express provides this capability for MSN Hotmail account users. These users can access their e-mail messages from any computer with an Internet connection and Outlook Express installed.

MSN Hotmail Integration

Outlook Express includes MSN Hotmail integration features, which enable you to do the following:

- Read your MSN Hotmail e-mail messages from within Outlook Express. Support for the HTTP protocol enables Outlook Express to communicate with MSN Hotmail e-mail servers.
- Configure your existing MSN Hotmail account for use with Outlook Express.
- Synchronize your Outlook Express and MSN Hotmail contacts.
- Sign up for a new MSN Hotmail account from within Outlook Express.

Productivity Features

Microsoft has added numerous features to make Outlook Express easier to use. Now you can perform the following tasks:

- Create multiple hierarchical folders and drag them and the messages they contain as needed to organize them.
- Easily save important e-mail addresses by using the Auto-Add feature, which automatically adds replied-to addresses to your Address Book.
- Enter a partial name of a recipient on the To: line. Outlook Express automatically compares it against your Address Book and fills in the rest of the name if it's found.
- Save e-mail messages in the Draft folder before they are sent, so you can easily keep track of messages in progress. The Draft folder ensures that important messages do not get overlooked among the e-mail in your Inbox.

- Execute the **Send** and **Receive** commands separately, so you can spend your time online efficiently. For example, if your connection is slow, you can choose only to send messages and not download large messages with attachments.

- Receive notification of unread messages and unfinished messages in your Draft folder when you start the application.

- Take advantage of several word-processor-like features, including changing font sizes, rich-text editing, and up to 150 levels of the **Undo** command.

Format for Message Stores

All Outlook Express messages are now stored in files with a .dbx extension. When you upgrade to Outlook Express 5 from a previous version (Outlook Express 4.0 or Internet Mail and News), a copy of the message store is converted to the new Outlook Express message format.

If you subsequently uninstall Outlook Express 5, you will see only the messages you received in Outlook Express 4.0 or Internet Mail and News.

Note If you were using Outlook Express 4.0 previously, you can import the Outlook Express 5 messages into Outlook Express 4.0. A message importer remains on your computer after you uninstall Outlook Express 5 (accessible by clicking **Import** on the **File** menu in Outlook Express 4.0).

Outlook Bar

Outlook Express offers the same style of navigational bar that Microsoft Outlook 97 introduced. Because you can use the Outlook bar to easily access different folders and modules, it is one of the most popular features of Outlook. You can also customize the Outlook bar by adding and deleting folders and changing the folder order according to your preferences.

Integration with Internet Explorer

Because Outlook Express is tightly integrated with the rest of the Internet Explorer components, you can easily use them together and switch between them seamlessly. Not only does Outlook Express share common menus and toolbars with the other Internet Explorer components, it also enables you to send an entire Web page to someone with a single click in the browser. The message embeds the page, not just a link to a Web site.

In addition, you can use the Internet Explorer Customization wizard to customize Outlook Express options as part of your custom browser package. You can specify the following information:

- The custom settings that apply to all users, including the default e-mail and news client, new account source information, and message rules
- The configuration for e-mail and news servers
- Whether users are required to log on by using secure password authentication (SPA) to access a server
- The default IMAP settings used to preconfigure IMAP accounts for users
- The LDAP directory services (in addition to standard Windows Address Book directories) that are available
- The custom views and default settings for the Outlook Express main windows, toolbar, and preview pane
- Whether HTML or plain text is used for e-mail and news messages
- The default signatures for e-mail messages and newsgroups
- Any other welcome message, in addition to the Outlook Express welcome message, that greets new users
- The custom content that appears in the Outlook Express InfoPane
- The presubscribed newsgroups for the default news server
- A menu item for users to sign up for a new mail account (Internet service providers only)

For More Information

Additional information about Outlook Express is available from the Microsoft Internet Explorer Web site.

Microsoft Windows Media Player

In the past, you needed to download and configure a separate media player for each type of multimedia content you wanted to play. This process wasted valuable time and system resources. The new Microsoft Windows Media Player solves this problem by enabling you to play different types of streaming multimedia content and local multimedia files from one easy-to-use application. Now, you can play all the popular multimedia formats and even develop your own filters to support other types of multimedia content.

The following illustration shows Media Player playing video content from MSNBC.

Microsoft Windows Media Player Features

You can use Windows Media Player to play popular multimedia formats and even develop your own filters to support other types of multimedia content. The following sections describe Media Player features.

Note If you choose not to install Windows Media Player with your browser package, you can use the Automatic Install feature of Internet Explorer to install this component when you need it.

Support for Multimedia File Formats

Windows Media Player can play most multimedia file formats, including the following:

- .asf
- .au
- .avi
- .midi
- .mov
- .mp3
- .mpeg 1

- .mpeg 2
- QuickTime®
- Real Video 4.0
- Real Audio 4.0
- .vod
- .wav

Also, this version of Media Player upgrades existing Media Player and Microsoft ActiveMovie content.

Customizable Media Playlists

Playlists provide quick access to your favorite content. Content authors can create entire shows that combine multiple pieces of media content using playlists and play them as a single program or continuous loop. Media Player can rapidly switch between the different multimedia streams without pausing between clips. The media can exist on different servers and can include different media types.

Fully Resizable Player

You can select video image sizes of 50%, 100%, 200%, and full screen, or resize the image to any percentage you want, depending on your preference for size and image quality.

Favorites

You can preload the **Favorites** menu with pointers to preferred content and add your own favorite Web site links.

Automatic Codec Download

When you attempt to play a new piece of media content, Media Player checks to see whether the required audio or video codec is installed. If the codec is not installed, Media Player automatically downloads the codec without user intervention.

Support for Multiple Bandwidths

Media Player enables you to play streams of speech-quality audio that range from 2.4 kilobits per second (Kbps) to full-screen, full-motion video at 8 megabits per second (Mbps).

Intelligent Streaming

Media Player can adjust the audio and video streams based on the capabilities of your computer. It chooses between one of two video streams depending on the available bandwidth. When the lower bit-rate stream cannot continue, Media Player requests that the server transmit only key frames. If the available bandwidth is insufficient to run video, Media Player stops the video stream but continues to play audio. Then, as network bandwidth conditions improve, the video stream is automatically restarted and optimized for your continued viewing.

Customizable Advertisement

Media Player provides space that you can use to display branding or advertising messages. Content authors can tailor the advertisements to specific users based on their preferences or other criteria. The advertisements can appear as a video stream or be displayed beside the main window.

Extendable Architecture

Because Media Player is based on Microsoft DirectShow™ architecture, developers can write filters that extend the functionality to support additional multimedia file types and content formats.

For More Information

Additional information about Windows Media Player is available from the Microsoft Windows Media Player Web site.

Microsoft NetMeeting

Microsoft NetMeeting 2.11 is a powerful application that supports real-time communication and collaboration over the Internet or intranet, providing standards-based audio, video, and multipoint data conferencing support. From a desktop running Windows 95, Windows 98, or Windows NT 4.0, you can communicate over the network with real-time voice and video technology. You can share data and information with many people using true application sharing, electronic whiteboard, text-based chat, and file-transfer features.

Connecting to other NetMeeting users is also made easy with the Microsoft Internet Locator Server (ILS), which enables participants to call each other from a dynamic directory within NetMeeting or from a Web page.

The Microsoft NetMeeting Current Call window is shown in the following illustration.

Designed for corporate communication, NetMeeting supports international communication standards for audio, video, and data conferencing. People can use NetMeeting to connect by modem, Integrated Services Digital Network (ISDN), or local area network by using Transmission Control Protocol/Internet Protocol (TCP/IP), and communicate and collaborate with users of NetMeeting and other standards-based, compatible products. In addition, support for custom settings in NetMeeting makes it easy for users to centrally control and manage the NetMeeting work environment.

The Microsoft NetMeeting 2.1 Software Development Kit enables developers to integrate NetMeeting conferencing functionality directly into their applications or Web pages. This open development environment supports international communication and conferencing standards and provides interoperability with products and services from multiple vendors.

Microsoft NetMeeting Features

As the leading Internet conferencing solution, NetMeeting has become the key building block for vendors of conferencing products and services. NetMeeting 2.11, the most recent product release, is designed to support new technology featured in Windows 98, including DirectX 5, Universal Serial Bus (USB) video cameras, and the new video device driver model. NetMeeting 2.11 is packaged as part of Windows 98, but it is also designed to run as a stand-alone product on Windows 95 and Windows NT 4.0 (with Service Pack 3 and later) operating systems.

NetMeeting 2.11 is fully compatible with NetMeeting 1.0 and 2.0, and with applications and solutions that use the NetMeeting SDK for the Windows 95 operating system. With its first release, NetMeeting 1.0 transformed the everyday telephone call into a richer and more effective communication tool. For the first time, people could use voice communication to interact and collaborate over the Internet. Also, this product was the first to introduce multipoint data conferencing capabilities based on the International Telecommunications Union (ITU) T.120 standard.

NetMeeting 2.0 was the next major release of this award-winning multimedia communication client. Building on NetMeeting 1.0 audio and data conferencing capabilities, NetMeeting 2.0 integrated a number of new features and provided improved functionality and an enhanced user interface.

The following sections describe the key features of NetMeeting 2.11.

H.323 Standards-Based Audio Support

Real-time, point-to-point audio conferencing over the Internet or corporate intranet enables you to make voice calls to associates and organizations around the world. NetMeeting audio conferencing offers many features, including half-duplex and full-duplex audio support for real-time conversations, automatic sensitivity-level settings for microphones to ensure that meeting participants hear each other clearly, and microphone muting, which enables you to control the audio signal sent during a call. NetMeeting audio-conferencing supports network TCP/IP connections.

The H.323 protocol provides interoperability between NetMeeting and other H.323-compatible audio clients. The H.323 protocol supports the ITU G.711 and G.723 audio standards and Internet Engineering Task Force (IETF) Real-Time Protocol (RTP) and Real-Time Control Protocol (RTCP) specifications for controlling audio flow to improve voice quality. On multimedia extensions (MMX)-enabled computers, NetMeeting uses the MMX-enabled audio codecs to improve performance for audio compression and decompression algorithms. This capability results in lower CPU use and improved audio quality during a call.

NetMeeting 2.11 infrastructure changes improve interoperability with new H.323 devices, including gateways and Multipoint Conferencing Units (MCUs). These changes include the ability to initiate a call by using the H.323 calling model rather than the T.120 calling model. You will not notice any visible differences resulting from these internal NetMeeting changes, although connections may occur more quickly in some cases.

H.323 Standards-Based Video Conferencing

NetMeeting enables you to send and receive real-time visual images with another conference participant using any video for Windows-compatible equipment. You can share ideas and information face-to-face, and use the camera to instantly view items, such as hardware or devices, that you choose to display in front of the lens. Combined with the audio and data capabilities of NetMeeting, you can both see and hear the other conference participant, as well as share information and applications. This H.323 standard-based video technology is also compliant with the H.261 and H.263 video codecs.

NetMeeting video conferencing includes the following features:

- Users can switch audio and video to another person during a meeting. This feature makes it easy for users to communicate with many different people.

- During a meeting, users can remotely adjust the video image quality, balancing the need for higher quality or faster performance.

- NetMeeting users can dynamically change the size of the video window to reduce or enlarge the image being sent to others.

- In the NetMeeting main window, the video preview and receive windows are located on the Current Call window. Users can view these video windows from Current Call, or they can drag them to a different location on the desktop.

- NetMeeting users can choose whether or not to transmit video immediately when a call starts. Also, they can pause or resume sending or receiving video by pressing a button in the video window frame.

- NetMeeting automatically balances the performance and quality of video during a meeting based on the speed of the network connection, providing the highest quality, lowest bandwidth video capabilities.

- Administrators can control access to video features by using NetMeeting custom settings.

- On MMX-enabled computers, NetMeeting uses the MMX-enabled video codecs to improved performance for video compression and decompression algorithms.

- NetMeeting support for H.323 conference servers and gateways enables users to take part in meetings with multiple audio and video connections.

Intelligent Audio and Video Stream Control

NetMeeting features intelligent control of the audio and video stream, which automatically balances the load for network bandwidth, CPU use, and memory use. This intelligent stream control ensures that audio, video, and data are prioritized properly so that NetMeeting maintains high-quality audio while transmitting and receiving data and video during a call. Using NetMeeting custom settings, IT organizations can configure the stream control services to limit the bandwidth used for audio and video for each client during a meeting.

Multipoint Data Conferencing

Two or more users can communicate and collaborate as a group in real time. They can share applications, exchange information through a shared clipboard, transfer files, collaborate on a shared whiteboard, and use a text-based chat feature. Also, the T.120 data conferencing standard provides interoperability with other T.120-based products and services.

The following features characterize multipoint data conferencing:

- **Application sharing**—You can share an application running on one computer with other participants in the conference. Participants can review the same data or information and see the actions as you work with the application (for example, as you edit content or scroll through information). Participants can share Windows-based applications transparently without any special knowledge of the application's capabilities.

The person sharing the application can choose to collaborate with other conference participants, and can take turns editing or controlling the application. Only the person sharing the application needs to have the given application installed.

- **Shared clipboard**—The shared clipboard enables you to exchange its contents with other participants in a conference by using familiar cut, copy, and paste operations. For example, you can copy information from a local document and paste the contents into a shared application as part of a group collaboration.

- **File transfer**—Using the file transfer capability, you can send a file in the background to one or all of the participants taking part in the conference. When you drag a file into the main window, the file is automatically sent to each person in the conference, who can then accept or decline receipt. This file-transfer capability is fully compliant with the T.127 standard.

- **Whiteboard**—You can simultaneously collaborate with many people by using the whiteboard to review, create, and update graphic information. Because the whiteboard is object-oriented (versus pixel-oriented), you can manipulate the contents by dragging and dropping. In addition, you can use a remote pointer or highlighting tool to point out specific contents or sections of shared pages.

- **Chat**—You can type text messages to share common ideas or topics with other conference participants, or record meeting notes and action items as part of a collaborative process. Also, participants in a conference can use chat to communicate without audio support. A new "whisper" feature enables you to have a separate, private conversation with another person during a group chat session.

Internet Locator Server

Replacing the NetMeeting 1.0 User Location Service (ULS), the Microsoft Internet Locator Server (ILS) for NetMeeting expands existing server technology to provide more advanced directory services, higher scalability, and better performance standards (such as LDAP). ILS enables you to locate other people for conferencing. You can view the ILS directory from within NetMeeting or a Web page and review a list of people currently running NetMeeting. Then, you can choose to connect to one or more of the listed users or select another user by typing the user's location information. For more information about ILS, see the Microsoft BackOffice Web site.

NetMeeting can detect whether a server is available and automatically attempt to log on in the background, without user intervention. If you log off and then log on again later, NetMeeting automatically connects to the specified ILS.

Support for the LDAP Standard

LDAP is an Internet standard that defines the protocol for directory access. NetMeeting uses LDAP to access the ILS and perform server transactions, including logging on and off, creating a directory listing of all available users, and resolving a particular user's address information, such as the IP address. This standards-based approach to directories facilitates interoperability and allows organizations to implement compatible servers.

Support for Windows NT 4.0

Windows NT 4.0 users can communicate and collaborate with each other, with NetMeeting 1.0 users, and with NetMeeting users running the Windows 95 operating system. The functionality of NetMeeting, including audio, video, and multi-user data conferencing for electronic whiteboard, text-based chat, and file transfer, is supported for Windows NT 4.0. Windows NT Service Pack 3 is required for a Windows NT 4.0 user to share applications.

Support for DirectX 5

DirectX is a set of technologies that provide faster access to hardware in Windows. DirectX 5, the latest version of DirectX, is available for Windows 95 and Windows 98. Installing the DirectSound component of DirectX 5 on your computer (with a compatible audio device) significantly speeds up sending or receiving audio over the Internet using NetMeeting. For example, Microsoft testing of a typical audio scenario in NetMeeting 2.0 showed an average delay of 590 milliseconds (ms) end-to-end. However, using NetMeeting 2.11 and DirectSound, the same scenario resulted in an average delay of 160 ms end-to-end.

DirectSound replaces your existing sound card driver with a new DirectX driver. The new DirectX driver supports DirectSound record and playback APIs (and also supports the existing driver functions). You can install the DirectSound component of DirectX 5 from the Microsoft NetMeeting Web site.

Because DirectX drivers are often installed with games, you may already have DirectX capabilities. You must upgrade to DirectX 5, though, because earlier versions of DirectX do not support NetMeeting 2.11.

Note Some DirectX sound drivers do not support full-duplex audio. When you upgrade your existing driver to a DirectSound driver, you may lose this capability. Removing DirectX restores your original configuration with full-duplex audio.

NetMeeting Custom Settings

Custom settings can be used to control access to NetMeeting components and features. These settings provide a standard configuration for the user community. For example, custom settings can prevent the use of audio and video features or limit the network bandwidth for audio and video streams. The NetMeeting Resource Kit wizard, Internet Explorer Customization wizard, and System Policy Editor all provide ways to configure these custom settings. To learn more about using the Customization wizard to preconfigure NetMeeting custom settings, see Appendix E, "Setting System Policies and Restrictions."

User Interface Enhancements

One of the goals of NetMeeting is to enhance the existing user interface so that features are easier to locate, view, and use. Enhancements focus on these areas:

- Four lists, which appear in the NetMeeting main window, make it easy for you to connect to other users and participate in calls:

    - **Directory list**—Shows all of the people currently logged onto the directory server and their audio and video capabilities

    - **SpeedDial list**—Displays entries and their status

    - **Current Call list**—Enumerates the users participating in the current call

    - **History list**—Provides a log of all received calls

- You can filter the directory entries to more easily find and connect with people. For example, you can filter the entries to identify only people currently participating in a call or only people who have audio and video capabilities. Also, you can choose one of three user categories—personal, business, or adults-only—as an additional filter to show only people who selected the same user category.

- A refined NetMeeting **Options** tab and wizards make it easier to set up and configure the NetMeeting environment. A new **Calling** tab enables you to choose directory and SpeedDial options. In addition, an H.323 gateway calling option enables you to connect to a person by using a telephone number.

- A graphical interface similar to the one in Internet Explorer, including a common toolbar, enables you to move easily between applications that are part of Internet Explorer. The toolbar is context-sensitive, displaying the most appropriate options based on the active window.

- The host computer allows the meeting originator to hang up on one or more meeting participants, so people can be removed from the call more easily within conference groups that you participate in.

- E-mail messaging provides you with the option of sending e-mail to people who are not available for conferencing. NetMeeting uses the Messaging Application Programming Interface (MAPI) to start an e-mail client of choice, automatically adds the subject information, and then includes a SpeedDial shortcut so that the person can easily call back later.

NetMeeting Mail Extension

NetMeeting includes a mail extension that works with Microsoft Outlook and Exchange e-mail clients, enabling you to place a call directly from a menu in the e-mail client based on entries in the mail address book. This feature gives you the flexibility to use your e-mail client to send a message or start a real-time meeting from the same mail address book. A NetMeeting custom setting enables you to specify the Exchange attribute for the NetMeeting address.

Outlook Bar

A new Outlook bar gives NetMeeting a look and feel that is consistent with Microsoft Outlook 97 and Outlook Express. This Outlook bar provides easy access to frequently used NetMeeting features, including the Directory, SpeedDial, Current Call, and History lists.

For More Information

Additional information about NetMeeting is available from the Microsoft NetMeeting Web site.

Microsoft FrontPage Express

Based on the full-featured Microsoft FrontPage 97 Web authoring and management tool, FrontPage Express features a graphical interface that makes creating HTML pages as easy as creating a document in a word processor. FrontPage Express enables you to create your own Web pages in a what-you-see-is-what-you-get environment, without knowing HTML. FrontPage Express includes all the features of the FrontPage 97 editor, except for premium features, such as Active Server Pages and some of the WebBot components (special preprogrammed scripts) that rely on specific server extensions.

The following illustration shows the FrontPage Express HTML editor.

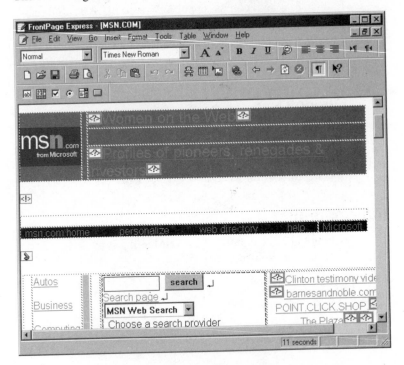

Microsoft FrontPage Express Features

You can use Front Page Express to author and publish your own Web pages and edit existing HTML documents. The following sections describe the features of the FrontPage Express editor.

Flexible Authoring Environment

FrontPage Express offers two ways to create and edit Web pages. The word-processing-style editor displays a graphical representation of what the Web page will look like when it's published. You can type the contents directly onto the page and highlight text to change the color, size, and style. You can also specify background colors and graphics, text and link colors, margins, and base location.

FrontPage Express enables authors to view the actual HTML code that is being generated. Color codes, indentation, and formats make it easy to read the HTML code. Authors who are comfortable working with HTML can even edit in this mode and instantly see the results in the FrontPage Express application.

Table Creation and Editing

The Insert Table feature enables you to generate tables effortlessly, because FrontPage Express creates all the HTML code automatically based on your input. You can insert the table into a Web page and then edit either the entire table or individual cells. This feature also makes it easy to create nested tables without knowing HTML.

Forms Creation

You can add forms to your Web page that people can fill out and return. Your forms can include text boxes, drop-down menus, images, and more. You must be connected to a server running FrontPage server extensions to use these form-related features.

Templates and Wizards

If you are connected to a server running FrontPage server extensions, you can also use form-related templates and wizards in FrontPage Express. Templates are preformatted Web pages that you can use as a guide to create your own pages and Web View folders. Wizards walk you through the step-by-step process of creating a Web page. Templates and wizards enable you to create the forms you want just by selecting the types of information you need. You can also create a survey to collect information from readers and store it on your Web server, or you can create a page to acknowledge that you have received the reader's input.

Support for Web Technologies

FrontPage Express support for standard Internet technologies means that you can make your pages more engaging without any programming knowledge. You can insert JavaScript, Java applets, Visual Basic Scripting Edition, and ActiveX objects. Also, you can add form elements, such as text boxes, buttons, and drop-down menus, to pages directly from the toolbar. Then, you can easily edit these properties.

For More Information

Additional information about FrontPage Express is available from the Microsoft Internet Explorer Web site.

Microsoft Chat

Microsoft Chat 2.5 enables you to conduct real-time conversations in an Internet chat room. This chat program gives you two ways to communicate and share ideas with other people:

- Text mode, which displays text only
- Comics mode, where your conversation appears as a combination of text and graphical features inside a comic strip

In comics mode, you and other chat participants are depicted as cartoon characters, and your conversation appears as word balloons inside the frames of a comic strip. A "wheel of faces" in the bottom right corner of your chat window displays facial expressions. As you type your chat responses, you can click the expression you want your character to make. Also, you can add sound effects to your chat. Pick a sound file, and Microsoft Chat inserts the sound effect into your conversation.

You can choose from one of more than twenty cartoon characters that Microsoft Chat provides for you, or you can create your own character by using the Microsoft Chat Character Editor. Using Microsoft Chat, you can create your own background for your comic strip as well. With its condensed file format, you can place the character and background files on a Web server for everyone in your chat room to download.

The following illustration shows Microsoft Chat in text mode.

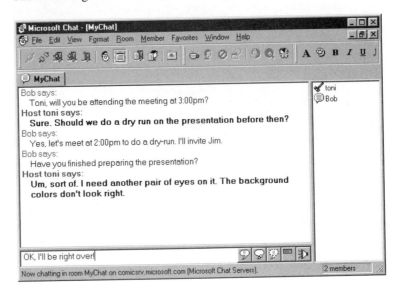

Microsoft Chat Features

Whether you chat in text or comics mode, you can take advantage of the Microsoft Chat features described in the following sections.

Toolbar Buttons

The toolbar buttons at the bottom of your chat room window—**Say**, **Whisper**, **Think**, **Action**, and **Sounds**—give you convenient one-click access to the Microsoft Chat features you use most often. For example, click the **Think** button to post a message that tells everyone what you're thinking. Use the **Action** button to tell the other chat participants what you are currently doing. Click the **Whisper** button to send private sounds and actions to a specific person rather than to the entire chat room.

Automation Rules

You can use automation rules to define responses for any event in the same way that you create Inbox rules for Microsoft Outlook. For example, you can make a rule that defines a specific message or sound that plays when someone whispers a message to you.

Automatic Logon and Friends Notification

When you start Microsoft Chat, the program automatically locates and connects you to the first available network server. As you chat, you can receive instant notification when friends log on and off your server.

Chat Room Member Lists

You can find out the names of all the participants in a chat room before you join by checking the member list for the room. The member list also enables you to view the participants' names in any available chat room and invite people to join your chat. You can also select a person from the list and whisper a secret message to that person.

Font Choices

In text mode, you can choose the fonts for any or all of the text that appears on the chat screen, including the message header and the message itself. When you click the **Set Font** button, a window displays the various message types you can format and a list of the fonts you can use. In comics mode, you can select the font you want for the text balloons.

Powerful Macros

Send complex actions, sounds, and multiple commands in a macro. You can easily set up one or more macros to insert your favorite bits of repartee into conversations with a simple keyboard shortcut. Select the keyboard combination you like, and give your macro a name so you can recognize it in the Macro List on the **View** menu. Then, press the key combination when you are ready to quickly post your remark into a chat room conversation.

NetMeeting Integration

You can fully integrate Microsoft Chat and NetMeeting if both you and the person you are calling have installed both applications. By using both Microsoft Chat and NetMeeting, you have a complete communication package that enables you to send chat messages while simultaneously holding NetMeeting voice and video conversations with friends, family, and business associates. In addition, you can share software applications or use the NetMeeting electronic whiteboard to collaborate with others in real time over the Internet or intranet.

Cross-Platform Solution

Although Microsoft Chat is available only for the Windows 95, Windows 98, and Windows NT 4.0 operating systems, you can still converse with Macintosh®, UNIX, and Windows 3.1 users. If users do not have a Java-enabled browser, they can download Microsoft Internet Explorer and then use Microsoft Chat 1.0 j. Also, Microsoft Chat can interoperate with other Internet Relay Chat (IRC) chat clients.

Development Platform

The *Microsoft Chat Software Development Kit* enables you to develop your own chat room. By inserting the Microsoft Chat controls (ActiveX-based controls) or Microsoft Chat 1.0 j or Microsoft Script Chat 1.0 (Java applets) controls into your Web pages, you instantly create a site where people can meet and chat with each other for hours.

For More Information

Additional information about Microsoft Chat is available from the Microsoft Chat Web site.

Additional Microsoft and Third-Party Components

In addition to the primary components described in the previous sections, Internet Explorer contains other Microsoft and third-party components that you can install. These additional components include the following:

- **Microsoft Offline Browsing Pack**—The Offline Browsing Pack enables users to view their favorite Web pages without being connected to the Internet. Offline browsing enables users to connect to the Internet periodically to download Web content, and then browse this content offline at their convenience.

- **Microsoft Internet Explorer Help**—Internet Explorer provides a comprehensive set of Help topics that users can access to find answers to questions, troubleshoot potential problems, or get additional product information.

- **Microsoft Virtual Machine**—The Virtual Machine (VM) enables users to browse Web pages that contain Java-enhanced content.

- **Microsoft Internet Explorer Connection wizard**—The Internet Explorer Connection wizard steps users through the process of signing up with and using an Internet service provider (ISP) to connect to the Internet.

- **Microsoft Internet Explorer core fonts**—This core set of TrueType® fonts has been optimized to provide maximum on-screen legibility.

- **Dynamic HTML data binding**—Data binding components allow Internet Explorer to access information from a database and display it in Web pages.

- **Microsoft Internet Explorer browsing enhancements**—Browsing enhancements include a graphical File Transfer Protocol (FTP) helper.

- **Microsoft Windows Media Player codecs**—These codecs support audio and video playback for Windows Media Player.

- **Media Player RealNetwork support**—This component is necessary for Microsoft Windows Media Player to play RealNetwork media files.

- **DirectAnimation**—This component provides animation and multimedia services for your computer, both for Web content and stand-alone products.

- **Vector Graphics Rendering (VML)**—This rendering tool enables users to view vector graphics images with Internet Explorer.

- **AOL Art Image Format Support**—This component enables you to view images from Internet Explorer that were created in AOL Art format.

- **Macromedia Shockwave Director**—With Director, you can create a variety of multimedia productions, including business presentations, Web content, interactive advertising pieces, Kiosk-mode productions, and CD-ROM titles.

- **Macromedia Flash**—Flash brings Web pages to life without the wait. Vector-based Flash movies offer compact, interactive Web interfaces, animations, buttons, advertising banners, logos, maps, cartoons, and more.

- **Microsoft Web Publishing wizard**—The Web Publishing wizard steps users through the process of uploading content and posting their Web site to almost any Web server available.

- **Web folders**—Web folders enable users to access FrontPage and Web servers for editing purposes.

- **Microsoft Visual Basic® scripting support**—This component provides support for viewing Web pages that use the VBScript scripting language.

- **Additional Web fonts**—This set of additional TrueType fonts enables users to read Web-page text that was designed for viewing with Arial, Comic, Courier, Impact, and Times New Roman fonts.

- **Microsoft Wallet**—This component makes the use of credit cards and mailing addresses for Web commerce secure. Users can employ the browser to purchase products or carry out banking and other financial transactions with complete safety and security.

- **Language auto-selection**—This feature enables Internet Explorer to automatically detect the language encoding of Web pages.

- **Japanese text display support**—The Japanese language pack includes TrueType fonts and other support files that enable Internet Explorer to display Japanese text.

- **Japanese text input support**—The Japanese Input Method Editor (IME) allows Japanese characters to be entered as text in other language versions of Windows.

- **Korean text display support**—The Korean language pack includes TrueType fonts and other support files that enable Internet Explorer to display Korean text.

- **Korean text input support**—The Korean IME allows Korean characters to be entered as text in other language versions of Windows.

- **Pan-European text display support**—The Pan-European language pack includes TrueType fonts and other support files that enable Internet Explorer to display Central European, Cyrillic, Greek, Turkish, and Baltic text.

- **Chinese (traditional) text display support**—The traditional Chinese language pack includes TrueType fonts and other support files that enable Internet Explorer to display traditional Chinese text.

- **Chinese (traditional) text input support**—The traditional Chinese IME allows traditional Chinese characters to be entered as text in other language versions of Windows.

- **Chinese (simplified) text display support**—The simplified Chinese language pack includes TrueType fonts and other support files that enable Internet Explorer to display simplified Chinese text.

- **Chinese (simplified) text input support**—The simplified Chinese IME allows simplified Chinese characters to be entered as text in other language versions of Windows.

- **Vietnamese text display support**—The Vietnamese language pack includes TrueType fonts and other support files that enable Internet Explorer to display Vietnamese text.

- **Hebrew text display support**—The Hebrew language pack includes TrueType fonts and other support files that enable Internet Explorer to display Hebrew text.

- **Arabic text display support**—The Arabic language pack includes TrueType fonts and other support files that enable Internet Explorer to display Arabic text.

- **Thai text display support**—The Thai language pack includes TrueType fonts and other support files that enable Internet Explorer to display Thai text.

C H A P T E R   3

Understanding Customization and Administration

This chapter describes how you can tailor Microsoft Internet Explorer 5 to fit the needs of your organization. Information in this chapter applies to corporate administrators, Internet service providers, Internet content providers, independent software vendors, and developers.

The Microsoft Internet Explorer Administration Kit (IEAK) provides a convenient way to alter the appearance and behavior of Internet Explorer and to customize Windows Update Setup for Internet Explorer 5 and Internet Tools. In addition, the IEAK enables corporate administrators to control many user actions, including file management, desktop behavior, and Internet usage. The IEAK also enables Internet service providers to develop tools and processes to sign up new customers.

In This Chapter

See Also

- For more information about developing deployment, training, and support plans, which you will test during the pilot installation, see Chapter 9, "Planning the Deployment."

- For more information about preparing graphics files and obtaining digital signatures, see Chapter 12, "Preparing for the IEAK."

- For more information about building custom packages, see Chapter 15, "Running the Internet Explorer Customization Wizard."

- For more information about deploying Internet Explorer to your users following the pilot program, see Chapter 19, "Deploying Microsoft Internet Explorer 5."

Reasons to Customize Internet Explorer

There are several reasons for customizing Internet Explorer. The benefits that you can gain from customization will vary depending on your role in your organization:

- If you're a corporate administrator, you can save time by centrally administering individual installations of Internet Explorer.

- If you're an Internet service provider, you can customize Internet Explorer so that customers can easily sign up for your services.

- If you're an Internet content provider, you can choose customization options for Internet Explorer that help showcase your content more effectively.

- If you're an independent software vendor or developer, you can easily distribute your program with Internet Explorer by customizing Windows Update Setup.

Customization Benefits for Corporate Administrators

You can control how Internet Explorer is installed, how the browsing software and Internet Explorer components get customized, and what browser, messaging, and conferencing options are available before installation begins. You can customize Internet Explorer for Windows 16-bit, Windows 32-bit, Apple Macintosh®, and UNIX platforms.

You can use automatic configuration and proxy files to change browser settings after you install Internet Explorer. If the needs of your organization change, you can use the IEAK Profile Manager to change the files that contain user options without leaving your office.

You can also set policies and restrictions for the browser, including security, messaging, and desktop settings. This can help you manage your organization's resources and bandwidth. Does your accounting department have different needs than your marketing department? You can create different profiles that contain settings and restrictions tailored for each department.

Customizing Windows Update Setup

You can customize Windows Update Setup in several ways. You can add Internet Explorer components or create up to 10 different setup options. This extends the Minimal, Typical, and Full options that come with default installations of Internet Explorer. Adding several setup options can be helpful if your employees have different usage needs and varying disk-space limitations.

Perhaps you want to reduce options so that certain setup choices are already made for users. You can configure Internet Explorer so that users can install it with little or no intervention from you. This setup option is sometimes referred to as a "silent install."

Installations with limited intervention are often used for setting up Internet Explorer after hours, when employees aren't at their desks. You can further adapt these types of installations by using command-line switches or batch files. Because you are making choices for the user, you can create only one "silent install" setup option.

If you suppress all user feedback, including error messages and status information, you should make sure your setup plan includes error handling. If you suppress restarting after installation, you'll need to handle restarting in your custom program or script to ensure that Internet Explorer is set up correctly. You can learn more about these issues in the IEAK online Help and in Chapter 16, "Customizing Setup," in this book.

You may find it convenient to install your own custom components—such as virus-checking programs or scripts—when you install Internet Explorer. You can include up to 10 custom components in your custom package.

You can also alter the appearance of the setup program by adding your own bitmap and including custom descriptions for your different setup options.

Note If you need to customize existing installations of Internet Explorer 4.01 Service Pack 1 and higher, you can use single-disk branding. This option creates a Setup.exe file in the BrndOnly folder of your build location. You can distribute this file on any media or server. When this file is run, it will customize Internet Explorer features without installing Internet Explorer. This option does not enable you to package and install custom components, however.

Customizing the Browser, Desktop, and Other Programs

You can customize the appearance and behavior of the browsing software, the user's desktop, and the Internet Explorer messaging and conferencing components. These customizations can help you create a standard corporate desktop that's easier to manage.

To customize the browser, you can add your organization's name or another message to the title bar. For example, the phrase "Microsoft Internet Explorer Provided by ABX Computer Corporation" could appear on your title bar. You can also customize the static and animated logos that appear in the upper-right corner of the browser.

You can preset the following Web pages and links:

- Corporate support page
- User's home page
- User's search page
- Links on the Links bar
- Links on the Favorites bar
- Channels (specialized ways of delivering Web content)
- Add-on Components page (for optional components)

The following illustration is an example of how you might customize a user's Favorites list with helpful links.

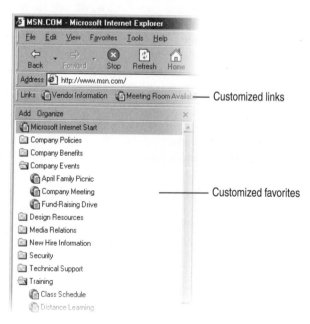

If your organization has standardized on the Active Desktop™ that was included with Internet Explorer 4.0, you can reinstall the desktop component with Internet Explorer 5. Even if only some of your users are running Internet Explorer 4.0, you can include the desktop component with Internet Explorer 5 so that all users have the same desktop. If your users are running Windows 98, they already have the new desktop.

You can also customize Internet Explorer components, such as Microsoft Outlook Express, Microsoft NetMeeting, and Microsoft Chat. You can preset server information for Outlook Express and customize the InfoPane that appears when users start Outlook Express. You can add a signature to all e-mail and newsgroup messages, such as a disclaimer that the sender's views don't represent your organization's policies.

In addition, you can customize remote dialing for your users, including the dialing settings they need, the icon they click, and the dialog box they see when they dial in to your services. Providing a preconfigured dialer, called a Connection Manager, can help reduce the amount of support that your help desk must provide for remote access services (RAS).

If your organization's messaging server doesn't automatically provide directory or address book services, you can use Lightweight Directory Access Protocol (LDAP) to set up those services for your network.

Maintaining Internet Explorer

If you will need to change settings after you install Internet Explorer, you should consider using automatic configuration, which enables you to change user settings globally at any time.

You can use the IEAK Profile Manager to create an installation (.ins) file containing user profile information. You then post the .ins file and custom cabinet (.cab) files on a server. When you use the Internet Explorer Customization wizard, which is part of the IEAK, you can point your users' browsers to the specific .ins file.

You can import connection settings, such as proxy servers, when you run the Customization wizard. You can also customize and maintain connection settings by using the IEAK Profile Manager. If your organization uses an automated program, such as a script in a proxy automatic configuration (.pac) file, a Jscript (.js) file, or a JavaScript (.jvs) file to control proxy settings, you can incorporate it into your Internet Explorer package.

For more information about using the IEAK, see Chapter 15, "Running the Internet Explorer Customization Wizard." For more information about automatic configuration, see Chapter 21, "Using Automatic Configuration and Automatic Proxy."

Setting Restrictions and Using System Policies

When users customize their programs, they sometimes create challenges for corporate administrators. Although some changes just reflect user preferences, other changes make it difficult for corporate administrators to manage resources, control security, or maintain consistent functionality. By using the IEAK, you can control user settings and, in some cases, disable browser features that don't fit your organization's needs.

You can "lock down" or control user settings by using the Internet Explorer Customization wizard or the IEAK Profile Manager. If you're familiar with system policies, you can import administration (.adm) files, and then customize them when you use the IEAK.

Both the Customization wizard and the Profile Manager have graphical interfaces that enable you to easily set and clear options. Just make sure to analyze whether you should control options on a "per computer" or "per user" basis. If you have roaming users who have different needs than other users, you may not want to lock down settings on a per-computer basis.

Customization Benefits for Internet Service Providers

You can customize the appearance of the browser and Setup, tailor Internet Explorer packages to meet various customer needs, and incorporate sign-up solutions. You can customize Internet Explorer for Windows 16-bit platforms and Windows 32-bit platforms by using the IEAK 5.

Customizing the Browser and Other Programs

You can customize the appearance and behavior of the browsing software and the Internet Explorer messaging and conferencing components.

To customize the browser, you can add your organization's name or another message to the title bar. For example, the phrase "Microsoft Internet Explorer Provided by ABX Computer Corporation" could appear on your title bar. You can also customize the static and animated logos that appear in the upper-right corner of the browser.

You can preset the following Web pages and links:

- Customer support page
- User's home page
- User's search page
- Links in the Links bar
- Links in the Favorites bar
- Channels (specialized ways of delivering Web content)

- Add-on Components page (for optional components)
- Sign-up and billing pages

The following illustration shows how you can customize the title bar, links bar, and logo.

Illustration 3.1   Internet Explorer with Customized Title Bar, Links Bar, and Logo

You can also customize Internet Explorer components, such as Microsoft Outlook Express. You can preset server information for Outlook Express and customize the InfoPane that appears when users start Outlook Express. You can add a signature to all e-mail and newsgroup messages, such as a disclaimer that the sender's views don't represent your organization's policies.

Tailoring Internet Explorer to Different Customer Needs

If you have customers who live in different parts of the world or who have different configurations, you can create different Internet Explorer packages to address those needs. You can create packages for different language versions of Internet Explorer, and you can determine which components to include with your packages.

If you distribute Internet Explorer in different countries, you can add the appropriate language packs, font packs, and versions of Internet Explorer components. You can also include different sets of sign-up pages using the appropriate languages.

You can add a custom component that you've created, such as an address book utility, for your customers to install when they set up Internet Explorer. You can include up to 10 custom components with your custom package.

Because customers often have different hard-disk limitations and advanced component needs, you can create up to 10 setup choices for them by using the IEAK. You can also design packages for different media, such as a Web server or a CD-ROM.

In addition, you can customize remote dialing for your customers by including the dialing settings they need, the icon they click, and the dialog box they see when they dial in to your services. This can give your Internet service a "branded" look so that customers have a consistent experience with your services.

Some of your users might have specialized logon needs as a result of their location or their hardware. If you're concerned that they will need to enter complicated settings manually each time they connect, you can create a logon script. The script can configure logon settings and can even manage pauses between dialing sequences so that users don't have to worry about their settings.

Notes If you need to customize existing installations of Internet Explorer 4.01 Service Pack 1 and higher, you can use single-disk branding. This option creates a Setup.exe file in the BrndOnly folder of your build location. You can distribute this file on any media or server. When this file is run, it will customize Internet Explorer features without installing Internet Explorer. This option does not enable you to package and install custom components, however.

If you are an Internet Service Provider, and plan to set up a sign-up server solution, you need to use Kiosk-mode sign-up for Internet Explorer 4.01 SP1 users. If you anticipate that some customers will have Internet Explorer 5 and others will have Internet Explorer 4.01 SP1,you can create an IEAK package that includes both types of sign-up server solutions.

Developing and Incorporating Sign-up Solutions

In addition to setting up Internet Explorer for customers, you probably also need to sign customers up and bill them for your services. The IEAK comes with sample sign-up pages and scripts that you can customize to create a complete sign-up solution for your customers.

You can use the IEAK to design server-based and serverless solutions. You can use a sign-up server to provide a new customer with a fully active account. If a customer already has an account with your service or another service, you can update the user's settings through single-disk branding.

You can also use a server-based solution to customize Internet Explorer for different sets of customers without having to create a separate IEAK package for each group. In this case, all of the compact discs you send out are the same, but they are branded differently when the customer signs up.

For more information about Internet sign-up, see Chapter 20, "Implementing the Sign-up Process."

Customization Benefits for Internet Content Providers

You can customize the appearance of the browser and Setup to showcase your content in a number of ways. You can customize Internet Explorer for Windows 16-bit, Windows 32-bit, and Apple Macintosh platforms.

Customizing the Browser

You can customize the appearance of the browsing software. That way, your organization's content can be more prominent when the user browses the Internet.

What are some reasons for customizing the browser? Perhaps you want to customize the customer's home page with content and links related to your business. By continually updating the content on your Web sites, you can keep your customers interested in and informed about your products or services.

To customize the browser, you can add your organization's name or another message to the title bar. For example, the phrase "Microsoft Internet Explorer Provided by ABX Computer Corporation" could appear on your title bar. You can also customize the static and animated logos that appear in the upper-right corner of the browser.

You can preset the following Web pages and links:

- Customer support page
- User's home page
- User's search page
- Links in the Links bar
- Links in the Favorites bar
- Channels (specialized ways of delivering Web content)
- Add-on Components page (for optional components)

Note If you need to customize existing installations of Internet Explorer 4.01 Service Pack 1 and higher, you can use single-disk branding. This option creates a Setup.exe file in the BrndOnly folder of your build location. You can distribute this file on any media or server. When this file is run, it will customize Internet Explorer features without installing Internet Explorer. This option does not enable you to package and install custom components, however.

Customization Benefits for Internet Developers

You can include Internet Explorer technologies, such as the WebBrowser control, with your custom program. You can redistribute Internet Explorer on Windows 16-bit, Windows 32-bit, and Apple Macintosh platforms.

You can use the Microsoft Internet Explorer Administration Kit (IEAK) to easily create Internet Explorer distribution media. You can also specify home and search pages and a favorites list. This enables you to create and distribute a Web browser that reflects your organization's specific needs and the needs of your users.

By using setup scripts or command-line switches, you can reduce or eliminate the user interaction required to install Internet Explorer. This helps ensure a smooth installation experience when users set up your custom program with Internet Explorer.

Note If you need to customize existing installations of Internet Explorer 4.01 Service Pack 1 and higher, you can use single-disk branding. This option creates a Setup.exe file in the BrndOnly folder of your build location. You can distribute this file on any media or server. When this file is run, it will customize Internet Explorer features without installing Internet Explorer. This option does not enable you to package and install custom components, however.

Using the Microsoft Internet Explorer Administration Kit

The Internet Explorer Administration Kit (IEAK) includes the Internet Explorer Customization wizard, the IEAK Profile Manager, the Connection Manager Administration Kit (CMAK), and the IEAK Toolkit.

You will find more information about using the IEAK in Chapter 15, "Running the Internet Explorer Customization Wizard." Before using the IEAK, however, you should spend some time planning your installation so that you'll know which decisions to make when you create your installation package.

You use the Internet Explorer Customization wizard to build custom packages. After you build custom packages, you distribute them to the appropriate user groups so that they can install customized versions of Internet Explorer on their desktops. Internet Explorer is installed with the settings and options that you specified when you built your custom package.

Preparing to Build Custom Packages

You'll get the most out of using the IEAK if you do some advance planning. You'll want to assess the needs of your users, analyze your organization's needs, and develop a deployment plan. You might also want to set up a deployment lab where you can test a pilot installation. For more information about getting ready to run the IEAK, see Chapter 12, "Preparing for the IEAK." For more information about developing an installation plan, see Chapter 9, "Planning the Deployment," and Chapter 11, "Setting Up and Administering a Pilot Program."

You'll also want to gather the URLs you'll need and create any custom graphics. For more information, see Chapter 12, "Preparing for the IEAK." For a preparation checklist and graphics resolutions and dimensions, see Appendix D, "Checklists for Preparing to Use the IEAK."

If your users will download your custom package over the Internet, you'll want to obtain a digital certificate to sign the custom .cab files that you create with the IEAK and any custom programs that you include. The .cab files are used to organize and compress installation files that are copied to the user's computer. If you have a publisher's certificate on your computer, you can sign your files when you run the Internet Explorer Customization wizard, which is included with the IEAK. For more information about signing files, see Chapter 12 "Preparing for the IEAK."

What's in the IEAK?

The following programs and tools come with the IEAK.

Internet Explorer Customization Wizard

The Customization wizard divides the customization process into five stages. Step-by-step screens for each stage guide you through the process of creating customized Internet Explorer packages.

IEAK Profile Manager

You can use the Profile Manager to change user settings and restrictions automatically after Internet Explorer is installed.

Connection Manager Administration Kit

The Connection Manager Administration Kit (CMAK) is a wizard that guides you through customizing and configuring the Microsoft Connection Manager dialer. The CMAK creates a self-extracting executable (.exe) file that installs itself on the user's computer. When the user clicks the custom icon to connect to the Internet, the custom dialer dialog box that you created appears. You can customize the dialer by building a custom service profile into your Internet Explorer packages.

IEAK Toolkit

The IEAK Toolkit contains helpful tools, programs, and sample files, such as the animated bitmap tools, IExpress wizard, and sample signup and add-on files. The Toolkit contents are located in the \Toolkit folder of the IEAK program folder.

IEAK Help

IEAK Help contains many conceptual and procedural topics that you can access by using the Index, Contents, and Search tabs. You can print topics from IEAK Help.

Starting the Internet Explorer Customization Wizard

Microsoft Internet Explorer 5 must be installed before you set up the IEAK. Before starting the installation process, make sure that you have enough disk space to download the Internet Explorer files and to build your IEAK packages. Information about how to use the IEAK is covered in detail in Chapter 12, "Preparing for the IEAK."

This procedure shows how to start the IEAK after you install it.

▶ **To start the Internet Explorer Customization wizard**

1. On the **Start** menu, point to **Programs**.

2. Point to **Microsoft IEAK**, and then click **Internet Explorer Customization Wizard**.

Integrating Your Custom Solutions

The IEAK gives you a high level of control over installation and customization. You can also use some of the tools that come with the IEAK to further tailor a solution for your organization.

The IEAK supports the use of batch files to further control Setup. For example, you can use a batch file if you need to temporarily download files from a location that isn't specified in your custom package.

The IExpress wizard, which is included in the IEAK Toolkit, can integrate command-line switches into your Internet Explorer package so they are run automatically during installation. The IExpress wizard provides graphical screens that enable you to control other setup options as well.

You can find more detailed information in Chapter 16, "Customizing Setup."

The IEAK Toolkit, which is installed on your hard disk when you set up the IEAK, contains additional samples that you can modify and tools that you can use to extend the IEAK functionality for your organization.

Sample Scenarios

You can customize Internet Explorer in many ways to accommodate different preferences and needs. To help you get started, here are just a few ideas about how an organization might customize Internet Explorer.

Corporate Administration Example

You can customize Internet Explorer to meet differing needs in your organization. For example, you might want to customize the following items:

- Include fewer components in custom packages used by employees in the field who might have limited disk space on their laptop computers.

- Include support for different character sets for employees who communicate with overseas departments, so they can correctly view Web pages in different languages.

- Create a CD-ROM setup for users in a remote country so that they do not need to connect to the local area network (LAN) or wide area network (WAN) used by most of your employees for downloading Setup.

- Increase the level of security for employees downloading from the Internet by creating a different IEAK package with enhanced security options or by using automatic configuration to modify their security settings.

Internet Service Provider Example

To accommodate different user preferences, you might want to customize the following items:

- Create an Internet Explorer package that includes several installation choices. That way, you can accommodate customers who want to use a different e-mail program than Microsoft Outlook Express, as well as experienced users who want to use more advanced components.

- Customize and control connection settings. For example, you can have a program run either before or after your users connect to the Internet. You can also add your organization's logo to the dialog box that appears when users dial in to the Internet.

- Customize Microsoft Outlook Express. You can modify the chat servers that appear in your customers' server list, specify a default server, and specify a default chat room. That way, your customers can get connected and start using their software more quickly and with less technical support from your organization.

Internet Content Provider Example

You might want to customize Internet Explorer to showcase your organization's information and services better on the Internet. For example, you could customize the following items:

- If your organization is a radio station, add links to your organization's Web sites, such as pages that highlight play lists and composers' biographies. You can also add your organization's name to the title bar and your organization's logo to the setup bitmap. In addition, you can replace the browser logo with a treble clef symbol, musical notes, or your organization's logo.

- Track usage of your customized browser by using a user agent string, which is a string of characters that a Web browser sends when it visits an Internet site. The custom string that you append to the user agent string enables Web sites to compile statistics about how many of your customers are using your browser to view the site.

Internet Developer Example

You might want to customize the following items:

- Create a custom program that uses, or "hosts," the WebBrowser control, but does not display the Windows Update Setup interface during installation.

- Use a batch file and command-line switches to install Internet Explorer in redistribution mode. This mode installs the underlying program files without overwriting the Internet Explorer icon, if Internet Explorer already exists on the user's computer. You can also suppress Windows Update Setup prompts, so that your custom program provides setup feedback to the user.

- Customize the Web browser with links to your organization's Web sites or to related technologies. Then you can use the IEAK to create a CD-ROM package that includes your custom program.

C H A P T E R   4

Working with Different Platforms

This chapter identifies the platforms on which you can install Microsoft Internet Explorer 5 and describes the deployment variations among the supported platforms. This information is particularly important if you are deploying Internet Explorer on multiple platforms.

In This Chapter

See Also

- For more information about planning your browser deployment for different platforms, see Chapter 9, "Planning the Deployment."

- For more information about building custom packages of Internet Explorer for different platforms, see Chapter 15, "Running the Internet Explorer Customization Wizard."

- For more information about installing Internet Explorer on different platforms, see Chapter 19, "Deploying Microsoft Internet Explorer 5."

Overview

You can install Internet Explorer 5 on the following platforms:

- Windows
    - Windows 32-bit versions, including Windows 95, Windows 98, Windows NT 3.51, and Windows NT 4.0
    - Windows 16-bit versions, including Windows 3.1 and Windows for Workgroups 3.11

Note Although Windows NT 3.51 is a 32-bit platform, it must run the 16-bit version of Internet Explorer.

- UNIX, including Sun Solaris 2.5.1, Sun Solaris 2.6, and Hewlett Packard HP-UX

If your organization uses several different platforms, you will need to deploy and maintain a separate version of Internet Explorer 5 for each platform. Internet Explorer 5 provides a single, standards-based set of technologies for Web authoring, browsing, communication, and collaboration for all supported platforms. The HTML rendering engine for Internet Explorer on Windows and UNIX platforms was derived from the same code base, so developers are assured that content developed for one platform will render the same on all platforms.

Note Although Macintosh is not included in this platform discussion, Internet Explorer for the Macintosh is also developed from the same standards-based set of technologies. If you have deployed Internet Explorer on the Macintosh platform or developed Web content for the Macintosh, you can expect the same benefits of this common browser across all platforms.

If you plan to install Internet Explorer on different platforms, you should consider the following issues:

- **Planning the deployment**—To successfully deploy Internet Explorer, you need to determine the platform and browser requirements for all groups targeted to migrate to Internet Explorer. For more information about planning your deployment on different platforms, see Chapter 9, "Planning the Deployment."
- **Conducting a pilot program**—Before you deploy Internet Explorer to your users, you should conduct a pilot program to test your browser packages for each platform. For more information about conducting a pilot program, see Chapter 11, "Setting Up and Administering a Pilot Program."

- **Building custom packages**—You can use the Internet Explorer Customization wizard, which is part of the Internet Explorer Administration Kit (IEAK) 5, to build custom packages of Internet Explorer for the Windows and UNIX platforms. For more information about the Internet Explorer Customization wizard, see Chapter 15, "Running the Internet Explorer Customization Wizard."

- **Maintaining browser versions**—You can use the IEAK Profile Manager to administer Internet Explorer for the Windows and UNIX platforms. The IEAK Profile Manager enables you to update browser settings and manage different versions of the browser from a single location. For more information about using the IEAK Profile Manager, see Chapter 22, "Keeping Programs Updated."

Windows Platform: 32-bit Versions

The 32-bit versions of Windows integrate Internet technology and browser features directly into the operating system. This browser-platform integration means that users who run Windows 32-bit versions can take advantage of advanced browsing capabilities. Users can browse their hard disk, local area network, or the Internet to quickly find the information they need. Using Internet Explorer, they can quickly navigate the Web using the Search, History, and Favorites bars, or get information delivered directly to their computers for offline viewing. For more information about this browser-platform integration, see the Microsoft Windows Web site at http://www.microsoft.com/windows/.

Some Internet Explorer customization features, deployment methods, and maintenance practices are specific to Windows 32-bit versions. You should consider the following issues when you deploy Internet Explorer on Windows 32-bit versions:

- **CD-ROM installation**—If you distribute your custom-browser package to users who run Windows 32-bit versions on a CD-ROM, a splash-screen Autorun program appears when users insert the disc. This program offers users the choice of installing your custom browser or viewing more information. If the current version of Internet Explorer is already installed, the Autorun program detects it. The browser appears in what is known as Kiosk mode (if this feature is enabled using the Internet Explorer Customization wizard), with the Start.htm file or your own custom start page loaded.

- **Administrative privileges**—For Windows NT, you must have privileges as an administrator to install and uninstall Internet Explorer. Users must, therefore, have administrative privileges the first time they start their computers after installing or uninstalling Internet Explorer.

- **Setup download folder**—You can find the IE5Setup.exe file in the media type folder created for your language and platform version. For example, the English version of Internet Explorer for Windows 32-bit versions would reside in the \Download\Win32\En folder of your build directory.

- **Code signing**—If you are distributing Internet Explorer 5 over the Internet or intranet, you should sign custom cabinet (.cab) files created by the Internet Explorer Customization wizard for Windows 32-bit versions. This is recommended unless you preconfigure the Local intranet zone with the Low security setting. You should also sign any custom components that you distribute with your browser package for this platform. Code signing lets users know that they can trust your code before downloading it to their computers. The default settings in Internet Explorer will reject unsigned code. If you have a digital certificate, the Internet Explorer Customization wizard can sign these files automatically.

- **Single-disk branding**—When you build custom packages using the Internet Explorer Customization wizard, you can choose the single-disk branding option for your media type. This option customizes an existing installation of Internet Explorer 4.01 Service Pack 1 (which is part of Windows 98) or higher. It does not install Internet Explorer 5.

Windows Platform: 16-bit Versions

Internet Explorer delivers a full set of browser features and functions for Windows 16-bit versions. The 16-bit versions of Internet Explorer were designed for computers with less than 12 MB of RAM and requires as little as 6.5 MB of hard-disk space to install, providing complete, standards-based Web-browsing and authoring capabilities even on lower-performance computers. Users can easily browse the Internet or intranet, use Internet standards-based e-mail and discussion groups, and benefit from the same secure browsing environment that is available to Windows 32-bit and UNIX users.

The Windows 16-bit browser also includes special features, such as the **Preview** button, which was designed to optimize the user's browsing experience on Windows 16-bit versions. The **Preview** button enables you to browse the Web faster by turning off images and formatting until you get to the page you want to see.

Some customization features, deployment methods, and maintenance practices for Windows 16-bit versions differ from Windows 32-bit versions. You should consider the following issues when you deploy Internet Explorer with Windows 16-bit versions:

- **Digital signatures**—Unlike Windows 32-bit versions with Authenticode technology, Windows 16-bit versions do not perform digital-signature verification. Windows 16-bit browsers do not support certificates, so automatic-configuration files are not signed. You do not need to sign your programs or cabinet files for this platform. You should, therefore, ensure that your automatic-configuration Web site has restricted access so that no one can tamper with your files.

- **Certification authorities**—For Windows 16-bit versions, you can import and install certificates for up to 20 certification authorities. If you have certificates for more than 20 certification authorities on your computer, you will need to identify the 20 certificates that you plan to install, and then remove the certificates for remaining certification authorities before you build your custom package.

- **File-naming format**—If you build a custom package for Windows 32-bit versions and then rebuild a custom package for Windows 16-bit versions in the same folder, the file names will automatically be converted to eight-character names with three-character extensions (8.3 format). If you rebuild a custom package for Windows 32-bit versions in the same location, the files will continue to be converted to 8.3 format. After rebuilding a custom package for Windows 16-bit versions, it is recommended that you build a new custom package for Windows 32-bit versions in a different location.

- **Dial-up access**—If your users need dial-up access, you must include the Stack and Dialer for Windows 3.1 as part of your setup package. If some users are running Windows NT 3.51 and some are running Windows 3.x, you should include at least two installation options: one with the dialer for Windows 3.1 and Windows for Workgroups 3.11, and one without it for Windows NT 3.51. For dial-up access, you must first configure Windows NT 3.51 computers for Remote Access Service (RAS).

- **Media selection**—When you build custom packages by using the Internet Explorer Customization wizard, you can choose the multiple floppy disks option for your media type. You can distribute custom packages on multiple floppy disks for Windows 3.1 and Windows for Workgroups 3.11, but not for Windows NT 3.51.

- **Microsoft Outlook Express**—With Windows 16-bit versions, you cannot use automatic configuration for Outlook Express.

- **Custom channels**—When you customize channels for Windows 16-bit versions, you should verify that any channels you include are displayed correctly for this platform. The channels will display in the Explorer bar, which appears in the left part of the browser window when the user clicks the **Channels** button, but they will not appear in a separate channel bar on the desktop.

- **Security options**—All security options apply to the Internet Explorer browser, but they are not necessarily applicable system-wide—that is, other programs may or may not respect these options. When you set the security options for Internet Explorer, you should be aware that the following options do not apply to the Windows 16-bit platform:

  - User authentication

  - Font download

  - Software channel permissions

  - Installation of desktop items

  - ActiveX® scripting

  - Launching applications and files from an IFRAME element

- **Setup download folder**—You can find the IE5Setup.exe file in the media type folder created for your language and platform version. For example, the English version of Internet Explorer for Windows 16-bit versions would reside in the \Download\Win16\En folder of your build directory.

- **Setup graphic file**—For Windows 16-bit versions, the Setup graphic that you use for a custom package must be a 16-color, 162-by-312-pixel bitmap (.bmp) file.

UNIX Platform

Internet Explorer for UNIX provides a full set of browser features that have been optimized for UNIX operating systems. Internet Explorer supports the primary UNIX installed systems. Users can also remotely use Internet Explorer for UNIX from other UNIX operating systems, such as Linux, Silicon Graphics IRIX, and IBM AIX.

Implementation of the Internet Explorer user interface is consistent with the standard UNIX design. Internet Explorer for UNIX takes advantage of UNIX interface standards and was developed using the Motif look. Users benefit from the power and flexibility of Windows, implemented in a way that is immediately familiar to UNIX users.

Internet Explorer also includes support for existing UNIX applications, such as Emacs, Elm, RN, and VI. This integration uses the UNIX features and functions that users are accustomed to. You can easily configure Internet Explorer to handle e-mail links or open a favorite e-mail client or news reader directly from the browser. Integration with existing applications also includes the ability to read UNIX-specific file types from Web sites without opening the application for that file separately.

Using Internet Explorer for UNIX, you can customize existing applications or Multipurpose Internet Mail Extension (MIME) types directly from the browser. This functionality allows you to configure existing applications to handle different content on the Internet, such as Adobe Acrobat file formats. For example, a user can click on a link to an Acrobat file and Internet Explorer automatically opens the Acrobat Reader.

Some customization features, deployment methods, and maintenance practices for UNIX differ from Windows 32-bit versions. You should consider the following issues when you deploy Internet Explorer for UNIX:

- **Custom packages**—You must build custom packages of Internet Explorer for UNIX from a Windows 32-bit computer. On the UNIX platform, the setup package will consist of one self-contained file rather than a collection of files or a set of floppy disks.

- **Digital signatures**—Unlike Windows 32-bit versions with Authenticode technology, UNIX does not perform digital-signature verification. UNIX browsers do not support certificates, so automatic-configuration files are not signed. You do not need to sign your programs or .cab files for UNIX. You should, therefore, ensure that your automatic-configuration Web site has restricted access so that no one can tamper with your files.

- **Server installations**—The UNIX functionality in the IEAK supports the common UNIX method of installing the customized product on only a few servers. Users can then run Internet Explorer from this location rather than installing the product locally. This configuration is recommended for UNIX installations. Windows Update Setup for Internet Explorer 5 and Internet Tools, which downloads .cab files, is not available on the UNIX platform.

- **Custom channels**—When you create custom packages for UNIX, you should verify that any channels you include are displayed correctly for this platform. The channels will display in the Explorer bar, which appears in the left side of the browser window when the user clicks the **Channels** button, but they will not appear in a separate Channel bar on the desktop.

- **Custom components**—For the UNIX platform, you should create a .cab file that contains your custom components and installation scripts. Then, specify the name of the .cab file, the script name, and size information when you run the Internet Explorer Customization wizard.

  When you install your customized IEAK package, it decompresses the .cab file, runs the script, and installs the components before it customizes the browser. After the setup script has run, it is deleted automatically. For more information, see the IEAK Help, which provides procedures and samples to help you create a script file and a .cab file so that you can prepare UNIX components for your custom package.

- **Security options**—All security options apply to the Internet Explorer browser, but they are not necessarily applicable system-wide—that is, other programs may or may not respect these options. When you set the security options for Internet Explorer, you should be aware that the following options do not apply to the UNIX platform:

  - ActiveX controls and plug-ins

  - Font downloads

  - Software channel permissions

  - Installation of desktop items

  - Launching applications and files from an IFRAME element

- **Setup download folder**—You can find the IE5Setup.exe file in the media type folder created for your language and platform version. For example, the English version of Internet Explorer for UNIX would reside in the \Download\Unix\En folder of your build directory.

- **File naming conventions**—You may need to change the case of file names on a UNIX FTP server.

Use the following conventions for UNIX operating systems:

Sun Solaris UNIX
If you are using a case-sensitive UNIX FTP server, the .cab directory must not be capitalized. You must, however, capitalize the following file names:

- BRANDING.CAB

- CUSTOM.CIF

- DESKTOP.CAB

- IE.CIF

- IECIF.CAB

- IE5SITES.DAT

AT&T UNIX
On an AT&T UNIX FTP server, all file names must be capitalized.

IRIX UNIX (Silicon Graphics)
For IRIX UNIX, you must capitalize the following file names:

- BRANDING.CAB

- CUSTOM.CIF

- DESKTOP.CAB

- IE.CIF

- IECIF.CAB

- IE5SITES.DAT

You should also use a text editor to modify the file names listed in the IE.CIF file to match the case of the files.

- **UNIX settings in the Internet Explorer Customization wizard**—If you are building custom packages of Internet Explorer for UNIX, the Internet Explorer Customization wizard provides several screens where you can enter UNIX-specific settings. The UNIX Programs screen enables you to specify which programs will run when the user performs tasks related to e-mail, newsgroups, or printing, or when the user views the HTML source of a page. The UNIX Mappings screen enables you to specify the options for associating extensions and MIME types with a program so that the appropriate program starts when a user clicks a link.

CHAPTER 5

Understanding Related Tools and Programs

When you use the Internet Explorer Customization wizard to build and install custom packages of Microsoft Internet Explorer 5, you can also include other tools and programs as part of the deployment process. This chapter describes the following related tools and programs and outlines how you can use them to support your rollout of Internet Explorer:

- Microsoft Systems Management Server (SMS)
- Microsoft Office 2000 Custom Installation wizard (CIW)
- Microsoft Internet Information Server (IIS)

See Also

- For more information about planning the deployment process, see Chapter 9, "Planning the Deployment."

- For more information about building custom packages of Internet Explorer, see Chapter 15, "Running the Internet Explorer Customization Wizard."

- For more information about installing Internet Explorer, see Chapter 19, "Deploying Microsoft Internet Explorer 5."

Microsoft Systems Management Server

Microsoft Systems Management Server (SMS) can help you automate a large-scale deployment of Internet Explorer by distributing and installing the browser on your users' computers. This automated installation requires no intervention from you or your users.

To distribute Internet Explorer by using SMS, you will need to complete the following tasks:

- **Create a package for Internet Explorer**—A package consists of a package source folder, which contains all the Internet Explorer installation files, and a package definition (.pdf) file. The .pdf file describes the setup commands that define how Internet Explorer is installed on users' computers.

- **Create and run a job to distribute the package**—A job consists of a package and a list of destination computers where you want Internet Explorer to be installed. SMS copies the package to distribution servers and then executes the job on the destination computers.

Note Before you use SMS to install Internet Explorer, you must create an administrative installation point on a server. SMS uses the administrative installation point as the package source folder.

Creating a Package for Internet Explorer

You can use the SMS Administrator program to import your Internet Explorer .pdf file and create a package for Internet Explorer installation. You need to manually copy this file to the administrative installation point.

Note The standard Internet Explorer .pdf file supports only local installations; it does not support installations that are run from a network server or that require sharing Internet Explorer components over the network.

The Internet Explorer .pdf file contains command-line definitions for the installation types and for the uninstall options. Each of these command-line definitions contains a setup command line that directs Windows Update Setup for Internet Explorer 5 and Internet Tools to run in batch mode with the specific installation type (except for Custom installations, which always run interactively). For a description of the available command-line options, see Appendix C, "Batch-Mode File Syntax and Command-Line Switches."

Creating and Running a Job to Distribute the Package

After you create your package, you must create a job to distribute it. This job includes the list of destination computers where you want Internet Explorer to be installed and the job schedule. When the job is executed, SMS copies all the files from the package source folder at the administrative installation point to a folder on one or more SMS distribution servers. These are the servers that support the users on your network. Windows Update Setup is then run from your distribution servers.

For More Information

For complete information about using SMS to deploy Internet Explorer, see the following:

- *Microsoft Systems Management Server Administrator's Guide*
- Microsoft BackOffice Web site
- Microsoft Internet Explorer Web site
- Chapter 9, "Planning the Deployment"
- Chapter 19, "Deploying Microsoft Internet Explorer 5"

Microsoft Office 2000 Custom Installation Wizard

The Microsoft Office 2000 Custom Installation wizard (CIW) enables you to customize how you install Office 2000 applications. To simplify the process of installing Internet Explorer with Office 2000, the Internet Explorer Customization wizard works with the CIW.

If you plan to include Internet Explorer with your custom Office package, you have the following two choices:

- If you do not want to customize Internet Explorer, you can choose to install Internet Explorer components by using the CIW. You do not need to use the Internet Explorer Customization wizard.
- If you want to customize Internet Explorer, you can specify this choice in the CIW. The CIW will then start the Internet Explorer Customization wizard so that you can customize the browser setup process.

To customize Internet Explorer, you must first install Internet Explorer 5 and the IEAK on the computer where you are creating your custom Office package. When you customize Internet Explorer settings, the Internet Explorer Customization wizard runs in corporate administrator mode with the following settings:

- The distribution media is CD.
- Two installation options are available: Minimal and Typical.
  You cannot change the names of these options, but you can specify which components will be installed with each installation option.

Note   The CIW installs Microsoft NetMeeting and Microsoft Outlook Express with all installation options.

- All of the cabinet (.cab) files and custom components that are created by the Internet Explorer Customization wizard are placed in the same folder.

When you run the CIW and customize Internet Explorer, user options from Windows Update Setup will not be displayed during the Office setup process. The user options for the setup are determined by the CIW.

Web Component Features

When you install Office 2000 and Internet Explorer 5, you can take advantage of new Office 2000 Web components, which integrate Office functionality with the Web. Most importantly, Web components make it possible for anyone with a browser to view the contents of Office files. Using Web components, you can easily create and share Web documents using the same Office tools that you use to create printed documents. For example, your Web pages can now include Microsoft Word documents or Microsoft Excel functions and formulas.

Web components include the following features:

- **HTML as a companion file format**—Office applications can save to and read from HTML files. HTML files are elevated to the same level as the proprietary file formats, including Microsoft Word (.doc) files, Microsoft Excel (.xls) files, and Microsoft® PowerPoint (.ppt) files. Office applications also intelligently manage companion files, such as embedded graphics and other objects that cannot be stored in HTML format.
- **Web-based collaboration**—Using Office Server Extensions (OSE) features, you can work with Office files and collaborate in a Web-based environment without needing expert knowledge of Web technologies and servers. For example, you can publish documents to available Web servers or view the contents of the Web server by using Windows Explorer.

- **Data access pages**—Using the new data access page designer, you can build data access pages (HTML pages with databinding capabilities) by using familiar Microsoft Access controls, or open any existing HTML file and add data-bound fields to the page. Data access pages also support Microsoft Visual Basic Scripting Edition (VBScript) or Microsoft JScript, so you can program in the language of your choice using a familiar development environment.

- **Save as a Web page**—This Web component feature enables you to save your current Office file in HTML format directly to a Web server. For example, you could create product pricing tables in Excel and then save them as Web pages on your server so that customers could view the tables using their browser.

- **Office themes and design templates**—You can easily create consistent-looking Web pages using themes and design templates, which have been created and coordinated between Office applications and the Microsoft FrontPage® Web site creation and management tool. For example, Microsoft Word and Microsoft Access provide themes, and the Microsoft PowerPoint presentation graphics program includes design templates consistent with these themes.

- **HTML file editing**—You can easily edit HTML files by using Office applications. When you click the **Edit** button in Internet Explorer, it launches the Office application that created the HTML file so that you can edit its contents.

- **HTML as a Clipboard format**—Office makes HTML a standard Clipboard format. Now you can easily copy and paste data between Office applications and the browser.

- **Web page preview**—Using your default browser, you can preview Web pages created in Office without saving the pages first.

- **Link handling and repair**—An improved link interface in Office applications makes it easier for you to create, edit, and remove links from Office documents. Also, when users save documents, Office applications check the links and repair those that are not working.

- **International text encoding**—Office applications save files by using international text encoding, which enables you to view the correct characters using any language.

For More Information

For more information about the CIW and deploying Internet Explorer with Office 2000, see the following:

- Microsoft Office 2000 Resource Kit
- Microsoft Office 2000 Web site
- Chapter 16, "Customizing Setup"

Microsoft Internet Information Server

Microsoft Internet Information Server (IIS) can help you deploy Internet Explorer and other business applications, host and manage Web sites, and publish and share information securely across a company intranet or the Internet. IIS can help you do the following:

- Manage the Web sites where you distribute and maintain your custom browser packages and other related files and programs.
- Generate dynamic Web pages by using Active Server Page (.asp) files.
- Customize Web site content, including custom error messages and content expiration.
- Capture user information in log files, which enables you to collect and analyze valuable customer and usage data.

Managing Web Sites

IIS management tools and flexible administration options can help you easily set up Web sites to distribute the browser and manage your custom packages and other content. Your organization can take advantage of these IIS site-management features:

- Built-in wizards step you through many common administrative tasks, such as creating a new Web site.
- From a single window, you can manage all network, Web, and application services.
- New configuration capabilities enable you to set properties independently for each Web site or file on the server.
- By running administration scripts from the command line, you can automate common administrative tasks across multiple servers.

Generating Dynamic Web Pages

You can create HTML page templates by using Active Server Page (.asp) files, which enable you to build dynamic Web pages for site information that is updated frequently. You can use .asp files to easily update the contents of Web pages without opening the HTML files. By keeping information, such as your site headlines, in a separate file, you can easily change the content or design of your site without updating every page. You can also keep frequently changing information in databases where it is easier to manage, and then build your Web pages from content dynamically extracted from the database. This capability means that Web sites of hundreds or thousands of pages can be reduced to a small number of .asp files.

Active Server Pages also make it easy to customize content for users. IIS Intrinsic Objects provide access to server variables, such as the user's browser type and screen resolution. An .asp file can use this information to select different graphics, layouts, or ActiveX components based on what the browser supports.

Customizing Web Site Content

You can easily customize the content on your Web site by taking advantage of the following IIS customization features:

- **Custom error messages**—Instead of using the default error messages, you can choose to send custom error messages (in a file or URL) to your users. You can also define custom .asp files to handle specific errors.

- **Content ratings**—You can configure content ratings for violence, nudity, sex, and offensive language by using embedded descriptive labels in the HTTP headers of Web pages on the server. Internet Explorer can detect these content labels and help users identify potentially objectionable Web content.

- **Content expiration**—You can set an HTTP header that determines how long a Web page should remain in the browser cache. For example, you can set the date for time-sensitive material, such as special offers or event announcements. The browser compares the current date to the expiration date and determines whether to display a cached page or request an updated page from the server.

- **Cache control**—You can set a tag in the HTTP header for secure Web sites that prevents Internet Explorer from caching the content. This capability prevents private information from being cached on a computer, where it could potentially be accessed by other people.

- **Custom headers**—You can send a custom HTTP header from the Web server to a browser. For example, you can send a custom HTTP header that allows the browser to cache a page, but prevents proxy servers from caching the same content.
- **Custom document footers**—You can configure the Web server to automatically insert a file that contains HTML formatting instructions for adding a logo image or text to the footer of Web pages on the server.

Capturing User Information

Using IIS logging features, you can gather detailed information about Web site visitors, such as the date and time the Web site is accessed, the client Internet Protocol (IP) address, and the browser type. IIS enables you to choose specific files for which you want to collect data, thereby reducing log file size and making it easier to interpret the log files. You can also create custom log files for processing specific user activities, such as tracking the Web site visitors who download your custom browser package.

Using Site Server Express analysis tools, you can easily identify basic trend and usage information from an IIS log file. The Usage Import and Report Writer modules of Site Server Express enable you to import an IIS log file and translate the entries into useful information about the client. Also, you can organize the information into over 20 predefined reports by using HTML or other business software file formats.

For More Information

For more information about using IIS to deploy Internet Explorer, see the following:

- Microsoft BackOffice Web site
- Chapter 13, "Setting Up Servers"
- Chapter 20, "Implementing the Sign-up Process"

CHAPTER 6

Digital Certificates

Microsoft Internet Explorer 5 uses digital certificates to authenticate clients and servers on the Web and to ensure secure browser communications. Read this chapter to learn about certificates and about how to configure settings for the certificates you trust.

In This Chapter

See Also

- For more information about configuring security zones and permission-based security, see Chapter 7, "Security Zones and Permission-Based Security for Microsoft Virtual Machine."

- For more information about Internet Explorer features that help ensure user privacy, see Chapter 8, "Content Ratings and User Privacy."

- For more information about planning for user security and privacy before Internet Explorer installation, see Chapter 9, "Planning the Deployment."

- For more information about digitally signing packages, see Chapter 12, "Preparing for the IEAK."

- For more information about using the Internet Explorer Customization wizard to preconfigure security settings, see Chapter 15, "Running the Internet Explorer Customization Wizard."

- For more information about using the IEAK Profile Manager to preconfigure security settings, see Chapter 22, "Keeping Programs Updated."

Understanding Digital Certificates

To verify the identity of people and organizations on the Web and to ensure content integrity, Internet Explorer uses industry-standard X.509 v3 digital certificates. Certificates are electronic credentials that bind the identity of the certificate owner to a pair (public and private) of electronic keys that can be used to encrypt and sign information digitally. These electronic credentials assure that the keys actually belong to the person or organization specified. Messages can be encrypted with either the public or private key, and then decrypted with the other key.

The following illustration shows the basic process of using public and private keys to encrypt and decrypt a message sent over the Internet.

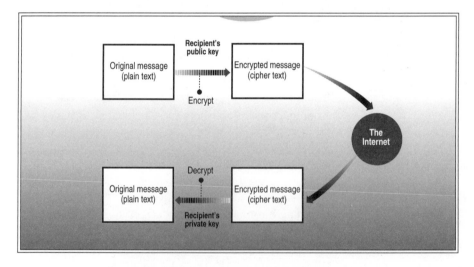

Illustration 6.1   How Public and Private Keys Work

Each certificate contains at least the following information:

- Owner's public key
- Owner's name or alias
- Expiration date of the certificate
- Serial number of the certificate
- Name of the entity that issued the certificate
- Digital signature of the entity that issued the certificate

Certificates can also contain other user-supplied information, including a postal address, e-mail address, and basic registration information, such as the country, postal code, age, and gender of the user.

Certificates form the basis for secure communication and client and server authentication on the Web. You can use certificates to do the following:

- Verify the identity of clients and servers on the Web.
- Encrypt secure communication channels between clients and servers.
- Encrypt messages for secure Internet e-mail communication.
- Verify the sender's identity for Internet e-mail messages.
- Sign executable code that users can download from the Web.
- Verify the source and integrity of signed executable code that users can download from the Web.

Certificates are authenticated, issued, and managed by a trusted third party called a certification authority (CA). The CA must provide a combination of three essential elements:

- Technology, such as security protocols and standards, secure messaging, and cryptography
- Infrastructure, including secure facilities, backup systems, and customer support
- Practices, including a defined model of trust and a legally binding framework for managing subscriber activities and resolving disputes

A commercial CA must be a trusted service. In addition to obtaining certificates from CAs, you can also implement a certificate server, such as Microsoft Certificate Server, and use it to provide certificate services for your Web infrastructure.

Commercial Certification Authorities

Commercial CAs issue certificates that verify the electronic identity of individuals and organizations on the Web. The primary responsibility of a CA is to confirm the identity of the people and organizations seeking certificates. This effort ensures the validity of the identification information contained in the certificate.

CAs perform the following types of services:

- Issue and renew certificates.
- Authenticate the identities of individuals and organizations.
- Verify the registrations of individuals and organizations.
- Publish and maintain a Certificate Revocation List (CRL) of all certificates that the CA has revoked.
- Handle legal and liability issues related to security.

Many commercial CAs offer certificate services for Microsoft products, as well as a wide range of other certificate services. For a current list of CAs that support Microsoft products, visit the Microsoft Security Advisor Web site. For a list of Microsoft Web sites that offer additional product support information related to Internet Explorer, see Appendix I, "Microsoft Internet Explorer 5 Resource Directory."

Commercial CAs issue various types of certificates, including the following:

- Personal certificates for people to digitally sign communications and assure secure transactions over the Internet and intranet
- Client authentication and server authentication certificates for managing secure transactions between clients and servers
- Software publisher certificates for people who digitally sign their software
- Software publisher certificates for commercial software companies that digitally sign their software

CAs can also issue many other types of certificates. Each CA operates within the charter of its Certification Practices Statement (CPS). You can visit the CA's Web site and read the CPS to understand the types of certificates issued by a specific CA and the operating procedures that the CA follows.

When you choose a CA, you should consider the following issues:

- Is the CA a trusted entity operating a certification practice that can both meet your needs and operate efficiently in your region? Other people should immediately recognize your CA as reputable and trustworthy. If you choose a CA with a questionable reputation, users may reject your certificate.
- Is the CA familiar with your organization's business interests? Look for a CA from which you can leverage technical, legal, and business expertise.

- Does the CA require detailed information from you to verify your trustworthiness? Most CAs require information, such as your identity, your organization's identity, and your official authority to administer the Web server for which you are requesting a certificate. Depending on the level of identification required, a CA may need additional information, such as professional affiliations or financial records, and the endorsement of this information by a notary.

- Does the CA have a system for receiving online certificate requests, such as requests generated by a key manager server? An online system can speed up the processing of your certificate requests.

- Does the CA give you enough flexibility and control over how certificates are issued and authenticated? Some commercial CA services and products may not integrate with your existing security model and directory services.

- Does the cost of the CA service meet your requirements? Substantial costs can be associated with obtaining a server certificate, especially if you need a high level of identification assurance.

Certificate Servers

You can implement a certificate server, such as Microsoft Certificate Server, to manage the issuance, renewal, and revocation of industry-standard certificates. You can use these certificates in conjunction with servers that support Secure Sockets Layer (SSL), Transport Layer Security (TLS), or Private Communications Technology (PCT) to build a secure Web infrastructure for the Internet or intranet. For large organizations with complex Web needs, certificate servers can offer many advantages over commercial CAs, including lower costs and total control over certificate management policies.

Depending on your relationship with your users, you can obtain server certificates from a commercial CA, or you can issue your own server certificates. For services on your intranet, user trust is typically not an issue, and you can easily configure Internet Explorer to trust server certificates issued by your organization. For services on the Internet, however, users may not know enough about your organization to trust certificates issued by your certificate server. Therefore, you may need to obtain server certificates that are issued by a well-known, commercial CA to ensure that users trust your Internet sites.

Authenticode Technology

Microsoft Authenticode™2.0 is client-side software that watches for the downloading of ActiveX control (.ocx) files, cabinet (.cab) files, Java applets, or executable files in order to provide reliable identity of the code. Authenticode displays certificate information, such as the name included in the digital signature, an indication of whether it is a commercial or personal certificate, and the date when the certificate expires. This information enables users to make a more informed decision before continuing with the download.

The software publisher digitally signs software (including .exe, .dll, .ocx, and .cab files) when it is ready for publication. Software publishers that obtain a code-signing certificate from a CA can use Authenticode signing tools to digitally sign their files for distribution over the Web. Authenticode looks for the signatures (or the lack of signatures) in the files that users attempt to download. For more information about how to digitally sign files by using Authenticode signing tools, see Chapter 12, "Preparing for the IEAK," and the MSDN Online Web site.

If a piece of software has been digitally signed, Internet Explorer can verify that the software originated from the named software publisher and that no one has tampered with it. Internet Explorer displays a verification certificate if the software meets these criteria. A valid digital signature, though, does not necessarily mean that the software is without problems. It just means that the software originated from a traceable source and that the software has not been modified since it was published. Likewise, an invalid signature does not prove that the software is dangerous, but just alerts the user to potential problems. When a digital signature fails the verification process, Internet Explorer reports the failure, indicates why the signature is invalid, and prompts the user about whether to proceed with the download.

You can configure Internet Explorer to handle software in different ways, depending on the status of its digital signature. Software can be unsigned, signed using valid certificates, or signed using invalid certificates.

For signed or unsigned software, you can configure Internet Explorer to do the following:

- Prevent users from downloading or running the software from a specific zone.
- Download and run the software without user intervention from a specific zone.
- Prompt users to make a choice about whether to download or run the software from a specific zone.

How you configure Internet Explorer to respond to certificates depends on various factors, such as the level of trust you have for the security zone where the content originated. If you are deploying Internet Explorer in an organization, you may also want to consider the level of trust you have for the intended user group and the level of technical expertise of the users. For example, you might trust unsigned software from your intranet, but not trust unsigned software from the Internet. In that case, you would configure Internet Explorer to automatically download and run unsigned active content from the intranet without user intervention and prevent the download of unsigned active content from the Internet.

Secure Client and Server Communications

Certificates can be used for secure communications and user authentication between clients and servers on the Web. Certificates enable clients to establish a server's identity, because the server presents a server authentication certificate that discloses its source. If you connect to a Web site that has a server certificate issued by a trusted authority, you can be confident that the server is actually operated by the person or organization identified by the certificate. Similarly, certificates enable servers to establish a client's identity. When you connect to a Web site, the server can be assured about your identity if it receives your client certificate.

The following sections describe security technologies that ensure secure communications between clients and servers.

Secure Channels

The exchange of certificates between clients and servers is performed using a secure transmission protocol, such as SSL, TLS, or PCT. SSL 2.0 supports server authentication only. SSL 3.0, TLS 1.0, and PCT 1.0 support both client and server authentication. Secure transmission protocols can provide these four basic security services:

- **Client authentication**—Verifies the identity of the client through the exchange and validation of certificates.
- **Server authentication**—Verifies the identity of the server through the exchange and validation of certificates.
- **Communication privacy**—Encrypts information exchanged between clients and servers by using a secure channel.
- **Communication integrity**—Verifies the integrity of the contents of messages that are exchanged between clients and servers by ensuring that messages have not been altered en route.

Note Encrypting all traffic over secure channels can put a heavy load on clients and servers. Therefore, secure channel encryption is typically used only for the transfer of small amounts of sensitive information, such as personal financial data and user authentication information.

You can change the set of protocols that are enabled for client and server authentication by clicking the **Tools** menu, clicking **Internet Options**, and then clicking the **Advanced** tab. For more information, see "Configuring Advanced Security Options for Certificate and Authentication Features" later in this chapter.

Server Gated Cryptography

For situations that require the highest-possible level of security, such as online banking, you can implement Server Gated Cryptography (SGC) to provide stronger encryption for communication between clients and servers. SGC enables a 128-bit server with an SGC certificate to communicate securely with all versions of Internet Explorer by using 128-bit SSL encryption. For example, SGC enables financial institutions with Microsoft Windows NT®–based Internet servers to use 128-bit SSL encryption for secure financial transactions.

Note 128-bit SSL encryption is available in the United States; internationally, it is restricted to approved SGC sites only.

The key benefits of SGC include the following:

- Banks and financial institutions can securely conduct financial transactions with their retail customers worldwide without requiring customers to change their standard Web browser or financial software.
- Online banking does not require any special client software. For example, customers can use all standard, off-the-shelf, exportable versions of Internet Explorer to connect to an SGC server and conduct secure transactions by using 128-bit encryption.
- SGC is fully interoperable with Netscape browsers and servers. Therefore, Internet Explorer users can communicate with Netscape servers using 128-bit encryption by means of SGC.

SGC is enabled in Internet Explorer 4.0 and later. It works with standard, off-the-shelf export-version servers and client applications that use an updated dynamic-link library named Schannel.dll and have an SGC certificate. For no charge, you can download the updated Schannel.dll from the Microsoft Web site. Users can enable their Internet Explorer browser for SGC by simply downloading the exportable 128-bit SGC add-on.

Banks can enable Microsoft Internet Information Server (IIS) for SGC if they have the standard, off-the-shelf version of IIS 3.0, which is part of Windows NT 4.0. First, they must download and apply the patch that updates their Schannel.dll file for IIS 3.0. Then they can use the Key Manager in IIS 3.0 to generate a request for a certificate, and submit the request to an authorized CA. After the certificate has been issued and installed, IIS will be fully SGC-enabled and can communicate with SGC-enabled Microsoft and Netscape clients.

CryptoAPI 2.0

CryptoAPI 2.0 provides the underlying security services for certificate management, secure channels, and code signing and verification (Authenticode technology). Using CryptoAPI, developers can easily integrate strong cryptography into their applications. Cryptographic Service Provider (CSP) modules interface with CryptoAPI and perform several functions, including key generation and exchange, data encryption and decryption, hashing, creation of digital signatures, and signature verification. CryptoAPI is included as a core component of the latest versions of Windows. Internet Explorer automatically provides this support for earlier versions of Windows.

Fortezza Support

Microsoft provides a Fortezza cryptographic service provider (CSP) plug-in for Internet Explorer that supports Fortezza security technology, which was created by the National Security Agency for the United States Department of Defense. Users can install the Fortezza CSP plug-in to ensure secure Internet Explorer communications based on Fortezza security standards; this support includes communications with Fortezza-secured Web sites.

Note To use the Fortezza CSP plug-in provided for Internet Explorer 5, users must have the necessary Fortezza hardware and CSP installed. For tools and instructions about installing and enabling Fortezza, users can contact their Fortezza hardware vendor.

Using Internet Explorer, users can log in using Fortezza credentials, and operate in Fortezza mode, which is identified by an "F" overlaid on the Internet Explorer lock icon. They can perform various Fortezza management functions, including selecting certificates and changing personalities (credentials). To enable this support, select the **Use Fortezza** check box. For more information about enabling advanced security options, see "Configuring Advanced Security Options for Certificate and Authentication Features" later in this chapter.

Server Certificate Revocation

Internet Explorer 5 adds support for server certificate revocation, which verifies that an issuing CA has not revoked a server certificate. This feature checks for CryptoAPI revocation when certificate extensions are present. If the URL for the revocation information is unresponsive, Internet Explorer cancels the connection.

Note Outlook Express also includes certificate revocation, which is controlled through a separate option within the e-mail program.

To enable server certificate revocation, select the **Check for server certificate revocation** check box. For more information about enabling advanced security options, see "Configuring Advanced Security Options for Certificate and Authentication Features" later in this chapter.

Publisher's Certificate Revocation

Internet Explorer 5 adds support for publisher's certificate revocation, which verifies that an issuing CA has not revoked a publisher's certificate. To enable publisher's certificate revocation, select the **Check for publisher's certificate revocation** check box. For more information about enabling advanced security options, see "Configuring Advanced Security Options for Certificate and Authentication Features" later in this chapter.

Using Digital Certificates

You can install certificates and configure certificate settings for Internet Explorer by using the following methods:

- Within the browser, you can use the Internet Explorer Certificate Manager by clicking the **Tools** menu, clicking **Internet Options**, and then clicking the **Content** tab. You can also configure advanced security options for certificates by clicking the **Tools** menu, clicking **Internet Options**, and then clicking the **Advanced** tab.

- You can use the Internet Explorer Customization wizard to create custom packages of Internet Explorer that include preconfigured lists of trusted certificates, publishers, and CAs for your user groups. If you are a corporate administrator, you can also lock down these settings to prevent users from changing them.

- After the browser is deployed, you can use the IEAK Profile Manager to manage certificate settings through the automatic browser configuration feature of Internet Explorer. You can automatically push the updated information to each user's desktop computer, enabling you to manage security policy dynamically across all computers on the network.

The options for configuring certificates are the same whether you access them from Internet Explorer 5, the Internet Explorer Customization wizard, or the IEAK Profile Manager. For more information about using the Internet Explorer Customization wizard and the IEAK Profile Manager, see Chapter 15, "Running the Internet Explorer Customization Wizard" and Chapter 22, "Keeping Programs Updated."

Note Outlook Express also includes certificates, called "digital IDs," which can be configured separately within the e-mail program.

Installing and Removing Trusted Certificates

The Internet Explorer Certificate Manager enables you to install and remove trusted certificates for clients and CAs. Many CAs have their root certificates already installed in Internet Explorer. You can select any of these installed certificates as trusted CAs for client authentication, secure e-mail, or other certificate purposes, such as code signing and time stamping. If a CA does not have its root certificate in Internet Explorer, you can import the root certificate into Internet Explorer. Each CA's Web site contains instructions describing how to obtain the root certificate. You may also want to install client certificates, which are used to authenticate users' computers as clients for secure Web communications.

▶ **To install or remove clients and CAs from the list of trusted certificates**

1. On the **Tools** menu, click **Internet Options**, and then click the **Content** tab.

2. Click **Certificates**.

3. Click one of the following tabbed categories for the type of certificates you want to install or remove:

   - **Personal**—Certificates in the Personal category have an associated private key. Information signed by using personal certificates is identified by the user's private key data. By default, Internet Explorer places all certificates that will identify the user (with a private key) in the Personal category.

   - **Other People**—Certificates in the Other People category use public key cryptography to authenticate identity, based on a matching private key that is used to sign the information. By default, this category includes all certificates that are not in the Personal category (the user does not have a private key) and are not from CAs.

   - **Intermediate Certification Authorities**—This category contains all certificates for CAs, including trusted root certificates.

   - **Trusted Root Certification Authorities**—This category includes only self-signing certificates in the root store. When a CA's root certificate is listed in this category, you are trusting content from sites, people, and publishers with credentials issued by the CA.

The following illustration shows the Certification Manager with the Intermediate Certification Authorities category selected.

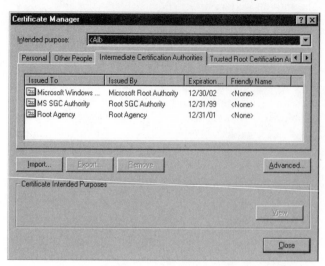

4. In the Intended Purpose box, select the filter for the types of certificates that you want to be displayed in the list.

5. To add other certificates to the list, click **Import**. The Certificate Manager Import wizard steps you through the process of adding a certificate.

   To export certificates from the list, click **Export**. The Certificate Manager Export wizard steps you through the process of exporting a certificate.

   To specify the default drag-and-drop export file format (when the user drags a certificate from the Certificate Manager and drops it into a folder), click **Advanced**.

The following illustration shows the Advanced Options dialog box.

To delete an existing certificate from the list of trusted certificates, click **Remove**.

To display the properties for a selected certificate, including the issuer of the certificate and its valid dates, click **View**.

Adding Trusted Publishers and Credentials Agencies

To designate a trusted publisher or credentials agency (also called certification authority and issuer of credentials) for Internet Explorer, use the Security Warning dialog box that appears when you attempt to download software from that publisher or credentials agency. Active content that is digitally signed by trusted publishers or credentials agencies with a valid certificate will download without user intervention, unless downloading active content is disabled in the settings for a specific security zone.

▶ **To add a trusted publisher or credentials agency**

1. Use Internet Explorer to download signed active content from the publisher or credentials agency.

2. When the Security Warning dialog box appears, select **Always trust content from** *publisher or credentials agency name.*

The following illustration shows the Security Warning dialog box.

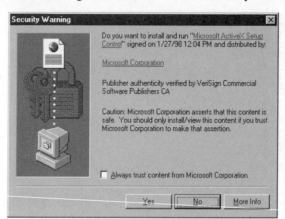

3. To download the software and control, and add the publisher or credentials agency to the list of trusted publishers and credentials agencies, click **Yes**.

Removing Trusted Publishers and Credentials Agencies

You can use the Authenticode Security Technology dialog box to remove publishers and credentials agencies from the list of trusted authorities.

▶ **To remove a trusted publisher or credentials agency**

1. On the **Tools** menu, click **Internet Options**, and then click the **Content** tab.

2. Click **Publishers**.

3. To remove a trusted publisher or credentials agency, select the name of the agency from the list, and then click **Remove**.

The following illustration shows a list of trusted publishers and credentials agencies.

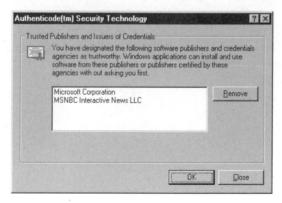

Configuring Advanced Security Options for Certificate and Authentication Features

You can easily configure options for certificate and authentication features that your users may need.

▶ **To configure advanced security options for certificates**

1. On the **Tools** menu, click **Internet Options**, and then click the **Advanced** tab.

2. In the Security area, review the options that are selected.

3. Depending on the needs of your organization and its users, select or clear the appropriate check boxes.

   For example, to enable Fortezza support for users with Fortezza Crypto Cards and the Fortezza CSP plug-in for Internet Explorer, select the **Use Fortezza** check box.

   The following illustration shows the Security check boxes.

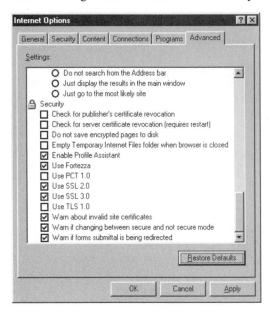

For information about security options for user privacy features, see Chapter 8, "Content Ratings and User Privacy."

CHAPTER 7

Security Zones and Permission-Based Security for Microsoft Virtual Machine

Microsoft Internet Explorer 5 provides comprehensive management and enforcement of Internet and network security. This chapter describes two key features of security management: security zones and permission-based security for Microsoft Virtual Machine. Read this chapter to learn how these security features can help protect access to individuals and information in your organization.

In This Chapter

See Also

- For more information about configuring digital certificates, see Chapter 6, "Digital Certificates."

- For more information about Internet Explorer features that help ensure user privacy, see Chapter 8, "Content Ratings and User Privacy."

- For more information about planning user security before Internet Explorer installation, see Chapter 9, "Planning the Deployment."

- For more information about Internet Explorer system policies and restrictions that enable you to preconfigure security settings, see Appendix E, "Setting System Policies and Restrictions."

Understanding Security Zones

Security zones offer you a convenient and flexible method for managing a secure environment. You can use security zones to enforce your organization's Internet security policies based on the origin of the Web content. Security zones enable you to:

- Group sets of sites together.
- Assign a security level to each zone.

Group Sets of Sites Together

Zone security is a system that enables you to divide online content into four categories, or zones. You can assign specific Web sites to each zone, depending on how much you trust the site's content. The Web content can be anything from an HTML or graphic file to an ActiveX control, Java applet, or executable file.

Important You should configure the Local intranet zone to correspond to the particular network and firewall configuration of your organization. The default settings for the Local intranet zone cannot be guaranteed to match your network configuration, and there is no method for automatically detecting your firewall and configuring the zone based on your specific settings. For more information, see "Setting Up the Local Intranet Zone" later in this chapter.

Internet Explorer includes the following predefined security zones:

- **Local intranet zone**—The Local intranet zone includes all sites inside an organization's firewall (for computers connected to a local network). The Local intranet zone also contains Web applications that need access to a computer's hard disk.

- **Trusted sites zone**—The Trusted sites zone can include all Internet sites that you know are trusted. For example, the Trusted sites zone might contain corporate subsidiaries' sites or the site of a trusted business partner.

- **Internet zone**—The Internet zone includes all sites on the Internet that are not in the Trusted sites or Restricted sites zones.

- **Restricted sites zone**—The Restricted sites zone can include all sites that you know are trusted.

- **My Computer zone**—The My Computer zone includes everything on the client computer, which is typically the hard disk and removable media drive contents. This zone excludes cached Java classes in the Temporary Internet Files folder.

  You cannot configure the My Computer zone through the security zone settings in Internet Explorer. However, you can configure My Computer zone settings by using the Microsoft Internet Explorer Administration Kit (IEAK).

Assign a Security Level to Each Zone

A security level assigned to each zone defines the level of browser access to Web content. You can choose to make each zone more or less secure. In this way, security zones can control access to sites based on the zone in which the site is located and the level of trust assigned to that zone. Also, you can choose a custom level of security, which enables you to configure settings for ActiveX controls, downloading and installation, scripting, cookie management, password authentication, cross-frame security, and Java capabilities. A custom level of security also enables you to assign administrator-approved control, which runs only those ActiveX controls and plug-ins that you have approved for your users.

Zone Architecture

When Internet Explorer opens an HTML page, a dynamic-link library named Urlmon.dll determines the zone from which the page was loaded. To do this, Urlmon.dll performs these two steps:

1. Determines whether a proxy server retrieved the HTML page. If it did, Urlmon.dll automatically recognizes that the page originated from the Internet.

2. Checks the registry to see whether the page is from a trusted or restricted location, and whether the security zone is set appropriately. If no proxy server is involved, the URL is then parsed to determine the origin of the page.

Setting Up Security Zones

You can use security zones to easily provide the appropriate level of security for the various types of Web content that users are likely to encounter. For example, because you can fully trust sites on your company's intranet, you probably want users to be able to run all types of active content from this location. To provide this capability, set the Local intranet zone to a low level of security. You might not feel as confident about sites on the Internet, so you can assign a higher level of security to the entire Internet zone. This higher level prevents users from running active content and downloading code to their computer. However, if there are specific sites you trust, you can place individual URLs or entire domains in the Trusted sites zone. For other sites on the Internet that are known to be sources of potentially harmful Web content, you can select the highest restrictions.

Note Outlook Express shares zone settings with Internet Explorer. You can also select zone settings in Outlook Express. For more information, see the Outlook Express Help files.

You can accept the default security settings for each zone, or you can configure the settings based on the needs of your organization and its users. The options for configuring security zones are the same whether you access them from Internet Explorer 5, the Internet Explorer Customization wizard, or the IEAK Profile Manager. For more information about using the Internet Explorer Customization wizard and the IEAK Profile Manager, see Chapter 15, "Running the Internet Explorer Customization Wizard" and Chapter 22, "Keeping Programs Updated."

Important Internet Explorer 5 maintains the existing security zone settings from previous browser versions.

Configuring Security Zones

You can configure security zones by using the following methods:

- In Internet Explorer, click the **Tools** menu, click **Internet Options**, and then click the **Security** tab.
- You can use the Internet Explorer Customization wizard to create custom packages of Internet Explorer that include security zone settings for your user groups. You can also lock down these settings to prevent users from changing them.
- After the browser is deployed, you can use the IEAK Profile Manager to manage security zone settings through the automatic browser configuration feature of Internet Explorer. You can automatically push the updated security zone settings to each user's desktop computer, enabling you to manage security policy dynamically across all computers on the network.

The following sections describe how to configure zone settings from within Internet Explorer.

▶ **To configure security zone settings**

1. On the **Tools** menu, click **Internet Options**, and then click the **Security** tab. The following illustration shows the Security tab.

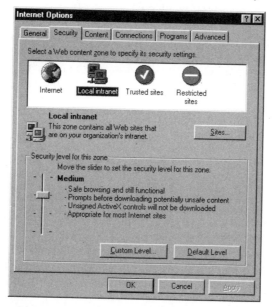

2. Click a security zone to select it and view its current settings.

3. As necessary, change the following settings:

   - **Security level**—To change the security level for the selected zone to **High**, **Medium**, **Medium-low**, or **Low**, move the slider. The on-screen description for each level can help you decide which level to select.

   - **Sites**—To add or remove Web sites from the zone, click the **Sites** button, and then click the **Add** or **Remove** button to customize your list of sites for the selected zone.

     If you are setting up the Local intranet zone, some additional site options are available. For more information about adding sites to the Local intranet zone, see "Setting Up the Local Intranet Zone" later in this chapter.

   - **Custom level**—For more precise control of your security settings, click the **Custom Level** button, and then select the options you want. At any time, you can click **Default Level** to return to the original security level for the selected zone. For more information about Custom Level security options, see "Selecting Custom Level Settings" later in this chapter.

The process required for setting up each security zone is described in the following sections.

Setting Up the Internet Zone

The Internet zone consists of all sites that are not included in the other zones. By default, the Internet zone is set to a Medium security level. If you are concerned about possible security problems when users browse the Internet, you might want to change the setting to High. If you raise the security setting, Internet Explorer prevents some Web pages from performing certain potentially harmful operations. As a result, some pages might not function or be displayed properly. Rather than use a High security setting, you might want to choose a Custom Level so that you can control each individual security decision for the zone.

Note   You cannot add Web sites to the Internet zone.

Setting Up the Local Intranet Zone

To ensure a secure environment, you must set up the Local intranet zone in conjunction with the proxy server and firewall. All sites in this zone should be inside the firewall, and proxy servers should be configured so that an external Domain Name System (DNS) name cannot be resolved to this zone. Configuring the Local intranet zone requires that you have a detailed knowledge of your existing networks, proxy servers, and firewalls. For more information, see the MSDN Online Web site.

By default, the Local intranet zone consists of local domain names, as well as domains that are specified to bypass the proxy server. You should confirm that these settings are secure for the installation, or adjust the settings to be secure. When you set up the zone, you can specify the categories of URLs that should be considered. You can also add specific sites to the zone.

▶ **To set up sites in the Local intranet zone**

1. On the **Tools** menu, click **Internet Options**, and then click the **Security** tab.

2. Click the **Local intranet** zone.

3. Click **Sites,** and then select the following check boxes that apply:

   - **Include all local (intranet) sites not listed in other zones**—Intranet sites, such as **http://local**, have names that do not include dots. In contrast, a site name that does contain dots, such as **http://www.microsoft.com**, is not local. This site would be assigned to the Internet zone. The intranet site name rule applies to File as well as HTTP URLs.

   - **Include all sites that bypass the proxy server**—Typical intranet configurations use a proxy server to access the Internet, but have a direct connection to intranet servers. The setting uses this kind of configuration information to distinguish intranet from Internet content for purposes of zones. If the proxy server is otherwise configured, you should clear this check box, and then use another means to designate Local intranet zone membership. For systems without a proxy server, this setting has no effect.

- **Include all network paths (UNCs)**—Network paths (for example, \\servername\sharename\file.txt) are typically used for local network content that should be included in the Local intranet zone. If some of your network paths should not be in the Local intranet zone, you should clear this check box, and then use other means to designate membership. For example, in certain Common Internet File System (CIFS) configurations, it is possible for a network path to reference Internet content.

The following illustration shows the Local intranet zone settings.

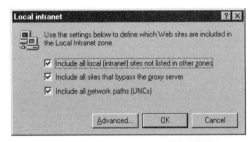

4. Click **Advanced**.

5. Type the address of the site you want to include in this zone, and then click **Add**.

   The following illustration shows where you would type the address to add a site to the Local intranet zone.

6. To require that server verification be used, select the **Require server verification (https:) for all sites in this zone** check box.

The Local intranet zone is intended to be configured by using the Internet Explorer Customization wizard or the IEAK Profile Manager, although you can also access Local intranet options by clicking **Internet Options** on the **Tools** menu, and then clicking the **Security** tab. After the Local intranet zone is confirmed secure, consider changing the zone's security level to Low so that users can perform a wider range of operations. You can also adjust individual security settings by using a Custom Level of security for this zone. If parts of your intranet are less secure or otherwise not trustworthy, you can exclude the sites from this zone by assigning them to the Restricted sites zone.

Setting Up the Trusted and Restricted Sites Zones

You can add trusted and untrusted Web sites to the Trusted sites and Restricted sites security zones. These two zones enable you to assign specific sites that you trust more or less than those in the Internet zone or the Local intranet zone. By default, the Trusted sites zone is assigned a Low security level. This zone is intended for highly trusted sites, such as the sites of trusted business partners.

If you assign a site to the Trusted sites zone, the site will be allowed to perform a wider range of operations. Also, Internet Explorer will prompt you to make fewer security decisions. You should add a site to this zone only if you trust all of its content never to perform any harmful operations on your computer. For the Trusted sites zone, Microsoft strongly recommends that you use the HTTPS protocol or otherwise ensure that connections to the site are completely secure.

By default, the Restricted sites zone is assigned a High security level. If you assign a site to the Restricted sites zone, it will be allowed to perform only minimal, very safe operations. This zone is for sites that you do not trust. To ensure a high level of security for content that is not trusted, pages assigned to this zone might not function or be displayed properly.

Note A user could copy content from one zone to another, potentially increasing or decreasing the level of security intended for that zone's content.

Working with Domain Name Suffixes

You can address Web content by using either the DNS name or the Internet Protocol (IP) address. You should assign sites that use both types of addresses to the same zone. In some cases, the sites in the Local intranet zone are identifiable either by local name or by IP addresses in the proxy bypass list. However, if you enter the DNS name but not the IP address for a site in the Trusted sites or Restricted sites zone, that site might be treated as part of the Internet zone if it is accessed by using the IP address.

If you want to reference a Web server by using a shorter version of its address that does not include the domain, you can use a domain name suffix. For example, you can reference a Web server named **sample.microsoft.com** as **sample**. Then you can use either **http://sample.microsoft.com** or **http://sample** to access that content.

To set up this capability, you must add the domain name suffix for TCP/IP properties to the domain suffix search order.

▶ **To add the domain name suffix for TCP/IP properties to the domain suffix search order**

1. Right-click the **Network Neighborhood** icon, and then click **Properties**.

2. On the **Configuration** tab, click **TCP/IP**, and then click **Properties**.

3. Click the **DNS Configuration** tab, and then select **Enable DNS** if it is not already selected.

4. In the **Domain Suffix Search Order** box, add the search order that you want.

   The following illustration shows the DNS Configuration tab.

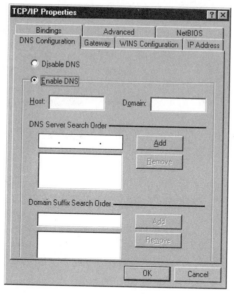

It is important to set up security zones correctly for this capability. By default, the URL without dots (**http://sample**) is considered to be in the Local intranet zone, while the URL with dots (**http://sample.microsoft.com**) is considered to be in the Internet zone. Therefore, if you use this capability and no proxy server bypass is available to clearly assign the content to the proper zone, you need to change the zone settings.

Depending on whether the content accessed by the domain name suffix is considered to be intranet or Internet content, you need to assign the ambiguous site URLs to the appropriate zones. To assign URLs, such as **http://sample**, to the Internet zone, clear the **Include all local (intranet) sites not listed in other zones** check box for the Local intranet zone, and include the site in the Internet zone.

Selecting Custom Level Settings

The **Custom Level** button on the **Security** tab gives you additional control over zone security. You can enable or disable specific security options depending on the needs of your organization and its users. For more information about how to use Custom Level security options, see "Setting Up Security Zones" earlier in this chapter.

The Custom Level security options for Internet Explorer are grouped into the following categories:

- ActiveX controls and plug-ins
- Cookies
- Downloads
- Java
- Miscellaneous
- Scripting
- User authentication

The following table identifies the default value for each Custom Level security option at each level of security.

Security option	Low	Medium-low	Medium	High
ActiveX controls and plug-ins				
Download signed ActiveX controls	Enable	Prompt	Prompt	Disable
Download unsigned ActiveX controls	Prompt	Disable	Disable	Disable
Initialize and script ActiveX controls not marked as safe	Prompt	Disable	Disable	Disable
Run ActiveX controls and plug-ins	Enable	Enable	Enable	Disable
Script ActiveX controls marked safe for scripting	Enable	Enable	Enable	Disable

Security option	Low	Medium-low	Medium	High
Cookies				
Allow cookies that are stored on your computer	Always	Always	Always	Disable
Allow per-session cookies (not stored)	Always	Always	Always	Disable
Downloads				
File download	Enable	Enable	Enable	Disable
Font download	Enable	Enable	Enable	Prompt
Java				
Java permissions	Low safety	Medium safety	Medium safety	High safety
Miscellaneous				
Access data sources across domains	Enable	Prompt	Disable	Disable
Drag and drop or copy and paste files	Enable	Enable	Enable	Prompt
Installation of desktop items	Enable	Enable	Prompt	Disable
Launching applications and files in an IFRAME	Enable	Enable	Prompt	Disable
Software channel permissions	Low safety	Medium safety	Medium safety	High safety
Submit non-encrypted form data	Enable	Enable	Prompt	Prompt
Userdata persistence	Enable	Enable	Enable	Disable
Scripting				
Active scripting	Enable	Enable	Enable	Enable
Allow paste operations via script	Enable	Enable	Enable	Disable
Scripting of Java applets	Enable	Enable	Enable	Disable
User authentication				
User Authentication - Logon	Automatic	Automatic	Prompt	Prompt

These Custom Level security options apply to Internet Explorer; other programs might not accept them. These security options are for Microsoft Windows 32-bit platforms, but some options might also apply to Microsoft Windows 16-bit or UNIX platforms. The following sections describe these settings in greater detail.

ActiveX Controls and Plug-ins

These options dictate how Internet Explorer approves, downloads, runs, and scripts ActiveX controls and plug-ins.

Note If a user downloads an ActiveX control from a site that is different from the page on which it is used, Internet Explorer applies the more restrictive of the two sites' zone settings. For example, if a user accesses a Web page within a zone that is set to permit a download, but the code is downloaded from another zone that is set to prompt a user first, Internet Explorer uses the prompt setting.

- **Download signed ActiveX controls**—This option determines whether users can download signed ActiveX controls from a page in the zone. This option has these settings:

  - **Disable**, which prevents all signed controls from downloading.

  - **Enable**, which downloads valid signed controls without user intervention and prompts users about whether to download invalid signed controls— that is, controls that have been revoked or have expired.

  - **Prompt**, which prompts users about whether to download controls signed by publishers who are not trusted, but still silently downloads code validly signed by trusted publishers. For more information about trusted publishers, see Chapter 6, "Digital Certificates."

- **Download unsigned ActiveX controls**—This option determines whether users can download unsigned ActiveX controls from the zone. This code is potentially harmful, especially when coming from an untrusted zone. This option has these settings:

  - **Disable**, which prevents unsigned controls from running.

  - **Enable**, which runs unsigned controls without user intervention.

  - **Prompt**, which prompts users about whether to allow the unsigned control to run.

- **Initialize and script ActiveX controls not marked as safe**—ActiveX controls are classified as either trusted or untrusted. This option controls whether a script can interact with untrusted controls in the zone. Untrusted controls are not meant for use on Internet Web pages, but in some cases they can be used with pages that can absolutely be trusted not to use the controls in a harmful way. Object safety should be enforced unless you can trust all ActiveX controls and scripts on pages in the zone. This option has these settings:

  - **Disable**, which enforces object safety for untrusted data or scripts. ActiveX controls that cannot be trusted are not loaded with parameters or scripted.

- **Enable**, which overrides object safety. ActiveX controls are run, loaded with parameters, and scripted without setting object safety for untrusted data or scripts. This setting is not recommended, except for secure and administered zones. This setting causes both untrusted and trusted controls to be initialized and scripted and ignores the **Script ActiveX controls marked safe for scripting** option.

- **Prompt**, which attempts to enforce object safety. However, if ActiveX controls cannot be made safe for untrusted data or scripts, users are given the option of allowing the control to be loaded with parameters or scripted.

For more information about how to make ActiveX controls safe, see the MSDN Online Web site.

- **Run ActiveX controls and plug-ins**—This option determines whether Internet Explorer can run ActiveX controls and plug-ins from pages in the zone. This option has these settings:

  - **Administrator approved**, which runs only those controls and plug-ins that you have approved for your users. To select the list of approved controls and plug-ins, use Internet Explorer system policies and restrictions. The **Control Management** category of policies enables you to manage these controls. For more information about selecting Control Management policies, see Appendix E, "Setting System Policies and Restrictions."

  - **Disable**, which prevents controls and plug-ins from running.

  - **Enable**, which runs controls and plug-ins without user intervention.

  - **Prompt**, which prompts users about whether to allow the controls or plug-ins to run.

- **Script ActiveX controls marked safe for scripting**—This option determines whether an ActiveX control that is marked safe for scripting can interact with a script. This option has these settings:

  - **Disable**, which prevents script interaction.

  - **Enable**, which allows script interaction without user intervention.

  - **Prompt**, which prompts users about whether to allow script interaction.

Note that safe-for-initialization controls loaded with PARAM tags are unaffected by this option. This option is ignored when **Initialize and script ActiveX controls that are not marked safe** is set to **Enable**, because that setting bypasses all object safety. You cannot script unsafe controls while blocking the scripting of the safe ones.

Cookies

These options determine the settings for per-session cookies (text files that store the user's preferences) and cookies that are stored on the client computer.

- **Allow cookies that are stored on your computer**—This option determines whether cookies are stored on the hard drive for future browsing sessions. For example, this setting can allow a list of preferences or a user's name to be retained for the user's next browsing session. This option has these settings:

  - **Disable**, which prevents persistent cookies from being created. If you disable persistent cookies, some Web sites will not retain their settings when users return to the sites.

  - **Enable**, which automatically accepts persistent cookies.

  - **Prompt**, which prompts users before persistent cookies are created.

- **Allow per-session cookies (not stored)**—This option determines how long cookies are stored when users browse a Web site. For example, this setting can allow a "virtual shopping cart" to be created while a user is shopping online. Per-session cookies do not remain on the hard disk. They are in effect only for the specific browsing session. This option has these settings:

  - **Disable**, which prevents cookies from being created. If you disable per-session cookies, some Web site information might not be displayed properly.

  - **Enable**, which automatically accepts cookies.

  - **Prompt**, which prompts users before cookies are created.

Downloads

These options specify how Internet Explorer handles downloads.

- **File download**—This option controls whether file downloads are permitted within the zone. Note that this option is determined by the zone of the page that contains the download link, not the zone from which the file originated. This option has these settings:

  - **Disable**, which prevents files from being downloaded from the zone.

  - **Enable**, which allows files to be downloaded from the zone.

- **Font download**—This option determines whether Web pages within the zone can download HTML fonts. This option has these settings:

  - **Disable**, which prevents HTML fonts from downloading.

  - **Enable**, which downloads HTML fonts without user intervention.

  - **Prompt**, which prompts users about whether to allow HTML fonts to download.

Java

These options control the permissions that are granted to Java applets when they are downloaded and run in this zone. Depending on the Internet Explorer components that you install, you might not be able to view or set these options.

Each option determines the following:

- The maximum permission level silently granted to signed applets downloaded from the zone.
- The permissions granted to unsigned applets downloaded from the zone.
- The permissions granted to scripts on pages in the zone that call into applets.

Note If a Java applet is downloaded from a different site than the page on which it is used, the more restrictive of the two sites' zone settings is applied. For example, if a user accesses a Web page within a zone that is set to allow a download, but the code is downloaded from another zone that is set to prompt a user first, Internet Explorer uses the prompt setting.

- **Java permissions**—This option has these settings:
  - **Custom**, which controls permissions settings individually. For more information about custom Java permissions, see "Configuring Java Custom Security" later in this chapter.
  - **Disable Java**, which prevents any applets from running.
  - **High Safety**, which enables applets to run in their sandbox (an area in memory outside of which the program cannot make calls).
  - **Low Safety**, which enables applets to perform all operations.
  - **Medium Safety**, which enables applets to run in their sandbox. In addition, applets are given other capabilities such as access to scratch space (a safe and secure storage area on the client computer) and user-controlled file input and output.

Note For Microsoft Windows 16-bit versions, the available settings are **Enable** and **Disable**.

Miscellaneous

These options control whether users can access data sources across domains, submit non-encrypted form data, launch applications and files from IFRAME elements, install desktop items, drag and drop files, copy and paste files, and access software channel features from this zone.

- **Access data sources across domains**—This option specifies whether components that connect to data sources should be allowed to connect to a different server to obtain data. This option has these settings:

  - **Disable**, which allows database access only in the same domain as the Web page.

  - **Enable**, which allows database access to any source, including other domains.

  - **Prompt**, which prompts users before allowing database access to any source in other domains.

- **Drag and drop or copy and paste files**—This option controls whether users can drag and drop, or copy and paste, files from Web pages within the zone. This option has these settings:

  - **Disable**, which prevents users from dragging and dropping files, or copying and pasting files, from the zone.

  - **Enable**, which enables users to drag and drop files, or copy and paste files, from the zone without being prompted.

  - **Prompt**, which prompts users about whether they can drag and drop files, or copy and paste files, from the zone.

- **Installation of desktop items**—This option controls whether users can install desktop items from Web pages within the zone. This option has these settings:

  - **Disable**, which prevents users from installing desktop items from this zone.

  - **Enable**, which enables users to install desktop items from this zone without being prompted.

  - **Prompt**, which prompts users about whether they can install desktop items from this zone.

- **Launching applications and files in an IFRAME**—This option controls whether users can launch applications and files from an IFRAME element (containing a directory or folder reference) in Web pages within the zone. This option has these settings:

  - **Disable**, which prevents applications from running and files from downloading from IFRAME elements on pages in the zone.

- **Enable**, which runs applications and downloads files from IFRAME elements on the pages in the zone without user intervention.

- **Prompt**, which prompts users about whether to run applications and download files from IFRAME elements on pages in the zone.

- **Software channel permissions**—This option controls the permissions given to software distribution channels. This option has these settings:

  - **High safety**, which prevents users from being notified of software updates by e-mail, software packages from being automatically downloaded to users' computers, and software packages from being automatically installed on users' computers.

  - **Low safety**, which notifies users of software updates by e-mail, software packages to be automatically downloaded to users' computers, and software packages to be automatically installed on users' computers.

  - **Medium safety**, which notifies users of software updates by e-mail and software packages to be automatically downloaded to (but not installed on) users' computers. The software packages must be validly signed; the user is not prompted about the download.

- **Submit non-encrypted form data**—This option determines whether HTML pages in the zone can submit forms to or accept forms from servers in the zone. Forms sent with Secure Sockets Layer (SSL) encryption are always allowed; this setting only affects data that is submitted by non-SSL forms. This option has these settings:

  - **Disable**, which prevents information from forms on HTML pages in the zone from being submitted.

  - **Enable**, which allows information from forms on HTML pages in the zone to be submitted without user intervention.

  - **Prompt**, which prompts users about whether to allow information from forms on HTML pages in the zone to be submitted.

- **Userdata persistence**—This option determines whether a Web page can save a small file of personal information associated with the page to the computer. This option has these settings:

  - **Disable**, which prevents a Web page from saving a small file of personal information to the computer.

  - **Enable**, which allows a Web page to save a small file of personal information to the computer.

Scripting

These options specify how Internet Explorer handles scripts.

- **Active scripting**—This option determines whether Internet Explorer can run script code on pages in the zone. This option has these settings:
  - **Disable**, which prevents scripts from running.
  - **Enable**, which runs scripts without user intervention.
  - **Prompt**, which prompts users about whether to allow the scripts to run.
- **Allow paste operations via script**—This option determines whether a Web page can cut, copy, and paste information from the Clipboard. This option has these settings:
  - **Disable**, which prevents a Web page from cutting, copying, and pasting information from the Clipboard.
  - **Enable**, which allows a Web page to cut, copy, and paste information from the Clipboard without user intervention.
  - **Prompt**, which prompts users about whether to allow a Web page to cut, copy, or paste information from the Clipboard.
- **Scripting of Java applets**—This option determines whether scripts within the zone can use objects that exist within Java applets. This capability allows a script on a Web page to interact with a Java applet. This option has these settings:
  - **Disable**, which prevents scripts from accessing applets.
  - **Enable**, which allows scripts to access applets without user intervention.
  - **Prompt**, which prompts users about whether to allow scripts to access applets.

User Authentication

This option controls how HTTP user authentication is handled.

- **Logon**—This option has these settings:
  - **Anonymous logon**, which disables HTTP authentication and uses the guest account only for Common Internet File System (CIFS).
  - **Automatic logon only in Intranet zone**, which prompts users for user IDs and passwords in other zones. After users are prompted, these values can be used silently for the remainder of the session.
  - **Automatic logon with current user name and password**, which attempts logon using Windows NT Challenge Response (also known as NTLM authentication), an authentication protocol between the client computer and the application server. If Windows NT Challenge Response is supported by the server, the logon uses the network user name and password for logon.

If Windows NT Challenge Response is not supported by the server, users are prompted to provide their user name and password.

For information about other secure connection options, see Chapter 8, "Content Ratings and User Privacy."

- **Prompt for user name and password**, which prompts users for user IDs and passwords. After users are prompted, these values can be used silently for the remainder of the session.

Understanding Permission-Based Security for Microsoft Virtual Machine

Permission-based security for Microsoft Virtual Machine (which is Java-compatible) is a Windows 32-bit security model that provides fine-grained management of the permissions granted to Java applets and libraries. This model uses Java cabinet (.cab) file-signing technology to ensure that an applet can perform actions only for which it specifically requests permissions.

Using permission-based security for Microsoft Virtual Machine, developers can precisely limit the section of code where permissions have been granted, and administrators can control the permissions granted to Java code, such as access to scratch space, local files, and network connections. Also, when used in conjunction with security zones, permission-based security for Microsoft Virtual Machine can simplify security decisions because it permits sets of Java permissions to be specified for each security zone.

Permission-based security for Microsoft Virtual Machine includes the following elements:

- **Permission-based security model**—This security model provides fine-grained control over the actions that Java classes can perform.

- **Security zones**—You can use security zones to assign security settings to a group of Web sites, such as all sites on a company intranet.

- **Permission signing**—You can use permission signing to associate specific security permissions with a Java package. You can specify the identity of the signer for the package's cabinet (.cab) file and the set of permissions being requested by the signed classes.

- **Permission scoping**—This feature enables you to precisely limit the sections of code for which a granted permission is enabled.

- **Package Manager**—The Package Manager allows classes to be installed with their associated permissions. Using the Package Manager, you can also control the permissions granted to local classes.

- **Trust User Interface**—This interface enables you to greatly simplify or eliminate the decisions that users need to make about the permissions granted to an applet.

The following sections describe these features of permission-based security for Microsoft Virtual Machine. For more information, see the MSDN Online Web site and the Microsoft Software Development Kit for Java.

Permission-Based Security Model

The permission-based security model for Microsoft Virtual Machine supports a set of parameterized and non-parameterized permissions that can individually be granted or denied. For an applet to obtain access to the desired set of resources, such as a file's input and output, the applet must be signed with the proper permissions. For more information about permission signing, see "Permission Signing" later in this chapter.

The following sets of permissions correspond to the standard Java sandbox:

- Allow thread access in the current execution context.
- Open network connections to the applet host.
- Create a top-level pop-up window with a warning banner.
- Access reflection application program interfaces (APIs) for classes from the same loader.
- Read base system properties.

Security Zones

Security zones integrate with the permission-based security model to create a configurable, extensible mechanism for providing security for users. Whenever users attempt to open or download content from the Web, Internet Explorer checks the security settings associated with that Web site's security zone. For more information about security zones, see "Understanding Security Zones" earlier in this chapter.

You can configure three different sets of permissions for each security zone for both signed and unsigned code:

- **Permissions that are granted without user intervention**—These permissions are available to applets from the zone without user intervention. They can be specified separately for signed and unsigned applets.

- **Permissions that are granted with user intervention**—Users are prompted about whether to grant these permissions to applets from the zone.

- **Permissions that are denied**—These permissions are considered harmful and are automatically denied to applets from the zone.

Only applets that have permissions granted without user intervention run automatically. An applet that has been denied permissions will not run. If an applet uses permissions granted with user intervention, Internet Explorer displays a dialog box with a list of all the permissions and their associated risks and prompts the user about whether to trust the applet. If the user chooses not to trust the applet, the applet can continue to run with alternate and limited functionality, but the applet is prevented from using the expanded set of permissions.

Note The user will be asked to confirm execution of the applet only if it requests more permissions than the zone can automatically grant. You can configure the specific permissions that Internet Explorer will automatically grant in each zone.

For more information about setting up permissions for each security zone, see "Configuring Java Custom Security" later in this chapter.

Permission Signing

Permission signing extends the signed .cab file functionality provided by previous versions of Internet Explorer. Under permission-based security, a signed .cab file can securely specify not only the identity of the signer, but also the set of permissions being requested for the signed classes.

When the signed .cab file is downloaded, the signature is examined for permission information before any code is permitted to run. By signing your applet with Java permission information, you request only the specific permissions that you need. Because your applet can perform only the actions that it specifically requests permission to perform, users can make informed decisions about the risks associated with running your applet.

Microsoft Virtual Machine uses the permissions requested in the signature and the user's general security preferences to determine whether to grant the requested access. If Microsoft Virtual Machine cannot automatically grant the requested access, it displays a dialog box prompting the user about whether the applet should be allowed to run. If the user approves, the applet is run with the permissions it requests. Otherwise, the applet is run in the sandbox. Because the set of permissions are fully defined and understood by Microsoft Virtual Machine, the requested permission information is displayed, and the user is warned about the risk of each requested access.

Note The .cab files can contain both Microsoft ActiveX controls and Java code. Because ActiveX controls must be fully trusted to be run, they are treated differently from Java code. For ActiveX controls to run when they are in a .cab file that uses permission signing, you must specify in the signature that the .cab file contains ActiveX controls.

Java code can be signed with the default capabilities of the following safety settings:

- **High Safety**—This setting is a restrictive set of capabilities that are the equivalent of "sandboxed" Java code. In addition, High Safety allows the applet to do the following:
  - Allow thread access in the current execution context.
  - Open network connections to the applet host.
  - Create a top-level pop-up window with a warning banner.
  - Access reflection APIs for classes from the same loader.
  - Read base system properties.
- **Medium Safety**—This setting includes the capabilities of High Safety. In addition, Medium Safety allows the applet to do the following:
  - Access scratch space.
  - Perform user-directed file input and output.
- **Low Safety**—This setting includes the capabilities of High and Medium Safety. In addition, Low Safety allows the applet to do the following:
  - Perform file input and output.
  - Execute other applications on the client computer.
  - Implement user-interface dialog boxes.
  - Provide thread group access in the current execution context.
  - Open network connections with computers other than the host.
  - Load libraries on the client computer.
  - Make native method calls.
  - Determine whether an applet can make native method calls.
  - Create a top-level pop-up window without a warning banner.
  - Exit the virtual machine.
  - Perform registry operations.
  - Perform printing operations.
  - Create a class loader.

Custom permissions can also be used if you need more fine-grained control of the types of permissions granted to the signed code. Custom permissions are defined in an initialization (.ini) file. The .ini file includes a section for each desired permission, which defines its necessary parameters. You can create the .ini file manually, or you can use the Piniedit tool provided with the Microsoft Software Development Kit for Java.

Permission Scoping

Permission scoping prevents permissions granted to a trusted component from being misused (either inadvertently or intentionally) by a less trusted component. A trusted class can precisely limit the range of code for which a granted permission is enabled. This is a particularly important feature because some methods that use enhanced permissions are designed to be safely called by anyone, while other methods are designed to be used internally by trusted callers only and should not expose their permissions to less trusted callers.

Permission-based security distinguishes between permissions that have been granted to a class and permissions that are actually enabled at a particular time. The granted permissions are determined by the administrative options for a class's zone and the permissions with which the class was signed. Enabled permissions are determined by the permissions granted to other callers on the call stack and whether any explicit calls to the **assertPermission**, **denyPermission**, or **revertPermission** methods have been made. If there are less trusted callers on the call stack, the enabled permissions can be more restrictive than the granted permissions.

Microsoft Virtual Machine follows two rules for permission scoping:

- Permissions are never inherited from the caller. If a class has not been directly granted a permission, then it can never make use of that permission, regardless of what permissions its callers have. This means that an untrusted class would never incorrectly be allowed to make use of the expanded permissions of its caller.

- Even if a class has been granted a permission, its methods must explicitly enable that permission using the **assertPermission** method whenever there is a caller on the call stack that has not been granted that permission.

    For example, permission P is enabled only if the following statements are true:

    - P is granted in all of the stack frames from the active frame up to the earliest frame on the stack.

    - P is granted in all of the stack frames up to a frame that has called **assertPermission** on P.

    - No intervening frame has called **denyPermission** on P.

Permission-based security for Microsoft Virtual Machine checks to see whether the code making the call to perform a trusted operation is signed with the proper level of permissions before honoring the **assertPermission** request. A security exception occurs if the caller was not signed with the permissions for the operation that it is trying to perform.

Package Manager

The Package Manager administers the installation of Java packages and classes and provides a database for storing them. The Package Manager uses permission signing to allow the installation of local class libraries that are not fully trusted. This is especially important for JavaBeans and class libraries. It is desirable to allow these components to reside locally and to have some expanded permissions, but not to give them unlimited power.

The Package Manager was designed to address the limitations of using the CLASSPATH environment variable. It does so in the following ways:

- **Security**—Packages and classes installed through the Package Manager are not implicitly trusted as system library classes. Any Java package installed through the Package Manager that requires access to certain resources on the user's computer must be signed with the desired permissions. The Package Manager, in coordination with the security manager in Microsoft Virtual Machine, enforces these signed permissions.

- **Versioning**—The Package Manager database stores the version number of every Java package it installs. By tracking version numbers, the Package Manager can upgrade Java packages if a newer version is being installed or downloaded from the network. The Package Manager can also eliminate any downgrading of Java packages.

- **Installing Java packages**—When Java packages are installed through the Package Manager, it is not necessary to update the CLASSPATH environment variable. Therefore, the user does not need to restart the computer.

- **Namespace**—To prevent namespace collision, Java packages can be installed under the global namespace or under an application namespace. Packages installed in the application namespace are visible only to applications running in that namespace. Packages in the global namespace are visible to all Java applications.

- **Load-time performance**—The Package Manager locally stores all of the packages it installs on the user's computer, which greatly speeds up class load time performance for Java applets. This improved performance occurs because the classes do not need to be downloaded from the network every time the user visits the Web page containing the applet.

  When the application classes are loaded from the user's computer, they will still be restricted to the permissions the application was originally signed with. The Java package includes specific system permission identifiers that are approved when the package is installed on the user's computer. These permission identifiers determine the maximum permissions that can be used by the classes in a specific package.

- **Upgrading**—When a user revisits a Web page that contains a newer version of a Java package (which was previously installed through the Package Manager), the new version is downloaded and the local classes are automatically upgraded. The Java applet or application must be packaged in a .cab file and signed with the permissions it needs to run.

Trust User Interface

The Trust User Interface defined by permission-based security for Microsoft Virtual Machine shields users from complicated trust decisions and reduces the number of dialog boxes they must respond to. The integration of permissions with security zones means that users need to make only a simple "Yes or No" choice when deciding whether to trust an application. The complex decisions about which permissions to allow have already been made by an administrator.

In addition, permission signing allows the security system to predetermine all the permissions required by a class. When a package is installed, the security system can use the signature to determine exactly the system permissions that it needs to provide, and a single trust dialog box can reliably present all of the permissions required by an application before running any code. Because the default system permissions are well defined and static, their level of risk can be determined and refined over time, ensuring that the level of risk is acceptable.

Setting Up Java Custom Security

You can deploy Internet Explorer with the default settings, or you can configure Java custom settings, which explicitly define the Java permissions for signed and unsigned applets. The options for configuring Java custom settings are the same whether you access them from Internet Explorer 5, the Internet Explorer Customization wizard, or the IEAK Profile Manager. For more information about using the Internet Explorer Customization wizard and IEAK Profile Manager, see Chapter 15, "Running the Internet Explorer Customization Wizard" and Chapter 22, "Keeping Programs Updated."

Important You can only configure Java custom settings if the Microsoft Virtual Machine is installed on your computer.

Configuring Java Custom Security

You can configure Java custom security by using the following methods:

- In Internet Explorer, click the **Tools** menu, click **Internet Options**, and then click the **Security** tab.

- You can use the Internet Explorer Customization wizard to create custom packages of Internet Explorer that include Java custom settings. If you are a corporate administrator, you can also lock down these settings to prevent users from changing them.

- After the browser is deployed, you can use the IEAK Profile Manager to manage Java custom settings through the automatic browser configuration feature of Internet Explorer. You can automatically push the updated security zone settings to each user's desktop computer, enabling you to manage security policy dynamically across all computers on the network.

You can view and change Java custom settings for each security zone. The following section describes how to configure Java custom settings.

▶ **To view and edit Java custom settings**

1. On the **Tools** menu, click **Internet Options**.

2. Click the **Security** tab.

3. Click a security zone.

4. Click **Custom Level**.

5. In the Java Permissions area, select **Custom**.

6. Click **Java Custom Settings**.

7. As necessary, perform the following tasks:

   - To view Java permissions, click the **View Permissions** tab.

     This tab displays permissions in a hierarchical tree that you can expand and collapse. Permissions are organized into the following categories:

     Permissions Given To Unsigned Content—Unsigned Java applets that request these permissions can run without user prompting.

     Permissions That Signed Content Are Allowed—Signed Java applets that request these permissions can run without user prompting.

     Permissions That Signed Content Are Denied—Signed Java applets are denied these permissions.

     The following illustration shows the Java permission categories.

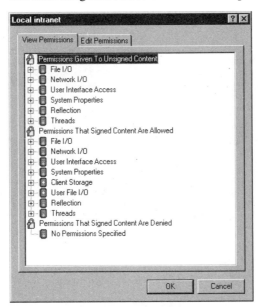

- To edit Java permissions, click the **Edit Permissions** tab, and then select the options you want for more precise control of Java permissions. At any time, you can click the **Reset** button to reset the Java custom settings to the last saved permissions or to the default high, medium, or low security settings. For more information about specific Java permissions, see "Selecting Java Custom Settings" later in this chapter.

The following illustration shows the options you can set for Java permissions.

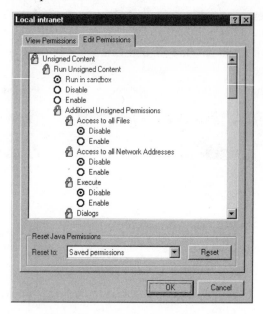

Selecting Java Custom Settings

The **Java Custom Settings** button on the **Security** tab gives you additional control over Java permissions. You can enable or disable specific Java permissions depending on the needs of your organization and its users. For more information about how to use the Java custom settings, see "Configuring Java Custom Security" earlier in this chapter.

Java custom settings for Internet Explorer are grouped into two categories: Unsigned Content and Signed Content. The following tables identify the default value for each option and the level of security.

Unsigned Content

Java custom option	High security	Medium security	Low security
Run Unsigned Content			
Run Unsigned Content	Run in sandbox	Run in sandbox	Run in sandbox
Additional Unsigned Permissions			
Access to all files	Disable	Disable	Disable
Access to all network addresses	Disable	Disable	Disable
Execute	Disable	Disable	Disable
Dialog	Disable	Disable	Disable
System information	Disable	Disable	Disable
Printing	Disable	Disable	Disable
Protected scratch space	Disable	Disable	Disable
User-selected file access	Disable	Disable	Disable

Signed Content

Java custom option	High security	Medium security	Low security
Run Signed Content			
Run Signed Content	Prompt	Prompt	Prompt
Additional Signed Permissions			
Access to all files	Prompt	Prompt	Disable
Access to all network addresses	Prompt	Prompt	Disable
Execute	Prompt	Prompt	Disable
Dialog	Prompt	Prompt	Disable
System information	Prompt	Prompt	Disable
Printing	Prompt	Prompt	Disable
Protected scratch space	Prompt	Enable	Disable
User-selected file access	Prompt	Enable	Disable

The following sections describe the settings for the **Unsigned Content** and **Signed Content** groups.

Unsigned Content

The **Run Unsigned Content** group determines whether unsigned applets can run in the zone. This group has the following settings:

- **Run in sandbox**, which runs unsigned Java applets for this zone in a Java sandbox that you specify. You can enable or disable individual options in the **Additional Unsigned Permissions** category.

- **Disable**, which disables running unsigned applets for this zone. All options in the Additional Unsigned Permissions category are disabled and shaded.

- **Enable**, which enables running unsigned applets for this zone. All options in the Additional Unsigned Permissions category are enabled.

The **Additional Unsigned Permissions** option determines whether unsigned applets can have additional permissions, such as access to network addresses and the ability to run other applications. If you disable the ability to **Run Unsigned Content**, Internet Explorer automatically disables all of these options.

- **Access to all files**—This option determines whether unsigned applets can have read access to all the files on the users' systems. This option has these settings:

  - **Disable**, which prevents unsigned applets from having read access to all the files on the users' systems.

  - **Enable**, which allows unsigned applets to have read access to all the files on the users' systems.

- **Access to all network addresses**—This option determines whether unsigned applets can access network addresses. This option has these settings:

  - **Disable**, which prevents unsigned applets from having access to network addresses.

  - **Enable**, which allows unsigned applets to have access to network addresses.

- **Execute**—This option determines whether unsigned applets can run other applications. This option has these settings:

  - **Disable**, which prevents unsigned applets from running other applications.

  - **Enable**, which allows unsigned applets to run other applications.

- **Dialogs**—This option determines whether unsigned applets can create file dialog boxes. This option has these settings:
  - **Disable**, which prevents unsigned applets from creating file dialog boxes.
  - **Enable**, which allows unsigned applets to create file dialog boxes.
- **System information**—This option determines whether unsigned applets can read system properties. This option has these settings:
  - **Disable**, which prevents unsigned applets from reading system properties.
  - **Enable**, which allows unsigned applets to read system properties.
- **Printing**—This option determines whether unsigned applets can access printer resources. This option has these settings:
  - **Disable**, which prevents unsigned applets from accessing printer resources.
  - **Enable**, which allows unsigned applets to access printer resources.
- **Protected scratch space**—This option determines whether unsigned applets can use storage space on the hard drive. This option has these settings:
  - **Disable**, which prevents unsigned applets from using storage area on the hard disk.
  - **Enable**, which allows unsigned applets to use storage area on the hard disk.
- **User-selected file access**—This option determines whether unsigned applets can access selected files. This option has these settings:
  - **Disable**, which prevents unsigned applets from accessing any files (users are not prompted for permission).
  - **Enable**, which prompts users about whether unsigned applets can access selected files.

Signed Content

The **Run Signed Content** option determines whether users can run signed applets. This option has these settings:

- **Prompt**, which sets individual options in the Additional Signed Permissions category to **Prompt**. You can disable or enable each individual option.

- **Disable**, which disables running signed applets for this zone. All options in the Additional Signed Permissions category are disabled and shaded.

- **Enable**, which enables running unsigned applets for this zone. All options in the Additional Signed Permissions category are enabled.

The **Additional Signed Permissions** options determine whether signed applets can have additional permissions, such as access to network addresses and the ability to run other applications. If you disable the ability to **Run Signed Content**, Internet Explorer automatically disables all of these options.

- **Access to all files**—This option determines whether signed applets can have read access to all the files on the users' systems. This option has these settings:

  - **Prompt**, which prompts users before signed applets can have read access to all the files on the users' systems.

  - **Disable**, which prevents signed applets from having read access to all the files on the users' systems.

  - **Enable**, which allows signed applets to have read access to all the files on the users' systems.

- **Access to all network addresses**—This option determines whether signed applets can access network addresses. This option has these settings:

  - **Prompt**, which prompts users about whether signed applets can access network addresses.

  - **Disable**, which prevents signed applets from accessing network addresses.

  - **Enable**, which allows signed applets to access network addresses.

- **Execute**—This option determines whether signed applets can run other applications. This option has these settings:

  - **Prompt**, which prompts users about whether signed applets can run other applications.

  - **Disable**, which prevents signed applets from running other applications.

  - **Enable**, which allows signed applets to run other applications.

- **Dialogs**—This option determines whether signed applets can create file dialog boxes. This option has these settings:
    - **Prompt**, which prompts users about whether signed applets can create file dialog boxes.
    - **Disable**, which prevents signed applets from creating file dialog boxes.
    - **Enable**, which allows signed applets to create file dialog boxes.
- **System information**—This option determines whether signed applets can read system properties. This option has these settings:
    - **Prompt**, which prompts users about whether signed applets can read system properties.
    - **Disable**, which prevents signed applets from reading system properties.
    - **Enable**, which allows signed applets to read system properties.
- **Printing**—This option determines whether signed applets can access printer resources. This option has these settings:
    - **Prompt**, which prompts users about whether signed applets can access printer resources.
    - **Disable**, which prevents signed applets from accessing printer resources.
    - **Enable**, which allows signed applets to access printer resources.
- **Protected scratch space**—This option determines whether signed applets can use storage space on the hard drive. This option has these settings:
    - **Prompt**, which prompts users about whether signed applets can use storage area on the hard disk.
    - **Disable**, which prevents signed applets from using storage area on the hard disk.
    - **Enable**, which allows signed applets to use storage area on the hard disk.
- **User-selected file access**—This option determines whether signed applets can access selected files. This option has these settings:
    - **Prompt**, which prompts users about whether signed applets can access selected files.
    - **Disable**, which prevents signed applets from accessing any files (users are not prompted for permission).
    - **Enable**, which prompts users about whether signed applets can access selected files.

C H A P T E R   8

Content Ratings and User Privacy

Using the content rating and user privacy features of Microsoft Internet Explorer 5, you can create a secure environment that protects users from inappropriate Web content and ensures the privacy of their information. This chapter describes these features and explains how you can configure rating and privacy settings.

In This Chapter

See Also

- For more information about managing your list of trusted digital certificates, see Chapter 6, "Digital Certificates."

- For more information about configuring security zones and Java custom security, see Chapter 7, "Security Zones and Permission-Based Security for Microsoft Virtual Machine."

- For more information about using the Internet Explorer Customization wizard to preconfigure security settings, see Chapter 15, "Running the Internet Explorer Customization Wizard."

- For more information about using the Internet Explorer Administration Kit (IEAK) Profile Manager to preconfigure security settings, see Chapter 22, "Keeping Programs Updated."

Using Content Ratings

Using the Internet Explorer Content Advisor, you can control the types of content that users access on the Internet. You can adjust the content rating settings to reflect the appropriate level of content in four areas: language, nudity, sex, and violence. For example, businesses might want to block access to sites that offer no business value to their employees, and parents might want to block access to sites that display inappropriate content for their children.

Historically, the motive for filtering sites on the basis of a site's content has been driven by a site's subject matter and the fact that some ideas and images are blatantly offensive to many people. In 1995, the World Wide Web Consortium (W3C) Platform for Internet Content Selection (PICS) began to define an infrastructure that would encourage Web content providers to voluntarily rate their sites. This is done by using a specific set of HTML meta tags that rate the content of Web sites. Software programs can then block access to Web sites based upon the values of those meta tags. Today, the most common content ratings are based on the PICS standard for defining and rating Web content. For more information about PICS, visit the W3C Web site.

RSACi Rating System

Internet Explorer is installed with a PICS-based content rating system known as the Recreational Software Advisory Council on the Internet (RSACi) system. This built-in PICS support can help you control the types of content that users can access on the Internet. When you enable Content Advisor, Internet Explorer reads the meta tags to determine whether Web sites meet your criteria for suitable content. You can also subscribe to independent ratings bureaus or use third-party ratings to control access to Web content.

RSACi is an open, objective, content ratings system for the Internet developed by the Recreational Software Advisory Council (RSAC), an independent, nonprofit organization. The RSACi system provides information about the level of sex, nudity, violence, and offensive language (vulgar or hate-motivated) in software games and Web sites. For more information about RSAC and the RSACi rating system, see the RSAC Web site.

The following table shows the five levels of the RSACi rating system and describes the content allowed for each level. Level 0 is the most restrictive, and Level 4 the least restrictive.

Level	Violence rating	Nudity rating	Sex rating	Language rating
4	Rape or wanton, gratuitous violence	Frontal nudity qualifying as provocative	Explicit sexual acts or sex crimes	Crude, vulgar language, or extreme hate speech
3	Aggressive violence or death of humans	Frontal nudity	Non-explicit sexual acts	Strong language or hate speech
2	Destruction of realistic objects	Partial nudity	Clothed sexual touching	Moderate expletives or profanity
1	Injury to a human being	Revealing attire	Passionate kissing	Mild expletives
0	None of the above	None of the above	None of the above or innocent kissing; romance	None of the above

You can set content ratings to any level for each of the four content areas. All content ratings are set to Level 0 by default. When Content Advisor is turned on and the PICS rating for a Web site exceeds the rating level you specify, Internet Explorer prevents users from accessing the site. Also, you can configure Internet Explorer to prevent or allow users to access unrated Web content. For more information, see "Configuring Content Advisor Settings" later in this chapter.

Web site publishers can obtain PICS content ratings from RSAC, as well as from a number of other nonprofit and fee-based ratings services. Publishers can voluntarily add PICS ratings to their Web sites. You can also obtain independent PICS ratings from ratings bureaus. Ratings bureaus are typically fee-based and specialize in rating Internet sites. You can specify a ratings bureau other than RSAC that Internet Explorer can use to obtain PICS ratings. Because Internet Explorer must contact the ratings bureau to obtain the ratings, using other ratings bureaus can slow access to Web pages considerably.

Other Rating Systems

Some Web publishers rate their sites using rating systems that are not based on PICS. To use these rating systems, you must subscribe to ratings services that support the non-PICS rating systems and then import the rating systems so that Internet Explorer can use them to rate Web content. For more information, visit the Web sites of the rating services. You can also review "Configuring Content Advisor Settings" later in this chapter to learn how to specify different rating systems for Internet Explorer.

Supervisor Password

The first time you turn on Content Advisor, you must specify a supervisor password. This password allows administrators or supervisors to turn Content Advisor on or off and to change Content Advisor settings for users.

In addition, you can configure Internet Explorer so that users can display restricted Web pages by typing the supervisor password. When users attempt to access restricted content, the Content Advisor dialog box prompts users to enter the supervisor password. For more information, see the next section.

Configuring Content Advisor Settings

You can configure Content Advisor settings in several ways:

- In Internet Explorer, click the **Tools** menu, click **Internet Options**, and then click the **Content** tab.

- You can use the Internet Explorer Customization wizard to create custom packages of Internet Explorer that include preconfigured Content Advisor settings for your user groups. You can also lock down these settings to prevent users from changing them.

- After Internet Explorer is deployed, you can use the IEAK Profile Manager to update Content Advisor settings through the automatic browser configuration feature of Internet Explorer. You can automatically push the updated security zone settings to each user's desktop computer, enabling you to manage security policy dynamically across all computers on the network.

You can accept the default Content Advisor settings, or you can configure the settings based on the needs of your organization and its users. The options for configuring Content Advisor are the same whether you access them from Internet Explorer 5, the Internet Explorer Customization wizard, or the IEAK Profile Manager. For more information about using the Internet Explorer Customization wizard and IEAK Profile Manager, see Chapter 15, "Running the Internet Explorer Customization Wizard," and Chapter 22, "Keeping Programs Updated."

After you enable Content Advisor, you can use it to do the following:

- Select content rating levels.
- Configure the list of approved and disapproved Web sites.
- Configure user options for content ratings.
- Change the supervisor password.
- Import new rating systems.
- Specify a different ratings bureau.

▶ **To enable Content Advisor**

1. On the **Tools** menu, click **Internet Options**, and then click the **Content** tab.

2. In the Content Advisor area, click **Enable**.

3. Type the password you want to use.

   The following illustration shows the Create Supervisor Password dialog box.

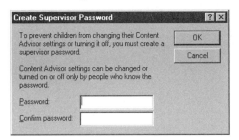

4. In the **Confirm password** box, type the same password again.

▶ **To select content rating levels**

1. On the **Tools** menu, click **Internet Options**, and then click the **Content** tab.

2. In the Content Advisor area, click **Settings**, and then click the **Ratings** tab.

3. Select the **Language**, **Nudity**, **Sex**, or **Violence** ratings category.

   The following illustration shows the ratings categories for Content Advisor.

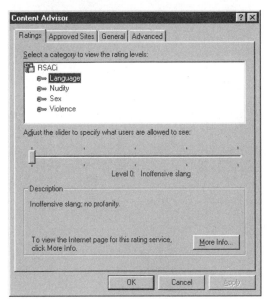

4. Drag the slider to the appropriate content level for the selected category.

The default setting for each category is Level 0, which is the most restrictive setting. For more information about ratings levels, see "RSACi Rating System" earlier in this chapter.

▶ **To configure the list of approved and disapproved Web sites**

1. On the **Tools** menu, click **Internet Options**, and then click the **Content** tab.

2. In the Content Advisor area, click **Settings**, and then click the **Approved Sites** tab.

The following illustration shows the **Approved Sites** tab for Content Advisor.

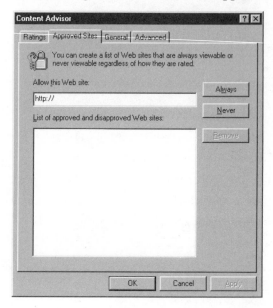

3. Type the URL for each Web site that your users can view regardless of its rating level, and then click **Always**.

4. Type the URL for each Web site that your users can never view regardless of its rating level, and then click **Never**.

Note If you want to delete an approved or disapproved Web site, click the URL in the list, and then click **Remove**.

▶ **To configure user options for content ratings**

1. On the **Tools** menu, click **Internet Options**, and then click the **Content** tab.

2. In the Content Advisor area, click **Settings**, and then click the **General** tab.

3. In the User Options area, select the settings you want.

   The following illustration shows the User Options area for Content Advisor.

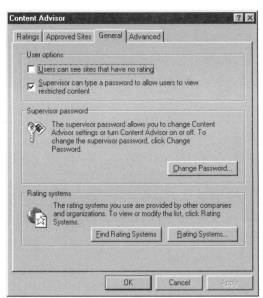

Option	Description
Users can see sites that have no rating	Select or clear this option depending on whether you want users to access Web pages that are not rated.
Supervisor can type a password to allow users to view restricted content	Select or clear this option depending on whether you want users to view restricted content by typing the supervisor password.

▶ **To change the supervisor password**

1. On the **Tools** menu, click **Internet Options**, and then click the **Content** tab.

2. In the Content Advisor area, click **Settings**, and then click the **General** tab.

3. Click **Change Password**.

The following illustration shows the Change Supervisor Password dialog box.

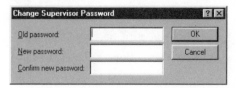

4. In the **Old password** box, type the current password to verify that you are authorized to change Content Advisor settings.

5. In the **New password** box, type the new password.

6. In the **Confirm new password** box, type the new password again.

▶   **To import new rating systems**

Important If necessary, install rating systems files following the directions provided by the ratings service. Then proceed with the following steps.

1. On the **Tools** menu, click **Internet Options**, and then click the **Content** tab.

2. In the Content Advisor area, click **Settings**, and then click the **General** tab.

3. Click **Rating Systems**.

The following illustration shows the Rating Systems dialog box.

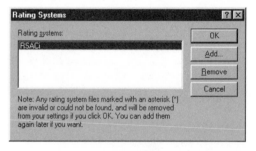

4. If the rating system you want to add is displayed on the list, click it, and then click **Add**.

If the rating system you want to add is not on the list, click **OK**, and then click **Find Rating Systems.**

▶ **To specify a different ratings bureau**

1. On the **Tools** menu, click **Internet Options**, and then click the **Content** tab.

2. In the Content Advisor area, click **Settings**, and then click the **Advanced** tab. The following illustration shows the **Advanced** tab for Content Advisor.

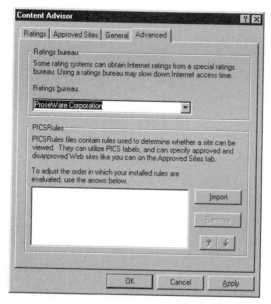

3. In the **Ratings bureau** box, type the name of the ratings bureau (other than RSAC) that Internet Explorer can use to obtain PICS ratings.

4. In the PICSRules area, click **Import**, and then type the name of the PICSRules (.prf) file used by the new ratings bureau.

Ensuring User Privacy

When you communicate over the Web, you want to know that other people cannot intercept or decipher the information you send and receive and cannot use your passwords and other private information. You also want to ensure that no one can access information on your computer without your knowledge. Internet Explorer protects your privacy in the following ways:

- It supports a wide range of Internet security and privacy standards that provide secure information transfer and financial transactions over the Internet or intranet.

- It provides encryption and identification capabilities to help users ensure the privacy of their information on the Web.

Secure Communications

Internet Explorer supports the latest Internet security standards, including Secure Sockets Layer (SSL), Transport Layer Security (TLS), and Private Communications Technology (PCT). Internet Explorer uses these protocols to create a secure channel for information exchange over the Web. In addition, Internet Explorer supports Fortezza security technology through the Fortezza Cryptographic Service Provider (CSP) plug-in. Users with Fortezza Crypto Cards can install the Fortezza CSP plug-in to ensure secure Internet Explorer communications based on Fortezza security standards.

When you browse a Web site that supports SSL, TLS, PCT, or Fortezza, Internet Explorer displays a lock icon in the browser's status bar at the bottom of your computer screen; in Fortezza mode, an "F" is overlaid on the lock icon. When you see this lock, you know that you can safely send information over the Internet to the site you are browsing.

For more information about Internet Explorer support for SSL, TLS, PCT, and Fortezza, see Chapter 6, "Digital Certificates."

Zone-Based Password Security Protection

Internet Explorer prompts you before transmitting your user name or password to sites that are designated as trusted in the security zones settings. You can, however, also configure security zones to send information from trusted sites without prompting you. For more information about configuring security zones, see Chapter 7, "Security Zones and Permission-Based Security for Microsoft Virtual Machine."

Control Over Cookies

An HTTP cookie is a small file that an individual Web site stores on your computer to provide customization features. For example, when you implement custom settings for MSN, that information is stored in a cookie file on your computer. MSN then reads the cookie each time you visit the site and displays the options you selected.

You can configure Internet Explorer to handle cookies in the following ways:

- Prevent cookies from being stored on your computer.
- Prompt you about whether to accept cookies from the site.
- Allow cookies to be stored on your computer without notifying you.

For more information, see Chapter 7, "Security Zones and Permission-Based Security for Microsoft Virtual Machine."

Note   Accepting a cookie does not give a Web site access to your computer or any personal information about you other than what you have specified in the customized settings for that site.

Profile Assistant

You can use Profile Assistant to securely share registration and demographic information with Web sites while maintaining your computer's privacy and safety. Profile Assistant supports the Internet privacy model defined by the Platform for Privacy Preferences (P3), a W3C project. You can maintain your personal information in a user profile, which provides a secure, encrypted information store on your computer.

A Web site can request information from your profile, but the Web site is not allowed to access profile information unless you specifically give your consent. Because Profile Assistant complies with the Internet's P3 privacy standards, it can also work with other Internet programs and servers.

For information about how to write scripts to access Profile Assistant information, see the Microsoft Internet Client Software Development Kit, which is part of the MSDN Online Web site.

When a Web site requests information from your user profile, the Profile Assistant dialog box opens. You can use the information in the Profile Assistant dialog box to verify which Web site is making the request, choose which information (if any) to share, and understand how the Web site intends to use the information.

The following table describes the information displayed in the Profile Assistant dialog box.

Option	Description
'Requester name' has requested information from you	Displays the name of the requester, which can be an individual or an organization.
Site	Displays the URL of the site requesting information from the user profile.
Profile information requested	Displays the list of information items requested. Clear the check boxes for any items you do not want to send to the requester.
Always allow this site to see checked items	Adds this site to a list of sites that you allow to access your user profile without notifying you.
Edit profile	Opens the My Profile dialog box so you can edit the profile information that will be sent to this Web site. For example, you might want to send a different fax number.
Privacy	Displays a message that explains whether the information you are sharing will be secure when it is sent over the Internet. It also displays a message describing how the requester intends to use the information.

Web sites can request up to 31 different items of information from your user profile. For more information, see "Configuring Profile Assistant" later in this chapter.

Microsoft Wallet 3.0

Microsoft Wallet 3.0 is a software payment program that you can use to conduct secure financial transactions over the Web with sites that support Wallet. You can use Wallet to securely store private information, such as credit card account data, for making payments over the Internet. Your private information is encrypted and stored in a protected storage area. You can decide what private information to put in Microsoft Wallet and who gets to view and use that information.

Note Wallet requires the Windows Address Book (WAB), which is included in the standard installation, but not the minimum installation, of Internet Explorer. If users attempt to start Wallet without the WAB, Internet Explorer can download this component using the Automatic Install feature.

Wallet supports all industry-standard payment methods, including SSL and Secure Electronic Transaction (SET), which enable the secure electronic use of credit cards. Wallet also supports add-on payment methods, such as digital cash and electronic checks, which some merchants and financial institutions might require. For instructions about how to install and use add-ons, contact the appropriate merchant or financial institution.

Wallet stores address and payment information separately. In the Addresses dialog box, you can enter, store, and access addresses that you want to reference for shipping and billing during online order entry. You can also view names, e-mail addresses, and telephone numbers of Wallet users in the Address Book.

In the Payments dialog box, you can enter, securely store, and access various types of payment methods for making online purchases. This information is protected by a password that you define. When you shop at an Internet store that supports Wallet, the site can prompt you to select payment methods stored in Wallet and to authorize payment by typing your password.

For more information, see "Configuring Microsoft Wallet 3.0" later in this chapter.

Configuring Privacy Options

To configure Internet Explorer privacy options, click the **Tools** menu, click **Internet Options,** and then click the **Content** and **Advanced** tabs. From these dialog boxes you can do the following:

- Configure Profile Assistant.
- Configure Microsoft Wallet 3.0.
- Configure advanced security options for user privacy.

Configuring Profile Assistant

You can use Profile Assistant to store or update the information you want to share with Web sites. Profile Assistant is used by other Internet programs, including NetMeeting and Outlook Express.

▶ **To create or update a user profile**

1. On the **Tools** menu, click **Internet Options**, and then click the **Content** tab.

2. Click **My Profile**.

   The following illustration shows the summary of profile properties.

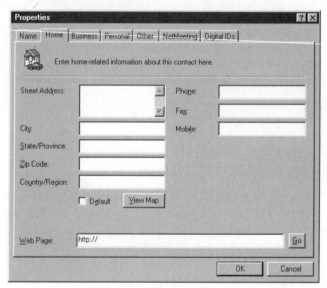

3. In the appropriate boxes on the **Personal**, **Home**, **Business**, and **Other** tabs, type the information you want to share.

Configuring Microsoft Wallet 3.0

You can use Microsoft Wallet 3.0 to store the information you want to use for payments over the Internet.

▶ **To add or update addresses used for payments**

1. On the **Tools** menu, click **Internet Options,** and then click the **Content** tab.

2. Click **Wallet,** and then click **Addresses**.

   The following illustration shows the **Addresses** tab for Microsoft Wallet.

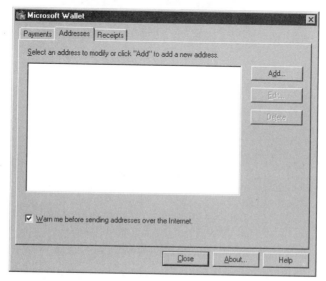

3. To add a new address, click **Add**.

   To update an existing address, click **Edit**.

The following illustration shows the Add a New Address dialog box.

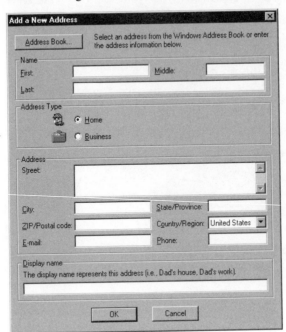

4. Type the name and address information, or click **Address Book** to select an existing address from the Address Book.

5. In the **Display name** box, type a display name for this address.

6. Click **Home** or **Business** depending on the type of address.

▶   **To add or update personal credit card information**

1. On the **Tools** menu, click **Internet Options**, and then click the **Content** tab.
2. Click **Wallet**, and then click **Payments**.

    The following illustration shows the **Payments** tab for Microsoft Wallet.

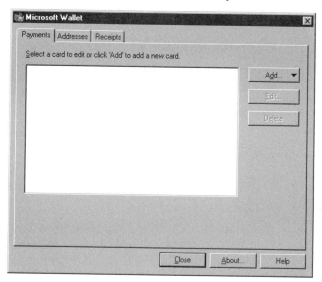

3. To add a credit card to the list of payment options, click **Add**.

    To update existing credit card information, click **Edit**.

4. Click the credit card you want to add or update, and then follow the instructions on your screen.

    You must provide your credit card account information and a password. You will need to enter this password before you can use the credit card to make a payment or edit the credit card information. This password ensures that other people cannot make purchases on the Internet using your credit card information. Internet Explorer encrypts and stores this information in the protected storage area in Wallet.

Configuring Advanced Security Options for User Privacy

You can configure a variety of user-privacy security options for Internet Explorer.

▷ **To configure advanced security options for user privacy**

1. On the **Tools** menu, click **Internet Options**, and then click the **Advanced** tab.

2. In the Security area, review the options that are selected.

   The following illustration shows the Security options on the **Advanced** tab.

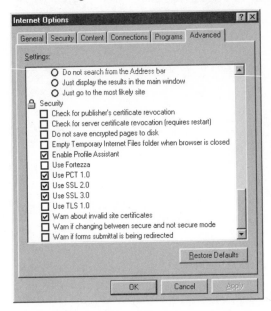

3. Depending on your needs, select or clear the Security check boxes. For example, if you want to enable Profile Assistant, select the **Enable Profile Assistant** check box.

P A R T 2

Preparing

Chapter 9: Planning the Deployment

To install Microsoft Internet Explorer 5 successfully, you must first plan your deployment processes and strategies. By understanding how to plan and automate your browser installation, you can reduce the cost of migration and ensure a smooth transition to Internet Explorer. This chapter describes how to plan your deployment.

Chapter 10: Accessibility Features and Functionality

This chapter describes the different ways that Internet Explorer supports enhanced accessibility and explains how to use the browser to accommodate different accessibility needs. In particular, Internet Explorer offers many features that enable users with disabilities to customize the appearance of Web pages to meet their own needs and preferences. Users without disabilities might also be interested in this functionality, which enables them to customize colors and fonts to their own tastes and to use time-saving keyboard shortcuts.

Chapter 11: Setting Up and Administering a Pilot Program

Before you deploy Internet Explorer to your users, it is recommended that you set up and administer a pilot program. Begin by testing the Internet Explorer installation in a lab, and then conduct the pilot program to refine your deployment configurations and strategies by using a limited number of pilot participants. This process will help you validate your deployment plan and ensure your readiness for full-scale deployment.

CHAPTER 9

Planning the Deployment

To install Microsoft Internet Explorer 5 successfully, you must first plan your deployment processes and strategies. By understanding how to plan and automate your browser installation, you can reduce the cost of migration and ensure a smooth transition to Internet Explorer. This chapter describes how to plan your deployment.

In This Chapter

See Also

- For more information about testing the deployment process before installation, see Chapter 11, "Setting Up and Administering a Pilot Program."

- For more information about building custom packages for installation, see Chapter 15, "Running the Internet Explorer Customization Wizard."

- For more information about deploying the browser to your users, see Chapter 19, "Deploying Microsoft Internet Explorer 5."

Evaluating Internet Explorer 5

The first steps in planning the deployment process are to evaluate the new and enhanced features and functions of Internet Explorer 5 and to understand how these features and functions can help you reduce the total cost of ownership.

Understanding New Features and Functions

To evaluate Internet Explorer 5, you should review the contents of this Resource Kit, which is a technical supplement to other browser product documentation. Each team member who assists with Internet Explorer planning and installation should obtain a copy to read and use during the deployment process. In particular, review the chapters in Part 1, "Getting Started," which provide an overview of the browser. These chapters can help you evaluate new features and functions so that you can better prepare for deploying Internet Explorer in your organization and training and supporting your users.

Reducing the Total Cost of Ownership

Microsoft has implemented Internet Explorer features and functions that can help you reduce the total cost of ownership while maximizing the return on your technology investment. Internet Explorer delivers both economic and business benefits without affecting browser scalability and flexibility. Your organization can quickly recover the time spent on Internet Explorer deployment and continue to realize cost savings by taking advantage of these features and functions:

- **Integrated, multiple-platform capabilities**—By integrating browser, desktop, network, messaging, and productivity applications, Microsoft offers a single desktop solution for users. The Internet Explorer Active Desktop enables users to browse the Internet, intranet, local network, or hard disk, and provides a standard method for accessing business-critical content, applications, and resources. Internet Explorer further enhances desktop integration by providing a common browser across multiple platforms, including Windows 32-bit, Windows 16-bit, Macintosh, and UNIX versions.

- **Internet Explorer Administration Kit**—You can use the Microsoft Internet Explorer Administration Kit (IEAK) to centrally customize, deploy, and manage Internet Explorer on your users' desktops from one central location. The IEAK includes the Internet Explorer Customization wizard, which enables you to create custom browser packages that you can distribute to your users, and the IEAK Profile Manager, which enables you to manage Internet Explorer settings after the browser is installed. These comprehensive, cross-platform tools work with your existing infrastructure without additional browser or server expenses.

  For more information about using the Internet Explorer Customization wizard, see Chapter 15, "Running the Internet Explorer Customization Wizard." For more information about using the IEAK Profile Manager, see Chapter 22, "Keeping Programs Updated."

- **System policies and restrictions**—Using the Internet Explorer Customization wizard or the IEAK Profile Manager, you can set system policies and restrictions to control user and computer access to Internet Explorer features and functions. System policies and restrictions enable you to customize the Internet Explorer work environment by deploying a standard configuration that best meets the requirements of your users. You can limit functionality to reduce browser complexity, or provide access to more advanced browser functions, as needed.

  These tools provide a simple, flexible method for customizing and administering user and computer settings. The system policies and restrictions you set are stored in a policy file, which overwrites default settings for HKEY_CURRENT_USER (user-specific policies) and HKEY_LOCAL_MACHINE (computer-specific policies) registry keys when users log on to the network. You can allow users to change these predefined settings, or you can choose to lock down all system policies and restrictions, which prevents users from making any changes. For more information about system policies and restrictions, see Appendix E, "Setting System Policies and Restrictions."

- **Channels**—You can use Internet Explorer channels to easily distribute and manage important information and software updates that your users receive on a regular basis. You can also use system policies and restrictions to predefine the channels that users can subscribe to, set limits on channel bandwidth usage, and control the frequency of channel updates. Organizations can use this technology to manage key business data and instantly notify users about important information and tools that can enhance their decision-making capabilities.

- **Security**—You can preconfigure Internet Explorer security settings to protect the work environment and the privacy of its users. These settings enable you to control the types of information and software that users can access, download, or run on the Internet or local intranet. You can set security zones to differentiate between trusted and untrusted content on the Internet and the intranet, so you provide rich browser functionality within the safety of the local firewall, while restricting incoming untrusted content from outside this environment. You can also manage security ratings, which control the users' access to undesirable content. For more information about Internet Explorer security, see Chapter 6, "Digital Certificates," Chapter 7, "Security Zones and Permission-Based Security for Microsoft Virtual Machine," and Chapter 8, "Content Ratings and User Privacy."

- **Application development**—Using Internet Explorer as a platform, you can develop your own custom Web-based applications that take advantage of state-of-the-art Web technologies based on Internet standards. Microsoft simplifies the development process by using familiar languages, such as HTML, Dynamic HTML, and Visual Basic. For more information about developing Web applications using Internet Explorer, see the MSDN Online Web site.

- **Usability features**—Users can benefit from the many usability features in Internet Explorer, which enable them to quickly and easily access important Web sites and desktop information. These features, which include the Search page, History bar, favorites, and Active Channel™ subscriptions, can help users complete tasks more efficiently and increase productivity. For more information about usability features, see Chapter 1, "What's New in Microsoft Internet Explorer 5?"

Assembling Project Teams

After you have a general understanding of Internet Explorer features and functions, you can assemble the people needed to plan and carry out the Internet Explorer deployment. Typically, a project manager oversees the deployment of Internet Explorer. That project manager assembles the necessary teams of system administrators and other information technology (IT) professionals to help plan, test, implement, and support the deployment.

Important   The size and number of teams will vary depending on the needs of your organization. For small organizations, only a few people who perform the roles of all the teams may be involved. Also, you can use external resources to supplement your internal teams.

Project teams can include:

- Planning teams that help determine the deployment requirements, develop deployment strategies, and write the deployment plan.

- Installation teams that set up the test lab and use it to test the deployment strategies.

- Training teams that develop the training plan and training documentation, promote Internet Explorer, and train the users during the pilot program and Internet Explorer deployment.

- Support teams that develop the support plan and assist users during and after the pilot program and Internet Explorer deployment.

When you set up your deployment planning teams, you should also include representatives from other groups involved in the deployment process. For example, you may include people from standards committees and finance groups.

Determining Time and Resource Requirements

The next step after assembling a team is to determine your project goals, including the number of computers on which to install Internet Explorer and the time expected for completion. Also, you should identify all the tools that you will need to complete the process within the stated time frame. If necessary, you can propose a formal budget for the company-wide implementation, including the cost for staff and additional resources, and present it to management for approval. Be sure to document all time and resource requirements in your deployment plan. For more information, see "Developing a Deployment Plan" later in this chapter.

After obtaining approval (if necessary), you should purchase any additional equipment or software you need to facilitate the installation. If you need additional staff, you might want to hire skilled Microsoft Certified Professionals to train your users, which can provide a cost-effective solution for many organizations.

Assessing System Requirements

The project teams should study the technical documentation for Internet Explorer and identify the system requirements for deployment. Sources of technical information include:

- This Resource Kit
- The Microsoft Windows Technologies Internet Explorer Web site
- Internet Explorer Help that is included with the product
- The Internet Explorer Customization wizard Help, which is included with the Microsoft Internet Explorer Administration Kit (IEAK)

The following sections describe the system requirements for installing and running Internet Explorer 5 and the Internet Explorer Customization wizard.

Requirements for Internet Explorer 5

Windows Update Setup for Internet Explorer 5 and Internet Tools offers four installation options: minimal, typical, full, and custom. The following table provides a list of components that are included with each of these options. If you select a custom installation, you can install only the Web browser—the minimal custom installation—or you can install the Web browser with as many other components as you like. In addition, you can use the Internet Explorer Customization wizard to build custom packages of Internet Explorer that include up to 10 additional custom components.

Internet Explorer 5 Components

This option	Includes these components
Minimal installation	Microsoft Internet Explorer 5 Web browser (all other components can be installed using the Automatic Install feature)
Typical installation	Microsoft Internet Explorer 5 Web browser, Microsoft Outlook Express 5, Microsoft Windows Media Player, and other multimedia enhancements
Full installation	Microsoft Internet Explorer 5 Web browser, Microsoft Outlook Express 5, Microsoft Windows Media Player, Microsoft NetMeeting 2.11, Microsoft Chat 2.5, Microsoft Wallet 3.0, and other multimedia enhancements
Custom installation	Microsoft Internet Explorer 5 Web browser and any of the following components: **Microsoft Internet Explorer 5:** Offline Browsing Pack, Microsoft Internet Explorer Help, Microsoft Virtual Machine, Microsoft Internet Connection wizard, Microsoft Internet Explorer core fonts, Dynamic HTML data binding, Microsoft Internet Explorer browsing enhancements **Communication components:** Microsoft NetMeeting 2.11, Microsoft Outlook Express 5, Microsoft Chat 2.5 **Multimedia components:** Microsoft Windows Media Player, Microsoft Windows Media Player codecs, Microsoft Media Player RealNetwork support, Microsoft DirectAnimation, Vector Graphics Rendering, AOL Art Image Format support, Macromedia Shockwave Director, Macromedia Flash **Web authoring components:** Microsoft FrontPage Express, Microsoft Web Publishing wizard, Web folders, Visual Basic scripting support, additional Web fonts **Additional components:** Microsoft Wallet 3.0 **Multi-language support:** Language auto-selection, Japanese text display support, Japanese text input support, Korean text display support, Korean text input support, Pan-European text display support, Chinese (traditional) text display support, Chinese (traditional) text input support, Chinese (simplified) text display support, Chinese (simplified) text input support, Vietnamese text display support, Hebrew text display support, Arabic text display support, Thai text display support

Disk space requirements depend on the components that you install. The following table lists the minimum hardware and software system requirements to deploy Internet Explorer 5 on Windows 32-bit versions. For information about requirements for other systems, including Windows 16-bit versions, UNIX, or Macintosh, see the Microsoft Windows Technologies Internet Explorer Web site.

Requirements for Windows 32-Bit Operating Systems

Item	Windows 95/Windows 98	Windows NT 4.0
Service pack	All	Service Pack 3 or later is required
Processor	486/66	486/66
Memory	16 MB	32 MB
Maximum disk space needed to accomplish installation	92 MB typical Web install 71 MB typical CD-ROM install 145 MB full Web install 112 MB full CD-ROM install	88 MB typical Web install 67 MB typical CD-ROM install 141 MB full Web install 109 MB full CD-ROM install

Requirements for the Internet Explorer Customization Wizard

The following table lists the system requirements that must be met to install and run the Internet Explorer Customization wizard. The Customization wizard is used to build custom packages of Internet Explorer.

Requirements for the Customization Wizard

Item	Requirements
Processor	486/66
Operating system	Windows 32-bit versions
Memory	16 MB for Windows 95 and Windows 98 16 MB for Windows NT 4.0
Disk space	8 MB to 70 MB to install 16 MB to 100 MB for each media type
Connection	A modem and Internet connection are needed to run the wizard the first time, if Internet Explorer is installed from a Web download site (not from CD-ROM)

Note Windows Desktop Update is included with Internet Explorer 4.0, but not with Internet Explorer 5. To install Windows Desktop Update with Internet Explorer 5, you must select this feature when you build your custom packages using the Internet Explorer Customization wizard.

You must install Internet Explorer 5 before running the Internet Explorer Customization wizard. If Internet Explorer 5 is not installed and you attempt to run the wizard, you will receive a message requesting that you install the browser first.

The disk space required to build custom browser packages varies considerably, depending on the number of components you plan to include. For example, a minimal installation, which includes only the Web browser, requires 16 MB of free disk space. A standard installation, which includes the Web browser, Outlook Express, Media Player, and other multimedia enhancements, requires 36 MB of free disk space. Also, you will need additional disk space for any custom components that you include with your browser installation.

The disk space required to install custom browser packages varies depending on the distribution method you use. If you plan to distribute Internet Explorer on CD-ROMs or floppy disks, the custom packages include the distribution files for the CD-ROMs or floppy disks. Therefore, CD-ROMs require about twice as much disk space, and floppy-disk packages require about three times as much disk space as packages that do not use these media.

Assessing Bandwidth Usage

Bandwidth usage and its impact on network traffic and server load can be a major concern for corporations that are implementing browser software. Microsoft designed Internet Explorer as a "bandwidth-smart" application with built-in mechanisms for caching and compressing data, as well as tools that optimize information dynamically. System policies to limit bandwidth and restrict access to bandwidth-intensive features, such as audiovisual components, provide additional control of bandwidth usage.

Internet Explorer achieves optimal bandwidth use by focusing on the most efficient methods for minimizing network traffic while maximizing performance. This occurs primarily by:

- Optimizing data through caching, compression, and other methods
- Using system policies and restrictions to control bandwidth

In addition, organizations that distribute Internet Explorer from Web download sites should consider the impact of this distribution media on bandwidth usage and server load. For more information about potential bandwidth issues, review "Assessing Network Performance and Bandwidth Issues" later in this chapter.

Optimizing Data Through Caching, Compression, and Other Methods

Internet Explorer uses the following methods to minimize the amount of data transmitted over the network and maximize the performance for the end user:

- **Caching content**—Internet Explorer optimizes bandwidth by caching Web content. The first time you connect to a Web page, Internet Explorer downloads the page and its supporting content to a cache stored in the Temporary Internet Files folder on your hard disk. By default, Internet Explorer uses the cached content instead of downloading new content when you return to browse a cached page. Using cached content provides faster performance for browsing Web sites, because the same content is not downloaded over and over again.

- **Providing data compression with the HTTP 1.1 protocol**—For faster, more efficient downloading of Web content, Internet Explorer supports the HTTP 1.1 protocol. This protocol compresses packets of data transferred with the HTTP protocol, which can boost performance as much as 50 to 100 percent over compressed data using HTTP 1.0. Web communications using HTTP 1.1 require fewer delays and consume less bandwidth, and Web content downloads faster to the browser. By default, HTTP 1.1 communications are enabled in Internet Explorer to optimize performance when the browser interacts with servers that support HTTP 1.1.

- **Supporting bandwidth-smart tools to develop Web content**—Internet Explorer supports the Portable Network Graphics (PNG) specification, Dynamic HTML, and the Microsoft DirectX multimedia extensions, which enable developers to design faster, more bandwidth-efficient graphics and interactive and animated Web content. Also, Internet Explorer includes the Microsoft Virtual Machine, which provides optimum performance for Java applets. For more information about these tools, see the MSDN Online Web site.

Using System Policies and Restrictions to Control Bandwidth

You can use Internet Explorer system policies and restrictions to control access to bandwidth-intensive features and to enforce a limit on bandwidth usage. For example, you can control the following capabilities:

- **Access to multimedia capabilities**—By default, Internet Explorer shows or plays a wide range of standard multimedia content, including graphics, video, and audio. Internet Explorer also uses image-dithering technology to smooth images, so they appear less jagged. However, multimedia content and dithering can use a significant amount of network bandwidth, causing Web pages to download and be displayed slowly.

Using system policies and restrictions, you can limit access to multimedia functions, such as Web pictures, animation, videos, and sound, which allows Web pages with multimedia content to download faster and use less bandwidth. You can also turn off image dithering to speed up image display time. Be aware, however, that when multimedia features are disabled, the pages will not appear as intended and you may miss some relevant content.

- **NetMeeting audio and video throughput**—NetMeeting intelligently manages the throughput (average bandwidth use) of audio, video, and data over the network on a client-specific basis. This process ensures the smooth operation of the separate NetMeeting components and the bandwidth resources of the network.

  You may want to further manage or restrict NetMeeting audio and video depending on the needs of your users and the capacity of your network systems. Using system policies and restrictions, you can set a specific number limit for the audio and video throughput, which controls bandwidth usage by restricting NetMeeting audio and video streams.

- **Access to offline features**—If you have many users who download Web content for offline browsing, you may be concerned about the server load. To address this concern, Internet Explorer provides system policies and restrictions that let you disable or limit access to offline functions. For example, you can reduce bandwidth usage by increasing the minimum number of minutes between scheduled updates of offline content and reducing the size of subscriptions that can be updated for offline viewing.

For more information about using Internet Explorer system policies and restrictions, see Appendix E, "Setting System Policies and Restrictions."

Identifying Client and Server Configurations

Because your deployment plan is dictated by your current system environments, you need to gather information about the existing client and server configurations for all groups that will migrate to Internet Explorer 5. You should interview the appropriate group managers, system administrators, and users for these groups. Be sure that you survey a representative sample so that you compile an accurate inventory of hardware and software used on client and server computers.

Specifically, you should consider the following configuration elements:

- **Minimum hardware requirements**—Computers may need to be upgraded to meet minimum hardware requirements for Internet Explorer, so review the hardware configurations currently in use by all groups.

- **Laptops and desktop computers**—Laptop and desktop computers have different configurations, including disk space and access to the network. You must select installation options that work for each type of computer.

- **Network access**—Users without network access need to install Internet Explorer locally from a CD-ROM or floppy disk. Users with network access can install Internet Explorer from a network.

- **Server load**—Many users installing the browser from a Web download site can impact server load. Microsoft Certified Professionals can provide information about server load patterns and how to distribute the server load by using multiple download sites.

For more detailed information about working with a large number of computers on a network, you can use system management programs, such as Microsoft Systems Management Server (SMS), to conduct the inventory. This tool can produce a report describing the computers' hardware and settings. In addition, you can use SMS to query the inventory database and quickly get information about equipment that might need to be upgraded. For more information about SMS, see Chapter 5, "Understanding Related Tools and Programs."

After you have identified the existing hardware and software for client and server computers, use that configuration information to do the following:

- Determine the preferred deployment strategies for the Internet Explorer custom package configurations.

- Evaluate migration issues, including the need for hardware and software upgrades to support migration.

- Simulate the organizational environment in the lab before full-scale deployment to your users.

Identifying Migration and Compatibility Issues

Whether your users currently run Internet Explorer or a competitive browser, planning how you want to migrate these users is critical. Determine in advance whether you need to convert existing files and custom programs. It's important to identify and solve migration issues, such as compatibility problems, before you attempt to migrate from your current browser software to Internet Explorer 5.

To identify migration issues, you should test the migration process using the actual user configurations. Testing enables you to identify solutions, such as the best method for upgrading existing, noncompatible systems. For more information about testing the migration process, see Chapter 11, "Setting Up and Administering a Pilot Program." After you have identified your migration solutions, you should also document them in your deployment plan.

The following sections discuss some of the general migration issues you should consider. For more information about migration issues:

- See the Internet Explorer 5 Release Notes, included with the browser software.
- Visit the Microsoft Internet Explorer Support Center on the Web.
- Contact the manufacturer of the existing software or hardware.

Upgrading from Internet Explorer Version 3.0 or Version 4.0

Windows Update Setup installs over existing versions of Internet Explorer 3.0 and Internet Explorer 4.0, and imports proxy settings, favorites, and cookies from the previous version. However, you must reinstall any add-ons that you want to keep. For more information about installing Internet Explorer 5, see Chapter 19, "Deploying Microsoft Internet Explorer 5."

Migrating from Netscape Navigator Version 3.0 or Version 4.0

Windows Update Setup imports proxy settings, bookmarks (called favorites in Internet Explorer), and cookies from Netscape Navigator version 3.0 and version 4.0. If you want helper applications to run when Internet Explorer calls them, add the applications' Multipurpose Internet Mail Extension (MIME) types and file extensions to the list of Windows file-type extensions. Also, specify the program that opens files with those extensions. For more information about migrating e-mail information, see "Using Previously Existing Internet E-Mail and News Programs" later in this chapter.

Using Previously Existing Browser Plug-ins or Add-ins

You can use most existing browser plug-ins and helper applications with Internet Explorer 5 by including them as custom components when you build your custom browser packages. For more information about building custom packages, see Chapter 15, "Running the Internet Explorer Customization Wizard."

Note Some earlier plug-ins and add-ins may not be compatible with Internet Explorer 5. The software manufacturer may be able to provide you with patches or updates to compatible versions.

Using Previously Existing Internet E-Mail and News Programs

Using the Internet Explorer Customization wizard, you can preconfigure Internet Explorer 5 to work with your previously existing e-mail and news applications. If the e-mail application is already installed, users can then select the application from within the browser.

▶   **To select a previously installed e-mail application**

1. On the **Tools** menu, click **Internet Options**, and then click the **Programs** tab.

2. In the E-mail box, select the application that you want to use.

If you want to introduce another e-mail or news application in conjunction with Internet Explorer, include each application as a custom component when you build your custom browser packages. For more information about building custom packages, see Chapter 15, "Running the Internet Explorer Customization Wizard."

You can also specify Outlook Express as your Internet e-mail and news program when you build custom packages of Internet Explorer. If you select a standard installation, Outlook Express is automatically included. If you select a custom installation, you can choose Outlook Express from the list of available components. If Outlook Express is selected, Windows Update Setup automatically imports folders from existing e-mail packages—such as Netscape Mail, Eudora Light, and Eudora Pro—into Outlook Express. Windows Update Setup also imports settings from Microsoft Exchange and Microsoft Outlook into Outlook Express, if they are appropriate for your configuration.

Dealing with Compatibility Problems

Some previously existing software may not be compatible with Internet Explorer 5. You can often correct compatibility problems with earlier software by obtaining upgrades or patches from the software manufacturer or by migrating to other compatible applications.

In addition, Web pages that were developed for other Web browsers and for proprietary HTML or scripting extensions may not function the same way in Internet Explorer 5. Test your Web pages to identify any compatibility problems with Internet Explorer 5. You may need to redesign any Web pages that do not function properly. For more information about third-party compatibility issues, see the Internet Explorer 5 Release Notes included with the Internet Explorer software.

Managing Multiple Browsers

Internet Explorer 5 can safely coexist on a computer with other versions of Internet Explorer, as well as different versions of competitive browsers.

Internet Explorer 4.0 Compatibility Mode

Internet Explorer 5 has an Internet Explorer 4.0 compatibility mode for evaluation and content-testing purposes only. Developers can test their Web sites using the rendering capabilities of Internet Explorer 4.0 or Internet Explorer 5 on a single computer, which simplifies the process of determining compatibility with previous browser versions.

Coexisting with Netscape Navigator

Internet Explorer 5 can coexist on the same computer with Netscape Navigator. If you install Internet Explorer 5 on a computer that already has Netscape installed, Windows Update Setup copies the Netscape plug-ins to the \Program Files\Internet Explorer\Plugins folder. Each time you launch the browser, the contents of this folder are loaded into memory.

Windows Update Setup looks for an installed browser that is specified as the current default browser. It then adopts the user-configurable settings—including proxy settings, dial-up connections, and favorites—from the current default browser. Windows Update Setup may also adopt additional settings if the corresponding optional components are installed.

For example, Windows Update Setup configures the following Outlook Express settings:

- SMTP server information
- POP3 server settings (POP3 server name and POP3 user name)
- Identity information (name, e-mail address, reply address, organization, and signature information)
- Personal address book
- Internet telephone program and Web-based phone book
- Send and post settings (8-bit characters in headers and MIME compliance) if different from the Netscape default
- Settings for **Check new message every x minutes** if different from the Navigator default

Windows Update Setup also configures the following Web Publishing wizard settings:

- Author name
- Document template location
- Publisher user name
- Publisher password

Specifying Custom Package Configurations

Using the Internet Explorer Customization wizard, you can select which components of Internet Explorer to install. This capability means that you can tailor client installations to include the best set of features for your users, while reducing the amount of disk space needed. The Customization wizard also enables you to specify a wide variety of configuration options. For example, you can specify security and proxy settings, and the media and setup options used to distribute the custom package to your users.

For more information about custom package configurations, review the following:

- Chapter 13, "Setting Up Servers," which provides information about setting up your servers to work with Internet Explorer and the components and options you select.
- Chapter 15, "Running the Internet Explorer Customization Wizard," which describes the components and options you can implement with your custom browser packages.
- "Considering User Needs," later in this chapter, which can help you determine whether any additional user requirements may affect your configuration choices.
- "Developing a Deployment Plan," later in this chapter, which describes documenting your components and options in a deployment plan.

Considering User Needs

When you are deciding which configuration options to install on your users' computers, you should consider the following user needs:

- Browser security and privacy requirements that your users may have
- Language versions of the browser that you will need to install for users
- Accessibility features needed to accommodate users with disabilities
- Training and support that your users will need during and after installation

Providing User Security and Privacy in the Corporate Environment

Note This section describes security and privacy options of Internet Explorer that are particularly important for administrators who need to protect the information, network, and users within their corporate environment. These options, though, may also be valuable for many other organizations and users.

Because Web browsers enable users to actively exchange important information and programs through the Internet and intranet, you must consider the security requirements needed to protect your users' privacy and the contents of their exchanges. You need to make educated choices about the types of browser security and privacy that you want to implement for your users.

Internet Explorer supports a wide range of Internet protocols for secure information transfers and financial transactions over the Internet or intranet. Internet Explorer also provides a variety of features to help users ensure the privacy of their information and the safety of their work environment. Users can set their own security and privacy options from within the browser, or you can preconfigure these options as part of your custom browser packages. When you preconfigure these settings, you have the option of locking them down, which prevents users from changing them. For more information about preconfiguring security options, see Chapter 15, "Running the Internet Explorer Customization Wizard."

You can implement the following options, depending on the security and privacy needs of your users:

- **Security zones**—Internet Explorer security zones enable you to divide the Internet and intranet into four groups of trusted and untrusted areas and to designate that specific Web content belongs to these safe and unsafe areas. This Web content can be anything from an HTML or graphics file to an ActiveX control, a Java applet, or an executable program.

  After establishing zones of trust, you can set browser security levels for each zone. Then you can control settings for ActiveX controls, downloading and installation, scripting, cookie management, password authentication, cross-frame security, and Java capabilities based on the zone to which a site belongs.

- **Digital certificates**—To verify the identity of individuals and organizations on the Web and to ensure content integrity, Internet Explorer uses industry-standard digital certificates and Microsoft Authenticode 2.0 technology. Together with security zones, certificates enable you to control user access to online content based on the type, source, and location of the content. For example, you can use security zones in conjunction with certificates to give users full access to Web content on their intranet but limit access to content from restricted Internet sites.

- **Content ratings**—The Internet Explorer Content Advisor enables you to control the types of content that users can access on the Internet. You can adjust the content rating settings to reflect the appropriate content in four areas: language, nudity, sex, and violence. You can also control access by specifying individual Web sites as approved or disapproved for user viewing.

- **Permission-based security for Java**—Internet Explorer provides permission-based security for Java with comprehensive management of the permissions granted to Java applets and libraries. Enhanced administrative options include fine-grained control over the capabilities granted to Java code, such as access to scratch space, local files, and network connections. These options enable you to give an application some additional capabilities without offering it unlimited access to every system capability.

For more information about Internet Explorer security, see Chapter 6, "Digital Certificates," Chapter 7, "Security Zones and Permission-Based Security for Microsoft Virtual Machine," and Chapter 8, "Content Ratings and User Privacy."

Addressing Language Needs

You may need to deploy Internet Explorer in more than one language, depending on the diversity of your user community. To do so, you must create and distribute a separate Internet Explorer custom package for each language version you want to deploy. When you create additional packages for different language versions, you do not need to reenter your setup and browser settings. For more information about selecting the language for your custom package of Internet Explorer, see Chapter 15, "Running the Internet Explorer Customization Wizard."

Internet Explorer also includes several Input Method Editors (IMEs), which you can deploy with your custom packages. IMEs enable users to input Chinese, Japanese, and Korean text into Web forms and e-mail messages using any Windows 32-bit language version. Then users can start any language version of Internet Explorer, Outlook Express, or Outlook, and write in Chinese, Japanese, or Korean without the need for a special keyboard or a different language browser. For example, a business based in New York could use its English version of the browser to send messages in Korean to an overseas affiliate, or a student attending classes in Paris could write home in Japanese.

Implementing Accessibility Features

You may need to address the needs of users who are affected by the following disabilities:

- Blindness
- Low vision
- Deafness
- Physical impairments that limit their ability to perform manual tasks, such as using a mouse
- Cognitive or language impairments
- Seizure disorders

Internet Explorer provides many features that benefit users who have disabilities, such as screen readers, customizable layout, and other accessibility aids. For more information about using accessibility features, see Chapter 10, "Accessibility Features and Functionality," and Internet Explorer 5 Help.

Providing User Training and Support

You may need to customize your user training and support to meet the different learning needs, backgrounds, and skill levels of your users. Consider these groups, which may be part of your user community:

- **Novice users**—Novice users have little or no experience using browser programs and browsing the Internet or intranet. They will require full training and support, starting with the most basic Internet Explorer features and functions. Also, these users may become overwhelmed by new information, so you should tailor your training and support for their special needs.
- **Intermediate users**—These users already have some experience using Internet Explorer or a competitive browser program, either at home or at work. Typically, these users require training and support for new browser features and job-specific functions that enhance their existing knowledge.
- **Advanced users**—Advanced users have expert knowledge of browser software and advanced features and functions. These users may include people who develop their own Web pages and Web applications. Training and support for these users should concentrate on adding new information to their existing knowledge.

After assessing your user groups, you may decide not to implement formal training and support, depending on the Internet Explorer components and features that you install. Instead, you can point your users to the built-in browser support. Help files included with Internet Explorer provide users with a comprehensive set of topics, which they can access from within the browser. Also, Microsoft offers complete support services through the **Online Support** option on the browser **Help** menu.

If you decide to offer formal training and support for your users, you will need to acquire the following resources:

- **Training and support methods**—Determine what training and support methods users need to master Internet Explorer, and structure those methods to meet their learning needs and anticipated use of the browser. If you are implementing custom browser packages, you need to tailor your training and support according to the features and functions that you will install.

  You may choose to offer a variety of learning methods—including online or in-person demonstrations, training and support Web pages, computer-based training (CBT), instructor-led training classes, self-paced learning materials, or desk-side support—depending on the needs of your users. Also, the types of training and support that you offer can depend on the amount of time that users can dedicate to those activities and the resources and facilities that are available.

  If in-house staff is not available, you might want to use outside vendors to develop and conduct your user training and support. The vendor must be able to meet your schedule and budget, and tailor training and support based on the needs of your organization and users.

- **Learning facilities, materials, and aids**—Decide what learning space, materials, and additional aids you need to train and support your users. These items can include videos, books, quick-reference cards, handouts, practice exercises and files, and multimedia presentations. You may choose to develop some materials internally or purchase them from an outside vendor, depending on the unique needs of your users, the type of installations you are planning, and the resources available. Also, to help your users learn more quickly, make these learning materials relevant by including information pertinent to your organization, such as job-specific policies and procedures and company software and templates.

- **Training and support schedule**—Decide how many users you need to train and support and the timeline for completing training and support tasks. You should schedule your first training sessions right before Internet Explorer deployment so that users can retain their knowledge by putting it to use immediately. Support services should also be in place before deployment.
- **Budget for training and support expenses**—Prepare a complete budget for training and support expenses. These expenses may include developing or purchasing learning materials and aids, renting external classroom facilities, and hiring an outside vendor for training and support.

After you have decided the best training and support strategies for your organization, you should document this information in formal training and support plans. For more information, see "Developing User Training and Support Plans" later in this chapter. Also, you should plan for ongoing training and support. For more information, see Chapter 23, "Implementing an Ongoing Training and Support Program."

Determining Installation Media and Methods

After you use the Internet Explorer Customization wizard to build custom packages, you can use several methods to distribute them to your users. You can automate installations of Internet Explorer with preselected components and browser settings so that no user action is required, or you can allow users to choose from up to 10 different installation options.

You can distribute Internet Explorer from:

- Download FTP or Web sites on the Internet or intranet
- Flat network shares (all files in one directory)
- CD-ROMs
- Multiple floppy disks
- A single floppy disk (Internet service providers only)
- Single-disk branding (customize existing installations of Internet Explorer 4.01 Service Pack 1, which is part of Windows 98, and higher)

The following sections discuss some of the factors to consider when you choose your distribution media and methods. For more information about selecting your media for distribution, see Chapter 15, "Running the Internet Explorer Customization Wizard."

Reaching Your Users

Identify the media that will work best for your users. For example, you may need to distribute your custom packages to the following types of users:

- **Stand-alone users**—For stand-alone users who are not connected to the local area network (LAN), you can distribute custom packages from the Internet, on CD-ROMs, or on floppy disks.

- **Remote-access users**—If your users access the Internet or intranet through remote-access modems, it can be time-consuming for them to download the Internet Explorer custom package over the modem. Instead of using the Internet or intranet, you can distribute the custom package to these users on CD-ROMs or floppy disks.

- **Local network users**—For corporate users who are connected to your network, you can distribute custom packages from download sites on your intranet.

Assessing the Size and Geographical Distribution of Your User Groups

The size and geographical distribution of your user groups will influence your distribution strategy. For example, consider these options:

- For a large number of users, you may want to produce and distribute custom packages on CD-ROMs at a volume discount.

- For a smaller number of users, it may be more economical to distribute custom packages over the intranet or the Internet.

- If your users are located worldwide, you may decide to distribute multiple-language versions of custom packages over the Internet.

Assessing Resources Available to Your Organization

The resources available to your organization will influence your distribution strategy. For example, if your organization does not have a wide area network (WAN), you may decide to distribute custom packages to your worldwide user community over the Internet.

Assessing Network Performance and Bandwidth Issues

When determining your distribution method, consider your network capacity, as well as the performance expectations of your users. If your users access the custom packages on the intranet, your distribution methods will affect network performance and the available bandwidth. Installing Internet Explorer over the network places different demands on network bandwidth, both in response time and connection time. Choose distribution methods that help optimize network performance and bandwidth.

For example, if you distribute custom packages over the Internet to users on your intranet, it can cause excessive loads on firewalls and proxy servers. If you distribute custom packages from only one download server on a large WAN, it can overload the server and cause traffic problems across the interconnecting routers and bridges of subnets and LANs. You can usually achieve the best network performance by distributing custom packages from download servers that are located in multiple domains or subnets of your intranet.

Note Using the Internet Explorer Customization wizard, you can specify up to 10 download sites that Windows Update Setup will automatically switch between during installations. This provides optimum download performance, as well as a distributed load across the intranet.

To help alleviate performance and bandwidth impact, you may also want to consider distributing a smaller package of Internet Explorer with only a limited number of browser components. For example, users can install an 8-MB browser-only version, which includes the majority of the components used on the Web, and then install additional components as needed using the Automatic Install feature of Internet Explorer.

Assessing Network Security Issues

The distribution methods available to you depend on the security configuration of your intranet, as well as the level of Internet access that you allow your users to have. You can distribute custom packages from the Internet to users on the intranet if you configure firewalls and proxy servers to allow users to download the Internet Explorer components. Internet Explorer components are authenticated when downloaded from the Internet. However, distributing custom packages over your intranet still provides maximum security and does not require additional configurations for firewalls and proxy servers.

If your organization does not provide the required level of Internet access to users, you do not have the option of distributing custom packages over the Internet. However, you still need to provide Internet access to the administrators who run the Internet Explorer Customization wizard to build the custom packages. The Internet Explorer Customization wizard must access the Internet to download the most current components of Internet Explorer from the Microsoft download site.

Developing a Deployment Plan

To ensure a successful Internet Explorer deployment, you should develop a written plan. Here's a suggested four-step process for completing your deployment plan:

1. **Get organization-wide input**. Collect information from your project teams, staff, and user groups. You may want to conduct surveys or interviews to determine the full scope of your organization's deployment requirements.

2. **Identify and document key topics**. Your deployment plan should include sections about the following topics:

   - Deployment goals
   - Critical success factors
   - Deployment tasks, resources, and tools
   - Task and resource dependencies
   - Budget for resources needed to meet deployment goals
   - Task responsibilities and timelines for completion
   - Significant risks and contingency plans

   As you read through the planning sections in this chapter, you can develop your deployment strategies and collect the information needed to write your plan. For example, as you read the "Identifying Client and Server Configurations" section, you should identify and document the number of computers for Internet Explorer installation, the software and hardware configurations, the best types of installations for these existing configurations, the time and cost for additional hardware upgrades, and any network access requirements for deployment.

3. **Test the plan**. After you write the plan, test it thoroughly. Verify all deployment strategies and identify any potential issues. Then update the plan based on your test results. For more information about testing your deployment plan in the lab, see Chapter 11, "Setting Up and Administering a Pilot Program."

4. **Review and accept the plan**. The deployment plan should be finalized before Internet Explorer deployment. All project teams should review and accept the contents of the plan before deployment begins.

Developing User Training and Support Plans

After you assess the training and support needs of your users (see "Providing User Training and Support" earlier in this chapter), it's time to prepare the training and support plans. The training and support teams should collaborate with the planning team to develop and review the plans. The purpose of these plans is to define the training and support objectives, tasks, resources, and methods you will use. You should finalize the training and support plans before you deploy Internet Explorer to your users.

You can follow the same four-step process used to develop your deployment plan. For more information, see the previous section, "Developing a Deployment Plan." In addition, consider the following items as you write your training and support plans:

- **Roles and responsibilities**—If you plan to use an outside vendor for training and support services, differentiate between tasks completed by internal staff members and tasks performed by a representative from the outside vendor. Make sure that you clearly assign responsibility for each task and identify any additional costs. For example, you should identify the people responsible for developing the curriculum and courseware, training the trainers and support staff, setting up equipment and classroom facilities, scheduling student training, and delivering training and user support.

- **Migration costs**—Carefully consider the costs for migration training and support. You may need to commit a percentage of your budget to preparing your users for Internet Explorer deployment, customizing training and support options to match their specific needs, and helping them learn how to use the new browser software. This investment is necessary to ensure that your users master browser skills quickly and to minimize additional migration support costs.

- **Ongoing training and support demands**—Anticipate increasing resource demands for ongoing support and training as users begin working with Internet Explorer. Determine a process for ensuring that users successfully complete training objectives. Also, decide how you will track and resolve support issues, and relay information about frequently asked questions to your users. For more information about ongoing training and support methods, see Chapter 23, "Implementing an Ongoing Training and Support Program."

CHAPTER 10

Accessibility Features and Functionality

This chapter describes the different ways that Microsoft Internet Explorer 5 supports enhanced accessibility and explains how to use the browser to accommodate different accessibility needs. In particular, Internet Explorer has many features that enable users with disabilities to customize the appearance of Web pages to meet their own needs and preferences. Users without disabilities might also be interested in this functionality, which enables them to customize colors and fonts to their own tastes and to use time-saving keyboard shortcuts.

In This Chapter

See Also

- For more information about planning accessibility features for users with disabilities, see Chapter 9, "Planning the Deployment."

- For more information about testing accessibility features before installing Internet Explorer, see Chapter 11, "Setting Up and Administering a Pilot Program."

- For more information about deploying Internet Explorer to your user groups, see Chapter 19, "Deploying Microsoft Internet Explorer 5."

Overview

Internet Explorer 5 makes the Web more accessible to computer users with disabilities. You can customize Internet Explorer for users with different types of disabilities, including users who are blind or have low vision, users who are deaf or hard-of-hearing, or users with physical impairments, seizure disorders, or cognitive or language impairments.

The sections in this chapter cover the following topics:

- Accessibility benefits offered by Internet Explorer

- Upgrade considerations for users transitioning from previous versions of Internet Explorer

- Suggested features that can benefit users with different types of disabilities

- Keyboard navigation within the Internet Explorer browser, Internet Explorer Help, the Windows Desktop Update (if installed), and Web pages

- Customization of fonts, colors, and styles on Web pages, the Windows Desktop Update (if installed), and Internet Explorer Help

- Advanced Internet accessibility options, such as disabling or enabling sounds, images, and animations; the use of smooth scrolling; and the treatment of links

- Accessibility features and keyboard shortcuts for Microsoft NetMeeting

- Other accessibility resources, including telephone numbers, postal addresses, and Web sites

Accessibility Benefits

Microsoft products are designed to make computers easier to use for everyone, including people with disabilities. In recent years, products have been further enhanced based on feedback from users who have disabilities, organizations representing those users, workers in the rehabilitation field, and software developers who create products for the accessibility market.

Internet Explorer offers many features that can benefit users with disabilities. These features enable users to perform the following tasks:

- **Control how Web pages are displayed**—Users can customize the colors of background, text, and links based on their preferences. By installing their own style sheets, users can control font styles and sizes for Web pages. Users can create style sheets that make headings larger or highlight italicized text with a different color. These Web-page preferences also apply to content within the Windows Explorer and Internet Explorer Help windows.

- **Work better with screen readers and other accessibility aids**—Internet Explorer 5 uses the HTML 4.0 standard, which enables Web-page designers to specify additional information on Web pages, such as the name of an image or control, for use by screen readers. Users can also turn off smooth scrolling and other effects that can confuse screen readers. In addition, the Dynamic HTML Object Model in Internet Explorer enables developers to create other accessibility aids for users with disabilities.

- **Reduce the amount of typing required**—With the AutoComplete feature turned on, Internet Explorer resolves partially typed URLs based on a cached history of sites that the user has visited. This feature makes it easier for users to type long or repetitive URLs. Explorer bars for Search, History, and Favorites also make it easier for users to find the items they need.

- **Perform tasks easily by customizing the desktop layout**—When Windows Desktop Update is installed, users can further customize their desktop, **Start** menu, and taskbar. They can choose from a range of desktop toolbars, or create their own. By clicking **Favorites** on the **Start** menu, users can quickly access preferred sites. Also, the Address bar enables users to enter URLs directly from the Windows desktop, without having to open the browser first.

- **Get better feedback**—Two sound events in Control Panel, Start Navigation and Complete Navigation, signal when a Web page begins loading and when the page finishes loading. These sounds can be helpful to users who are blind or have low vision. Users can also set the appearance of links to show when they are activated or hovered over with a mouse.

- **Use a mouse with greater ease**—When Windows Desktop Update is installed, users can choose to single-click rather than double-click the mouse to initiate common computer operations, such as opening folders. Also, users can put the most commonly used commands and shortcuts on desktop toolbars so that they can be accessed with a single mouse click.

- **Communicate with Internet conferencing**—The Internet conferencing features of Microsoft NetMeeting can improve accessibility for users with disabilities. NetMeeting users can employ real-time, multipoint communication, which enables them to collaborate and share information with two or more conference participants at the same time.

- **Navigate with the keyboard**—Using their keyboards, users can navigate through Web pages, panes, links, toolbars, and other controls. Keyboard shortcuts also make it easy for users to work with Favorites, use the Address bar, and perform editing functions, such as cut and paste.

- **Replace images with textual descriptions**—Users with disabilities might want to turn off the display of pictures in Internet Explorer and read the textual description of the image instead.

- **Turn off animation, pictures, videos, and sounds**—Users who are blind or have low vision might want to turn off animation, pictures, videos, and sounds to improve computer performance. Sounds can interfere with screen readers that read text aloud. Users with cognitive disabilities or users who are sensitive to motion or sound might also want to disable these functions.

- **Use the High Contrast option**—High contrast enables users to choose a simple color scheme and omit images that make text difficult for them to read.

Upgrade Considerations

Changes in software architecture might affect the functionality of certain accessibility aids that were written for previous versions of Internet Explorer. You should test Internet Explorer 5 with those aids to determine if the behavior differs from previous versions. Also, you can contact vendors to find out how the different accessibility aids function with Internet Explorer 5.

Depending on their specific needs, users with disabilities might find challenges using the different features of Internet Explorer 5. They can easily customize those features by installing or uninstalling components based on the functionality that works best for them. Many features can also be turned on or off, according to user preferences.

The following list provides some general tips to consider when upgrading to Internet Explorer 5:

- When Windows Desktop Update is installed with Internet Explorer 5, it replaces the traditional **Start** menu with a scrolling **Start** menu that supports dragging so that users can rearrange menu items. However, this type of menu limits the number of menu commands that are visible at one time to those commands that fit in a single column. Although long menu lists do not display all of the commands at once, users can navigate to them all by using the keyboard.

  Users who need to keep as many options as possible available on the screen at one time and who currently have many commands on their **Start** menu might want to remove some commands from the **Start** menu. They might also want to use the desktop toolbar, the Quick Launch toolbar, or the custom toolbar feature to make the commands available from other places on the desktop.

- Internet Explorer 5 uses menus and check boxes that might not be described correctly by some screen readers. If Windows Desktop Update is installed with Internet Explorer, these menus will also be used in Windows Explorer. To determine the level of support, you should test these features with your accessibility aids. Also, contact the vendors of your aids to find out about upgrades that might better support Internet Explorer 5.

Suggested Features for Different Types of Disabilities

The following sections suggest features that can benefit users with certain types of disabilities. The list of features for each type of disability is not complete, because the needs and preferences of individuals vary and some people have a combination of disabilities or varying abilities.

To learn more about these features or to find procedures that explain how to configure a specific setting, see "Using Keyboard Navigation," "Customizing Fonts, Colors, and Styles," and "Configuring Advanced Internet Accessibility Options" later in this chapter.

Features for Users Who Are Blind

Many users who are blind depend on screen readers, which provide spoken or Braille descriptions of windows, controls, menus, images, text, and other information that is typically displayed visually on a screen. Internet Explorer 5 provides improved functionality for screen readers and offers a range of other features that can be helpful to individuals who are blind.

Users who are blind can benefit from these features:

- Use the keyboard to navigate Internet Explorer, Web pages, Internet Explorer Help, and NetMeeting.
- Ignore colors specified on Web pages.
- Ignore font styles and sizes specified on Web pages.
- Format documents by using an individualized style sheet.
- Expand alternate text for images.
- Move the system caret with focus and selection changes.
- Disable smooth scrolling.
- Choose not to show pictures, animations, and videos in Web pages.
- Disable smart image dithering.
- Assign a sound to the Start Navigation and Complete Navigation events.

Features for Users Who Have Low Vision

Common forms of low vision are color blindness, difficulty in changing focus, and impaired contrast sensitivity. Users with color blindness might have difficulty reading colored text on a colored background. Users who have difficulty changing focus or who experience eye strain with normal use of a video display might have difficulty reading small text, discriminating between different font sizes, or using small on-screen items as targets for the cursor or pointer. Users with impaired contrast sensitivity might have difficulty reading black text on a gray background.

Users who have low vision can benefit from these features:

- Use the keyboard to navigate Internet Explorer, Web pages, Internet Explorer Help, and NetMeeting.
- Ignore colors specified on Web pages.
- Ignore font styles and sizes specified on Web pages.
- Format documents by using an individualized sheet.
- Expand alternate text for images.
- Move the system caret with focus and selection changes.
- Disable printing of background colors and images.

- Choose text and background colors for Web pages (or create custom colors).
- Choose the visited and unvisited colors for Web links (or create custom colors).
- Display Web pages in the Windows High Contrast color scheme (click the **Accessibility Options** icon in Control Panel), which offers a simple color palette and omits images that make text difficult to read.
- Assign a sound to the Start Navigation and Complete Navigation events.
- Add the **Size** button to the browser toolbar so font sizes can be changed easily.
- Display large icons.

Features for Users Who Are Deaf or Hard-of-Hearing

Sound cues in programs are not useful to users with hearing impairments or users working in a noisy environment. Users who are deaf might have sign language as their primary language and English as their secondary language. As a result, they might have difficulty reading pages that use custom fonts, depart from typographical convention (that is, the standardized use of uppercase and lowercase letters), or use animated text displays.

Note Users who are deaf might also be interested in the features recommended for users with cognitive or language impairments.

Users who are deaf or hard-of-hearing can benefit from these features:

- Select **SoundSentry**, which generates visual warnings when the computer makes a sound.
- Select **ShowSounds**, which displays captions for the speech and sounds the computer makes.
- Integrate NetMeeting.
- Disable sounds in Web pages.

Features for Users with Physical Impairments

Users with physical impairments might perform certain manual tasks with difficulty, such as manipulating a mouse or typing two keys at the same time. They might also hit multiple keys or "bounce" fingers off keys, making typing difficult. These users could benefit from adapting keyboards and mouse functions to meet their requirements.

Users who have physical impairments can benefit from these features:

- Use the keyboard to navigate Internet Explorer, Web pages, Internet Explorer Help, and NetMeeting.
- Use Explorer bars.
- Ignore font sizes specified on Web pages.
- Format documents by using an individualized style sheet.
- Add hover colors to links.
- Expand alternate text for images.
- Move the system caret with focus and selection changes.
- Use inline AutoComplete for Web addresses.
- Use inline AutoComplete in the integrated shell.
- Use inline AutoComplete for Web forms.
- Underline links when hovering.
- Add the **Size** button to the browser toolbar so font sizes can be changed easily.
- Display large icons.

Features for Users with Seizure Disorders

Users with seizure disorders, such as epilepsy, might be sensitive to screen refresh rates, blinking or flashing images, or specific sounds.

Users who have seizure disorders can benefit from these features:

- Use the ESC key to immediately turn off animations.
- Disable animation.
- Disable video.
- Turn off sounds.

Note Even if users turn off sounds in Internet Explorer, sounds might still play if RealAudio is installed or if a movie is playing.

Features for Users with Cognitive and Language Impairments

Cognitive impairments take many forms, including short-term and long-term memory loss, perceptual differences, and developmental disabilities. Dyslexia and illiteracy are also common types of language impairments. People who are learning the language used by their computer software as a second language might also be considered to have a form of language impairment.

Users who have cognitive or language impairments can benefit from these features:

- Use the keyboard to navigate Internet Explorer, Web pages, Internet Explorer Help, and NetMeeting.
- Use Explorer bars.
- Ignore colors specified on Web pages.
- Ignore font styles and sizes specified on Web pages.
- Format documents by using an individualized style sheet.
- Choose text and background colors for Web pages (or create custom colors).
- Choose the visited and unvisited colors for Web links (or create custom colors).
- Display Web pages in the Windows High Contrast color scheme (click the **Accessibility Options** icon in Control Panel), which offers a simple color palette and omits images that make text difficult to read.
- Choose a hover color for links.
- Expand alternate text for images.
- Move the system caret with focus and selection changes.
- Choose to launch the browser in full-screen mode, which removes all toolbars and scrollbars from the screen. This capability enables users with cognitive disabilities to have more information on the screen at one time or to remove distractions from peripheral controls.
- Choose to display friendly URLs.
- Use inline AutoComplete for Web addresses.
- Use inline AutoComplete in the integrated shell.
- Choose not to use smooth scrolling.
- Disable images.
- Disable animation.
- Disable video.
- Add the **Size** button to the browser toolbar so font sizes can be changed easily.
- Display large icons.

Using Keyboard Navigation

One of the most important accessibility features is the ability to navigate by using the keyboard. Keyboard shortcuts are useful for people with a wide range of disabilities, as well as anyone who wants to save time by combining key commands with mouse control. This section describes the following keyboard navigation features:

- Internet Explorer shortcut keys
- AutoComplete shortcut keys
- Keyboard navigation of Web pages
- Keyboard navigation of the Windows Desktop Update (if it is installed)
- Keyboard navigation of Internet Explorer Help

Internet Explorer Shortcut Keys

Shortcut keys can make it easier for users to move between screen elements, choose commands, and view documents. The following tables describes common tasks and the associated shortcut keys.

Shortcut Keys for Viewing and Exploring Web Pages

To	Press
View Internet Explorer Help	F1
Switch between the regular and full-screen views of the browser window	F11
Move forward through the Address bar, Links bar, Explorer bars, and the items, menus, and toolbars on a Web page	TAB
Move backward through the Address bar, Links bar, Explorer bars, and the items, menus, and toolbars on a Web page	SHIFT+TAB
Move forward between frames	CTRL+TAB
Move backward between frames	SHIFT+CTRL+TAB
Activate a selected link	ENTER
Display a shortcut menu for the page or link	SHIFT+F10
Go to the previous page	ALT+LEFT ARROW
Go to the next page	ALT+RIGHT ARROW
Scroll toward the beginning of a document	UP ARROW
Scroll toward the end of a document	DOWN ARROW
Scroll toward the beginning of a document in larger increments	PAGE UP or SHIFT+SPACEBAR
Scroll toward the end of a document in larger increments	PAGE DOWN or SPACEBAR

To	Press
Move to the beginning of a document	HOME
Move to the end of a document	END
Stop downloading a page and stop animation	ESC
Refresh the current page only if the timestamps for the Web version and the locally stored version are different	F5 or CTRL+R
Refresh the current page even if the timestamps for the Web version and the locally stored version are the same	CTRL+ F5
In the History or Favorites bar, open multiple folders	CTRL+CLICK
Open Search in the Explorer bar	CTRL+E
Find on this page	CTRL+F
Open History in the Explorer bar	CTRL+H
Open Favorites in the Explorer bar	CTRL+I
Go to a new location	CTRL+O or CTRL+L
Open a new window	CTRL+N
Print the current page or active frame	CTRL+P
Save the current page	CTRL+S
Close the current window	CRTL+W

Shortcut Keys for Using the Address Bar

To	Press
Move the mouse pointer to the Address bar	ALT+D
Display the Address bar history	F4
When in the Address bar, move the cursor left to the next logical break character (. or /)	CTRL+LEFT ARROW
When in the Address bar, move the cursor right to the next logical break character (. or /)	CTRL+RIGHT ARROW
Add **www.** to the beginning and **.com** to the end of the text typed in the Address bar	CTRL+ENTER
Move forward through the list of AutoComplete matches	UP ARROW
Move backward through the list of AutoComplete matches	DOWN ARROW

Shortcut Keys for Working with Favorites

To	Press
Add the current page to the Favorites menu	CTRL+D
Open the Organize Favorites dialog box	CTRL+B

Shortcut Keys for Editing

To	Press
Select all items on the current Web page	CTRL+A
Copy the selected items to the Clipboard	CTRL+C
Insert the contents of the Clipboard at the selected location	CTRL+V
Remove the selected items and copy them to the Clipboard	CTRL+X

For additional information about using the keyboard with Windows, visit the Microsoft Accessibility Web site.

AutoComplete Shortcut Keys

With the AutoComplete feature turned on, Internet Explorer automatically completes Web page addresses and directory paths as the user types them in the Address bar. Internet Explorer resolves this information based on the Web pages or local files that the user has visited. AutoComplete also works with the **Run** command on the **Start** menu.

For example, if the user starts typing **http://www.home.micr** and has recently visited http://www.home.microsoft.com, AutoComplete suggests http://www.home.microsoft.com. The user can accept the match, view other potential matches, or override the suggestion by typing over it. AutoComplete also adds prefixes and suffixes to Internet addresses.

Users can turn AutoComplete on or off in the Internet Options dialog box.

▶ **To turn AutoComplete on or off**

1. On the **Tools** menu, click **Internet Options**, and then click the **Advanced** tab.

2. Select or clear the following check boxes:

   - **Use inline AutoComplete for Web addresses**—Specifies whether you want Internet Explorer to complete Web addresses automatically as you type them in the Address bar.

   - **Use inline AutoComplete in integrated shell**—Specifies whether you want Internet Explorer to complete file names, paths, or folders automatically as you type them in the Address bar or the **Open** box in the **Run** command.

The following illustration shows the AutoComplete options.

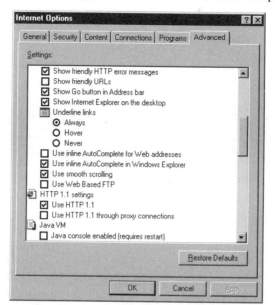

AutoComplete includes the following shortcuts:

- To add to the string that Internet Explorer has automatically completed, press the RIGHT ARROW key, and then type the additional characters.

- To skip to break characters or separator characters in URLs (such as the forward slash (/)), press and hold CTRL, and then use the LEFT ARROW or RIGHT ARROW keys.

- To search a history file, type the beginning of an address, and then press the UP ARROW or DOWN ARROW keys to complete it.

- To add a prefix or suffix to a partial URL, press CTRL+ENTER to add **http://www.** before the entry and **.com** after it.

Keyboard Navigation of Web Pages

Users can move forward and backward through the items in the browser window by using the TAB and SHIFT+TAB keys. A one-pixel-wide border (called the focus box) appears around links, so the user can identify the selected item.

Note Screen readers do not recognize the TAB and SHIFT+TAB keys for toolbars.

When users press the TAB key, the selection rotates forward through the browser window in the following order:

1. Address bar

   - To display the Address bar, on the **View** menu, point to **Toolbars**, and then click **Address Bar**.

2. Links bar

   - To display the Links bar, on the **View** menu, point to **Toolbars**, and then click **Links**.

   - To move between the links, use the LEFT ARROW and RIGHT ARROW keys. To open a link, press ENTER, or to display the shortcut menu for a link, press SHIFT+F10.

3. Explorer bar

   - If an Explorer bar is open, users will see an entry highlighted on the bar.

   - To display an Explorer bar, on the **View** menu, point to **Explorer Bar**, and then click **Search**, **Favorites**, or **History**. Or, on the Internet Explorer toolbar, click the **Search**, **Favorites**, or **History** icon.

   - To move between the items on the Explorer bar, use the LEFT ARROW, RIGHT ARROW, UP ARROW, and DOWN ARROW keys. To activate a link on the Explorer bar, press ENTER, or to open a shortcut menu for a link, press SHIFT+F10.

4. Links on the page, moving left to right, and then down

   - As links are highlighted, the link's URL appears on the message bar.

   - To activate the link, press ENTER, or to open a shortcut menu for the link, press SHIFT+F10.

Note Web-page designers might specify a different order for their links than the standard left-to-right and top-to-bottom order.

5. Internet Explorer menus

- To move between the items on the Internet Explorer menus, use the LEFT ARROW, RIGHT ARROW, UP ARROW, and DOWN ARROW keys.

- To select a menu item, press ENTER.

6. Internet Explorer toolbar

- To move between the buttons on the Internet Explorer toolbar, use the LEFT ARROW, RIGHT ARROW, UP ARROW, and DOWN ARROW keys.

- To select a toolbar button, press ENTER.

Note In order to navigate through the Internet Explorer menus and toolbar by using the TAB and SHIFT+TAB keys, you must select the **Show extra keyboard help in programs** check box. (To access this option from Control Panel, click **Accessibility Options**.)

To move between the same areas in reverse order, press SHIFT+TAB. Using reverse order, the focus stops on the page as a whole before reaching the links on the page. To quickly skip to the next frame, press CTRL+TAB, or to go to the previous frame, press CTRL+SHIFT+TAB.

Keyboard Navigation of the Windows Desktop Update

If Windows Desktop Update is installed, users can press TAB and SHIFT+TAB to move forward and backward through the desktop elements. A focus box appears around the selected item.

When users press the TAB key, the selection rotates forward through the desktop elements in the following order:

1. **Start** button

2. Quick Launch toolbar

- One of the Quick Launch icons appears selected.

- To move between the toolbar icons, press the LEFT ARROW, RIGHT ARROW, UP ARROW, and DOWN ARROW keys. After the focus is on an icon, to open the application, press ENTER, or to display the shortcut menu for the toolbar, press SHIFT+F10. (All the toolbars on the desktop share the same shortcut menu.)

- To bring the focus back to the left-most icon, continuously press the RIGHT ARROW key.

3. Taskbar

- A selection will not appear on the taskbar. To display the shortcut menu for the toolbar, press SHIFT+F10. (All the toolbars on the desktop share the same shortcut menu.)

- To select an application, press the RIGHT ARROW key. To open the selected application, press ENTER, or to display the shortcut menu for that application, press SHIFT+F10.

- To move between the applications, press the LEFT ARROW, RIGHT ARROW, UP ARROW, and DOWN ARROW keys.

4. Desktop icons

- An icon on the desktop appears selected.

- To move between the icons on the desktop, press the LEFT ARROW, RIGHT ARROW, UP ARROW, and DOWN ARROW keys. To open the application or document, press ENTER, or to display the shortcut menu for that icon, press SHIFT+F10.

- To select or deselect the current icon, press CTRL+SPACEBAR. To display the shortcut menu for the entire desktop when no icon is selected, press SHIFT+F10.

5. Desktop items

- A desktop item appears selected.

- To move forward through the links in that item and on to the other items on the desktop, press TAB. To activate a link, press ENTER.

6. Desktop Channel bar

- The topmost button on the Channel bar appears selected.

- To move between the icons on the Channel bar, press the LEFT ARROW, RIGHT ARROW, UP ARROW, and DOWN ARROW keys. To display a channel by using Internet Explorer, press ENTER.

Note Internet Explorer 5 does not include the desktop Channel bar; this feature is a part of previous browser versions.

7. **Start** button

To move between the same areas in reverse order, press SHIFT+TAB. If you add other bars, such as the Address bar, Quick Links toolbar, desktop toolbar, or a custom toolbar, you can also navigate to these bars by pressing TAB and SHIFT+TAB. Note that you can reach the Channel bar only by pressing TAB; the Channel bar is skipped when you navigate in reverse order by using SHIFT+TAB.

Keyboard Navigation in Internet Explorer Help

Internet Explorer Help displays Help information as Web pages. This tool offers several significant accessibility advantages (explained in detail in this section), but it also introduces a few changes for users who navigate by using the keyboard:

- When a user displays a topic in the right pane, it continues to be displayed until the user replaces it with another selection—that is, when the user highlights another topic and then presses ENTER. This display can be confusing during navigation, because the topic name currently selected in the left pane might not match the topic shown in the right pane.

- The **Hide** button on the Help toolbar hides the left pane (used for Contents, Index, and Search). When the left pane is hidden, users cannot navigate through Help. To return to the **Contents**, **Index**, or **Search** tab, press ALT+C, ALT+I, or ALT+S, respectively.

The following procedures describe how to navigate through the Internet Explorer Help **Contents**, **Index**, and **Search** tabs by using the keyboard.

▶ **To navigate through the Help Contents by using the keyboard**

1. To view the **Contents** tab in Internet Explorer Help, press ALT+C.

   The following illustration shows the **Contents** tab for Internet Explorer Help.

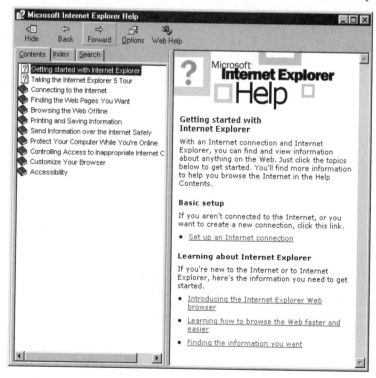

2. To scroll through the list of Contents topics, press the UP ARROW and DOWN ARROW keys.

3. To display the expanded list of subtopics for a main topic, highlight the main topic and then press ENTER or the RIGHT ARROW key. An open main topic is represented by an open-book icon. A subtopic is represented by a page icon. To close the main topic, press ENTER or the LEFT ARROW key; the list of subtopics collapses and a closed book icon appears.

4. To view topic information, highlight the subtopic, and then press ENTER. Internet Explorer Help displays the topic you select in the right pane, and the keyboard focus moves to the topic. Within the topic, you can do the following:

   - To scroll up and down or left and right in the topic pane, press the UP ARROW and DOWN ARROW keys or the LEFT ARROW and RIGHT ARROW keys.

   - To display information about a linked topic, highlight the link, and then press ENTER.

   - To scroll to the beginning or end of the topic, press HOME or END.

   - To display the shortcut menu for the topic, press CTRL+F10.

5. To return to the **Contents** tab to select another topic, press ALT+C.

6. To exit Help, press ALT+F4.

▶   **To navigate through the Help Index by using the keyboard**

1. To view the **Index** tab in Internet Explorer Help, press ALT+I. Initially, the keyboard focus is in the keyword box, and the box is empty.

The following illustration shows the **Index** tab for Internet Explorer Help.

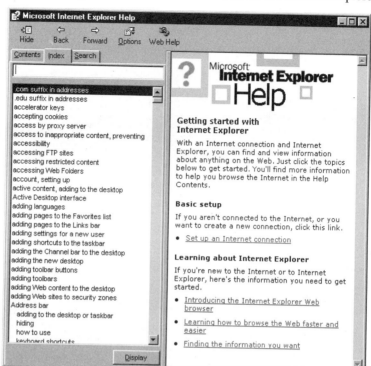

2. To scroll through the list of index topics, press the UP ARROW and DOWN ARROW keys. As you scroll, each highlighted topic appears in the keyword box.

   You can also type the name of the topic you want to view in the keyword box. As you type, the Index list scrolls to highlight matching topics.

3. To display information about a highlighted topic, press ENTER or ALT+D. Internet Explorer Help displays the topic you select in the right pane, and the keyboard focus moves to the topic. Within the topic, you can do the following:

   - To scroll up and down or left and right in the topic pane, press the UP ARROW and DOWN ARROW keys or the LEFT ARROW and RIGHT ARROW keys.

   - To display information about a linked topic, highlight the link, and then press ENTER.

   - To scroll to the beginning or end of the topic, press HOME or END.

   - To display the shortcut menu for the topic, press CTRL+F10.

4. To return to the **Index** tab to select another topic, press ALT+I.

5. To exit Help, press ALT+F4.

▶ **To navigate through the Help Search by using the keyboard**

1. To view the **Search** tab in Internet Explorer Help, press ALT+S. The keyboard focus moves to the keyword box.

   The following illustration shows the **Search** tab for Internet Explorer Help.

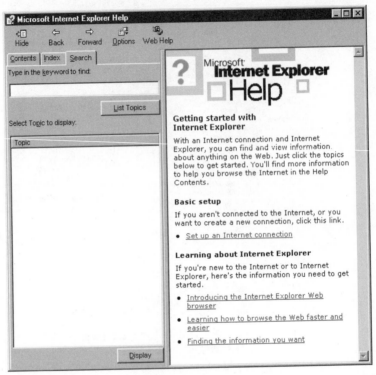

2. Type the keyword you want, and then press ENTER or ALT+L. The Select Topic to Display list shows topics that contain the keyword you typed.

3. To move the keyboard focus to the first item in the Select Topic to Display list, press ALT+T and then the DOWN ARROW key.

4. To highlight a topic, press the UP ARROW and DOWN ARROW keys.

5. To display information about a highlighted topic, press ENTER or ALT+D. Internet Explorer Help displays the topic you select in the right pane, and the keyboard focus moves to the topic. Within the topic, you can do the following:

   ▪ To scroll up and down or left and right in the topic pane, press the UP ARROW and DOWN ARROW keys or the LEFT ARROW and RIGHT ARROW keys.

   ▪ To display information about a linked topic, highlight the link, and then press ENTER.

   ▪ To scroll to the beginning or end of the topic, press HOME or END.

   ▪ To display the shortcut menu for the topic, press CTRL+F10.

6. To return to the **Search** tab to select another topic, press ALT+S, or to begin another search, press ALT+K.

7. To exit Help, press ALT+F4.

Customizing Fonts, Colors, and Styles

When Web authors and designers create Web pages, they often specify particular fonts, colors, and styles. They might specify the settings for each coded item on the Web page, or they might define the settings in a style sheet. A style sheet provides a template for specifying how different styles should appear throughout a Web site.

Internet Explorer 5 enables users to override any or all of these settings. Users can specify their own font and color preferences for all Web pages. They can also use their own style sheet or select the Windows High Contrast option. If users have installed the Windows Desktop Update, these font, color, and style options will also affect the Windows desktop and file folders.

Because Internet Explorer Help information is also displayed as Web pages, most of the browser accessibility features are also available for viewing Help topics. Users can override and customize formatting and color settings, display text instead of images, disable animation, and even apply their own style sheet to control how Help is presented. When users adjust these options in Internet Explorer and then restart Help, the settings automatically apply to all Help topics.

Overriding Web-Page Formatting

Because of the different methods Web authors and designers can use to format Web pages, some pages might not be affected by customizing the font, color, and style options within the browser. To change the appearance of these pages, users must override the page formatting.

▶ **To override page formatting**

1. On the **Tools** menu, click **Internet Options**.

2. On the **General** tab, click **Accessibility**.

3. Select any of the following options:

   - **Ignore colors specified on Web pages**
   - **Ignore font styles specified on Web pages**
   - **Ignore font sizes specified on Web pages**
   - **Format documents using my style sheet**

The following illustration shows these accessibility options.

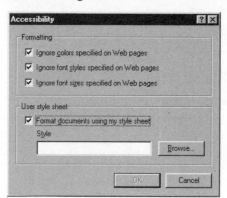

Changing Font Size

When users browse a Web page, they can immediately change the size of the displayed text.

▶ **To immediately display all text in a larger or smaller font size**

1. On the **View** menu, click **Text Size**, or click the **Size** button on the toolbar.

2. Choose the size you want. A check mark appears next to your choice, and the change takes effect immediately.

If the **Size** button is not displayed, users can add it to the toolbar.

▶ **To add the Size button to the toolbar**

1. On the **View** menu, click **Toolbars**, and then click **Customize**.

2. In the Available Toolbar Buttons list, select **Size**, and then click **Add**.

   The following illustration shows **Size** after it has been added to the Current Toolbar Buttons list.

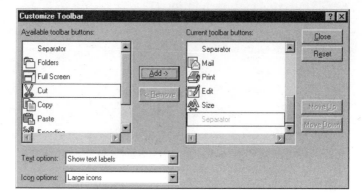

3. Click **Close**.

The changes created by the **Text Size** menu option and **Size** button are active for current and future sessions.

For more information about changing font sizes, see "Understanding Font-Size Changes" later in this chapter.

Creating a Style Sheet

This section shows a sample style sheet that adjusts the display of Web pages and Help topics to be read more easily by users who have certain types of low vision. In particular, it overrides normal formatting of all displayed pages in the following ways:

- All items on the Web page appear in high contrast, with a black background and brightly colored text. Body text is white, highlighted text is yellow, and links are brighter versions of their normal blue and purple.
- All text is displayed in a large, sans serif font. Body text is 24 point, and headings are 32 point.
- All bold, italic, and underlining, which might be difficult to read, are replaced by normal text with a single highlight color.
- The keyboard focus is emphasized by showing the active link in a bright, light green, sometimes called "low-vision green."

These settings affect all pages viewed in Internet Explorer, as well as pages displayed by other programs, such as HTML Help.

Note The style sheet in the following example is just one possible solution for increasing the readability of Web pages. By editing the style sheet, users can change the background color and the size, color, and style of the fonts according to their preferences.

▶   **To create a high-visibility style sheet**

1. Open Notepad.

2. Type the following text into a new file:

```
<STYLE TYPE="text/css">
<!--
BODY, TABLE {
    font-size: 24pt;
    font-weight: normal;
    font-family: sans-serif;
    background: black;
    color: white;}

B, I, U {color: yellow; font-weight: normal; font-style: normal;}
H1 {font-size: 32pt;}
H2 {font-size: 32pt;}
H3 {font-size: 32pt;}
H4 {font-size: 32pt;}
H5 {font-size: 32pt;}

a:visited {color: #FF00FF}
a:link {color: #00FFFF}
a:active {color: #B1FB17}
-->
</STYLE>
```

3. Save the file with a .css file name extension (for example, Mystyle.css) to the folder of your choice.

4. In Internet Explorer, on the **Tools** menu, click **Internet Options**.

5. On the **General** tab, click **Accessibility**.

6. Click **Format documents using my style sheet**.

    The following illustration shows this option selected.

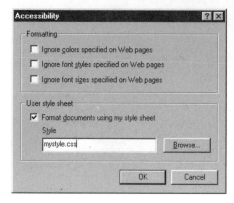

7. Type the path of the style sheet file you just created, or click **Browse** to navigate to the file's location.

Caution Use care when experimenting with the **Format documents using my style sheet** option. Errors in style sheets can cause serious problems with Internet Explorer. If possible, use style sheets that have been created by professional designers. When trying out new style sheets, keep the style-sheet files on a floppy disk that can be removed if a problem occurs.

Changing Colors of Text, Backgrounds, and Other Objects

Users can select the colors they prefer for text, backgrounds, links, and objects that the mouse pointer hovers over on Web pages.

▶ **To change the color of text, backgrounds, links, and objects that the mouse pointer hovers over**

1. On the **Tools** menu, click **Internet Options**.

2. On the **General** tab, click **Colors**.

3. Clear the **Use Windows colors** check box.

4. Click the **Use hover color** check box. The **Hover** button is enabled with the default color.

    The following illustration shows **Use hover color** selected in the Colors dialog box.

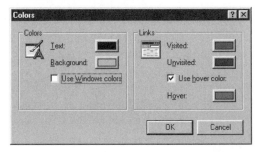

5. Click the **Text**, **Background**, **Visited**, **Unvisited**, or **Hover** button to display the Color dialog box, which includes the Basic colors and Custom colors palettes.

6. In the Color dialog box, click the color of your choice from the color palettes. (To create custom colors, see "Creating Custom Colors" later in this section.)

Creating Custom Colors

Users can create custom colors for fonts, text background, links, and objects that the mouse pointer hovers over.

▶ **To create custom colors**

1. On the **Tools** menu, click **Internet Options**, and then click the **General** tab.

2. Click the **Colors** button.

3. In the Colors dialog box, click the **Text**, **Background**, **Visited**, or **Unvisited** button to display the Color dialog box, which includes the Basic colors and Custom colors palettes.

4. In the Color dialog box, click **Define Custom Colors**. The dialog box expands to include the Custom colors palette.

   The following illustration shows the expanded dialog box for the Custom colors palette.

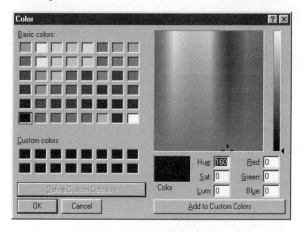

5. Select a custom color by using either of two methods:

   - Type values for either **Hue**, **Sat** (Saturation), and **Lum** (luminescence), or type values for **Red**, **Green**, and **Blue**. The sample box changes color to reflect your choices.

   - Click within the color box to select a color, and then move the slider (on the right) up or down to select the luminescence level. The sample box changes color to reflect your choices.

6. Click **Add to Custom Colors**.

Selecting the High Contrast Color Scheme

Instead of creating their own customized color scheme, users can choose to view their Web pages by using the Windows High Contrast color scheme.

▶ **To view Web pages by using Windows High Contrast**

1. On the **Start** menu, point to **Settings**, and then click **Control Panel**.

2. Click the **Display** icon, and then click the **Appearance** tab.

3. In the Scheme list, select one of the high contrast options.

   The following illustration shows the **Appearance** tab with **High Contrast Black** selected.

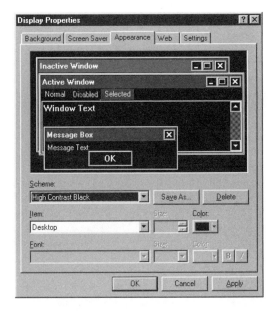

4. In Control Panel, click the **Internet Options** icon.

5. On the **General** tab, click the **Accessibility** button.

6. Select the **Ignore colors specified on Web pages** check box, and then click **OK**.

7. On the **General** tab, click the **Colors** button.

8. Select the **Use Windows colors** check box.

Note   You must restart Internet Explorer before these changes can take effect.

Selecting a Full-Screen Browser Window

When users browse a Web page, they can choose to immediately change the size of the browser window to full screen.

▶ **To immediately change the size of the browser window to full screen**

- On the **View** menu, click **Full Screen**, click the **Full Screen** button on the toolbar, or click **F11** (shortcut key).

If the **Full Screen** button is not displayed, you can add it to the toolbar.

▶ **To add the Full Screen button to the toolbar**

1. On the **View** menu, click **Toolbars**, and then click **Customize**.

2. In the Available Toolbar Buttons list, select **Full Screen**, and then click **Add**.

   The following illustration shows **Full Screen** after it has been added to the Current Toolbar Buttons list.

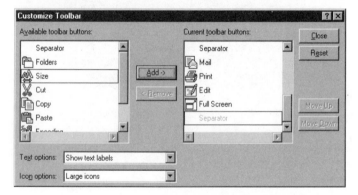

Note   The changes created by the **Full Screen** menu option or the **Full Screen** button are active only for the current session.

Changing Button Size and Text Labels on the Toolbar

Users with disabilities might want to change the button size and text labels on the Internet Explorer toolbar. Some users might want to view large buttons on the toolbar rather than the smaller Microsoft Office-style buttons. Users who have low vision might prefer these larger buttons. Users can also choose whether to show text labels for the buttons.

▶ **To change button size and text labels on the toolbar**

1. On the **View** menu, click **Toolbars**, and then click **Customize**.

2. In the Icon Options list, select the button size that you want to display on the toolbar.

3. In the Text Options list, select whether to display text labels for the toolbar buttons.

   The following illustration shows the Customize Toolbar dialog box with **Show text labels** and **Large icons** selected.

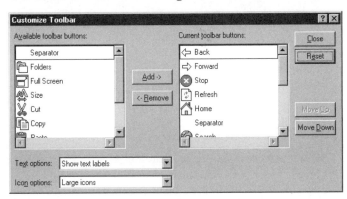

Understanding Font-Size Changes

The following list identifies the factors that affect font size and describes how these factors are applied in Internet Explorer. The factors are listed in the order they are applied when the browser displays a page.

1. The Internet Explorer display defaults (for example, P is size 3 and H1 is size 6).

2. A user-specified style sheet (if one is provided) and whether **Format documents using my style sheet** is selected in the Accessibility dialog box.

3. Style-sheet information in the document, unless **Ignore font sizes specified on Web pages** is selected in the Accessibility dialog box.

4. FONT tags in the document, unless **Ignore font sizes specified on Web pages** is selected in the Accessibility dialog box. Selecting this option does not override relative sizes that are implied by structural tags. For example, a top-level heading (H1) will still be larger than body text, even when **Ignore font sizes specified on Web pages** is turned on.

5. A scaling factor determined by the **Text Size** options accessible from the **View** menu, except in those cases where the font is specified in an absolute size, such as 12 point.

▶ **To set the font-scaling factor**

- For current and future sessions, click the **Tools** menu, click **Internet Options**, click the **General** tab, and then click the **Fonts** button.

- For the current session only, click the **View** menu, point to **Text Size**, and then click the option you want.

Users can specify font sizes in three ways:

- As an index value (1–7)

- As a relative value (+1, +5)

- Using an absolute size unit, such as point or pixel (for example, 12pt, 32px)

Font sizes that are set by using index or relative values are affected by the **View** menu font options, while fonts set in absolute size units are not.

Configuring Advanced Internet Accessibility Options

Users can configure many accessibility features by using the **Advanced** tab in the Internet Options dialog box.

▶ **To configure advanced Internet accessibility options**

1. On the **Tools** menu, click **Internet Options**, and then click the **Advanced** tab.

   The following illustration shows the **Advanced** tab.

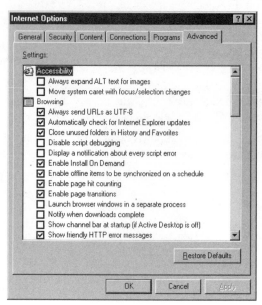

2. Scroll through the check list, and clear or select the options you want.

For recommendations on selecting options for different types of disabilities, see "Suggested Features for Different Types of Disabilities" earlier in this chapter.

Users might want to select the following options, depending on their disabilities:

- **Move system caret with focus/selection changes**—Specifies whether to move the system caret whenever the focus or selection changes. Some accessibility aids, such as screen readers or screen magnifiers, use the system caret to determine which area of the screen to read or magnify.

- **Always expand alt text for images**—Specifies whether to expand the image size to fit all of the alternate text when the **Show Pictures** check box is cleared.

- **Use inline AutoComplete for Web Addresses**—Specifies whether to automatically complete Web addresses as the user types them in the Address bar. The AutoComplete feature suggests a match based on the Web sites the user has visited. Some users with cognitive disabilities might want to turn this option off to avoid distractions. Also, some users who have low vision might want to turn this option off if their accessibility aid reads the suggestions as they appear, making typing difficult.

- **Use inline AutoComplete in integrated shell**—Specifies whether to automatically complete names of files, paths, or folders as the user types them in the Address bar or the **Open** box in the **Run** command. The AutoComplete feature suggests a match based on the names of files, paths, or folder the user has visited. Some users with cognitive disabilities might want to turn this option off to avoid distractions. Also, some users with low vision might want to turn this option off if their accessibility aid reads the suggestions as they appear, making typing difficult.

- **Show friendly URLs**—Specifies whether to show the full Internet address (URL) for a page on the status bar.

- **Use smooth scrolling**—Specifies whether to scroll through Web pages, which gradually slides information up or down the screen when the user clicks on the scroll bar or presses navigation keys, such as DOWN ARROW. Users who have low vision might want to turn this option off if it causes timing problems. People with certain cognitive disabilities might also want to turn this option off if the scrolling motion is distracting.

- **Underline links**—Specifies whether to underline links on Web pages. Older screen readers rely on underlining to recognize links. Users can select one of the following settings:

  - **Always**, which underlines all links.

  - **Never**, which does not underline links.

  - **Hover**, which underlines links when the mouse pointer is placed over the link.

- **Show pictures**—Specifies whether to include images when pages are displayed. When available, alternate text is displayed in place of the image. When this check box is cleared, users can still display an individual image by right-clicking the icon that represents the image and then clicking **Show Picture**. If images are turned on or the textual description is cut off by space limitations, users can view the full description by moving the mouse over the image.

  Turning off images allows older screen readers to read the textual description for images aloud. However, newer readers can use Microsoft Active Accessibility® to identify and read descriptions, even when the images are displayed on the screen. Turning off images speeds up browser performance, although it might interfere with the functionality and effectiveness of some Web sites.

- **Play animations**—Specifies whether animations can play when pages are displayed. Internet Explorer displays alternate text in place of the animations if the text is supplied on the Web page. When this check box is cleared, users can still play an individual animation by right-clicking the icon that represents the animation and then clicking **Show Picture**. Users who are blind, as well as users with seizure disorders, might want to turn off animations (especially blinking). Users with cognitive disabilities might also want to turn off animations or selectively download them to prevent distractions.

- **Play videos**—Specifies whether to play video clips. When this check box is cleared, users can still play an individual video by right-clicking the icon that represents the video and then clicking **Show Picture**. Users who are blind, as well as users with seizure disorders, might want to turn off videos. Users with cognitive disabilities might also want to turn off videos or selectively download them to prevent distractions.

- **Play sounds**—Specifies whether to play audio sounds. If RealAudio is installed or if a movie is playing, sounds might play even if users clear this check box. Users who are deaf or hard-of-hearing, as well as users with seizure disorders, might want to turn off sounds. Users with cognitive disabilities might also want to turn off sounds or selectively download them to prevent distractions. Users who are blind might want to turn off sounds or selectively download them so that they do not conflict with the screen reader when it is reading text aloud.

- **Print background colors and images**—Specifies whether to print background colors and images when users print Web pages. Users who have low vision or those wanting to speed up print time might want to turn this option off. Users might also want to turn this option off if they are preparing text to be scanned—for example, to provide the text to a text reader.

Accessibility Resources

The Microsoft Accessibility Web site contains information about Microsoft products and accessibility. This site also discusses how to design accessible Web pages that take advantage of new features in Internet Explorer 5 and offers information about tools and utilities that make Internet Explorer even more accessible.

The following sections describe additional resources that are available for people with disabilities.

Microsoft Services for People Who Are Deaf or Hard-of-Hearing

If you are deaf or hard-of-hearing, complete access to Microsoft product and customer services is available through a text telephone (TTY/TDD) service.

You can contact the Microsoft Sales Information Center on a text telephone by dialing (800) 892-5234 between 6:30 A.M. and 5:30 P.M. Pacific time.

For technical assistance in the United States, you can contact Microsoft Product Support Services on a text telephone at (425) 635-4948 between 6:00 A.M. and 6:00 P.M. Pacific time, Monday through Friday, excluding holidays. In Canada, dial (905) 568-9641 between 8:00 A.M. and 8:00 P.M. Eastern time, Monday through Friday, excluding holidays. Microsoft support services are subject to the prices, terms, and conditions in place at the time the service is used.

Microsoft Documentation in Other Formats

In addition to the standard forms of documentation, many Microsoft products are available in other formats to make them more accessible. Many of the Internet Explorer documents are also available as online Help or online user's guides, or from the Microsoft Web site. You can also download many Microsoft Press® books from the Microsoft Accessibility Web site.

If you have difficulty reading or handling printed documentation, you can obtain many Microsoft publications from Recording for the Blind & Dyslexic, Inc. Recording for the Blind & Dyslexic distributes these documents to registered, eligible members of their distribution service, either on audio cassettes or on floppy disks. The Recording for the Blind & Dyslexic collection contains more than 80,000 titles, including Microsoft product documentation and books from Microsoft Press. For information about the availability of Microsoft product documentation and books from Microsoft Press, contact:

Recording for the Blind & Dyslexic, Inc.
20 Roszel Road
Princeton, NJ 08540

Phone: (609) 452-0606
Fax: (609) 987-8116

Microsoft Products and Services for People with Disabilities

Microsoft provides a catalog of accessibility aids that can be used with the Windows and Windows NT® operating systems. You can obtain this catalog from the Microsoft Web site or by phone at the Microsoft Sales Information Center.

For more information about this catalog, contact:

Microsoft Sales Information Center
One Microsoft Way
Redmond, WA 98052-6393

Voice telephone: (800) 426-9400
Text telephone: (800) 892-5234

Computer Products for People with Disabilities

The Trace R&D Center at the University of Wisconsin-Madison publishes a database containing information about more than 18,000 products and other topics for people with disabilities. The database is available on their Web site. The database is also available on a compact disc, titled the *Co-Net CD*, which is issued twice a year. The Trace R&D Center also publishes a book, *Trace Resourcebook,* which provides descriptions and photographs of approximately 2,000 products.

To obtain these directories, contact:

Trace R&D Center
University of Wisconsin
S-151 Waisman Center
1500 Highland Avenue
Madison, WI 53705-2280

Fax: (608) 262-8848

Information and Referrals for People with Disabilities

Computers and accessibility devices can help people with disabilities overcome a variety of barriers. For general information and recommendations about how computers can help you with your specific needs, consult a trained evaluator. For information about locating programs or services in your area that might be able to help you, contact:

National Information System
University of South Carolina
Columbia, SC 29208

Voice/text telephone: (803) 777-1782
Fax: (803) 777-9557

CHAPTER 11

Setting Up and Administering a Pilot Program

Before you deploy Microsoft Internet Explorer 5 to your users, it is recommended that you set up and administer a pilot program. Begin by testing the Internet Explorer installation in a lab, and then conduct the pilot program to refine your deployment configurations and strategies using a limited number of pilot participants. This process will help you validate your deployment plan and ensure your readiness for full-scale deployment. This chapter describes how to set up a computer lab to test your deployment process and outlines the steps necessary to conduct a successful pilot program.

Important Although the processes described in this chapter are based on a corporate business model for deployment, it is recommended that Internet service providers and Internet content providers follow similar procedures when they administer a pilot program.

In This Chapter

See Also

- For more information about developing deployment, training, and support plans, which you will test during the pilot installation, see Chapter 9, "Planning the Deployment."

- For more information about building custom packages for the pilot installation, see Chapter 15, "Running the Internet Explorer Customization Wizard."

- For more information about rolling out Internet Explorer to your users following the pilot program, see Chapter 19, "Deploying Microsoft Internet Explorer 5."

Overview

Typically, a pilot program is preceded by a period of lab testing, which enables you to experiment with deployment processes and methods by building and installing custom browser packages on lab computers. You should develop a separate plan and checklist for lab testing, because it encompasses only a subset of actual deployment tasks. Your users do not need to participate in lab testing, so no user training and support are required.

When you are comfortable with the installation process in the lab, you should plan and conduct a pilot program. This program uses a small group of pilot users to simulate the activities that will occur during final deployment. During this trial run, you should complete the tasks for deploying Internet Explorer, which are identified in your deployment, training, and support plans. Also, you should finalize your deployment plan based on the results of your pilot program. For more information about planning your deployment, including choosing browser configurations, selecting training and support staff, and developing formal, written plans, see Chapter 9, "Planning the Deployment."

Important This chapter assumes that an optimum budget, time frame, staffing, and resources are available for testing and pilot program tasks. Smaller companies might need to implement a scaled-down version, with fewer computers and participants. For example, if you do not have a designated support team that is available on-site to address user questions and issues during the pilot program, you may need to rely on other knowledgeable staff members or Microsoft Technical Support for browser support services.

Preparing the Test Plan and Checklist

First, prepare a test plan and checklist. Use the checklist as a guide when you test the deployment process in the computer lab before conducting your pilot program. On the checklist, mark the tasks that are completed satisfactorily, and note any problems with the process.

Your checklist should include each of the following sets of tasks:

Prepare custom packages for deployment

✓ Install and run the Microsoft Internet Explorer Customization wizard.

✓ Build custom packages containing the distribution files.

✓ Configure automatic browser configuration and automatic detection process files.

✓ Configure download sites and install the distribution files.

✓ Copy distribution files to compact discs and floppy disks, if needed.

Deploy custom packages to lab computers

✓ Run Windows Update Setup for Internet Explorer 5 and Internet Tools to install the custom package on each lab computer.

✓ Install Internet Explorer using each available user option.

Test browser software after custom packages are installed

✓ Run the sign-up server process, if applicable.

✓ Run Internet Explorer to test all add-ins and features.

✓ Run other desktop and business applications to make sure they work properly.

Restore lab computers to their original state

✓ Uninstall Internet Explorer and add-ins.

✓ Verify that Internet Explorer components have been removed.

✓ Test the desktop and business applications.

Testing the Deployment Process in the Lab

To ensure that your deployment of Internet Explorer is as smooth as possible, test the proposed deployment process on lab computers that are configured to represent your typical user groups. If your user groups are large or have very different computing environments or requirements, you may need to prepare multiple labs and conduct tests at several different sites.

Preparing the Lab

Set aside physical space for each computer lab. Acquire a mix of computers that accurately reflects the hardware and software environments of your users' computers. Also, set up lab computers to represent existing browser configurations so that you can accurately test the migration process.

Make sure that all lab computers are functioning properly before you install Internet Explorer:

- Select a production computer that meets the system requirements for the Internet Explorer Customization wizard. For more information about system requirements for the wizard, see Chapter 9, "Planning the Deployment."

- Check to see that each computer has enough disk space, memory, and processing speed to run Internet Explorer. For more information about hardware requirements for Internet Explorer, see Chapter 9, "Planning the Deployment."

- Test basic operating system functions, including starting each computer and connecting to the server.

- Run virus detection, disk scanning, and defragmentation programs on each computer to prevent problems that might occur during testing. Although the computers might appear to be operating properly, software upgrades often uncover hardware or software problems because of the way they read and write data to the hard disk. Checking the computers before installing Internet Explorer helps you to focus on issues related to deployment.

- Make sure you have the appropriate network connection hardware. If your users dial in from remote locations using portable computers or you need to use additional servers or mainframe computers for business data, equip the lab computers with an analog phone line and appropriate network access. Also, you might need power supplies and surge protectors, depending on the number of computers you use for testing. Be sure to research and eliminate potential problems related to overheating or frequency distortion from the location.

- When the system hardware is ready, verify that the existing network is fully operational.

Important   Make a backup copy of critical data and configuration files in case the installation fails or you need to restore the original configuration. If you want to automate the process of restoring the original configuration, consider using a commercial backup program instead of copying the files manually.

Make sure to document the lab setup completely. Maintain a record of any changes you make so that you can repeat the same setup process for the pilot program.

Conducting the Lab Tests

To test the deployment process in the lab, perform all the tasks identified on the test checklist. Install Internet Explorer on the lab computers in the same way that you plan to install Internet Explorer on your users' computers. In some cases, this might mean setting up the network installation location on the server and then installing Internet Explorer on the lab computers from the server.

Automating your installation is an important step in reducing the cost of migration. You can choose to run the installation process from start to finish without user intervention. Also, you can run the installation from the server so that you don't need to configure individual computers when Internet Explorer is installed. You should complete this automation work in the lab before you conduct the pilot program. For more information about automating the installation process, see Chapter 16, "Customizing Setup."

When you run the Internet Explorer Customization wizard, you can predefine a number of options for your users. Be sure to test the Internet Explorer configuration you select and any changes you make before you run your pilot program. Depending on how the test installation proceeds, you may want to modify the configuration by adding or removing components or features. If you are considering several different configurations, you can evaluate them side by side in the lab. For more information about using the Internet Explorer Customization wizard to predefine user options, see Chapter 15, "Running the Internet Explorer Customization Wizard."

After you install Internet Explorer on the test computers, you need to verify that the software runs correctly and that you can perform basic browser tasks, such as navigating to a Web page or adding a Web page to the favorites list. After you are sure that the basic configuration works as expected, be sure to test any optional features and components, such as FrontPage Express or NetMeeting, that you install.

During the testing process, maintain a record of all issues and problems. These records will help you design solutions to correct the problems you encounter. Then test each solution using this same process.

Testing the Uninstall Process

After you have successfully completed the Internet Explorer installation process, you should uninstall the browser and restore the lab computers to their original state. Using the Add/Remove Programs dialog box in Windows Control Panel, you can remove Internet Explorer 5. You also have the option to restore the previous version of Internet Explorer that was installed on the computer.

Using the Internet Explorer Customization wizard (in corporate administrator mode), you can choose not to install the files needed to uninstall the browser. This reduces the amount of hard disk space required for the custom package installation, but users will not be able to uninstall the browser from Control Panel. Also if you are using system management programs, such as Microsoft Systems Management Server (SMS), to install Internet Explorer, you cannot uninstall the browser using Control Panel.

Important Because of the large number of changes made to the system by Windows Update Setup, a manual uninstall would be a time-consuming process requiring many steps. Attempting a manual uninstall is not recommended.

For troubleshooting information about the uninstall process, see Appendix B, "Troubleshooting."

Planning the Pilot Program

After you test the deployment process in the lab, plan your pilot program. The pilot program is a scaled-down version of the final deployment. The goal of the pilot program is to further test and refine deployment strategies and configurations in everyday use among a limited group of users (for example, between 15 and 50 people).

In this phase, appointed project teams determine the best methods for installing your custom package configurations. Even though you are only testing the installation process, the pilot program sets a precedent for the final deployment; therefore, it is important that all participants are completely prepared. For more information about assembling project teams and selecting your custom package configurations, see Chapter 9, "Planning the Deployment."

To plan the pilot program, you will need to:

- Select appropriate pilot groups.
- Identify the resources and tasks for the pilot program.
- Create a database to document your progress.

Selecting Pilot Groups

First, you will need to identify your pilot groups and prepare them for the pilot program. If your user groups are large or have very different computing environments or requirements, you may need to select several pilot groups. Select groups that represent the diversity of your computer users. Make sure that the participants have enough time in their schedules and are willing to cooperate in the pilot program. Consider asking for volunteers—you should not ask people to participate who might be too busy meeting deadlines.

Identifying Resources and Tasks

Next, identify the resources and tasks you need to conduct the pilot program. Because the pilot program is your rehearsal for the final deployment, the tasks and resources should be similar to those identified in your deployment plan.

Creating a Database to Document Progress

Before the actual pilot installation begins, create a central database to monitor your progress and document any areas that may require further action. You can use the database to track open items and issues and to measure your actual progress against the original objectives documented in your deployment plan.

Conducting the Pilot Program

The pilot program helps you identify problems that may impede or delay deployment and also helps you determine the resources you will need. A successful pilot program can help your final deployment of Internet Explorer run more smoothly. To conduct the pilot program, you need to:

- Prepare the training and support teams.
- Prepare the pilot groups.
- Implement the pilot installation of Internet Explorer.

Preparing the Training and Support Teams

Before the pilot installation begins, the training and support teams must become skilled users of Internet Explorer and any additional browser components that you plan to install. First, give the teams access to the browser software so that team members can explore the functions and features on their own. Then, decide how you want to train the teams.

Some team members might already be proficient with earlier versions of Internet Explorer or third-party browser software, while others may not be skilled in this area. Consider self-paced and instructor-led training options, based on the skill levels of your team members and the types of information you want to present. A classroom that allows hands-on practice is recommended when you instruct teams about more complex browser functions. If an external company is instructing your training and support teams, make sure that their representative is informed about any company- or job-specific policies or applications for Internet Explorer.

After training, encourage team members to work with Internet Explorer every day. Continue to provide follow-up information and practice exercises so that team members are confident in their knowledge and ability before you start the pilot program.

Preparing Pilot User Groups

Inform the users about the pilot program. Explain the benefits of migrating to Internet Explorer 5, and describe the overall plan and process by which each group or department will make the move. Then, users can anticipate and plan for the Internet Explorer installation.

Announce the pilot program well in advance of the start date, and follow up your announcement with several reminders. Conduct meetings with the pilot group managers and with the entire group to set their expectations and to answer any questions. Provide a deployment presentation that explains how users will install Internet Explorer. Describe any installation options that users can select, and explain how users can get support if they have any questions or issues.

Conduct Internet Explorer training. Training and support for the pilot program should simulate—on a smaller scale—the user training for the final deployment.

Encourage users to visit the Microsoft Windows Technologies Internet Explorer Web site for more information. If you implement a training Web page on the Internet or intranet, use a memo or e-mail letter to broadcast the URL and a description of the training page to users. Be sure to explain how users can benefit from visiting your training page.

Implementing the Pilot Installation

The schedule for the pilot installation should simulate the schedule for the final deployment. As you conduct the pilot installation, you may need to revise the schedule because certain tasks take more or less time than expected, some tasks need to be added, or some tasks can be eliminated. Use the revised pilot schedule for projecting the final deployment timetable, and then update the deployment plan with the new schedule information.

Before you begin the pilot installation, make a backup copy of all files on the pilot computers. Then, perform the pilot installation in the same way that you expect to install Internet Explorer during the final deployment.

To implement the pilot installation, you will perform the following tasks:

- Deploy custom packages to pilot users.
- Test Internet Explorer performance and capabilities on pilot computers.
- Monitor and support pilot users as they install Internet Explorer.

Deploying Custom Packages

Use the appropriate distribution methods to deploy the custom package of Internet Explorer that you created and tested in the lab. For example, you can send an e-mail message to users that directs them to the download site where they can follow instructions to download the custom package. Another option is to include a batch file as an e-mail attachment and instruct users to double-click the batch file to install the custom package. If you are using compact discs or floppy disks, you can distribute them to the users and provide e-mail instructions about how to install the custom package from this media.

Testing Internet Explorer Performance and Capabilities

In addition to the technicians responsible for conducting the pilot installation, you might want to assign additional technicians to measure, observe, and test the installation. By tracking the time per installation, handling problems that arise, and identifying areas for improvement or automation, these individuals can help ensure the success of both the pilot and final installations.

After Internet Explorer is installed, these technicians can test system capabilities, such as remote administration, to make sure that all functions are operating correctly. They should monitor the pilot computers for performance, stability, and functionality, and highlight any inconsistencies with the lab configuration. Also, they should document ways to improve the installation, training, and support processes.

Monitoring and Supporting Pilot Users

Staff the support team with some of your best technicians and dedicate them to the pilot program for the first few weeks. These technicians could be members of your existing help desk, staff members that you have trained as subject matter experts, or representatives from an external vendor that you have hired to provide support services to browser users. The assigned technicians should carry pagers or be available by phone to assist users at all times. The support team should also monitor the progress of the pilot program.

Track the volume of support calls during the pilot program to gauge the effect of deploying Internet Explorer on your support staff. Make sure to document all user trouble calls and problems, as well as the staff resources required to support pilot users. Then, use your experience during the pilot program to plan the support resources for the final deployment. You may want to plan for additional staffing, or use this information to revise the final deployment schedule.

Finalizing the Deployment Plan

The results of the pilot installation provide the basis for developing a final plan for deploying Internet Explorer to your user groups. To finalize your deployment plan, you need to:

- Incorporate feedback from all participants in the pilot program.
- Determine the time and resource requirements for the final rollout.
- Update company policies and standards regarding Internet Explorer use.

Incorporating Feedback

Survey the pilot users to measure their satisfaction and proficiency with the new installation and to evaluate the level of training and support provided. Test users' proficiency by having them perform a few common tasks or use several of the new Internet Explorer 5 features.

Obtain feedback from all participants, including pilot users, trainers, and support technicians, and document the lessons learned during the pilot program. Based on this initial feedback, record changes that will increase the satisfaction level and the effectiveness of the installation process.

Continue to monitor the pilot installation for a week or more to ensure that everything runs smoothly. Track open items and issues using the database you created for the pilot installation. Then, incorporate the feedback into your deployment, training, and support plans. If the pilot program did not run smoothly or if feedback was negative, conduct additional pilot installations until the process works well.

Determining Time and Resource Requirements for Final Deployment

Using the actual time and resource requirements from the pilot program, teams can make projections about the time and resources required for the final deployment. If additional resources are needed, identify and acquire them at this time.

Updating the Policies and Practices Guidelines

Before beginning the final deployment, update all company policies regarding the use of browser software and Internet and intranet access by employees. In addition, update the corporate standards lists for software usage, and ensure that all computers are compliant.

P A R T   3

Customizing

Chapter 12: Preparing for the IEAK

If you plan to use the Microsoft Internet Explorer Administration Kit (IEAK), you should take some time to gather information, set up your computers, and prepare custom files. This advance preparation will help you use the IEAK programs more effectively.

This chapter applies to corporate administrators, Internet service providers (ISPs), Internet content providers (ICPs) and developers, and independent software vendors (ISVs) who are planning to use the IEAK to customize and distribute Microsoft Internet Explorer 5.

Chapter 13: Setting Up Servers

As you customize the browser and prepare for deployment, you should also prepare any servers that you will need to support your deployment of Internet Explorer. This chapter covers preparing for proxy servers, roaming user profiles, Internet sign-up by using the Internet Connection wizard, and using Microsoft NetMeeting.

Chapter 14: Customizing Connection Management and Settings

This chapter describes how to manage dial-up connections for your users. Using the Connection Manager Administration Kit (CMAK) wizard, which is part of the IEAK, you can customize connections and service profiles and the ways in which they are managed.

Chapter 15: Running the Internet Explorer Customization Wizard

You can use the Microsoft Internet Explorer Customization wizard, which comes with the IEAK, to customize the appearance and functionality of the browser, its components, and Windows Update Setup for Internet Explorer 5 and Internet Tools. You can also preset browsing options and, if you are a corporate administrator, set system policies and restrictions.

This chapter will help you understand how to use the Customization wizard to create custom Internet Explorer packages that you can distribute to your users.

Chapter 16: Customizing Setup

You can customize Microsoft Windows Update Setup for Internet Explorer 5 and Internet Tools to fit the needs of your organization.

To customize Windows Update Setup, you can use the IEAK or you can use a batch file or command-line switches. The following information applies to anyone who wants to modify Windows Update Setup, including ISPs, ICPs, corporate administrators, developers, and ISVs.

Chapter 17: Time-Saving Strategies That Address Diverse User Needs

If your users or customers have diverse needs—for example, your marketing department requires different Internet Explorer settings than your finance department—there are ways that you can address those needs without repeating all customization steps.

This chapter provides some strategies that corporate administrators and ISPs can use to efficiently address diverse user needs.

Chapter 18: Working with .inf Files

Although you can use the IEAK, batch files, command-line switches, and third-party programs to customize setup, you can also extend the setup program by using setup information (.inf) files. Scripts based on .inf files take advantage of the setup engine built into the Microsoft Windows operating system.

C H A P T E R   1 2

Preparing for the IEAK

If you plan to use the Microsoft Internet Explorer Administration Kit (IEAK), you should take some time to gather information, set up your computers, and prepare custom files. This advance preparation will help you use the IEAK programs more effectively.

This chapter applies to corporate administrators, Internet service providers (ISPs), Internet content providers (ICPs) and developers, and independent software vendors (ISVs) who are planning to use the IEAK to customize Microsoft Internet Explorer 5.

In This Chapter

See Also

- For more information about customizing Internet Explorer, see Chapter 3, "Understanding Customization and Administration."

- For more information about using the IEAK, see Chapter 15, "Running the Internet Explorer Customization Wizard."

- For a checklist of specific information you need to gather before running the Internet Explorer Customization wizard, see Appendix D, "Checklists for Preparing to Use the IEAK."

Preparing to Customize Internet Explorer

You can make a wide variety of changes to Internet Explorer to fit your needs. You can modify the setup program, preset Internet options, and make visual changes. If you're a corporate administrator, you can control, or "lock down," many important settings to prevent users from changing them. If you're an ISP, you can provide sign-up solutions for your customers.

You should evaluate your organization's needs and then determine the preparation steps you'll need to take.

Determining Which Features to Customize

This section outlines the customization options for Internet Explorer and gives the steps you need to follow when preparing to use those options. To see a checklist of specific options, see Appendix D, "Checklists for Preparing to Use the IEAK."

Digital Signatures

If you are deploying 32-bit versions of your programs over the Internet, you must ensure that your programs are digitally signed. If you are deploying your programs over an intranet and you do not want to specially configure settings in your users' browsers, you must also ensure your programs are digitally signed. This is one of the first preparation steps you should consider, because you'll need to obtain a digital certificate from a certification authority (CA), if you don't already have one.

Digital signatures show where programs come from and verify that they haven't been altered. If you have a publisher certificate from a CA, the Internet Explorer Customization wizard can use it to sign your programs automatically.

If you are an ISP, you can specify a root certificate, so that all certificates lower in the hierarchy inherit the same level of trust and the user isn't continually prompted with security messages.

For more information about digitally signing your programs, see Chapter 6, "Digital Certificates."

Preparation

- To prepare certificates for use by the Customization wizard, you can import them onto your computer by using the Certificate Manager Import wizard. If you have received a file with a software publishing certificate (.spc) extension, you can start the Certificate Manager Import wizard by double-clicking the .spc file in Windows Explorer or My Computer. You can also open the Certificate Manager from Internet Explorer. To do this, click the **Tools** menu, click **Internet Options**, click the **Content** tab, and then click **Certificates**. Click **Import** to start the Certificate Manager Import wizard, and then follow the steps in the wizard.

- Specify the company name, descriptive text, a URL that the users can click for more information, the .spc file name, and the private key (.pvk) file name.

- If you are an ISP and plan to specify a root certificate, you'll need to specify its URL when you run the Customization wizard.

- Although the Customization wizard provides an automated method of signing files, you can sign files manually as well, if you have a digital certificate. To use the manual method, you'll need to sign any custom files or programs that you are including in your custom package (also commonly known as an IEAK package). In addition, you'll need to sign any custom files created by the Customization wizard.

  You need to sign the following custom files:

  - Branding.cab

  - Desktop.cab

  - IEcif.cab

  - IE5Setup.exe

  - Any cabinet (.cab) files that are created by using the IEAK Profile Manager

    By default, the .cab files created by the IEAK Profile Manager will be preceded by the root name of the corresponding Internet settings (.ins) file. For example, if your .ins file is named Finance.ins, the corresponding default file name for the Configuration cabinet file would be Finance_Config.cab.

For more general information about digital signatures, contact your CA.

Windows Update Setup

You can add custom components to Windows Update Setup for Internet Explorer 5 and Internet Tools. In addition, you can create ten setup combinations, control whether users can customize the setup prompts, suppress user prompts during the setup process, and modify the appearance and functionality of the Windows Update Setup wizard. For 32-bit versions of Internet Explorer, you can add a custom Autorun screen for CD-ROM installations.

Preparation

- Prepare custom components and decide which setup combinations you'll need.

- If you want the user to be able to uninstall your component by using the **Add/Remove Programs** icon in Control Panel, create an uninstall script.

- Determine how you want to customize the appearance and functionality of the Windows Update Setup wizard. This includes preparing any custom graphics you want to use for the wizard.

- If you are creating CD-ROM packages, prepare the graphics and any text you want for the Autorun screen.

- You can also use a batch file to customize Windows Update Setup. If you want to include the batch file with your custom package, you should create it before you run the Customization wizard.

For more detailed information about Windows Update Setup, see Chapter 16, "Customizing Setup."

CD-ROM Autorun Screen

If you are creating a CD-ROM version of your customized browser, you can create an Autorun screen that is displayed when the user inserts the compact disc into the CD-ROM drive.

You can also provide a text file that gives additional or late-breaking information to users; this file is sometimes called a readme file. In addition, you can specify a Web page that appears in full-screen, or "Kiosk," mode after the user installs Windows Update Setup.

Preparation

If you want to include an Autorun screen:

- Provide a background bitmap.

- Provide labels for two buttons: one for installing Windows Update Setup and one for displaying more information.

- Determine whether you want to customize the title bar and the text color.

For more information about creating the Autorun splash screen, see "Creating CD-ROM Autorun Splash-Screen Graphics" later in this chapter.

If you plan to add an informational file or specify a Web page for Kiosk mode, you'll need to prepare the files and know their paths before you run the Customization wizard.

Browser Toolbar Buttons

You can specify a custom toolbar button that appears in the toolbar of the user's browser. The toolbar button can launch a custom program or script, including opening a custom Explorer bar.

Preparation

If you want to prepare a browser toolbar button:

- Create two icon files that contain color and gray-scale images for active and inactive states.
- Specify the script or custom program that you want to run when you start the browser.

For more information about creating the icons, see "Designing Browser Toolbar Icons for Internet Explorer 5" later in this chapter.

For more information about creating custom programs, see the MSDN Online Web site.

Connection Manager

Corporate administrators and ISPs can use the Microsoft Connection Manager Administration Kit (CMAK) to customize the appearance and functionality of the Connection Manager, a tool that enables users to dial up to the Internet or an intranet.

Preparation

You can import a connection profile that you've already created, or you can start the CMAK from the Customization wizard. Either way, you'll want to determine the settings that you want to customize.

For more information, see Chapter 14, "Customizing Connection Management and Settings" and online Help in the CMAK.

Appearance

You can customize the title bar, animated and static logos, and the toolbar background of the browser. You can add a custom toolbar button or custom icons for the Favorites list. You can also customize the appearance of the Windows Update Setup wizard and Outlook Express.

If you're an ISP or a corporate administrator, you can customize the appearance of the Connection Manager, the dialog box that provides users with a connection to the Internet. ISPs can also customize the appearance of the Internet Connection wizard, which sets connection options and helps users sign up for Internet services.

Preparation

- Determine how you want to customize title bars.
- Gather any custom graphics. For a list of all the graphics you can customize, see Appendix D, "Checklists for Preparing to Use the IEAK."

For more information about using IEAK programs to create the animated logo, see "Creating an Animated Logo" later in this chapter.

Links, Favorites, and Important URLs

You can customize the links to Web pages that appear in the user's Links bar, across the top of the browser, and in the Favorites list, which appears in the left part of the browser when the user clicks the **Favorites** button. You can also customize the user's search, home, and support pages.

Preparation

- Gather up to 200 URLs and determine whether you want to use URL titles that differ from the current ones. Instead of specifying the links and favorites when you run the wizard, you can import them from the computer where you build your custom package.
- If you want graphics for the Favorites list, create custom 16-by-16-pixel icons before running the Customization wizard.
- Know the URLs for the search, home, and support pages. The pages don't have to be created before you run the Customization wizard, but you'll need to make sure they're in place when you deploy Internet Explorer.

Channels

You can add a channel or a channel category, which is a folder of related channels. The channels feature enables you to specify what content is downloaded and when. For example, you can provide the latest news reports and company information through a channel.

The technology that makes this possible is the Channel Definition Format (.cdf) file. You can use content you already have, such as Web pages and graphics, for channels. You might, however, want to structure your content differently, so you are sure that users receive the right amount of content in an organized way.

Preparation

For channel file specifications, see Appendix D, "Checklists for Preparing to Use the IEAK." For more information about creating channels, see the MSDN Online Web site.

User-Agent String

Some companies track site statistics, such as how many times their content is accessed and by which types of Web browsers. User-agent strings help identify the browser type.

Here's an example of a user-agent string:

Mozilla/4.0 (compatible; MSIE 5.0; WindowsNT; *YourCustomString***)**

Preparation

If you want to append a custom string to the user-agent string generated by Internet Explorer, you need to determine what the customizable part of the string will be.

Internet Sign-up

If you're an ISP, you can specify whether your customers will sign up for Internet services when they install Windows Update Setup. You can use a server-based sign-up process and post your sign-up files on an Internet server. You can have customers use the Internet Connection wizard, or they can use the browser in Kiosk mode as the interface for signing up using a server-based solution. You can also use a serverless, or local, solution that you include in your custom package.

Preparation

For a server-based sign-up process, you'll need to:

- Customize sign-up files—such as Signup.htm or Icwsign.htm—that will point to your sign-up server.

- Post sign-up and settings files on your servers before you deploy Internet Explorer.

- Customize all the sign-up and settings files that you want to include in your custom package. The Customization wizard can generate .ins files to post to your server (for a server-based sign-up process) or to include in your custom package (for a serverless, or local, sign-up process). If you want the Customization wizard to generate these files for you, you'll need to know the settings that you plan to specify, such as area code, gateway, and connection settings.

For more information about setting up servers, see Chapter 13, "Setting Up Servers." For more information about the sign-up process, see Chapter 20, "Implementing the Sign-up Process."

Address Book Directory Services

Corporate administrators and ISPs can provide custom directory or "address book" services using the Lightweight Directory Access Protocol (LDAP).

You can specify your own LDAP server and Web site, and you can customize the bitmap that appears when users access directory services.

Preparation

To customize LDAP settings:

- Know the service name, server name, service Web site, search base, and service bitmap path.

- If you plan to customize the service bitmap, prepare it before you run the Customization wizard.

Microsoft Outlook Express

Corporate administrators and ISPs can customize many settings for Outlook Express. Some key settings include account and server information, the InfoPane that appears when users start the program, and advanced settings, such as service information for obtaining additional accounts and for determining whether Outlook Express is the default e-mail program.

Preparation

To customize Outlook Express, you need to gather the following information:

- **Incoming mail server**—This can be a Post Office Protocol (POP3) or Internet Mail Access Protocol (IMAP) server. POP3 is used by most Internet subscribers for e-mail. An example is pop01.microsoft.com. IMAP is used mainly by corporate users who want to read their e-mail from a remote location. POP3 servers allow access to a single inbox, but IMAP servers provide access to multiple server-side folders.

- **Outgoing mail server**—This is a Simple Mail Transfer Protocol (SMTP) server. An example is smtp.microsoft.com.

- **Internet news server**—This is a Network News Transfer Protocol (NNTP) server that is used to distribute network news messages to NNTP servers and to NNTP clients (news readers) on the Internet. An example server name is nntp.microsoft.com.

- **InfoPane**—This is the page that appears along the bottom of the Outlook Express window. You can specify a local Web page that you include with your custom package, or a Web page on the Internet or intranet that you can continue to customize. You can also include an image for the InfoPane. If you do, you'll need to provide the path to the image.

- **HTML welcome message**—This is a custom message that appears in the users' inbox when they first install Outlook Express. You'll need to specify the location of the .htm message, the sender (your name or your group's name) address, and the recipient's name (the group of users you will send the message to).

- **Subscribed newsgroups**—This is the list of newsgroups that the user will automatically be subscribed to. You should collect these names before you run the Customization wizard.

- **Service for additional accounts**—This is the menu item that users can access to get an additional mail account. You'll need to know the service name and service URL of the account provider. This entry is added to the New Account From menu in Outlook Express. When the user selects this service name from the menu, the Web page is opened. An account number, which can be specified in the .ins file, and a unique identifier for the user will be sent to the ISP when the Web page is opened.

- **Compose settings**—This is the default signature that you can add to each e-mail or news message. Often, this is a disclaimer that shows that messages submitted by employees over the Internet do not represent official company policies. The maximum size of the signature is 1 KB.

Component Update and Update Notification Pages

You can specify and host a custom Web page from which users can download components. By default, this is the Microsoft site that appears when the user clicks the **Tools** menu, and then clicks **Windows Update**. If you choose to customize this page, you'll need to know its URL before you run the wizard. For more information, see Chapter 16, "Customizing Setup."

You can specify a page that temporarily replaces the user's home page at a time interval you designate. You'll need to know the URL of this page before you run the Internet Explorer Customization wizard. The default notification page is the Microsoft Windows Update page. For ideas about how you can use this page, see Chapter 22, "Keeping Programs Updated."

For a checklist of specific information you need to gather before running the Customization wizard, see Appendix D, "Checklists for Preparing to Use the IEAK."

My Computer and Control Panel

If you are a corporate administrator, you can customize how My Computer and Control Panel appear on your company's computers by customizing the files that serve as templates for them. Then, if the user installs the Windows Desktop Update, My Computer and Control Panel can appear as Web pages, or Webviews. You can customize these folders to provide instructions, a company logo, or links to support or corporate sites.

To provide Webviews, you must include the Windows Desktop Update in your browser package and be running the desktop on your build computer.

Preparation

To customize the templates, you use the following files:

- Mycomp.htt for My Computer
- Controlp.htt for Control Panel

If you have installed the Windows Desktop Update on your computer, these files are located in the C:\Windows\Web or C:\Windows\NT folder. You can open them using a text editor, such as Notepad, or an HTML editor. It's recommended that you make a back-up copy of these files before working with them, so you can restore them to their original state if needed.

You can modify these files in several ways to suit your company's needs. You can add your own links or graphics, change colors, and even determine which icons and file names are displayed. For example, you could choose not to display the icons in Control Panel. Instead, you could provide graphical buttons that the user can click for the settings you choose to make available.

The .htt files use active scripting, such as JavaScript, JScript, or Visual Basic Scripting Edition (VBScript). The existing Mycomp.htt and Controlp.htt files, and other files related to the desktop (Folder.htt and Printers.htt), use JavaScript. You can modify some aspects of these files without scripting, or if you're familiar with scripting, you can add to or change the scripting to meet your needs.

The desktop template files are very similar to HTML (.htm) files, except for three variables: %THISDIRNAME%, %THISDIRPATH%, and %TEMPLATEDIR%, which are processed through a Multipurpose Internet Mail Extensions (MIME) filter and replaced with the correct file or path information. These variables are useful when you specify links to external files, such as graphics. Although the template files are located in the C:\Windows\Web or C:\Windows\NT folder, they are processed in the Temp folder, so the path information is necessary to ensure that links to other items work.

It's important to ensure that the customized versions of My Computer and Control Panel resize the display in accordance with users' screen resolutions, and that they appear correctly. In the Mycomp.htt and Controlp.htt files, the following syntax is used to ensure proper resizing:

```
<script language="JavaScript">
window.onresize = fixSize;
</script>
```

In My Computer and Control Panel, Infotips from the registry are displayed when the user points to an item. The Infotips provide a brief description of the item.

You can also modify the Printers.htt (Printers folder) and Folder.htt (default Web view for folders) template files in the C:\Windows\Web or C:\Windows\NT folder on your computer or on your users' computers. These files cannot be included in your custom package.

If you want, you can provide .htm files instead of modifying the *.htt files. To do this, you need to change the associated **PersistMoniker** references in the registry to **PersistFile**, and point the references to your customized file.

Caution Editing the registry can cause harm to the operating system. You are responsible for any risks associated with editing registry entries.

Developing Custom Graphics

Some custom graphics used with the Customization wizard are simple bitmaps sized to the appropriate dimensions and resolutions. Other graphics, however, require more complex preparation. This section discusses how to produce those graphics.

Creating CD-ROM Autorun Splash-Screen Graphics

When the user inserts a CD-ROM into a computer running a 32-bit version of Windows, an Autorun splash screen can appear. The splash screen provides installation instructions and other helpful information.

The following procedure for creating an Autorun splash screen assumes that you are starting with a 24-bit RGB bitmap file. If your file is not a 24-bit RGB bitmap, you must convert it.

▶   **To create an Autorun bitmap**

1. Create a 256-color bitmap image (540-by-357 pixels).

   This bitmap should provide an introduction to the product and should contain labels for two buttons: one for installing Windows Update Setup and one for displaying more information.

   Note The dimensions of the bitmap are important, because the dialog box resizes to the bitmap dimensions. If the bitmap isn't wide enough, text in the dialog box may appear clipped.

2. In your graphics program, create a working file for your palette. To do this, paste both your background and button files into a single file. Make sure to paste the files side by side, not overlapping.

3. Save the file as Palette.bmp.

Creating an Animated Logo

Two separate tools are included with the IEAK to help you create customized animated bitmaps for your browser:

- The Animated Bitmap Creator takes a series of sequentially numbered bitmaps and stacks them into one bitmap using the correct format for animation.

- The Animated Bitmap Previewer allows you to preview the animation of the bitmap. This tool can also be used to display any correctly formatted bitmap.

Note These tools are not to be distributed as supported Microsoft products. Both tools can be found in the \Toolkit\Tools\Animate folder.

▶ **To use the Animated Bitmap Creator (Makebmp.exe)**

- To run this tool, type the following at the command line:

makebmp *basename numfiles outputname*

Where:

- **makebmp** is the executable file
- *basename* is the root file name (without numbers and an .bmp extension)
- *numfiles* is the number of bitmaps to sequentially add
- *outputname* is the output file name (you must include the .bmp extension)

Example:

To combine the files Bitmap0.bmp through Bitmap19.bmp, you would type the following:

makebmp bitmap 20 final.bmp

Note The files you use should be numbered sequentially beginning with 0. For example, if you were using 25 files, they would be numbered as: IEbmp0.bmp IEbmp1.bmp IEbmp2.bmp ... IEbmp24.bmp. When typing *basename* at the command line, you would use **IEbmp**.

▶ **To use Animated Bitmap Previewer (Animbmp.exe)**

- Start the previewer either from a command line or from Windows Explorer.

After Animbmp.exe is started, you can preview an animated bitmap by dragging the file into the box, or by clicking the **File** menu and then clicking **Open**. The lead-in frames are shown only once, and then the bitmap loops continuously.

Designing Browser Toolbar Icons for Internet Explorer

To create a custom browser toolbar icon, you will need to provide each image in two sizes for two toolbar states (grayscale for the default state and color for the active state, when the user's mouse is pointing to it), and in two color depths. The following summary describes the image icons that you need:

- One 20-by-20-pixel color image (256-color Windows half-tone palette)
- One 20-by-20-pixel gray image (256-color Windows half-tone palette)
- One 20-by-20-pixel color image (16-color Windows palette)
- One 20-by-20-pixel gray image (16-color Windows palette)
- One 16-by-16-pixel color image (16-color Windows palette)
- One 16-by-16-pixel gray image (16-color Windows palette)

For example, if you used the image of a house as the icon, the images would look similar to this:

Designing Toolbar Icons

Keep the following points in mind when designing toolbar icons:

- Make sure the visual transitions between your default and active images are smooth. An easy way to test this is to create separate layers for the default and active images in a photo imaging program so that you can view the images on top of each other.

- When you design 16-color icons, use the Windows 16-color palette. For both the default and active states, a black border should appear around the icon, except where the readability of the image might be affected, such as for an arrow or an "X." The images should have little shading and appear flat.

- When you design 256-color icons, use the Windows half-tone palette. For both the default and active states, the icons should have icon-style borders with gray or color top and left borders, and black bottom and right borders. They can have more shade and visual depth than 16-color images, with a light source from the upper left and shading where appropriate.

Creating .ico Files

You will need to create two .ico files for one icon:

- The first .ico file contains the active images (color) in the appropriate sizes and color depths.

- The second .ico file contains the default images (grayscale) in the appropriate sizes and color depths.

It is recommended that you use a graphics program to draw your icons and a development environment, such as Microsoft Visual C++® Development Studio, to create the .ico files.

The two icon files would contain the following graphics:

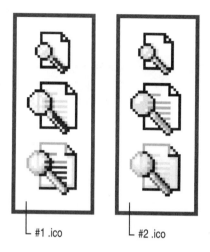

To draw images for your icons

1. After drawing your images in a graphics program, place the 16-color and 256-color images in separate files.

2. Index each file to the appropriate palette, either the Windows 16-color palette or the Windows half-tone palette.

3. Save each file as a .bmp file.

To create your icon files in Visual C++

1. Open each .bmp file.

2. On the **File** menu, click **New**, and then click **Icon**. By default, the icon window that opens displays a standard 32-by-32-pixel device image.

3. In the Icon window, click **New Device Image**. Click **Custom**, and then create the following images:

   - One 22-by-20-pixel 16-color image

   - One 22-by-20-pixel 256-color image

   - One 18-by-16-pixel 16-color image

Note The device images are two pixels wider than your original images, which reflects the actual width of the button. Center your images in the device image area.

4. Delete the default 32-by-32-pixel device image.

5. Copy and paste the color images from your .bmp files into a device image with the appropriate size and color depth.

6. To make the background transparent, select the transparent color in the color palette and fill the background of each image where you want transparency.

7. Save this file as an .ico file.

8. To create your default (grayscale) .ico file, follow the same steps (steps 1 through 7).

Setting Up Your Computers

The next stage in preparing for running the Customization wizard is to ensure that your build computer and your users' computers meet the appropriate system requirements. You should also prepare any settings on your build computer that you plan to import into your custom package.

Preparing Your Build Computer

You can build browser packages and use the IEAK Profile Manager for the Windows 16-bit, Windows 32-bit, and UNIX platforms. You must build the packages and run the Customization wizard from a computer running a Windows 32-bit operating system.

Before you start the Customization wizard, check the amount of disk space available in the Program Files folder and on the destination drive (where you build your custom package). The destination drive can be, but isn't required to be, on the same computer.

For each media type that you build, you will need to have additional space on your build computer. For more information about system requirements for the IEAK and Internet Explorer, see Chapter 9, "Planning the Deployment."

Understanding IEAK Build Locations

You can build a custom package on the computer where you are running the Customization wizard, and then move the files to servers where users will download them. Or, you can build on a network server on your Local Area Network (LAN) or on a Web server, such as Microsoft Internet Information Server (IIS).

When you build custom packages, folders for each media type are created in your build folder. For flat (network) and download (Web) packages, you can build at the location where files will be available for downloading. For CD-ROM packages, you can drag the appropriate folder from Windows Explorer to a CD-recording program. For floppy disk packages, you can drag the appropriate folders to the drives for the floppy disks.

If you are building directly on a Web or network server, you should have the necessary folder structure in place before building your custom packages. For more information about deploying your packages, see Chapter 19, "Deploying Microsoft Internet Explorer 5."

Importing Your Settings

You can import some settings directly from your computer. Importing settings can save time if your computer already contains settings or options you want to use. For some customizations, such as your Favorites list and channels, you can import items from your computer as a starting point, and then further customize them while you are using the Customization wizard.

It's a good idea to prepare your computer before you run the Customization wizard. However, if last-minute adjustments are necessary, you can switch away from the wizard by pressing ALT+TAB, change the settings on your computer, and then switch back to the wizard to import your settings.

Here are the items you can import from your computer:

- **Links and favorites**—You can import the URLs and titles for your Links bar and Favorites list. You can also import any custom graphics that you've used for items in your Favorites list. To see your current Favorites list, click the **Favorites** button in your browser. To see your current links, point to **Toolbars** on the **View** menu in the browser, and then click **Links**.

- **Channels**—You can import Channel information from your computer, and then further customize it as necessary. The channels that you will import are located in the Channels folder on your Favorites list.

- **Certification authorities (corporate administrators only)**—You can import your certification authorities, and then use the Certificate Manager to further customize settings (if necessary). To see the current settings in Internet Explorer, click the **Tools** menu, and then click **Internet Options**. Click the **Content** tab, and then click **Certificates**.

- **Authenticode security (corporate administrators only)**—You can import Authenticode settings, which designate software publishers and credentials agencies as trustworthy, from your computer. To see the current settings in Internet Explorer, click the **Tools** menu, click **Internet Options**, click the **Content** tab, and then click **Publishers**.

- **Content ratings (corporate administrators only)**—You can import your content ratings. Ratings provide a way to control the type of content that your users can access on the Internet. To see the current settings in Internet Explorer, click the **Tools** menu, click **Internet Options**, click the **Content** tab, and then click **Settings**. If you have not yet enabled Content Advisor, click **Enable**, and then set the options you want.

- **Connection settings (corporate administrators only)**—You can import your connection settings, such as proxy server information. To see the current settings in Internet Explorer, click the **Tools** menu, click **Internet Options**, and then click the **Connections** tab. To see network and proxy settings, click **LAN Settings**.

- **System policies and restrictions**—Corporate administrators can import their settings, policies, and restrictions. ISPs and ICPs can import their settings.

- **Desktop toolbar settings**—If you are a corporate administrator and you are including the Windows Desktop Update with your custom package, you can import your desktop toolbar settings. The desktop could be installed with Internet Explorer 4.0 and is part of Windows 98.

CHAPTER 13

Setting Up Servers

As you customize the browser and prepare for deployment, you should also prepare any servers that you will need to support your deployment of Microsoft Internet Explorer 5. This chapter covers preparing for proxy servers, roaming user profiles, Internet sign-up with the Internet Connection wizard, and Microsoft NetMeeting.

In This Chapter

See Also

- For more information about testing the deployment process before the final rollout, see Chapter 11, "Setting Up and Administering a Pilot Program."

- For more information about preparing to use the Internet Explorer Administration Kit (IEAK), see Chapter 12, "Preparing for the IEAK."

- For more information about building custom browser packages for installation, see Chapter 15, "Running the Internet Explorer Customization Wizard."

- For more information about rolling out Internet Explorer to your users, see Chapter 19, "Deploying Microsoft Internet Explorer 5."

- For more information about automatic configuration, see Chapter 21, "Using Automatic Configuration and Automatic Proxy."

- For more information about updating programs after deployment, see Chapter 22, "Keeping Programs Updated."

Preparing Servers

Depending on your situation, you may need to set up servers as part of your deployment. When setting up servers, you should plan for your users' needs in terms of deployment, browser use, and updating of software. If you are an Internet service provider (ISP), you should also plan how users will sign up for your services.

If you distribute files over the Internet or an intranet, consult your Web server documentation for specific information about how to set up your servers. Regardless of your Web server type, consider the following issues that can impact how smoothly users are able to install your software:

- **Security**—Certain security levels prevent files that are not digitally signed from being downloaded, and some security levels prompt the user with warning messages. For general information about digital certificates, see Chapter 6, "Digital Certificates." For information about preparing digital certificates for use with the Internet Explorer Customization wizard, see Chapter 12, "Preparing for the IEAK."

- **Bandwidth**—Setting up servers in different locations or staggering rollouts might be necessary to avoid an overwhelming demand on a specific server. For example, you could schedule installation for different divisions or regions a few days or weeks apart, depending on the size of your organization and resources. For more information about deployment, see Chapter 19, "Deploying Microsoft Internet Explorer 5."

You can use the Customization wizard to specify up to 10 locations from which users can download and install Internet Explorer. This information is stored in the IE5Sites.dat file. If one server is down, an attempt is made to download files from the next site in the list. You can choose only one site, however, if you are installing Internet Explorer silently—that is, with no user interaction.

If you are a corporate administrator, you can help offset some of the load associated with Internet usage by specifying and setting up key user pages, such as the home, support, and search pages, on your intranet. You can preconfigure these pages before deployment on the Important URLs screen in Stage 4 of the Customization wizard.

If you are a corporate administrator and you don't have Internet access, you must set up these pages on your intranet.

If your deployment plan also includes software updates, you might want to schedule them during off-hours or stagger updates among groups of users to minimize server load. For more information about software updates, see Chapter 22, "Keeping Programs Updated."

In addition to general deployment issues, you may need to address additional server needs for your organization. This chapter covers the following specific server issues:

- Automatic browser configuration servers and automatic detection of browser settings (corporate administrators)
- Proxy servers
- Automatic searching
- Roaming user profiles (corporate administrators)
- Internet sign-up servers (ISPs)
- NetMeeting servers

Configuring Central Automatic Configuration Servers

Automatic configuration and automatic proxy enable you to change user settings from a central location after you deploy Internet Explorer. This can be useful if you expect the needs of your users or your organization to change frequently.

On the **Connections** tab in the Internet Options dialog box, you can specify that Internet Explorer should check periodically for changes to the automatic configuration files, and then refresh user settings as needed.

You can also set these options before deployment by using the Internet Explorer Customization wizard. The following illustration shows the Automatic Configuration screen of the wizard, where you can set automatic detection, automatic proxy, and automatic configuration settings.

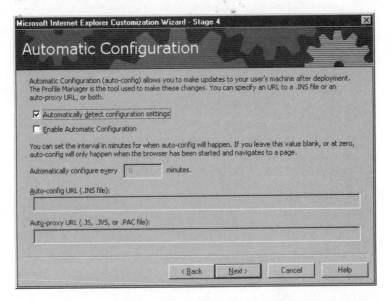

Information about setting up your servers for this feature is contained in this chapter. Information about setting options in the browser and in the Customization wizard are contained in Chapter 21, "Using Automatic Configuration and Automatic Proxy. If you plan to use automatic configuration, you will need to configure servers on your intranet. To configure central management servers, you need to have the following:

- Web-server software, such as Microsoft Internet Information Server (IIS)
- Automatic configuration and automatic proxy files on the server at the URLs necessary for automatic browser configuration

The number of automatic browser configuration servers you require can vary according to the size and demands of your organization. If your organization is large, you might need to configure automatic browser configuration servers for each domain. For example, you could specify automatic browser configuration for user groups in domain 1 as follows:

```
http://domain1_server/autoconfig/<usergroup>.ins
http://domain1_server/autoconfig/proxy1.pac
```

You would install a Web server at http://domain1_server/ and then copy the *<usergroup.ins* and *<usergroup>*.cab files and proxy1.pac to the server at http://domain1_server/autoconfig/. When users in domain 1 start Internet Explorer, it reads the appropriate automatic configuration files and the auto-proxy file residing at http://domain1_server/autoconfig/.

Note   Whenever you update and post an Internet settings (.ins) file to a server, you should also copy any cabinet (.cab) files that have also changed.

Automatic Detection of Browser Settings (Corporate Administrators)

You can configure your network so that Internet Explorer is customized automatically the first time it is started. This can help reduce administrative overhead and potentially reduce help desk calls about browser settings.

Automatic detection of browser settings, which is based on Web Proxy AutoDiscovery (WPAD), is supported by both Dynamic Host Configuration Protocol (DHCP) and Domain Name System (DNS). With the appropriate settings, DHCP servers that support the DHCPINFORM message and DNS servers can automatically detect and configure a browser's settings.

Automatic detection of settings builds on existing automatic configuration technologies, in which a browser can be configured from a central location with an IEAK profile or a JavaScript proxy configuration (.js, .jvs, or .pac) file.

With automatic detection, the browser can now be automatically configured when it is started, even if the browser was not first customized by the administrator. For example, if a user were to download a noncustomized browser from the Internet, instead of installing a customized version from the corporate servers, automatic detection can automatically configure and customize the user's browser.

To specify in the IEAK that you want to set up automatic detection of browser settings, select **Automatically detect settings** on the Automatic Configuration screen of the Internet Explorer Customization wizard.

Automatic Detection of Browser Settings for DHCP and DNS

A DHCP server enables the administrator to centrally specify global and subnet-specific TCP/IP parameters and to define parameters for clients by using reserved addresses. When a client computer moves between subnets, it is automatically reconfigured for TCP/IP when the computer is started.

DNS is a set of protocols and services on a TCP/IP network that allow users to search for other computers by using hierarchical user-friendly names, often known as "hosts," instead of numeric IP addresses.

Using DHCP with automatic detection works best for local area network-based (LAN-based) clients, while DNS enables computers with both LAN-based and dial-up connections to detect their settings. Although DNS can handle network and dial-up connections, DHCP provides for faster access to LAN users and allows greater flexibility in specifying configuration files.

To enable automatic detection of browser settings, you need to configure specific settings on DNS servers, DHCP servers, or both.

Enabling Automatic Detection of Browser Settings on DHCP

To set up automatic detection of browser settings on a DHCP server, you need to create a new option type with a code number of 252. Your DHCP server must support the DHCPINFORM message.

Note Depending on your type of DHCP server, the option names may vary slightly.

▶   **To add a new DHCP option type**

1. On the **DHCP Options** menu, click **Defaults**.

2. In the Option Class list, click the class for which you want to add a new option type, and then click **New**.

3. In the **Name** box, type a new option name.

4. In the Data Type list, click the **String** data type.

   For the default value of the string, type the URL that points to your configuration file. This file can be a .pac, .jvs, .js, or .ins configuration file.

   Examples:
   http://www.microsoft.com/webproxy.pac
   http://marketing/config.ins
   http://###.#.###.#/account.pac

5. In the **Identifier** box, type the code number **252** to associate with this option type.

6. In the **Comment** box, type a description.

Enabling Automatic Detection on DNS

To enable automatic detection of browser settings on DNS, you need to configure either the host record or CNAME "alias" record in the DNS database file.

Host Record

A host record is used to statically associate host (computer) names to IP addresses within a zone. A host record contains entries for all hosts that require static mappings, such as work stations, name servers, and mail servers.

The syntax for a host record has this form:

```
<host name> IN A <ip address of host>
```

The following list shows some examples.

Host name	IN	A	Host IP address
corserv	IN	A	192.55.200.143
nameserver2	IN	A	192.55.200.2
mailserver1	IN	A	192.55.200.51

CNAME Record

These records are sometimes called "aliases" but are technically referred to as "canonical name" (CNAME) entries. These records allow you to use more than one name to point to a single host. Using canonical names makes it easy to do such things as host both an FTP server and a Web server on the same computer.

▶ **To configure a DNS database file for automatic detection of browser settings**

- In the DNS database file, enter a host record named **wpad** that points to the IP address of the Web server that contains the .pac, .jvs, .js, or .ins automatic configuration file.

    -or-

    Enter a CNAME alias named **wpad** that points to the name (the resolved name, not the IP address) of the server that contains the .pac, .jvs, .js, or .ins automatic configuration file.

    Note After the record is added and the database file is propagated to the server, the DNS name wpad.*domain*.com should resolve to the same computer name as the server that contains the automatic configuration file.

When using DNS, Internet Explorer constructs a default URL template based on the host name **wpad**—for example:

http://wpad.domain.com/wpad.dat

Therefore, on the Web server **wpad**, you must set up a file or redirection point named wpad.dat, which delivers the contents of your automatic configuration file.

Working with Proxy Servers

A proxy server acts as an intermediary between your computer and the Internet. It is most frequently used when there is a corporate intranet and users are connected to a LAN. It can also work with a firewall to provide a security barrier between your internal network and the Internet. In addition, corporate administrators can balance proxy loads and block undesirable sites. Proxy servers are becoming more advanced in their ability to reduce network traffic by caching content that is frequently requested by the browsers they serve.

A key benefit of Internet Explorer 5 is that users can have multiple connection configurations. Proxy and other LAN settings can be altered for each connection configuration, and a friendly name can be assigned to each configuration—for example, "docking station."

The following section covers two key issues that you should consider if your organization uses proxy servers:

- Configuring proxy port settings
- Configuring proxy bypass lists

Proxy Configuration (Corporate Administrators and ISPs)

Corporate administrators and ISPs can preset proxy server settings by entering the settings in Stage 4 of the Internet Explorer Customization wizard. The following illustration shows the Proxy Settings screen.

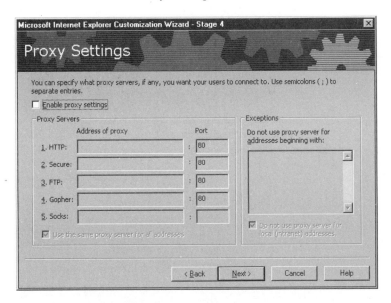

These settings in the Customization wizard correspond to proxy settings in the browser. To see these settings in the browser, click the **Tools** menu, and then click **Internet Options**. Click the **Connections** tab, and then click **LAN Settings**. To see addresses of specific proxy servers, click **Advanced**.

Selecting the **Use the same proxy server for all protocols** check box in the browser or the **Use the same proxy server for all addresses** check box in the Customization wizard makes all the other entries unavailable and copies the proxy information in the HTTP setting into the other protocol settings. Selecting the check box also hides the information in the **Socks** setting.

The **Secure** setting is for HTTPS requests based on the Secure Sockets Layer (SSL) technology.

Proxy locations that do not begin with a protocol (such as http:// or ftp://) are assumed to be a CERN-type HTTP proxy. For example, when the user types **proxy**, it's treated the same as if the user typed **http://proxy**. For FTP gateways, such as the TIS FTP gateway, the proxy should be listed with the ftp:// in front of the proxy name. For example, an FTP gateway for an FTP proxy would have this format:

```
ftp://ftpproxy
```

When you enter proxy settings, use the following syntax, where <address> is the Web address of the proxy server and <port> is the port number assigned to the proxy server:

```
http://<address>:<port>
```

For example, if the address of the proxy server is proxy.example.microsoft.com and the port number is 80, the setting in the **Proxy Server** box for LAN settings in the Proxy Settings dialog box or the Proxy Settings screen of the Customization wizard should read as follows:

```
http://proxy.example.microsoft.com:80
```

Note If you are using the Internet Protocol (IP) address of your proxy server, make sure not to type leading zeros. For example, use 130.25.0.1 instead of 130.025.000.001.

Key proxy registry settings are as follows:

```
HKEY_CURRENT_USER\SOFTWARE\MICROSOFT\WINDOWS\CURRENTVERSION\
Internet Settings\
"ProxyEnable"="01 00 00 00"
"ProxyServer"="data"
"ProxyOverride"="local"
```

The proxy bypass list in the Exceptions area of the Proxy Settings dialog box allows users to specify addresses that will bypass the proxy server and be accessed directly.

Corporate administrators can also preset proxy settings or manage proxy settings by using an automatic proxy configuration file in .js, .jvs, or .pac format. For more information about automatic proxy configuration, see Chapter 21, "Using Automatic Configuration and Automatic Proxy."

Using the Proxy Bypass List

Some network requests need to bypass the proxy. The most common reason to bypass the proxy is for local (intranet) addresses. Generally, these addresses do not contain periods in them. By selecting the **Bypass proxy server for local (intranet) addresses** check box, all addresses without a period (for example, http://compserv) will bypass the proxy and be resolved directly.

To bypass more complex addresses, you can set up exceptions for specific addresses or wildcards. If you are configuring settings by using the Customization wizard, enter the addresses into the **Do not use proxy server for addresses beginning with** check box in the Exceptions area of the Proxy Settings dialog box. If you are configuring proxy settings on a user's computer after deployment, click the **Tools** menu, and then click **Internet Options**. Click the **Connections** tab, click **LAN Settings**, and then click **Advanced**. Enter the addresses into the **Do not use proxy server for addresses beginning with** check box in the Exceptions area. Use a semicolon (;) between entries in the Customization wizard and in the browser.

A proxy bypass entry may begin with a protocol type: http://, https://, ftp://, or gopher://. If a protocol type is used, the exception entry applies only to requests for that protocol. Note that the protocol value is case insensitive. Multiple entries should be separated by semicolons.

If no protocol is specified, any request using the address will be bypassed. If a protocol is specified, requests with the address will be bypassed only if they are of the indicated protocol type. As with the protocol type, address entries are case insensitive. If a port number is given, the request is processed only if all previous requirements are met and the request uses the specified port number.

The Exceptions area of the Proxy Settings dialog box allows a wildcard (*) to be used in the place of zero or more characters. The following list contains examples showing how to use wildcards:

- To bypass servers, enter a wildcard at the beginning of an Internet address, IP address, or domain name with a common ending. For example, use ***.example.com** to bypass any entries ending in .example.com (such as some.example.com and www.example.com).

- To bypass servers, enter a wildcard in the middle of an Internet address, IP address, or domain name with a common beginning and ending. For example, the entry **www.*.com** matches any entry that starts with www and ends with com.

- To bypass servers, enter a wildcard at the ending of an Internet address, IP address, or domain name with a common beginning. For example, use **www.microsoft.*** to bypass any entries that begin with www.microsoft. (such as www.microsoft.com, www.microsoft.org, and www.microsoftcorporation.com).

- To bypass addresses with similar patterns, use multiple wildcards. For example, use **123.1*.66.*** to bypass addresses such as 123.144.66.12, 123.133.66.15, and 123.187.66.13.

Although wildcards are powerful, they must be used carefully. For example, the entry **www.*.com** causes Internet Explorer to bypass the proxy for most Web sites.

If you need to bypass the proxy for a local domain, try using ***.domain.com**. This will not use the proxy for any computer name ending in .domain.com. You can use the wildcard for any part of the name.

Using FTP with CERN-Compliant Proxy Servers

Users can access FTP sites through a CERN-compliant proxy server. To access an FTP site, users would type the Internet address (URL) for the FTP site they want to connect to, as shown in the following example:

ftp://ftp.microsoft.com

If the site requires a user name and password, users also need to include that information in the address:

ftp://username:password@ftp.microsoft.com

If your system uses a CERN proxy server, users can only download files from and view files at FTP sites. To enable users to perform other services, such as uploading files, you need to provide another proxy solution.

Working with Automatic Search

You can customize automatic search, which enables users to type a conversational word into the Address bar to search for frequently used pages. Users do not need to remember the URLs for the pages that you specify, so key information is easier to find.

For example, you could enable a Web page about invoices to appear when a user types the term "invoice" into the Address bar, even if the URL of the page doesn't contain this term. If you are a corporate administrator, the following topic shows you how you can customize automatic searching. If you are an ICP or ISP, send e-mail to autosrch@microsoft.com for more information.

This feature is already enabled for the Internet. For example, typing certain distinct, popular terms into the Address bar causes a Web site associated with that term to appear. When a Web site cannot distinctly be associated with that term— for example, if there are several apparent matches—then a Web page showing top search results is displayed.

The Web site that appears does not necessarily contain the exact search term in its URL. If a Web site whose domain is the same as the term is not the best match for the search term (for example, if the search term is the same as the URL without www. and .com), then the user is redirected to the site that is the best match for that term. By default, the user is prompted when a redirection occurs.

The Automatic Search URL is configurable by using two parameters denoted by a percent (%) sign. These two values must be part of the URL itself. The value %1 represents what the user typed in the Address bar. The value %2 represents the type of search option chosen by the user. Possible values for %2 are 3, 2, 1, and 0, where:

- 3 = Display the results and go to the most likely site.
- 2 = Just go to the most likely site.
- 1 = Just display the results in the main window.
- 0 = Do not search from the Address bar.

▶ **To set up Automatic Search**

1. Create a script and post it to an intranet server.

    The search page can be a script file, such as an Active Server Page (.asp) file, that conditionally checks for search terms. The script needs to be hosted at this location: http://ieautosearch/response.asp?MT=%1&srch=%2. If you are not using IIS, then you would need to remap this URL to the address where your script is located.

2. If you are setting this option on the System Policies and Restrictions screen in Stage 5 of the Customization wizard, click **Internet Settings**.

    If you are setting this option in the Profile Manager, click **Policies and Restrictions**, and then click **Internet Settings**.

3. Click **Advanced Settings**, and then in the Searching area, type **intranet** into the **Search Provider Keyword** box.

    If you're just redirecting users to another site rather than returning search results, then select **Just go to the most likely site** in the **When Searching From The Address Bar** box.

Note If you are a corporate administrator, you are not customizing search, and your organization doesn't have Internet access, you may want to disable automatic searching. To do this, in the Searching area on the Advanced Settings screen, select **Never search from the Address bar**.

Sample .asp AutoSearch Script

The following is a script that shows how search queries on an intranet can be redirected to the appropriate Web page.

```
<%@ Language=VBScript %>
<%
' search holds the words typed in the Address bar by the user, without
' the "go" or ' "find" or any delimiters like "+" for spaces.
' If the user types "Apple pie," search = "Apple pie."
' If the user types "find Apple pie," search = "Apple pie."
search = Request.QueryString("MT")
search = UCase(search)
searchOption = Request.QueryString("srch")


' This is a simple if/then/else script to redirect the browser
' to the site of your choice based on what the user typed.
' Example: expense report is an intranet page about
' filling out an expense report
if (search = "NEW HIRE") then
Response.Redirect("http://admin/hr/newhireforms.htm")
elseif (search = "LIBRARY CATALOG") then
Response.Redirect("http://library/catalog")
elseif (search = "EXPENSE REPORT") then
Response.Redirect("http://expense")
elseif (search = "LUNCH MENU") then
Response.Redirect("http://cafe/menu/")
else
' If there is not a match, use the
' default IE autosearch server
Response.Redirect("http://auto.search.msn.com/response.asp?MT="
+ search + "&srch=" + searchOption +
"&prov=&utf8")
end if
%>
```

Working with Roaming User Profiles (Corporate Administrators)

The roaming user profiles feature allows multiple users to use a single installation of Internet Explorer while retaining unique individual settings for each user. This feature also allows settings to follow a user to another computer. Corporate administrators should consider how best to configure roaming user profiles for network configuration and user needs.

If a network is used, user profiles can roam. This means that the user's copy of User.dat is stored on a central server and downloaded to any workstation that the user logs on to. This way, users can see the same environment no matter what workstation they use. It also allows administrators to have central control over individual user settings.

Internet Explorer and the Internet Explorer Customization wizard include options for caching temporary Internet files. These options can be useful when you are using roaming user profiles on a network. If you do not use these options, all temporary Internet files are copied to the user's profile folder when the user logs off. The temporary Internet files are then copied back to the local computer the next time the user logs on. This can be time-consuming and can use a lot of server space.

Caching Options

You can use a caching option in Internet Explorer to delete all cached Internet files when a user quits the browser. This option does not delete cookie information. Cookie information (which is usually small) is copied when the profile is saved. To set this option in the browser, carry out the following procedure:

▶ **To set caching options in Internet Explorer**

1. On the **Tools** menu in Internet Explorer, click **Internet Options**.

2. Click the **Advanced** tab.

3. In the Security area, select the **Empty Temporary Internet Files folder when browser is closed** check box.

You can also use the System Policies and Restrictions screen of the Internet Explorer Customization wizard or the Internet Restrictions screen of the IEAK Profile Manager to set this option before deployment. In the Security area, select the **Delete saved pages when browser closed** check box.

Understanding Roaming Profiles

The Personalized Item Settings dialog box in Control Panel can control the content and settings saved on a per-user basis. This control is especially useful for conserving disk space and for avoiding excessive network traffic. Even if a server might have unlimited disk space to store content, it is not always practical for content in a profile to pass back and forth between the server and a client. Thus, to minimize the amount of data stored in profiles, you can specify personalized item settings as follows:

- **Desktop folder and Documents menu**—If the Active Desktop is part of the corporate installation, this setting can be left on.

- **Start Menu and Program folders**—Because these folders are dependent on the programs installed in a standard corporate installation, this setting can be turned off.

- **Favorites folder**—This setting should be left on so that users can maintain a personal Favorites list.

- **Downloaded Web pages**—This setting affects the Temporary Internet Files folder, which contains Cookies and History. If strict size limitations are necessary, this setting can be left on, but in most cases it can be left off.

- **My Documents folder**—Network traffic can be minimized if this setting is turned off and a network share is used for document storage.

If roaming profiles are already enabled on a computer, installing Internet Explorer does not automatically move the new folders to the profile. You need to select the items from the User Profiles Manager by clicking the **Users** icon in Control Panel in Windows. If you run Internet Explorer on Windows NT 4.0, the **Users** icon does not appear in Control Panel. Windows NT 4.0 either uses a preconfigured profile or creates a local user profile automatically when you log on.

Note Because roaming profiles are handled by the operating system, they are bound by the differences between user profiles for specific operating systems.

Creating User Profiles

Before you can create a user profile, you first need to enable them on the **User Profiles** tab of the Passwords Properties dialog box (to access this dialog box, click the **Passwords** icon in Control Panel.)

To create a new profile in Windows, just log on using a user name that is new to the system and, therefore, has no corresponding password list (.pwl) file. The system prompts you to confirm the new user password and asks whether you would like to use global settings or per-user settings.

Instead of logging on with a new user name, you can click the **Users** icon in Control Panel to run the User Profile wizard, which you can use to add and configure user profiles. This is an alternate user interface for creating a new profile.

Understanding Advanced User Profile Functionality

If a path is stored in the per-user registry, it probably points to a folder with contents that are also per-user. You should consider whether these contents also should roam from one computer to another. Keep in mind that although any file can be made to roam, not all files should. In addition to performance issues when large numbers of files are copied to and from the user's logon server, there are security issues. For example, a user may not want or expect sensitive documents to be copied to any workstation on which they log on and to remain there even after they log off.

You need to be particularly careful with links to programs. Links usually contain hard-coded paths (such as a shortcut to C:\Program Files\Internet Explorer\IExplore.exe), which may not roam well. If you want the contents of a folder full of shortcuts to roam, create shortcuts that don't contain absolute paths.

When working with roaming profiles, there are several ways you can use folder settings:

- **Not per-user**—The setting is the same for all users and does not follow the user to other computers.

- **Optionally per-user**—The user or network administrator can choose whether users get their own version of the setting. Note that it's possible for this optional configuration to be per-user. That is, either all users get their own version of the setting or none of them do, or some users get their own setting and others use the default.

- **Optionally both per-user and roaming**—Either all users get the same setting and the contents do not follow them from computer to computer, or users get their own settings and the contents follow them. This is how the **Desktop** and **Start** menus work in Windows 95. Whether a particular user gets a unique copy or uses the default is determined on a per-user basis.

- **Always per-user, optionally roaming**—All users on a computer get their own version of the setting, but the contents of the folder do not follow the user to other computers on the network.

- **Always per-user, always roaming**—Users each get their own content because their individual content always follows them. This is the way typical per-user registry items work; it is also how the user's Favorites, Cookies, and History folders are expected to work.

Preparing Servers for Internet Sign-up (ISPs)

An Internet sign-up server is an HTTP server that automates the task of adding new customers to an ISP's customer database. The Internet sign-up server collects information from each new customer, adds the information to the ISP's customer database, and then passes a configuration packet back to the customer's desktop computer. The configuration packet contains information that is used to configure the customer's Internet browser for subsequent connection to the ISP's services.

To add a new customer to the ISP's database, the Internet sign-up server:

- Causes the client computer to establish an HTTP connection with the sign-up server.
- Collects sign-up information from the customer.
- Handles the customer's acceptance or refusal of the ISP's services.

When using the IEAK, three options are available for performing Internet sign-up:

- Server-based sign-up by using the Internet Connection wizard (ICW)
- Server-based sign-up by using the browser in Kiosk mode
- Serverless sign-up

Server-based sign-up is preferred, unless you can't provide a sign-up server, because settings are easier to change on the server than on the client. Of the two server-based options, the ICW method is recommended, because it uses a standard wizard interface that can be customized to fit your needs. This section will help you prepare for Internet sign-up by using the ICW.

If you're an ISP, you can specify the ICW as the tool that customers use to sign up for Internet services and configure their computers.

Important If you are using single-disk branding and you anticipate that some of your users will have Internet Explorer 4.01 Service Pack 1, you should not use ICW mode sign-up; you should Kiosk-mode sign-up instead. If you think some customers will have a later version of Internet Explorer, then you can create an IEAK package that contains both sign-up solutions.

Customizable solutions for Internet sign-up are located in the IEAK Toolkit. The code is provided in Active Server Pages as well as in Perl format, allowing you to build an ICW sign-up process for Web servers on different platforms with a minimum of effort. If you use the sample code, the only work you need to do is to integrate the sign-up server with your registration and billing systems. In the Windows 98 Referral Server Program, the sign-up server code is similar for both IEAK sign-up and Referral Server registrations.

The following sections describe how to develop a sign-up process for the ICW. Although these sections describe a tested, comprehensive sign-up solution, which is recommended in most cases, you can customize the sign-up process further to meet the needs of your organization.

Note Because the IEAK solution includes multiple Internet sign-up (.isp) files for different customer needs, you must also include the Dynamic HTML Data Binding component in your custom package.

For general information about Internet sign-up and implementing the sign-up process, see Chapter 20, "Implementing the Sign-up Process."

Meeting Coding and Accessibility Requirements for Internet Sign-up by Using the ICW

To prepare your Internet server, you need to design HTML pages on your server that will interact with the customer during Internet sign-up.

The new ICW-mode sign-up mechanism in the IEAK is designed so that an Internet sign-up server looks and acts like a standard Windows wizard. Although the ICW uses the power and flexibility of HTML, it does not use the same formatting as HTML.

HTML pages in the ICW must use the Windows system colors and fonts and also must meet accessibility requirements. Unless otherwise specified, the ICW HTML pages cannot contain any special HTML formatting, such as tables with visible borders, images, or anchors. Only plain text and FORM elements (where required) are allowed. Tables with invisible borders can be used for layout.

To match the user's system colors, all HTML pages except the Icwsign.htm page should contain no color or font attributes unless otherwise specified.

The only requirement for implementing forms within the HTML pages is that the forms use the NAME attribute in FORM elements defined in the specification.

Back and Next Button Functionality

ICW-mode sign-up has specific requirements that must be met for the **Back** and **Next** buttons in the Internet Connection wizard to work correctly.

Back Button

For the **Back** button to work correctly, you must add a FORM element to the sign-up server page that specifies the URL of the **Back** button. To retain the data previously collected in the sign-up process, you must append it to the URL for the **Back** button page.

The following example shows the FORM element that's used with the **Back** button for sending the user to the previous page of the sign-up process. Note that the data for the first and last names is appended to the URL in name/value pairs:

```
<FORM
NAME="BACK"ACTION="http://myserver/page2.asp"?firstname=bob&lastname=smi
th&address=..."></FORM>
```

Note All letters in the NAME attribute and its value must be capitalized because the ICW is case-sensitive.

Next Button

For the **Next** button to work properly, you must add a FORM element to the sign-up server page that specifies the URL of the **Next** button. For the data collected to be passed to the next page in the sign-up process, you must add hidden FORM fields on each of your sign-up server pages that contain the data elements collected on this and all previous pages. The URL you reference must contain code that collects the data from the previous page and displays the next page of the sign-up process.

The following example shows the FORM element that's used with the **Next** button for sending the user to the next page of the sign-up process:

```
<FORM NAME="NEXT" ACTION="http://myserver/page2.asp"></FORM>
```

The sample sign-up server code included in the IEAK already conforms to these requirements.

Accessibility

To ensure that the elements on the page are accessible by using only the keyboard, you should check that each FORM element meets the following requirements:

- An access key (hot key) must be associated with the FORM element. Use the Internet Explorer ACCESSKEY attribute in the INPUT element. The access-key character should be highlighted with an underline by using an Underline tag. The letters b, f, g, n, and o are reserved for the ICW and cannot be used as access keys. For more information about the ACCESSKEY attribute, see the MSDN Online Web site.

- Each FORM element on the page must be part of the ICW tab-key order. To be included in the ICW tab-key order, the element must have a unique ID in the INPUT element.

- Each FORM element should have a label associated with it. To associate a label for the different FORM input types, use the Internet Explorer LABEL attribute.

The following example shows a radio button FORM element that meets these accessibility requirements:

```
<input ID="option2"
type="radio"
name="billing"
value="hour"
accesskey="h"
checked>

<label for="option2">
5 <u>H</u>ours per month for $10.
</label>
```

Designing HTML Pages for ICW Sign-up

Each page of the Internet Connection wizard should have the following design elements and adhere to the following design conventions.

Style Sheet

If you use a style sheet, do not specify any font style or color attributes in it. The parent wizard sets these attributes. If you use a TABLE element in your error pages, the element must include a STYLE attribute—for example:

```
<TABLE style="font: 8pt 'ms sans serif' buttontext"> </TABLE>
```

Design Restrictions

Only text and FORM elements are allowed. Do not use images, links, or scroll bars in your design.

Required Form Elements

The HTML page must include four FORM elements that specify different page properties:

- **The unique PAGEID for the page**—The NAME attribute for the FORM element must be "PAGEID" (case sensitive). The ACTION attribute of the FORM element must be a unique ID that does not match the PAGEID of any other page in the ISP section of the wizard, as shown in this example:

  ```
  <FORM NAME="PAGEID" ACTION="page4"></FORM>
  ```

- **The Back button function**—The NAME attribute for the FORM element must be "BACK" (case sensitive). The ACTION attribute for the FORM element should be the absolute URL for the previous page, as shown in this example:

  ```
  <FORM NAME="PAGEID" ACTION="HTTP://signup/bin/page1.cgi"></FORM>
  ```

  Note, however, that no data is posted to this page.

- **The characteristics of the page**—The NAME attribute for the FORM element must be "PAGETYPE" (case sensitive). Because this is a standard frame where the ISP defines the entire space, the ACTION attribute for the FORM element must be an empty string, as shown in this example:

  ```
  <FORM NAME="PAGETYPE" ACTION=""></FORM>
  ```

- **The Next button function**—The NAME attribute for the FORM element must be "NEXT" (case sensitive). There are no restrictions on the token names for the INPUT elements within the FORM element. The ACTION attribute for the FORM element should be the absolute URL where the form information should be posted. The URL that you post on your server should contain a script that receives the data and then displays the next HTML page of the wizard.

Working with the ICW Sample Sign-up Files

If you want to simulate the sign-up process before creating your own files, you can use the sample files from the IEAK Toolkit. The sample files can give you a general idea of how the sign-up process works and the type of information that you'll need to provide.

▶ **To test the sample sign-up files on your server**

1. Create a subfolder named Signup in the wwwroot folder on your server.

2. Copy the files from the Toolkit folder to the Signup subfolder.

3. In the files, change all the references to point to your sign-up server.

4. In the HTML code of the sign-up server pages, change all the references from the sample company name to your organization's name.

5. Modify the last sign-up server page to reflect your .ins settings.

Creating Initial, Error, and Finish Pages for ICW Sign-up

For ICW sign-up, you need to design the initial page the user sees (Icwsign.htm), error pages, and the finish page.

Initial Page (Icwsign.htm)

The initial page that the user sees after installing Internet Explorer 5 and restarting the computer is the branded Icwsign.htm page. This page is specified in the IEAK and is included in your build of Internet Explorer 5. It is not hosted on your sign-up server.

On the Icwsign.htm page, the user sees welcome information from the ISP and is asked to either click **Next** to begin the sign-up process (if there is only one ISP file needed for sign-up) or to select the city and state being dialed from so that the

ICW can select the appropriate sign-up server ISP file to use. When the user clicks **Next**, the ICW dials and connects the user to the ISP sign-up server.

Error Pages for ICW Sign-up

If the data submitted to the sign-up server is invalid at any time during the sign-up process, the server can display an HTML page with a friendly error message. An example would be if the user requests an e-mail name that is already in use.

The error HTML page that is sent by the ISP's sign-up server is displayed in a floating frame within the wizard. The frame is 444 pixels wide by 273 pixels high. Scroll bars do not appear if the HTML page exceeds these dimensions.

The frame should contain text that lets the user know that the data entered was invalid and provides the FORM elements required for the user to enter new data.

For information about HTML design and required FORM elements, see "Designing HTML Pages for ICW Sign-up" earlier in this chapter.

Finish Page for ICW Sign-up

When the user clicks **Next** on the ISP finish page, the .ins file is processed and the computer is configured for the new Internet account. After this is done, the ICW displays its final page, which informs the user that the Internet connection is ready and tells the user how to begin browsing the Internet. There is no ISP-configurable interface on this page.

The finish page also provides the option of beginning browsing immediately when the user selects the **Begin browsing immediately** check box. You can use the StartURL value in the .ins file to specify the page the browser displays when it first opens.

Note After the user has finished the sign-up process, your sign-up server must return information about how to configure the user's computer for Internet access. The .ins file, downloaded at the end of your sign-up process, contains this information.

Creating the Name and Address Page for ICW Sign-up

When a user connects to your sign-up server, the first page the user sees is the name and address page.

The name and address HTML page is displayed in a frame within the wizard. The frame is 444 pixels wide by 273 pixels high. Scroll bars do not appear if the HTML page exceeds these dimensions.

For information about HTML design and required form elements, see "Designing HTML Pages for ICW Sign-up" earlier in this chapter.

Creating the Billing Options Page for ICW Sign-up

On the Billing Options page, you can present the service billing options from which the user can choose. The options are presented using an HTML form within a frame in the wizard window.

The user should be able to select an option by clicking an HTML radio button, and one of the radio-button options must be selected by default. If the user needs to make multiple selections, you can also include HTML check boxes in the frame.

The billing-option HTML page that you supply is displayed in a floating frame within the wizard. The frame is 444 pixels wide by 273 pixels high. Scroll bars do not appear if the HTML page exceeds these dimensions.

For information about HTML design and required form elements, see "Designing HTML Pages for ICW Sign-up" earlier in this chapter.

Creating the Method of Payment Page for ICW Sign-up

The Method of Payment page is where users specify how they want to pay for the Internet service. Each ISP controls which payment methods are available in the Payment Method list. Payment information is collected in the form that appears in a frame below the selection, which changes depending on the payment method selected in the list.

You can choose to offer any type of payment method:

- Credit card (you can specify the type of card, such as Visa or American Express)
- Debit card
- Invoice
- Phone bill charges

For information about HTML design and required form elements, see "Designing HTML Pages for ICW Sign-up" earlier in this chapter.

Creating the ISP Account Login/E-Mail Screen for ICW Sign-up

The account login/e-mail page enables the user to select an account login and/or e-mail ID and password.

The HTML page that is sent by your sign-up server for account login and e-mail is displayed in a floating frame within the wizard. The frame is 444 pixels wide by 273 pixels high. Scroll bars do not appear if the HTML page exceeds these dimensions.

For information about HTML design and required form elements, see "Designing HTML Pages for ICW Sign-up" earlier in this chapter.

Creating the ISP POP Selection Page for ICW Sign-up

The POP selection page is where the user selects a local phone number for Internet access.

The HTML page that is sent by the ISP's sign-up server for POP selection is displayed in a floating frame within the wizard. The frame is 444 pixels wide by 273 pixels high. Scroll bars do not appear if the HTML page exceeds these dimensions.

The user should not be asked to enter an area code or phone number a second time. Any area code or phone number fields in the frame should be prepopulated using the information already sent to the ISP's sign-up server from the name and address page.

For information about HTML design and required form elements, see "Designing HTML Pages for ICW Sign-up" earlier in this chapter.

Creating the ISP Terms and Conditions Page for ICW Sign-up

The ISP Terms and Conditions page is where the ISP displays the legal agreement that the user must read to subscribe to the service. To ensure that the user accepts the agreement, the **Next** button of the ICW is not available until the user clicks the **I accept the agreement** check box.

The user can save the HTML page for ISP terms and conditions for viewing later by clicking the **Save Copy** button. After clicking the button, the user is prompted to enter a file name and path for where the file should be saved. The actual terms and conditions HTML file from the ISP's sign-up server will be saved to that location.

The HTML page that is sent by the ISP's sign-up server for Terms and Conditions is displayed in a floating frame with a 2-pixel border within the wizard. The frame's width is 426 pixels (without the 2-pixel border and vertical scroll bar). A horizontal scroll bar does not appear if the HTML page exceeds the width dimension.

The Terms and Conditions page should begin with the document's title and instructions explaining how users can find a copy of the legal document on the ISP's Web site if they want to view it again or print it.

For information about HTML design and required form elements, see "Designing HTML Pages for ICW Sign-up" earlier in this chapter.

Note There are no accessibility requirements for this page because no HTML form elements are allowed on the page.

Using ICW Automatic Reconfiguration for ISP Sign-up

ICW Automatic Reconfiguration enables users who already have an Internet account with an Internet service provider to have an account setting automatically reconfigured. When users buy a new computer, this feature helps them configure it for the same Internet account they had on a previous computer or on a computer at work. It also helps users whose Internet settings have become corrupted. The Automatic Reconfiguration feature restores the user's settings; the user needs to know only the user name, password, and POP server.

In a custom version of Internet Explorer, the user reaches the automatic reconfiguration server by clicking a link on the Icwsign.htm page. This link connects the user to the registration server.

After the user is connected to your sign-up server, you can ask for the user name, password, and POP server. With this information, you can send an .ins file to the user's computer to reconfigure the user's account.

Supporting ICW Automatic Reconfiguration

You can use two methods with ICW Automatic Reconfiguration to restore user accounts:

- Ask the user for the user name, password, and POP server. This should be sufficient information for you to recreate the .ins file, send it to the user, and reconfigure the account. If you are concerned about abuse of this feature, you might want to recollect the user's credit card number and run a check against the registration database.

- Store .ins files in the same location as the rest of the user's account information. When a user connects to the Automatic Reconfiguration server, the user can obtain the .ins file by providing only the user name and password. The server would then look up the user's account and deliver a copy of the user's original .ins file. As noted for the previous method, if you are concerned about abuse of this feature, you might want to recollect the user's credit card number and run a check against the registration database.

To set up ICW Automatic Reconfiguration, follow the coding and accessibility requirements for ICW sign-up and design the ISP account login/e-mail page, the ISP POP selection page, and the ISP finish page.

Working with the Sample Sign-up Automatic Reconfiguration Files

If you want to simulate the Automatic Reconfiguration process before creating your own files, you can use the sample files from the IEAK Toolkit. To do this, carry out the following steps:

▶ **To work with the sample sign-up pages for Automatic Reconfiguration**

1. Create a folder named Autocfg in the wwwroot folder on your server.
2. Copy the files from the Toolkit folder to the Autocfg folder.
3. In the files, change all the references to point to your sign-up server.
4. In the HTML code of the sign-up server pages, change all the references from Acme ISP to your organization's name.
5. Modify the last sign-up server page to reflect your .ins settings.

The following sample files can give you a general idea of how the sign-up process works and the type of information that you'll need to provide.

- **ISP Account Login/E-mail page**—This is the first page on the Automatic Reconfiguration server, which asks the user to provide the account login and/or e-mail ID and password. It is similar in design to the ISP Account Login/E-mail page for traditional ICW sign-up.

- **ISP POP selection page**—The POP selection page is where the user selects a local phone number for Internet access. After the user provides this information, the ISP should have sufficient information to recreate the .ins file. It is similar in design to the ISP Account Login/E-mail page for traditional ICW sign-up.

- **ISP finish page**—This is the last page of the Automatic Reconfiguration account restoration. The text provided by your HTML page is purely informational with no visible FORM elements. The check box and text at the bottom of the page are provided by the ICW. If the user selects the check box and clicks **Next**, the HTML code from your sign-up server shown on this page is saved to the user's desktop as an HTML file. The user can refer to this file to remember passwords or service information.

You can also decide whether you want to display the **Save Information** check box and text. By default, it is not shown. To turn on the check box, add the following form type to the HTML code for the finish page:

```
<FORM NAME=PAGEFLAG ACTION=1></FORM>
```

Sign-up Server Considerations for Internet Information Server

If you are using IIS as your sign-up server, you must configure the Internet sign-up server to provide a DHCP IP address to the client when the client connects to the server. Because the sign-up process is relatively short, the expiration time for the IP address lease can be small, possibly only a few minutes.

The sign-up processing is intended to be used over a point-to-point dial-up connection, so the IP addresses allocated for the DHCP server need not be formally assigned IP addresses. It is your responsibility to determine whether the DHCP IP addresses will be valid Internet addresses or arbitrary addresses.

For the client to process the .ins file automatically, you must register a Multipurpose Internet Mail Extensions (MIME) type for the .ins file with the sign-up server. The .ins file has been assigned the "application/x-Internet-signup" Type. When the client requests an .ins file, the sign-up server responds with this MIME type, which starts the associated installation application on the client side.

Server Considerations for NetMeeting

When configuring your network for NetMeeting, you should consider how to handle standardization requirements:

- Particularly in the corporate environment, communication between local and remote locations is a necessity. To support these user communities, products must interoperate in a standard fashion across platforms and networks.

- Products of varying levels of functionality must be able to communicate; standards enable compatibility of applications that have a variety of functions and features.

- As more vendors develop standards-based products, customers benefit from competitive pricing, improved quality, and product upgrades.

The following sections describe the specific types of products and services, including clients, servers, and gateways, that interoperate with NetMeeting. Interoperability testing is described for two International Telecommunications Unions (ITU) standards that NetMeeting currently supports: T.120 for data conferencing and H.323 for audio and video conferencing. This section also discusses the elements that make T.120 and H.323 standards-based products interoperate.

Interoperability Scenarios and NetMeeting

For corporate and home users, many interoperability scenarios are possible between NetMeeting and compatible, standards-based clients, servers, bridges, and gateways:

- Within an organization, NetMeeting users can connect with each other over the corporate intranet. A T.120 or H.323 conferencing server can provide inbound and outbound connectivity with compatible clients for data, audio, or video conferencing.

- An H.323 gateway can be used to bridge internal and external networks over a corporate firewall, supporting connections for audio and video conferencing.

- NetMeeting users can initiate multipoint connections with third-party T.120 clients. T.120 servers can provide administration services for this data conferencing scenario.

- NetMeeting users can initiate point-to-point connections with H.323 clients. T.120 data conferencing can be supported in conjunction with H.323 audio and video conferencing. H.323 servers can provide administration services for this data conferencing scenario.

- Through an H.32x gateway, NetMeeting users can connect to H.320 and H.324 systems. Also, an H.320 server can be used for connectivity with multiple H.320 systems.

- An H.323 gateway also enables NetMeeting users to connect to people over public switched telephone network (PSTN) lines.

Internet Locator Server

Internet Locator Server (ILS) offers a standards-based, dynamic directory solution to the user location problem on the Internet. ILS supports LDAP conferencing servers and directory servers. These server types are described in following sections.

ILS provides organizations with a directory server for NetMeeting users. Like User Location Service (ULS), which was developed for NetMeeting 1.0, ILS provides a memory-resident database for storing dynamic directory information. This database enables users to find dynamic information, such as an IP address, for people currently logged on to an Internet service or site. The ILS database maintains the entries, which clients update periodically. This process ensures that clients can always access the most current information about each user's Internet location.

The following features distinguish ILS:

- **Support for industry-standard protocols**—ILS provides both an LDAP interface for NetMeeting support and a proprietary user location protocol (ULP) interface for legacy support of NetMeeting 1.0. Through these built-in protocols, ILS provides directory server support for NetMeeting. These interfaces allow NetMeeting to access the server for dynamic directory information and facilitate point-to-point Internet communication sessions. Other clients can access ILS through the LDAP interface. For more information, see the Microsoft NetMeeting Software Development Kit. All client applications must migrate to LDAP to access dynamic directory information.

- **Performance monitoring**—ILS supports Windows NT Server administration features—including performance monitoring (Perfmon counters), Simple Network Management Protocol (SNMP) monitoring, and event logs—to measure activity and system performance. Operators can make use of administration features, such as transaction logs that collect usage statistics, track messages and transactions, and allow administrators to examine usage patterns. These tools enable administrators to proactively monitor server performance and identify potential problems.

- **Stable, robust server capabilities**—As a standards-based Internet directory server, ILS was designed to provide stable, robust directory services. ILS uses thread pooling and connection management to enable more efficient handling of system resources. ILS users experience better performance, because ILS uses binary data packets to optimize performance. Also, the server uses a spanning tree architecture to support many concurrent users in a single server configuration.

- **Customization through Active Server Pages**—Using Active Server Pages (.asp files), administrators can combine HTML and scripting components to customize their ILS interface. They can create scripts to display a specific group of NetMeeting users currently online, enable user searches, and initiate real-time communication sessions with other users.

- **Easy setup and administration**—ILS provides a graphical setup program so that administrators can install server components quickly and easily. Then, administrators can set options for user logon, security, and server access through the Microsoft Internet Service Manager.

- **Microsoft product support**—Microsoft provides worldwide product support through the Microsoft Support Network. ILS users can choose from standard or priority support.

For information about setting up and implementing ILS, see the *Microsoft Internet Locator Server Operations Guide* or its companion, the *Microsoft Internet Locator Service Operations Reference*.

LDAP Conferencing Servers

ILS supports the IETF Lightweight Directory Access Protocol (LDAP) version 2 standard for NetMeeting directory services. LDAP servers support the same LDAP protocol, but each server extends LDAP for a particular purpose. For example, ILS applies LDAP for use with dynamic records.

LDAP version 3 designers have proposed dynamic directory services as part of the LDAP protocol. When version 3 is finalized and implemented within NetMeeting, developers can access standards information from the IETF Web site for developing compatible servers. Currently, vendors can develop interoperable servers for NetMeeting by obtaining information about the LDAP extension from Microsoft.

In addition, many people use ULS for locating and connecting to other NetMeeting users. Third-party vendors have developed many interoperable ULSs, such as uls.four11.com, which users can log on to from NetMeeting.

Directory Servers

ILS, an optional component of IIS, supports directory servers that enable NetMeeting users to locate each other on the Internet or corporate intranets. These servers create a directory of NetMeeting users. From this directory, users can select participants for real-time conferencing and collaboration. ILS provides all of the ULS functionality, as well as introducing advanced server technology not previously available. Users can benefit from enhanced features and functions, better performance, and higher scalability to support more NetMeeting users.

Firewall Configuration for NetMeeting

Microsoft NetMeeting can be configured to work with most organizations' existing firewall security. However, because of limitations in most firewall technology, few products are available that allow you to securely transport inbound and outbound NetMeeting calls containing audio, video, and data across a firewall. You might want to consider carefully the relative security risks of enabling different parts of a NetMeeting call in your firewall product. You must especially consider the security risks involved when modifying your firewall configuration to enable any component of an inbound NetMeeting call.

NetMeeting and Firewalls

A firewall is a set of security mechanisms that an organization implements, both logically and physically, to prevent unsecured access to an internal network. Firewall configurations vary from organization to organization. Most often, the firewall consists of several components, which can include a combination of routers, proxy servers, host computers, gateways, and networks with the appropriate security software. Very rarely is a firewall a single component, although a number of newer commercial firewalls attempt to put all of the components in a single package.

For most organizations, an Internet connection is part of the firewall. The firewall identifies itself to the outside network as a number of IP addresses—or as capable of routing to a number of IP addresses—all associated with DNS server entries. The firewall might respond as all of these hosts (a virtual computer) or pass on packets bound for these hosts to assigned computers.

You can configure firewall components in a variety of ways, depending on your organization's specific security policies and overall operations. Although most firewalls are capable of allowing primary (initial) and secondary (subsequent) TCP and User Datagram Protocol (UDP) connections, they might be configured to support only specific connections based on security considerations. For example, some firewalls allow only primary TCP connections, which are considered the most secure and reliable.

To enable NetMeeting multipoint data conferencing (application sharing, whiteboard, chat, file transfer, and directory lookups), your firewall only needs to pass through primary TCP connections on assigned ports. For NetMeeting to make calls that use audio and video conferencing, your firewall must be able to pass through secondary TCP and UDP connections on dynamically assigned ports. Some firewalls can pass through primary TCP connections on assigned ports, but cannot pass through secondary TCP or UDP connections on dynamically assigned ports.

Note   NetMeeting audio and video features require secondary TCP and UDP connections. Therefore, when you establish connections through firewalls that accept only primary TCP connections, you are not able to use the audio or video features of NetMeeting.

Establishing a NetMeeting Connection with a Firewall

When you use NetMeeting to call other users over the Internet, several IP ports are required in order to establish the outbound connection. If you use a firewall to connect to the Internet, it must be configured so that the following IP ports are not blocked.

This port	Is used for
389	Internet Locator Server (TCP)
522	User Location Service (TCP)
1503	T.120 (TCP)
1720	H.323 call setup (TCP)
1731	Audio call control (TCP)
Dynamic	H.323 call control (TCP)
Dynamic	H.323 streaming (Real Time Protocol over User Datagram Protocol)

To establish outbound NetMeeting connections through a firewall, the firewall must be configured to do the following:

- Pass through primary TCP connections on ports 389, 522, 1503, 1720, and 1731

- Pass through secondary TCP and UDP connections on dynamically assigned ports (1024-65535)

The H.323 call setup protocol (over port 1720) dynamically negotiates a TCP port for use by the H.323 call control protocol. Also, both the audio call control protocol (over port 1731) and the H.323 call setup protocol (over port 1720) dynamically negotiate UDP ports for use by the H.323 streaming protocol, which is the Real Time Protocol (RTP). In NetMeeting, two UDP ports are determined on each side of the firewall for audio and video streaming, for a total of four ports for inbound and outbound audio and video. These dynamically negotiated ports are selected arbitrarily from all ports that can be assigned dynamically.

NetMeeting directory services require either port 389 or port 522, depending on the type of server you are using. ILS, which supports LDAP for NetMeeting, requires port 389. ULS, developed for NetMeeting 1.0, requires port 522.

Firewall Limitations for NetMeeting

Some firewalls cannot support an arbitrary number of virtual internal IP addresses, or cannot do so dynamically. With these firewalls, you can establish outbound NetMeeting connections from computers inside the firewall to computers outside the firewall, and you can use the audio and video features of NetMeeting. Other people, though, cannot establish inbound connections from outside the firewall to computers inside the firewall. Typically, this restriction is due to limitations in the network implementation of the firewall.

Note Some firewalls are capable of accepting only certain protocols and cannot handle TCP connections. For example, if your firewall is a Web proxy server with no generic connection-handling mechanism, you will not be able to use NetMeeting through the firewall.

C H A P T E R   1 4

Customizing Connection Management and Settings

This chapter describes how to manage dial-up connections for your users. Using the Connection Manager Administration Kit (CMAK) wizard, which is part of the Internet Explorer Administration Kit (IEAK), you can customize connections and service profiles, and the ways in which they are managed.

Important The information in this chapter is an extension of, not a substitute for, the information found in the *CMAK Guide*. Before building your first service profile, you should print the *CMAK Guide* and be familiar with the information contained in the six-phase process found there for developing custom Connection Manager service profiles. Many of the technical details required to develop custom elements for your service profiles are found only in the *CMAK Guide*.

In This Chapter

See Also

- For more information about the Internet Explorer Customization wizard, see Chapter 12, "Preparing for the IEAK," and Chapter 15, "Running the Internet Explorer Customization Wizard."

- For more information about using the Internet Connection wizard for Internet sign-up, see Chapter 20, "Implementing the Sign-up Process."

- For more information about planning and implementing Connection Manager service profiles, see the CMAK folder on the CD-ROM.

Connection Management Overview

The Internet Explorer Administration Kit (IEAK) supports the use of Connection Manager to establish and maintain connections to your service. Previously, Dial-Up Networking connections were a primary method for establishing and maintaining connection capabilities for users. Connection Manager supports managed connections to the Internet or a corporate intranet, and it offers more features than standard Dial-Up Networking connections, including customization features, extensible functionality, greater scalability, and enhanced security.

Note Most of this chapter relates specifically to Connection Manager service profiles and connections, except where otherwise noted. All references to a "profile" in this chapter refer to a Connection Manager service profile. Unless otherwise specified, all references to an "installation package" in this chapter refer to an Internet Explorer installation package created by using the Internet Explorer Customization wizard.

Creating, customizing, and implementing your Connection Manager service profiles, discussed in the following six sections, includes:

- **Using the CMAK wizard to create Connection Manager service profiles that present the image that you want to provide to your users**—You can support managed dial-up access to Internet service providers (ISPs) and corporate networks, as well as establish virtual private network (VPN) connections to corporate networks, by creating custom Connection Manager service profiles. The scenarios provided in this section can assist you in determining how to effectively implement service profiles for these types of accounts.

- **Using advanced customization techniques to provide additional functionality and features in your Connection Manager service profiles**— Functions and features that cannot be customized by using the CMAK wizard can still be edited manually. You also can set up custom programs to run automatically during a user's connection to the service, and you can merge multiple phone books to provide maximum Points of Presence (POPs) for your users.

- **Importing connection settings**—By using the Internet Explorer Customization wizard, you can incorporate previously created connection settings from a Connection Manager connection, or from another Dial-Up Networking connection on your computer, to your installation package.

- **Setting system policies and restrictions for connections, including Connection Manager connections**—You can control the initial setup of automatic dialing for users. If you are a corporate administrator, you can specify whether users can change the connection settings for your service. Use the Internet Explorer Customization wizard to set these restrictions, but evaluate carefully how to specify these settings when implementing all of the procedures contained in this chapter.

- **Using the Internet Connection wizard for signup and setup**—You can use the Internet Connection wizard (ICW) to enable users to sign up for your service by using your online sign-up server. To simplify log on and connection for your users after they receive your installation package, you can also use the ICW to populate your Connection Manager service profile with the appropriate user data. Users who have the latest version of the ICW can even download an initial Connection Manager service profile from your sign-up or registration server.

- **Customizing profile delivery and installation to meet other support requirements**—If you want to distribute a Connection Manger service profile in an installation package other than the one you create by using the Internet Explorer Customization wizard, you can invoke command-line parameters from within your installation package to install Connection Manager as a part of that package.

Using the Connection Manager Administration Kit (CMAK) wizard, you can customize Connection Manager by creating service profiles that include the functions and look that you want for your service. When you run the CMAK wizard, it automatically builds a custom service profile. The profile is packaged in a self-installing executable file that, when installed by the user, appears to them as a customized version of Connection Manager and enables them to connect to your service.

Using the CMAK wizard, you specify the custom elements that you want Connection Manager to support, such as branded graphics; access numbers for dial-up connections; direct VPN connections; automatic programs (connect actions and automatic applications) that run during a connection; and other features specific to your service. You can include your custom Connection Manager service profile in an Internet Explorer installation package, so that both are automatically installed when your users install Internet Explorer.

Using the wizard to create a Connection Manager service profile is not difficult, but if you want to incorporate custom graphics and programs, many of the elements that you include must be developed before you run the wizard. The *CMAK Guide* provides a six-phase process that details how to create and implement a custom Connection Manager service profile and how to incorporate custom elements. The following six steps summarize this process:

- **Phase 1**—Decide what you want to customize and document it by using the worksheet provided in the planning section.
- **Phase 2**—Develop the custom elements, such as custom graphics, for your profile.
- **Phase 3**—Run the CMAK wizard to build the profile.
- **Phase 4**—Prepare for delivery, either as part of the IEAK installation package or as a separate installation package.
- **Phase 5**—Test your deliverables and resolve problems before distribution.
- **Phase 6**—Support your customers after distribution.

To access the *CMAK Guide*, open the Cmak_ops.chm file or click **Help** when you are running the CMAK wizard.

If you want to include your Connection Manager service profile in your Internet Explorer installation package, you can do so directly from the Internet Explorer Customization wizard. However, to ensure that the Connection Manager service profile works the way you want it to, it is recommended that you create and test the service profile before you include it in your custom installation package.

After you have created your Connection Manager service profiles, you may want to further customize them. Using advanced customization techniques to edit the service-profile files, you can further refine the service profiles by providing additional functionality, such as support for data encryption. You can also include your service profiles in another installation package by programmatically customizing installation options.

Options for Creating a Service Profile

Using the CMAK wizard, you can develop multiple service profiles to support a wide variety of connection requirements. The number of options available can make it seem difficult to determine what you need to include in your service profile to best support your needs. This section provides an overview of how to develop service profiles to support two of the most common scenarios:

- Providing access to an Internet service provider (ISP)
- Providing corporate access

These scenarios show the differences between two very different types of enterprises and how to customize a Connection Manager service profile to support their requirements. These are only two possible scenarios. You should review these two scenarios and review the Phase 1 information in the *CMAK Guide* to decide which options are best for your service.

You can make a copy of the planning worksheet and mark it up as you go through the scenarios to clarify how the options are defined. The worksheet is designed to match the structure of the CMAK wizard, so it is a good way to document the information required when running the wizard.

Important The following information provides an overview of methods of structuring Connection Manager service profiles to support the most common scenarios. This information is not sufficient to enable you to build service profiles. The details required to develop custom elements for a service profile and the rules for specifying each option are covered in the *CMAK Guide*. You should print the *CMAK Guide* and use it to determine how to set up your service profile. You can access the *CMAK Guide* by clicking **Help** from any page of the CMAK wizard.

Scenario 1: Providing Access to an Internet Service Provider

If you are an ISP that provides local access and participates in a consortium that enables your users to access the Internet from remote locations, you can create service profiles that contain multiple phone books—one for your local service and one or more for other access points provided by other members of the consortium. Merging multiple phone books into your service profile enables more effective phone-book maintenance than would be possible if all access numbers were maintained in a single phone book.

The *CMAK Guide* provides information about how to merge service profiles by using the CMAK wizard. The following information provides insight on how you can use merged phone books to effectively support an ISP account.

Step 1: Create the Phone Books and Dial-Up Networking Entries

Before running the CMAK wizard to create your service profile, create one or more phone books. For example, you could create a separate phone book for each ISP in the consortium to maintain on its own. To simplify the scenario, this example uses only two phone books (one for the local service and one for all of the other ISP access numbers supported by the consortium).

The phone books that you create contain all of the phone numbers that can be used to access the Internet. Each phone number in a phone book is known as a Point of Presence (POP). Microsoft Connection Point Services (available in the Windows NT 4.0 Option Pack) provides a Phone Book Administrator tool that simplifies the creation and maintenance of phone books in the format required by Connection Manager. Connection Point Services also includes Phone Book Service software that can be used to maintain the phone book and automatically update users' phone books when they connect to your service. For more information about creating the phone book, see Connection Point Services Help; also see the topics "Providing phone book support" and "Merging phone books and other features from existing service profiles" in Phase 2, "Developing custom elements," of the *CMAK Guide*.

For this example, create two phone books, one that contains the POPs for local access to your service and one that contains POPs for all fifty states in the United States. Because the POPs in the second phone book are provided by various remote ISPs, each with their own configuration requirements, each POP can have its own configuration settings. To specify the way in which a POP is handled, label the POP in the phone book with a specific Dial-Up Networking entry. In Step 2 (following), when you use the CMAK wizard to create the service profile, you specify how each Dial-Up Networking entry is handled. Before creating the service profile, determine how each POP is handled:

- Decide whether it will use preassigned addresses or server-assigned addresses.
- Specify the script, if any, associated with the entry.
- Determine additional customization requirements (such as encryption requirements implemented by using advanced customization techniques).

Each phone book (.pbk) file that you create must have a region file (.pbr) with the same file name. For example, the two phone books in this example might have the names LocalISP.pbk and RemISP.pbk, so the region files are named LocalISP.pbr and RemISP.pbr.

Step 2: Create the Connection Manager Service Profile That You Want to Merge

To merge multiple phone books, you must create one service profile for each phone book. For example, using the two-phone-book example, you would create a service profile for the remote ISPs by entering the following information:

- **Service and File Names**—In this example use the service name, Remote Internet Service Providers, because a service name is required to build a service profile. However, the service name is not used by Connection Manager when this service profile is merged into another service profile. In that case, you would use the file name, RemISP. The file name is used for the folder and many of the files created when CMAK builds the service profile.

- **Realm Name**—If no realm name is specified in the primary service profile (see Step 3 following), Connection Manager uses the realm name specified in the merged service profile for connections that use those phone numbers. In this example, assume that no realm name is required.

- **Dial-Up Networking Entries**—Specify the Dial-Up Networking entries associated with the remote ISP access numbers (POPs) that are contained in the RemISP.pbk file.

- **Connect Actions**—Click only the **Run post-connect actions** option.

- **Post-Connect Actions**—Click only the **Automatically download phone-book updates** option. All other connect actions specified for this service profile are ignored when the profile is merged into another service profile.

- **Phone Book**—Browse to the RemISP.pbk file to select it as the phone book. (If you do not want to provide the phone book in the service profile, leave this box empty and specify the name in the Phone-Book Updates dialog box instead, in order to download it at a later time.)

- **Phone Book Updates**—In the **Connection Point Services server** box, enter the name of the URL where the phone book for the remote ISPs is maintained and available for downloading.

You can specify other options when running the CMAK wizard to create this service profile, but only the options listed previously are used when a service profile is merged with another service profile.

Step 3: Create the Primary Connection Manager Service Profile

After you create the service profile that you want to merge, create the primary service profile, which is known as the referencing service profile. In this profile, specify the following information:

- **Service and File Names**—Specify the names for the referencing service profile. In this example, these might be Internet Service Provider and LocalISP. The service name you specify here is used for all of the connections that your users make, even if they are using POPs from the merged service profile.

- **Realm Name**—For this example, do not specify a realm name.

- **Merged Service Profiles**—In the Existing Service Profile list, select the file name of the profile you want to merge. In this example, the file is RemISP. To add it to the Service Profiles To Be Merged box, click **Add**.

- **Other options**—Specify all other options as appropriate. The options you specify here are used for all connections, except that the options previously specified in Step 2 will override these options when users connect by using the merged phone book.

Step 4: Implement Your Service Profiles

After you have completed step 3, thoroughly test your service profiles to ensure that they work as you expect. The Connection Manager service profile that you create can be incorporated in an installation package that is created by using the Internet Explorer Customization wizard. You also can distribute the service profile individually on a disk or use a Web server to download it to your users. For information about configuring profiles from your sign-up server, see "Using the Internet Connection Wizard for Sign-up and Setup" later in this chapter.

Scenario 2: Providing Corporate Access ·

You can create Connection Manager service profiles that provide corporate access to users by using either private dial-up connections to your corporate LAN or by using VPN connections that tunnel through a public network (such as the Internet). If you want to use ISPs to access your corporate account, it is recommended that you specify support for VPN connections to secure the data that you send over the Internet. Although you could set up corporate access without VPN support and use only a single service profile (a single phone book), for this example, assume that the service profile will support VPN connections and that you need two service profiles: one containing the phone book for your private corporate numbers and one containing the ISP phone book.

Step 1: Create the Phone Books and Dial-Up Networking Entries

Similar to the first scenario, create the phone books before creating the service profiles. In this example, create the phone book and region files for the corporate numbers (such as Corp.pbk and Corp.pbr) and the phone book and region files for the ISPs (such as Isp.pbk and Isp.pbr). Determine the requirements for Dial-Up Networking entries for the POPs in both Corp.pbk and Isp.pbk. (For more information about Dial-Up Networking Entries, see step 1 of "Providing Access to an Internet Service Provider," earlier in this chapter.)

When corporate numbers and ISP numbers are both included (by merging service profiles), the users get a single view of the network. If you prefer that some phone numbers for a geographic area are used only as emergency or secondary-access numbers, you can use the **Surcharge** option in Phone Book Administrator to distinguish them from numbers to be used for routine access.

Step 2: Set Up a VPN Server

To support VPN connections, you must set up a VPN server at the egress point from the Internet to your private network. For more information about setting up a VPN server, visit the Microsoft Windows NT Server Communication Services Web site.

Step 3: Create the Connection Manager Service Profile To Be Merged

Similar to the first scenario, create the merged service profile before creating the referencing service profile. In this example, create a service profile to provide corporate access through ISPs by entering the following information:

- **Service and File Names**—In this example use the name, Internet Service Providers, because a service name is required to build a service profile. However, this name is not used by Connection Manager when this service profile is merged into another service profile. In that case, you would use the file name, ISP.

- **Realm Name**—Some ISPs allow you to authenticate your users against your own authentication server at the time they connect by using the Remote Authentication Dial-In User Service (RADIUS) protocol. This gives the corporation full control of who is allowed to access the ISP on the corporation's behalf and eliminates the need to administer separate accounts and credentials for each user with the ISP. If your ISP supports this feature, you can use the Microsoft Internet Authentication Services (IAS), which is available in the Windows NT 4.0 Option Pack, to authenticate users against your Windows NT domain controller.

When you do this, you normally have to append routing information to each authentication request to the ISP so that the request can be sent to the corporate server. This routing information is specified in Connection Manager as the realm name. If a realm name is specified in the referencing service profile, it will be used in all instances (including all merged service profiles). If no realm name is specified in the referencing service profile, the realm names specified in the merged service profile is used for connections that are made using entries from the merged service profile. In this example, specify a realm name in the merged service profile.

- **Dial-Up Networking Entries**—Specify all of the Dial-Up Networking entries associated with the ISP access numbers (POPs) that are contained in the Isp.pbk file. In this example, in the Dial-Up Networking Entry dialog box, click **Add**, type **Pre-Authorization** in the Phone book Dial-Up Networking Entry box, click **Allow the server to assign addresses**, and then browse to the PreAuth.scp file to enter the script name in the Dial-Up Networking Script box.

- **Connect Actions**—Click only the **Run post-connect actions** option.

- **Post-Connect Actions**—Click only the **Automatically download phone-book updates** option. All other connect actions specified for this service profile are ignored when the profile is merged into another service profile.

- **Phone Book**—Browse to the Isp.pbk file and select it to be included as the phone book in the service profile. (If you prefer to download the phone book at a later time, leave this box empty and enter the file name in the Phone-Book Updates dialog box instead.)

- **Phone Book Updates**—In the **Connection Point Services server** box, enter the name of the URL where the phone book for the ISPs is maintained and available for downloading.

Other options specified in this service profile will be ignored when it is merged into another service profile.

Step 4: Create the Primary Connection Manager Service Profile

After you have created the service profile that you want to merge, you can create the primary service profile, which is known as the referencing service profile. In this profile, specify the following information:

- **Service and File Names**—Specify the names for the referencing service profile. In this example, these might be Corporate Account and CorpAcct. The service name you specify here is used for all connections your users make, even if they are using POPs from the merged service profile.

- **Merged Service Profiles**—In the Existing Service Profile list, select the file name of the profile that you want to merge. In our example, this is ISP. Click **Add** to add it to the Service Profiles To Be Merged box.

- **Realm Name**—For this example, do not specify a realm name in this service profile, because it is specified in the merged service profile. If you specify a realm name here, the realm name specified in the merged service profile is ignored.

- **VPN Support**—To support VPN connections for the merged service profile, select the **Merged service profiles** check box.

- **VPN Connection**—To send user data (for dial-up connections) with the realm name (when your users log on to your corporate network by using a VPN connection through an ISP POP), select the **Use the same user name and password for a VPN connection as for a dial-up connection** check box.

- **Phone Book**—All numbers designated as surcharge numbers appear in the More Access Numbers box in the Connection Manager Phone Book dialog box. If you have surcharge numbers in your phone books, you might want to specify a line of text to appear next to the More Access Numbers box. Specify the text by typing it in the CMAK wizard Phone Book dialog box in the More Text box.

- **Other options**—Specify all other options as appropriate. The options you specify here are used for all connections, except for the options that were specified in step 2, which will override these options when users connect by using the merged phone book.

Step 5: Implement Your Service Profiles

After you have completed step 4, thoroughly test your service profiles on all supported platforms to ensure that they work as you expect. You can then distribute the service profiles to corporate users by posting them to a file or to Web servers.

Advanced Customization Options for Connection Manager

The CMAK wizard supports most of the customization features that administrators need to build a custom Connection Manager service profile. However, you can customize additional features by editing the service-profile files and changing the manner in which Connection Manager implements certain functions.

You can edit service-profile files to customize functions and features that are not controlled through the CMAK wizard. To do this advanced customization, you can edit two sets of service-profile files:

- The template files that are used by the CMAK wizard to build all service profiles
- The files that are built when you run the CMAK wizard to create a specific service profile

Service-profile files consist of the following file types:

- **Service provider (.cms) files**—These files specify the configuration of the phone book and most of the other functions of your service profiles. Most advanced customization for a service profile is done by editing the .cms file for that service profile.

- **Connection profile (.cmp) files**—These files contain information specified by the user. You should not edit the .cmp files because any changes you make can be overwritten by the user.

- **Information (.inf) files**—These files specify the installation information for your service profiles. Although you can edit some setup and removal information in an .inf file, you must be extremely cautious to avoid installation problems.

- **Connection profile (.sed) files**—These files contain the instructions for building a self-extracting executable (.exe) file for your service profiles. You should never edit any .sed file.

Important Be careful when you modify these files. Troubleshooting the changes made to these files is difficult. Never modify the original file, and always make backup copies. A basic understanding of system-configuration files is assumed.

Editing Service-Profile Files

You can edit either the template files or the specific service-profile files, or both, depending on whether you want your customization options applied globally to all service profiles or only to a specific service profile.

Template Files

When you install the CMAK, the following template files are installed in the \Program Files\CMAK\Support folder:

- Template.cms
- Template.cmp
- Template.inf
- Template.sed

These files contain the default settings that the CMAK wizard uses to build the service profiles. If you want to incorporate custom functions in all service profiles that you build, edit the template files before building the service profiles.

Generally, you should edit only the .cms template file.

Built Files

When you use the CMAK wizard to build a service profile, the wizard creates a self-extracting .exe file and several other files that contain the settings that you specify. The service-profile files are saved in the following folder: \Program Files\CMAK\Profiles*ServiceProfileFileName*

All service-profile files have the name *ServiceProfileFileName*, which you specify in the CMAK wizard. In addition to the .exe file, the wizard creates the following files for each service profile:

- *ServiceProfileFileName*.cms
- *ServiceProfileFileName*.cmp
- *ServiceProfileFileName*.inf
- *ServiceProfileFileName*.sed

For all files except the .cmp files, the built files take precedence over the template files. After editing a service-profile file, you must run the CMAK wizard again to rebuild the service profile with your customized settings.

Formats and Conventions

Connection Manager creates service (.cms) files, which use the same format as Windows .ini files and information (.inf) files. In these files:

- Each file is divided into sections, with specific entries assigned to the sections. A section heading is enclosed within brackets ([ ]). For example, **[Strings]** is a section that contains text strings for messages. The entries for a section are not enclosed within brackets.

- Each value specified for a numeric entry must be an integer. Any noninteger value is truncated to an integer or ignored as invalid data. For example, 1.1 is truncated to 1, or ignored.

- The order in which sections appear is not important; a particular section can be placed anywhere in the file.

- Any comment in the file begins with a semicolon (;).

For more information about these formats and conventions, see the Microsoft Platform Software Development Kit.

Customizing Functions

You should customize the entries only in the .cms and .inf files, and only as specified in this chapter.

Information (.inf) File Entries

By editing an .inf file, you can specify commands that run when the user sets up or removes your service profile. For example, you can specify:

- Setup programs that integrate any custom software that you include

- Programs that automatically display a readme file

- Configuration utilities or cleanup programs

To add custom set-up and uninstall commands to your service profile, you must first create the service profile by running the CMAK wizard and incorporate any files needed to run your custom commands by specifying each of them as an additional file. After you have built the service profile, specify the custom commands in the appropriate sections of the .inf file.

The .inf file contains the following four sections that you can edit to incorporate setup and uninstall commands, each of which controls the commands that are run at a specific point in the process. Use only file names of eight characters or less (do not use spaces).

- **RunPreSetupCommands**—Commands specified in this section run before installation of your service profile.

- **RunPostSetupCommands**—Commands specified in this section run after the setup program finishes the service profile.

- **RunPreUnInstCommands**—Commands specified in this section run before the uninstall program begins.

- **RunPostUnInstCommands**—Commands specified in this section run after the uninstall program runs.

Each command should include the name of the program to be run and any command-line parameters. Each command specified in the .inf file is run only once during an installation or removal process.

Important   Incorrectly specified entries can cause significant installation problems. You should not edit any of the entries in the .inf file except those previously specified. Thoroughly test all service profiles that contain custom .inf entries for version, file, or other conflicts. Be sure that the file location is specified correctly.

When upgrading to a new version of the Connection Manager Administration Kit, the new .inf file replaces the previous .inf file. After the upgrade, you must add your custom entries to the new .inf file if you want to continue using your custom setup and uninstall commands in the service profiles that you build.

Long file names are not supported.

Service Provider (.cms) File Entries

Editing a .cms file can change the implementation of many of the Connection Manager functions. For example, you can do the following:

- Edit the **RedialDelay** entry, which controls the delay between redials.

- Edit the **PasswordHandling** entry, which specifies case sensitivity for passwords.

- Edit the **HideRememberPassword** entry, which controls whether the **Save password** check box appears.

- Edit the **HideDialAutomatically** entry, which controls whether the **Connect automatically** check box appears.

- Edit the **ResetPassword** entry, which controls whether a **New** button appears in the Connection Manager logon dialog box.

- Edit the **HideDomain** entry, which controls whether the **Logon domain** field appears.

- Edit settings in the **[Server&*EntryName*]** and **[TCP/IP&*EntryName*]** sections, which enables you to specify additional settings that control the way in which Dial-Up Networking entries are handled in Connection Manager. Many of these settings are controlled through the CMAK wizard; however, some must be edited in the .cms file, such as the **IP_Header_Compress** setting.

The following table shows the valid entries for each section of the .cms and .cmp files, the function and use of each entry, and where each entry can be set—in the CMAK wizard, .cms file, and/or .cmp file.

Notes

- Do not edit any entry in the .cms file if it can be set by using the CMAK wizard, because the CMAK wizard may overwrite entries in the .cms file.

- If an entry is valid in both .cms and .cmp files, edit only the .cms entry.

- Make sure that locations are specified either as the full path or in reference to the location of the .cmp file.

[Section] or entry	Specifies	Set in
[Connection Manager]	Miscellaneous service-profile settings.	.cms .cmp
Dialup	Whether dial-up connections are supported. 0 = No. 1 (default) = Yes.	.cms
Direct	Whether direct connections are supported. 0 = No. 1 (default) = Yes.	.cms
ConnectionType	The connection method used. 0 (default) = Connect by using a dial-up connection—for example, a modem. 1 = Connect by using a direct connection—for example, a LAN. The first time the service profile is run, the user is prompted to select the appropriate option. The user can change this option on the **General** tab in the Properties dialog box. The setting in the .cmp file represents the current state.	.cms .cmp

[Section] or entry	Specifies	Set in
PBMessage	Text in the Phone Book dialog box next to the **More access numbers** box when the phone book is displayed and alternate access numbers are available for the selected geographic region. Maximum = approximately 100 characters.	CMAK .cms
CMSFile	Name of the service-profile file (*Path\ServiceProfileFileName.cms*).	CMAK .cmp
ServiceName	Text appearing in the Connection Manager logon dialog box as the service name, and as the name of the connection object. This is the key identifier for the profile.	CMAK .cms
	Maximum = approximately 35 characters.	
	If the Connection Manager service profile is to be included in a Microsoft Internet Explorer installation package created with the IEAK, this name must be the same as the name specified in the **[Entry]** section of the Internet Explorer .ins file.	
ServiceMessage	Connection Manager logon dialog box service message, usually a customer-support number for the service.	CMAK .cms
	Maximum = approximately 50 characters.	
UserName	User name typed by the user.	.cmp
UserNamePrefix	Prefix appended to the user name. Enables access to a service requiring a realm name as a prefix.	CMAK .cms
UserNameSuffix	Suffix appended to the user name. Enables access to a service requiring a realm name as a suffix.	CMAK .cms
MaxUserName	Maximum length of the user name that can be typed by the user. UserNamePrefix and UserNameSuffix are not included.	.cms
	Default = 256 bytes.	
UserNameOptional	Whether the user must type a user name at the Connection Manager logon dialog box.	.cms
	0 (default) = User name required. 1 = User name not required.	
HideUserName	Whether the **User name** box appears in the Connection Manager logon dialog box when using dial-up connections.	.cms
	0 (default) = Display the box. 1 = Do not display the box.	
	If the field is hidden, the data is considered optional.	
Password	Password typed by the user.	.cmp

[Section] or entry	Specifies	Set in
PasswordHandling	Method of handling the password during the logon process. 0 (default) = Normal (case sensitive). 1 = Lowercase password. 2 = Uppercase password.	.cms
MaxPassword	Maximum length of the password that can be typed by the user. Default = 256 bytes.	.cms
PasswordOptional	Whether the user must specify a password in the Connection Manager logon dialog box. 0 (default) = Password required. 1 = Password not required.	.cms
RememberPassword	Whether the user selected the **Save password** check box in the Connection Manager logon dialog box. 0 (default) = User did not select the check box. 1 = User selected the check box. However, if the Connection Manager service profile is included in an Internet Explorer installation package created with the IEAK, it simplifies user logon if this entry is set to 1.	.cmp
HidePassword	Whether the Password box appears in the Connection Manager logon dialog box when using dial-up connections. 0 (default) = Display the box. 1 = Do not display the box. If the field is hidden, the data is considered optional.	.cms
HideRememberPassword	Whether to display the **Save password** check box in the Connection Manager logon dialog box of Connection Manager and on the **Internet Logon** tab. Service profiles built to support VPN connections contain this additional tab. 0 (default) = Display the check box. 1 = Do not display the check box. If **HideRememberPassword** is set to **1**, it overrides the **HideDialAutomatically** setting, even if **HideDialAutomatically** is not set to **1**.	.cms
Domain	Logon domain name typed by the user.	.cmp
MaxDomain	Maximum length of the domain name that can be typed by the user. Default = 15 bytes.	.cms

[Section] or entry	Specifies	Set in
HideDomain	Whether the Logon Domain box appears in the Connection Manager logon dialog box when using dial-up connections.	.cms
	0 = Display the box. 1 (default) = Do not display the box.	
	The default is 1 only if the profile supports VPN connections; otherwise, the default is 0. If the field is hidden, the data is considered optional.	
HideInternetUsername	Whether the Username box appears on the **Internet Logon** tab in the Properties dialog box.	.cms
	0 (default) = Display the box. 1 = Do not display the box.	
	If the field is hidden, the data is considered optional. If **HideInternetPassword** and **HideInternetUsername** are both 1, the tab is not displayed.	
HideInternetPassword	Whether the **Password** box appears on the **Internet Logon** tab in the Properties dialog box.	.cms
	0 (default) = Display the box. 1 = Do not display the box.	
	If the field is hidden, the data is considered optional. If **HideInternetPassword** and **HideInternetUsername** are both 1, the tab is not displayed.	
DialAutomatically	Whether the user selected the **Connect automatically** check box in the Connection Manager logon dialog box.	.cmp
	0 (default) = User did not select the check box. 1 = User selected the check box.	
HideDialAutomatically	Whether the **Connect automatically** check box appears in the Connection Manager logon dialog box.	.cms
	0 (default) = Display the check box. 1 = Do not display the check box.	
InternetUserName	User name for VPN connections, typed by the user.	.cmp
InternetPassword	Password for VPN connections, typed by the user.	.cmp
RememberInternetPassword	Whether the user selected the **Save password** check box in the **Internet Logon** dialog box.	.cmp
	0 = (default) User did not the select check box. 1 = User selected the check box.	
Phone0	Primary phone number typed or selected by the user.	.cmp

[Section] or entry	Specifies	Set in
PhoneCanonical0	The canonical format of the primary phone number last selected from the phone book or typed in using the canonical format.	.cmp
PhoneCountry0	TAPI country/region code for the primary phone number.	.cmp
UseDialingRules0	How dialing rules are applied to the primary phone number.	.cms .cmp
	0 = Use the form of the number exactly as it appears in the phone book or as it is typed. 1 (default if no values are specified) = Apply dialing rules to the canonical form of the number when displaying and dialing.	
	The value in the .cmp file, if there is one, takes precedence over the value in the .cms file.	
PhoneSource0	Service profile for the primary phone number.	.cmp
Description0	Description of the primary phone number. Appears in the Phone Book dialog box as a POP name.	.cmp
DUN0	Dial-Up Networking entries used for the primary phone number.	.cmp
Phone1	Backup phone number, entered by the user.	.cmp
PhoneCanonical1	The canonical format of the backup number last selected from the phone book or typed in using the canonical format.	.cmp
PhoneCountry1	TAPI country/region code for the backup phone number.	.cmp
UseDialingRules1	How dialing rules are applied to the backup number.	.cms .cmp
	0 = Use the form of the number exactly as it appears in the phone book or as it is typed. 1 (default if no values are specified) = Apply dialing rules to the canonical form of the number when displaying and dialing.	
	The value in the .cmp file, if there is one, takes precedence over the value in the .cms file.	
PhoneSource1	Service profile for the backup phone number.	.cmp
Description1	Description of the backup phone number. Appears in the Phone Book dialog box as a POP name.	.cmp
DUN1	Dial-Up Networking entries used for the backup phone number.	.cmp
Modem0	Name of the modem device to use for the primary phone number.	.cmp

[Section] or entry	Specifies	Set in
Modem1	Name of the modem device to use for the backup phone number.	.cmp
NoPromptReconnect	Whether the user is prompted for reconnection. 0 (default) = Prompt the user. 1 = Do not prompt the user.	.cms
ServiceType0	Service type that the user most recently selected from the phone book for the primary phone number.	.cmp
ServiceType1	Service type that the user most recently selected from the phone book for the backup phone number.	.cmp
Region0	State or province that the user most recently selected from the phone book for the primary phone number.	.cmp
Region1	State or province that the user most recently selected from the phone book for the backup phone number.	.cmp
Version	Version of the phone book.	.cms
DUN	Dial-Up Networking entries used when Dial-Up Networking in the phone book is blank. Default = *ServiceProfileServiceName*.	.cms
RedialCount	Number of redials to attempt. Default = 3.	.cms .cmp
RedialDelay	Delay (in seconds) between dials. The delay is the elapsed time between the point of failure of the first call and the dialing of the first digit of the next phone number. Default = 5 seconds.	.cms
IdleTimeout	Length of time (in minutes) that the connection must be idle before disconnecting. Default = 10 minutes. If set to 0, no timeout occurs.	.cms .cmp
IdleThreshold	Maximum bytes per minute that can be received if an idle state is to be detected for the connection. Default = 0. (This entry is for Windows 95 and Windows 98 operating systems.)	.cms
Logo	Location of the .bmp file displayed in the Connection Manager logon dialog box. Default = the standard Connection Manager logon bitmap.	CMAK .cms

[Section] or entry	Specifies	Set in
PBLogo	Location of the .bmp file for the Phone Book dialog box.	CMAK .cms
	Default = the standard Phone Book bitmap.	
Icon	Location of the icon (.ico) file for the large program icon.	CMAK .cms
	Default = the standard Connection Manager icon.	
SmallIcon	Location of the .ico file for the small title-bar icon.	CMAK .cms
	Default = the standard Connection Manager icon.	
TrayIcon	Name of the .ico file for the status-area icon.	CMAK .cms
	Default = the Connection Manager icon.	
HideTrayIcon	Whether to display the status-area icon in the Windows taskbar.	.cms
	0 (default) = Display the icon. 1 = Do not display the icon.	
	If you choose not to display a status-area icon, edit the Help file to remove references to it.	
HelpFile	Location (including name) of the custom Help file.	CMAK .cms
	Default Help file = the standard service-profile Help file.	
DownloadDelay	Time (in seconds) to delay before downloading phone book updates.	.cms
	Default = 15 seconds when a profile (%Profile%) is passed to the download connect action.	
	This entry is valid only when, in the CMAK wizard, in the Setup Post-Connect Actions dialog box, **Automatically download phone book updates** is selected.	
HideDelay	Time (in seconds) to delay before displaying the Phone-Book Updates dialog box (with progress indicators and message).	.cms
	Default = Do not display the dialog box.	
PBUpdateMessage	Text that appears in the dialog box during a phone book update.	.cms
	Default = "Downloading new phone book."	
Tunnel	Whether VPN connections are enabled for the service profile.	CMAK .cms
	0 (default) = Not enabled. 1 = Enabled.	

[Section] or entry	Specifies	Set in
TunnelDUN	Dial-Up Networking entries used for VPN connections. Default = *ServiceProfileServiceName* Tunnel.	.cms
TunnelAddress	IP address or domain name for the VPN server.	CMAK .cms
TunnelReferences	Whether VPN connections are enabled for phone numbers taken from referenced phone books. 0 (default) = Do not use phone numbers. 1 = Use phone numbers.	CMAK .cms
UseSameUserName	Whether to use a separate user name and password when connecting to the Internet service provider (for a VPN connection). 0 (default) = Use the separate user name and password as specified by the user on the **Internet Logon** tab of the Properties dialog box. 1 = Use the same user name and password when connecting to the Internet service provider as the name specified in the Connection Manager logon dialog box for logging on to the private service.	CMAK .cms
ResetPassword	Whether the **New** button appears in the Connection Manager logon dialog box to enable a user to reset the password. You can use this button to set up a custom password option. Type the location (including name) of the executable program you use to support this process. You must provide an executable program for this option and include it as an additional file when you run the CMAK wizard.	.cms
AnimatedLogo	Whether an animation is used instead of a static bitmap in the Connection Manager logon dialog box. 0 (default) = Do not use animated graphic. 1 = Use animated graphic. The **[Animated Logo]** section specifies the location of the animation (.spl or .swf) file. This function is provided for compatibility with Connection Manager 1.0, which supports Macromedia Flash animation files. If you add this option to the service profile, users will be prompted to restart their computers after installing the service profile.	.cms

[Section] or entry	Specifies	Set in
CheckOSComponents	Whether Connection Manager checks the operating-system components.	.cms
	0 (default) = Check the operating-system components only when an error occurs. 1 = Always check the operating-system components on startup.	
DoNotCheckBindings	Whether to include the TCP/IP bindings in the TCP/IP check.	.cms
	0 (default) = Include the TCP/IP bindings in the TCP/IP check and bind all that are not bound. 1 = Do not include the TCP/IP bindings in the TCP/IP check.	
	(This entry applies only to Windows 95 and Windows 98.) TCP/IP shims are protected from checking only if this option is set to **1** in all installed service profiles. This option does not prevent bindings from being checked by other service profiles or programs.	
AutoReconnect	Whether Connection Manager attempts to re-establish a connection that is dropped by the network.	.cms
	0 (default) = Do not attempt to re-establish dropped connections. 1 = Connection Manager automatically attempts to re-establish any connection dropped by the network, unless the connection was torn down—for example, by a timeout.	
	However, in Windows NT, Connection Manager always attempts to reconnect regardless of the timeout settings. If **AutoReconnect** is set to **1** (attempt reconnection), Connection Manager attempts to re-establish the connection without prompting the user.	
LanaTimeout	The time (in seconds) to wait before attempting connection to a VPN server.	.cms
	Default = 20 seconds.	
	Increase this value if the connection consistently fails to find a domain controller.	
[Profile Format]	Service-profile version.	.cms .cmp
Version	Format version of the profile or service file.	.cms .cmp

[Section] or entry	Specifies	Set in
[ISP]	Service types (such as Modem or ISDN) that you want to list in the Phone Book dialog box, and how you want phone numbers to appear for each service type. The Mask and Match lines control where a phone number is listed in the Phone Book dialog box. You can specify whether the number is listed under Access Numbers or under More Access Numbers. Each Mask and Match line has a corresponding service option in Phone Book Administrator.	.cms
PBFile	Location of the phone book (.pbk) file used by the service profile.	CMAK .cms
RegionFile	Location of the region (.pbr) file used by the service profile.	CMAK .cms
PBURL	Uniform Resource Locator (URL) for the phone book update.	CMAK .cms
Mask&*FilterName*	Mask value for *FilterName*.	.cms
Match&*FilterName*	Match value for *FilterName*.	.cms
FilterA&*ServiceProfile*	List of filter names to be applied to the access numbers' phone-book settings field—for example, FilterA& = NosurchargeSignon. The selected phone numbers are listed in the Access Numbers box in the Connection Manager Phone Book dialog box. Default = NosurchargeSignon.	.cms
FilterB&*ServiceProfile*	List of filter names to be applied to the referenced phone book options field—for example, FilterB& = SurchargeSignon. The selected phone numbers are listed in the More Access Numbers box in the Connection Manager Phone Book dialog box. Default = SurchargeSignon.	.cms
References	Service profiles merged through the CMAK wizard. Profile names are separated by commas or spaces. Each name is used as a reference to that profile.	CMAK .cms
CMSFile&*MergedProfile*	Location of the merged service file (.cms file). The format is CMSFile&*MergedProfile*=*Location*, where *MergedProfile* is the name of the merged service profile and *Location* is the location of the .cms file for the merged service profile— for example: CMSFile&Awesome1 = Awesome1\ AwesomeE.cms	CMAK .cms

[Section] or entry	Specifies	Set in
FilterA&*MergedProfile*	List of filter names to be applied to the referenced phone book options field. The format is FilterA&*Reference* = *FilterName*, where *MergedProfile* is the name of the merged service profile, as specified in the CMSFile*MergedProfile* entry, and *FilterName* is the name of the filter to be applied—for example: FilterA&AwesomeE = NoSurchargeSignon The selected phone numbers are merged into the list in the Access Numbers box in the Connection Manager Phone Book dialog box.	CMAK .cms
FilterB&*MergedProfile*	List of filter names to be applied to the referenced phone book options field. The format is FilterB&*MergedProfile* = *FilterName*, where *MergedProfile* is the name of the merged service profile, as specified in the CMSFile*Reference* entry, and *FilterName* is the name of the filter to be applied—for example: FilterB&AwesomeE = SurchargeSignon The selected phone numbers are merged into the list in the More Access Numbers box in the Connection Manager Phone Book dialog box.	CMAK .cms
[Service Types]	Items that are listed in the Phone Book dialog box under Service Type.	.cms
ServiceType	A service type as a filter name to be applied to the referenced phone book options field. The format of the entry is *ServiceType=FilterName*, where *ServiceType* is the name as it appears in the Service Type list in the Phone Book dialog box, and *FilterName* is the name of the filter to be associated with the entry—for example: ISDN Multicast = MulticastISDN It is recommended that a service type name include no more than 25 characters. If you need to add a service type, copy and edit an existing line in the **[Service Types]** section.	.cms

[Section] or entry	Specifies	Set in
[Pre-Connect Actions]	Optional pre-connect actions to run before a connection is established. The following environment variables are set in Connection Manager and can be implemented in connect actions as command-line options: Profile, UserName, UserPrefix, UserSuffix, ServiceName, DialRasPhoneBook, TunnelRasPhoneBook, AutoRedial, PopName, RasErrorCode, DialRasEntry, TunnelRasEntry. (Other settings are available through the RAS connection.)	.cms
#	A single pre-connect action. The format of the entry is # = *Program*, where # is a number from 0 to *x*, and *Program* is the complete name of the program (including the .exe or .dll file and associated parameters). Programs start in sequence: 0 first, 1 next, and so on.	CMAK .cms
#&Flags	Whether a pre-connect action runs when a specific type of connection is established. The format of the entry is #&options = *x*, where # is the number of a defined pre-connect action and *x* is a value indicating how dial-up and direct connections for that pre-connect action are handled: If *x* = 0, both dial-up and direct connections include this pre-connect action. If *x* = 1, only direct connections include this pre-connect action. If *x* = 2, only dial-up connections include this pre-connect action. Default = 2.	CMAK .cms
#&Description	A short description of a pre-connect action. The format of the entry is #&Description = *text*, where # is the number of a defined pre-connect action and *text* is the descriptive information for that pre-connect action. This option can provide useful information when a synchronous connect action does not run properly. Default = name specified using # = *Program* for the pre-connect action. Default = program name specified using # = *Program* for the pre-connect action.	CMAK .cms

[Section] or entry	Specifies	Set in
[Pre-Tunnel Actions]	Optional pre-tunnel actions to run after a connection is established but before a VPN connection is established. Pre-tunnel actions use the same format as other connect actions (as shown in the **[Pre-Connect Actions]** section, the #, #&option, and #&Description entries).	.cms
[Connect Actions]	Optional post-connect actions to run after a connection is established and, if using a VPN connection, after the tunnel is established. Post-connect actions use the same format as other connect actions (as shown in the **[Pre-Connect Actions]** section, the #, #&option, and #&Description entries).	.cms
[Disconnect Actions]	Optional disconnect actions to run immediately before disconnecting. Disconnect actions use the same format as other connect actions (as shown in the **[Pre-Connect Actions]** section, the #, #&option, and #&Description entries).	.cms
[Pre-Dial Actions]	Optional pre-dial actions to run immediately before dialing. Pre-dial actions use the same format as other connect actions (as shown in the **[Pre-Connect Actions]** section, the #, #&option, and #&Description entries), but they cannot be set in the CMAK wizard.	.cms
[On-Cancel Actions]	Optional on-cancel actions to run when the user cancels a session after the connection has been started. On-cancel actions use the same format as other connect actions (as shown in the **[Pre-Connect Actions]** section, the #, #&option, and #&Description entries), but they cannot be set in the CMAK wizard.	.cms
[On-Error Actions]	Optional on-error actions to run when an error occurs. On-error actions use the same format as other connect actions (as shown in the **[Pre-Connect Actions]** section, the #, #&option, and #&Description entries), but they cannot be set in the CMAK wizard.	.cms
[Auto-Applications]	Optional auto-applications to run during a connection. Auto-applications are similar to connect actions, but they cause the connection to close as soon as the final auto-application finishes. (Auto-applications use the same format as shown in the **[Pre-Connect Actions]** section, the # entry). Unlike pre-connect actions, auto-applications do not use the #&option or #&Description entries.	.cms

[Section] or entry	Specifies	Set in
[Menu Options]	Shortcut menu that appears when a user right-clicks the status-area icon for your service.	.cms
MenuItemName	Command to be run from the shortcut menu. Shortcut menu commands use the format *MenuItemName = Program*, where *MenuItemName* is the descriptive name that appears on the shortcut menu and *Program* is the name of the executable file (.exe or .dll), including any parameters required for the program. For example, if you wanted to add Notepad to the menu with the command name "Editor," the **[Menu Options]** line would be **Editor = Notepad.exe**.	CMAK .cms
	Default commands = **Status** and **Connect**.	
	These programs are available in a shortcut menu that appears when a user right-clicks the status-area icon. Applications are listed in the menu in sequence: 0 first, 1 next, and so on.	
[Animated Logo]	Animation for the Connection Manager logon dialog box. **AnimatedLogo** in the **[Connection Manager]** section determines whether an animation is used.	.cms
Movie	Location of the optional animation file displayed in place of the static bitmap in the logon dialog box. Settings in the **[Animated Actions]** section control how the optional animation plays based on the connection state.	.cms
Parameter	Other animation parameters passed from software used to create the animation, such as Quality = 3.	.cms
[Animated Actions]	When to play segments of the animation.	.cms
Initial	Starting frame number; plays when Connection Manager starts.	.cms
Dialing0	Starting frame number; plays while the primary phone number is dialed.	.cms
Pausing	Starting frame number; plays during pauses between dials.	.cms
Dialing1	Starting frame number; plays while the backup phone number is dialed.	.cms
Authenticating	Starting frame number; plays during user authentication.	.cms
Tunneling	Starting frame number; plays while establishing a VPN connection.	.cms
Connected	Starting frame number; plays when a connection is established.	.cms

[Section] or entry	Specifies	Set in
Error	Starting frame number; plays at any connection error.	.cms
[Server&*EntryName*]	Dial-Up Networking configuration. To store settings for multiple Dial-Up Networking entries, the name of the Dial-Up Networking entry is appended to each section header for that entry—for example, Server&Awesome1.	.cms
NetworkLogon	Whether to log on to the network. 0 (default) = Do not log on. 1 = Log on.	.cms
SW_Compress	Whether to negotiate PPP software compression of data. 0 = Do not negotiate. 1 (default) = Negotiate.	.cms
Disable_LCP	Whether to enable Link Control Protocol (LCP) extensions. 0 = Enable. 1 (default) = Disable.	.cms
PW_Encrypt	Whether to encrypt password when authenticating. 0 (default) = Do not encrypt. 1 = Encrypt.	.cms
Negotiate_TCP/IP	Whether to negotiate TCP/IP. 0 = Do not negotiate. 1 = Negotiate. Always set to 1.	.cms
Negotiate_IPX	Whether to negotiate IPX protocol. 0 = Do not negotiate. 1 (default) = Negotiate.	.cms
Negotiate_NetBEUI	Whether to negotiate NetBEUI protocol. 0 (default) = Do not negotiate. 1 = Negotiate.	.cms
[TCP/IP&*EntryName*]	Dial-Up Networking configuration. The name of the Dial-Up Networking entry is appended to each section header for that entry—for example, **[TCP/IP&Awesome1]**.	.cms
Specify_IP_Address	Whether to specify a static IP address. 0 (default) = Do not specify. 1 = Specify.	.cms
IP_Address	Static IP address.	.cms

[Section] or entry	Specifies	Set in
Specify_Server_Address	Whether to specify static DNS and WINS addresses. 0 (default) = Do not specify. 1 = Specify.	CMAK .cms
DNS_Address	DNS address.	CMAK .cms
DNS_Alt_Address	Alternate DNS address.	CMAK .cms
WINS_Address	WINS address.	CMAK .cms
WINS_Alt_Address	Alternate WINS address.	CMAK .cms
IP_Header_Compress	Whether to enable IP header compression. 0 = Not enabled. 1 (default) = Enabled.	.cms
Gateway_On_Remote	Whether to use the default gateway on the remote private network. 0 = Do not use. 1 (default) = Use.	.cms
[Networking&*EntryName*]	Dial-Up Networking configuration. The name of the Dial-Up Networking entry is appended to each section header for that entry—for example, **[Networking&Awesome1].**	.cms
VpnStrategy	Which tunneling protocol to use when establishing a VPN connection. 0 (default) = Automatically select the primary protocol. 1 = Use PPTP only. 2 = Try PPTP first. 3 = Use L2TP only. 4 = Try L2TP first. If this value is not specified, the RAS default value of 0 (currently 0) is used. **Note** PPTP is currently the primary protocol.	.cms
[Scripting&*EntryName*] Section	Location (path and file name) of the script (.scp) file for the Dial-Up Networking entry. The name of the Dial-Up Networking entry is appended to each section header for that entry—for example, **[Scripting&Awesome1].**	.cms
Name	Location (including file name) of the script (.scp) file for the Dial-Up Networking entry.	CMAK .cms

Importing Connection Settings into a Custom Package

By preconfiguring connection settings and then importing them to a custom package by using the Internet Explorer Customization wizard, you can affect how a user connects to the Internet or intranet. You can import connection settings from your computer on the Connection Settings screen of the Customization wizard. To see which settings you can import, on the **Tools** menu in Internet Explorer, click **Internet Options**, and then click the **Connections** tab.

The following illustration shows the **Connections** tab.

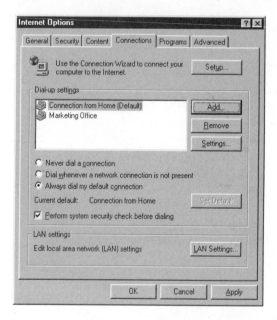

Internet Explorer 5 supports multiple connection settings. When you create connection settings, you import the settings for all connections in your configuration, including proxy servers, automatic configuration, and proxy automatic detection.

Stage 4 of the Internet Explorer Customization wizard enables you to determine whether to import your connection settings.

▶ **To specify whether you will import connection settings**

1. In Stage 4 of the Internet Explorer Customization wizard, click **Next** until the Connection Settings screen appears.

2. Select the options that you want.

The following illustration shows the Connection Settings screen.

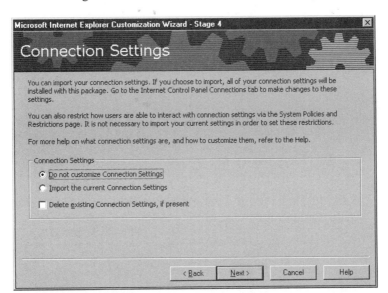

Note Corporate administrators also have the option of clearing any existing settings on their users' computers. This ensures that no incorrect settings remain in users' configurations.

Setting System Policies and Restrictions for Connections

If you are an ISP, an Internet content provider (ICP) or developer, or a corporate administrator, you can enable or disable automatic dialing in Stage 5 of the Customization wizard. This setting doesn't affect whether users can change this option, but it enables you to preset the option before you deploy Internet Explorer 5.

▶ **To preset automatic dialing options**

1. In Stage 5 of the Internet Explorer Customization wizard, click **Next** until the System Policies and Restrictions screen appears.

2. Click **Internet Settings** to expand the category, click **Modem settings**, and then select or clear the **Enable Autodialing** check box.

If you are a corporate administrator, you can set system policies and restrictions to determine whether users can change their connection settings. You can set policies and restrictions in Stage 5 of the Internet Explorer Customization wizard or by using automatic configuration and the IEAK Profile Manager.

▶ **To set connection restrictions (corporate administrators only)**

1. In Stage 5 of the Internet Explorer Customization wizard, click **Next** until the System Policies and Restrictions screen appears.

2. Click **Corporate Restrictions** to expand the category, and then click **Connections Page**.

3. Select the options that you want to restrict.

The following illustration shows the Connection options available in the Corporate Restrictions area.

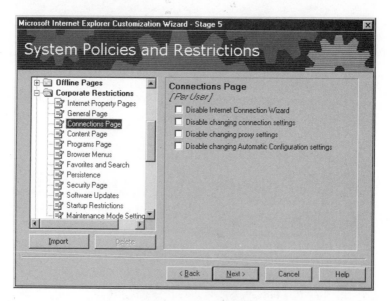

For more information about the IEAK Profile Manager and automatic configuration, see Chapter 21, "Using Automatic Configuration and Automatic Proxy," and Chapter 22, "Keeping Programs Updated."

For more information about the Internet Explorer Customization wizard, see Chapter 15, "Running the Internet Explorer Customization Wizard."

For more information about system policies, see Appendix E, "Setting System Policies and Restrictions."

Using the Internet Connection Wizard for Sign-up and Setup

If you are an Internet service provider and you are using server-based Internet sign-up, your users can use the Internet Connection wizard (ICW) to sign up for your services. You can customize the ICW to meet your needs.

A user can start the ICW from the Windows interface (at installation) or from Internet applications, such as Internet Explorer or Outlook Express, that have not been run before so there is no evidence of an existing Internet configuration.

This section generally discusses how the ICW can be customized by ISPs. For specific information about Internet sign up, see Chapter 13, "Setting Up Servers," and Chapter 20, "Implementing the Sign-up Process."

If you are an ISP in the Microsoft Referral Server Program and you have customized the Internet Connection wizard, your server code can easily be modified for Internet sign-up for IEAK users.

Internet sign up is also available by using Kiosk mode of Internet Explorer. If you are an ISP and you have already created a solution that uses Kiosk mode, you can continue to use your existing server solution or you can switch to Internet sign-up with the ICW. You should evaluate whether changing your server solution is cost-effective for your organization.

The ICW is designed to help users configure their Internet settings for the first time. Here's how the ICW works with the sign-up process:

- If the ICW has not already been successfully completed on the client computer, it configures the computer as necessary for dial-up access to the Internet and verifies the user's area or city code. Items configured by the ICW include the TCP/IP protocol stack, a provision for dynamically obtaining an IP address, modem settings, dialing properties, and a Dial-Up Networking entry.

- An Internet sign-up server is a Web-based application that automates the task of adding new subscribers to an ISP subscriber database. The Internet sign-up server collects information from each new subscriber, adds that information to the ISP subscriber database, and then generates a customized .ins file on the subscriber's computer.

- The .ins file contains information that configures the subscriber's Internet Explorer connection, Domain Name Service (DNS) address, news server address, mailbox, protocol stack, and dialer for subsequent connection to the ISP services. This configuration file also contains the phone numbers required to connect to the ISP Internet access network.

- When the client computer receives the .ins file, the ICW executes the configuration specified in the .ins file and completes the sign-up process. After that, when the user starts Internet Explorer, a connection to the ISP Internet access network is established.

Customizing the ICW and the sign-up process requires two steps: making any changes to brandable screens of the Internet Connection wizard, and setting up a sign-up server to work with the ICW. The IEAK Toolkit comes with Active Server Page (.asp) and PERL solutions that you can modify to fit your needs. For more information, see Chapter 20, "Implementing the Sign-up Process."

You can use the ICW for two specific set-up procedures:

- If your users already have the Connection Manager service profile, they can use the ICW to update the service profile, by populating it with user data (user name, password, and phone number) to provide a simpler logon sequence for the user.

- If your users have the latest version of the ICW, they can download an initial Connection Manager service profile

These two processes are covered in the following sections.

Populating User Data in a Connection Manager Profile

The .ins file is either shipped with the installation package or, more often, dynamically created by the online sign-up server. When using a sign-up server, the Internet service provider (ISP) should change the online sign-up server code to create .ins files with these new settings. Use the following procedure to synchronize the .ins file with the service profile delivered in the installation package:

▶ **To customize the .ins file to support integration of the Connection Manager service profile**

1. Create your Connection Manager service profile and then, in the Connection Manager Customization dialog box in the Stage 3 - Customizing Setup section of the Internet Explorer Customization wizard, include the service profile for the installation package.

2. In the **[Entry]** section of the .ins file, specify a service name that is identical to the **ServiceName** entry specified in the **[Connection Manager]** section of the Connection Manager .cms file.

3. In the **[Custom Dialer]** section of the .ins file, type the following two items, which enable Connection Manager to be used as the default dialer for Internet Explorer (although users will still need to set the default on their computers):

   - **Auto_Dial_DLL=cmdial32.dll**
   - **Auto_Dial_Function=_InetDialHandler@16**

4. In the **[Custom]** section of the .ins file, type the following:

   - **Run=icwconn2.exe**
   - **Keep_Connection=yes**

5. In the **[ClientSetup]** section of the .ins file, specify the following two items:

   - **Done_Message=***End of Signup Message*
   - **Explore_Command=***URL/Window to Launch for Initial CM Connection*

Note If you do not specify both, your users may receive error messages.

---

6. In the .ins file, to set the user data, create Connection Manager **[Entry]**, **[User]**, **[Phone]**, and **[Backup Phone]** sections and specify the information for each, as appropriate.

   - **[Entry]**
     Entry_Name=*ServiceProfileServiceName*

   - **[User]**
     Name=*UserName*
     Password=*UserPassword* (in plain text)
     Tunnel_Domain=*LogonDomain* (for logon dialog box, if appropriate)
     Tunnel_Name=*UserName* (for VPN, if appropriate)
     Tunnel_Password=*UserPassword* (in plain text, for VPN, if appropriate)
     UserNamePrefix=*RealmNameToBePrefixedToUserName*
     UserNameSuffix=*RealmNameToBeSuffixedToUserName*

   - **[Phone]**
     Phone_Number=*PrimaryAccessNumber*
     Dial_As_Is=*YesOrNo*
     Country_ID=*TAPICodeForCountry/Region* (use only if Dial_As_Is=Yes)
     Area_Code=*AreaCodeAppendedToNumber* (use only if Dial_As_Is=Yes)

   - **[Backup Phone]**
     Phone_Number=*BackupAccessNumber*
     Dial_As_Is=*YesOrNo*
     Country_ID=*TapiCodeForCountry/Region* (use only if Dial_As_Is=Yes)
     Area_Code=*AreaCodeAppendedToNumber* (use only if Dial_As_Is=Yes)

Downloading an Initial Connection Manager Service Profile

If your users are running the latest version of the ICW (available with Internet Explorer 5), you can use the ICW to download a complete Connection Manager service profile from the sign-up server to your users. This is useful when a user employs the ICW to connect to a referral service for Internet Service Providers (ISPs) and selects your service as the provider.

Because of security, ICW does not support the downloading of executable files. However, it does support incorporation of all Connection Manager service-profile information in the .ins file, which it then uses to create the service profile and install the profile on the user's computer. After the initial Connection Manager service profile is downloaded and installed, the user can use it to connect to your service and obtain another service profile (a full service profile that includes all required attached files).

To provide this support, create the initial Connection Manager service profile by using the CMAK wizard, and then copy the information from the service-profile files directly into the appropriate sections in the .ins file by using the following procedure. When the ICW downloads the .ins file, it recognizes information in these sections that belong to the .cmp, .cms, .pbk, .pbr, and .inf files and uses them to create the appropriate service-profile files.

Note Do not use this procedure if the user already has the service profile. To update an existing service profile, use the previous procedure. (See "Populating User Data in a Connection Manager Profile" earlier in this chapter.)

▶ **To download an initial Connection Manager service profile by using the ICW**

1. Use the latest version of the CMAK wizard to create your Connection Manager service-profile files and, if appropriate, use advanced customization techniques to further customize it. (For information about customizing the service-profile files after they are created, see "Advanced Customization Options for Connection Manager" earlier in this chapter.) Test your service profile on all supported platforms.

2. Create your Internet Explorer installation package, but do not incorporate the Connection Manager service profile.

3. In your Internet Explorer .ins file, create a **[Connection Manager CMP]** section, and then copy the information from the .cmp file (created in step 1) into this section. Change all section titles from the .cmp file so that, instead of being enclosed with square brackets, they are enclosed with braces (curly brackets). For example, change **[Profile Format]** to **{Profile Format}.** This indicates that they are subsections, not sections, of the .ins file. For example:

[Connection Manager CMP]
{Profile Format}

.
.
.

{Connection Manager}

Note The **[Connection Manager CMP]** section contains user-configurable data such as the user name, domain, password, phone numbers, and so on. Specify the appropriate entries in this section in order to populate a profile with this data.

---

4. In the .ins file, create a **[Connection Manager CMS 0]** section, specify the name of your .cms file instead of the placeholder (*ServiceProfileFileName*), and then copy the information from the .cms file into this section. Remember to change the brackets in the .cms file to braces, as covered previously in step 3. For example:

[Connection Manager CMS 0]
CMSFile=*ServiceProfileFileName*
Contents from this .cms file

Note If you have merged service profiles, you must create a section for the .cms file of each merged service profile. Specify a section name of **[Connection Manager CMS 1]** for the first merged service profile, **[Connection Manager CMS 2]** for the second merged profile, and so on.

---

5. In the .ins file, create a **[Connection Manager PBK 0]** section, specify the name of your .pbk file instead of the placeholder (*PhoneBookFileName*), and then copy the information from the .pbk file into this section. Remember to change the brackets in the .pbk file to braces, as covered previously in step 3. For example:

[Connection Manager PBK 0]
PbkName=*PhoneBookFileName*
Contents from this .pbk file

Note If you have merged service profiles that contain phone books, you must create a section for each additional phone book (.pbk) file. Specify a section name of **[Connection Manager PBK 1]** for the first merged phone book, **[Connection Manager PBK 2]** for the second one, and so on.

6. In the .ins file, create a **[Connection Manager PBR 0]** section, specify the name of your .pbr file instead of the placeholder (*PhoneBookRegionFileName*), and then copy the information from the .pbr file into this section. Remember to change the brackets in the .pbr file to braces, as covered previously in step 3. For example:

[Connection Manager PBR 0]
PbrName=*PhoneBookRegionFileName*
Contents from this .pbr file

Note If you have merged service profiles that contain phone books, you must create a section for each additional phone book region (.pbr) file. Specify a section name of **[Connection Manager PBR 1]** for the first merged phone book, **[Connection Manager PBR 2]** for the second one, and so on. Remember that each .pbk file must have a corresponding .pbr file of the same name.

7. In the .ins file, create a **[Connection Manager INF]** section, and then copy the information from the .inf file into this section. Remember to change the brackets in the .inf file to braces, as covered previously in step 3. For example:

[Connection Manager INF]
Contents from the .inf file

8. Before posting the .ins file to your sign-up server, test it on all supported platforms.

Supporting Other Distribution and Installation Methods by Using Command-Line Parameters

If you want to distribute a Connection Manager service profile but don't want to include it in an Internet Explorer installation package, you can use the CMAK wizard separately from the Internet Explorer Connection wizard to build a service profile. You can then distribute this service profile separately or as part of another custom installation package. You will find the information you need to build and distribute a stand-alone service profile in the *CMAK Guide* (see CMAK Help, available by clicking **Help** in the CMAK wizard). However, you may want to customize the distribution and installation method for your service profile. For example, you might want to:

- Distribute and install the Connection Manager service profile over a corporate network using Microsoft Systems Management Server (SMS) to automatically handle the process without user intervention.

- Integrate the Connection Manager service profile with another product's installation package and install them both in a single process.

- Post the Connection Manager service profile to a Web site to enable users to access and install the service profile in a standard way (specifying certain installation options for the user).

These distribution and installation options can be set up programmatically after you have used the CMAK wizard to build your service profile. The Connection Manager installer, Cmstp.exe, supports command-line parameters that can be used to do the following:

- Install a service profile.
- Remove a service profile.
- Remove the Connection Manager software.

The command-line format for Cmstp.exe is as follows:

ServiceProfileFileName.exe /q:a /c:"cmstp.exe *ServiceProfileFileName*.inf *Parameters*"

where:

- *ServiceProfileFileName* is the name of the service profile you build with the CMAK wizard.

- The parameter, q:a, suppresses the prompt that asks users whether they want to install the profile.

- The command, /c:cmstp.exe, tells the extraction program to override the installation defaults.

- *ServiceProfileFileName*.inf is the full path to the file.

- *Parameters* are the command-line parameters supported by the Cmstp.exe installer.

- The following parameters are supported for installation:

  - **/ni**—Do not create a desktop icon (valid only on Windows 95, Windows 98, and Windows NT 4.0) The desktop icon is the only method provided by Connection Manager to enable users to delete a profile. If you use this command-line parameter, you must provide your users with a different way to delete the service profile, such as using an **Add/Remove Programs** script or program. See the /u parameter for information about how to programmatically delete a service profile.

  - **/nf**—Do not install the support files. CMAK automatically incorporates the required support files (.dll files) in each service profile if the service profile contains the Connection Manager software. If you distribute a Connection Manager service profile separately from the Internet Explorer installation package, you can use this option to prevent the support files from being installed. Use this option only if you are sure that your users already have the required support files on their computers (that is, if they already have Windows 98 or Internet Explorer 3.02, or later, installed on their computers).

  - **/s**—Install silently. This option allows automatic installation of the service profile without requiring user action to complete the installation.

  - **/I**—A combination of the /nf and /s parameters, used by the IEAK to install a Connection Manager profile as part of an Internet Explorer installation package.

- The parameters supported for uninstalling and migrating are as follows:

  - **/x**—Uninstall Connection Manager.

  - **/u**—Uninstall the service profile.

Note   To display Help for the command-line installation parameters, type **cmstp.exe /?**.

If you do not specify parameters for the Cmstp.exe file, the following defaults are used on computers running Windows 95, Windows 98, and Windows NT 4.0: the installation is not silent, support files are automatically installed with the profile, and a desktop icon is created. The profile launches upon installation.

CHAPTER 15

Running the Internet Explorer Customization Wizard

You can use the Microsoft Internet Explorer Customization wizard, which comes with the Internet Explorer Administration Kit (IEAK), to customize the appearance and functionality of the browser, its components, and Windows Update Setup for Internet Explorer 5 and Internet Tools. You can also preset browsing options and, if you are a corporate administrator, set system policies and restrictions.

This chapter will help you understand how to use the Customization wizard to create custom Microsoft Internet Explorer 5 packages that you can distribute to your users.

In This Chapter

See Also

- For more information about testing the deployment process before the final rollout, see Chapter 11, "Setting Up and Administering a Pilot Program."

- For more information about preparing to run the Internet Explorer Customization wizard, see Chapter 12, "Preparing for the IEAK."

- For more information about rolling out Internet Explorer to your users, see Chapter 19, "Deploying Microsoft Internet Explorer 5."
- For a list of preparation steps for running the Customization wizard, see Appendix D, "Checklists for Preparing to Use the IEAK."

Understanding How the Customization Wizard Works

The Internet Explorer Customization wizard enables you to create custom packages of Windows Update Setup that you can distribute on various types of media. It also enables Internet service providers (ISPs) to customize existing installations of Internet Explorer.

In addition to ISPs, corporate administrators, and Internet content providers (ICPs) and developers can use the IEAK to customize Internet Explorer. For more information about your role, see the IEAK Web site.

You can create packages in multiple languages. You'll need to create a different package for each language that you will need. For more information about how to create multiple packages efficiently, see Chapter 17, "Time-Saving Strategies That Address Diverse User Needs."

Before you run the Customization wizard, you'll need to plan your deployment and prepare any custom files. For information about planning the deployment, see Chapter 9, "Planning the Deployment." For more information about preparing files for the IEAK, see Chapter 12, "Preparing for the IEAK," and Appendix D, "Checklists for Preparing to Use the IEAK."

Depending on your situation, you might also need to set up servers, such as a network, intranet, or Internet server that users can download files from, proxy servers, an automatic configuration server, and (if you are an ISP you may need a sign-up server. For more information about configuring servers, see Chapter 13, "Setting up Servers."

When you use the Customization wizard, you can choose which features you need. That way, you won't have to view or supply answers to Customization wizard screens that don't apply to your situation. For more information, see "Stage 1: Gathering Information" later in this chapter.

The Customization wizard can either create a package from scratch or import settings from an existing Internet settings (.ins) file. Either way, when you click **Finish** in the wizard, the Customization wizard will build the package.

The custom package includes the following:

- Program files that you have downloaded
- The setup file (IE5Setup.exe, which is based on IESetup.inf)
- The branding cabinet file (Branding.cab, which consists of custom files, including .ins files, information (.inf) files, and any custom files that you have specified)
- The component information cabinet file (IEcif.cab, which includes components and component settings)

The following illustration shows how custom-package generation works.

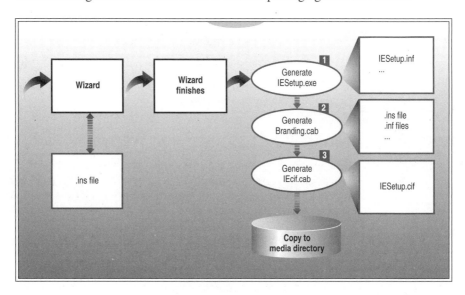

Illustration 15.1   How the IEAK Generates Custom Packages

After the Customization wizard creates these files, you copy them (if needed) to your deployment media. For more information about deployment, see Chapter 19, "Deploying Microsoft Internet Explorer 5."

Stages of the Customization Wizard

You use the Internet Explorer Customization wizard to create packages that install customized versions of Internet Explorer for user groups. The Customization wizard guides you step by step through the customization process.

Running the Customization Wizard

After you install the IEAK, you can run the Customization wizard from the **Start** menu.

▶ **To run the Internet Explorer Customization wizard**

1. On the **Start** menu, point to **Programs**.

2. Point to **Microsoft IEAK**, and then click **Internet Explorer Customization Wizard**.

3. Follow the steps in the wizard.

Navigating Through the Customization Wizard

The Customization wizard provides step-by-step screens that prompt you for the necessary information and files to customize Internet Explorer. For information about preparing information and files, see Chapter 12, "Preparing for the IEAK," and Appendix D, "Checklists for Preparing to Use the IEAK."

After you select a role (corporate administrator, ISP, or ICP/developer) and a platform, the Customization wizard displays the relevant screens for your situation. If you need to return to a wizard screen before you finish the wizard, click **Back** until the screen appears. After you have completed all of the wizard screens, the Customization wizard can build your custom package.

Because the Customization wizard provides a wide range of custom options, some of the wizard screens might not apply to your situation. You need to view only the wizard screens that are necessary for the options you want to customize. In Stage 1 of the wizard, you can clear the options that you don't want to use. This will help you proceed through the wizard more quickly.

Note If you have inadvertently selected options that you don't need and a wizard screen appears that doesn't apply to your situation, just click **Next** to proceed to the next screen.

You specify the feature information that you want to see on the Feature Selection screen of the wizard, as shown in the following illustration.

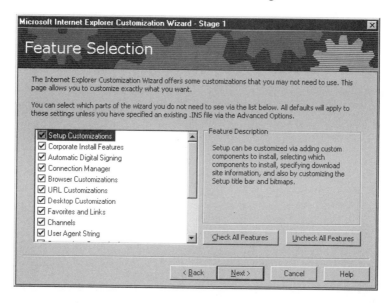

If you've already built a custom package, you can save time when building additional packages that use many of the same options. You can import your settings from the .ins file associated with that package. For more information, see Chapter 17, "Time-Saving Strategies That Address Diverse User Needs."

Note If you run the Internet Explorer Customization wizard from the Microsoft Office Custom Install wizard (CIW), or if you install Internet Explorer "silently" (that is, without user interaction), you will have fewer choices when you run the Internet Explorer Customization wizard. You can select only one setup type, such as **Typical** or **Minimal**, and some options will not be available.

After you have entered all the information in the Internet Explorer Customization wizard, the wizard can create your custom package. You will then need to prepare the distribution media needed by your users. For more information about preparing distribution media for deployment, see Chapter 19, "Deploying Microsoft Internet Explorer 5."

Running the Customization Wizard

The Customization wizard is a step-by-step process organized into five stages:

- Stage 1: Gathering Information
- Stage 2: Specifying Setup Parameters
- Stage 3: Customizing Setup
- Stage 4: Customizing the Browser
- Stage 5: Customizing Components

The following sections provide summaries for the five wizard stages. They cover key information about each stage. You can obtain information about wizard options by clicking **Help** on each screen of the wizard.

Before running the wizard, you should consider reviewing Appendix D, "Checklists for Preparing to Use the IEAK." The checklist specifies the information and files you need to supply depending on your role.

Stage 1: Gathering Information

The Stage 1 options are as follows:

- **Company Name and Customization Code**—First, enter your customization code, provided to you by Microsoft, and your company name. You also need to select your role in this step. The roles—based on your license agreement—are corporate administrator, ISP, or ICP/developer. If you are an independent software vendor (ISV), choose the ICP/developer role.

- **Platform Options**—Determine the platforms that you need to support. All IEAK users can build browser packages for Windows 32-bit and 16-bit versions of Internet Explorer. Corporate administrators can also build UNIX browser packages. For more platform-specific information, see Chapter 4, "Working with Different Platforms."

- **File Locations**—Select the destination folder. You can build a custom package on the computer where you are running the Internet Explorer Customization wizard, and then move the files to servers where users will download them. Another option is to build the files on a network server on your local area network (LAN) or on a Web server, such as Microsoft Internet Information Server (IIS).

  When you build a custom package, folders for each media type are created in your build folder. For flat (network) and download (Web) packages, you can build at the location from which the files will be downloaded.

If your build computer is also set up as a Web server, you can build in a folder from which your users can download the files. For example, if you use IIS, the Web server structure on your local hard disk could be: C:\Inetpub\Wwwroot\Build1. If you build your custom packages in that folder and add a Web page that links to the IE5Setup.exe file in the \Download*platform**language* folder, users can download and install the setup program from your Web server.

To see more options, click the **Advanced Options** button, which will display the Advanced Options dialog box, as shown in the following illustration.

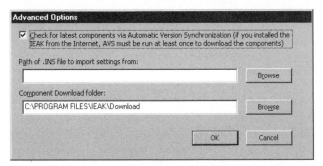

In the Advanced Options dialog box, you'll find the following settings:

- **Check for latest components via Automatic Version Synchronization**—
  Select this check box to indicate that the Customization wizard should check on the Internet for the latest versions of components when you create your custom package. By default, this setting is selected. In most cases, this default is the recommended setting. If you have downloaded the IEAK from the Internet, you must run the Customization wizard with Automatic Version Synchronization (AVS) at least once, so that the wizard can check for updated versions of components. For more information about AVS, see Chapter 16, "Customizing Setup."

- **Path of .INS file to import settings from**—To use an existing .ins file as the starting point for a new custom package, enter the full path to the .ins file. You can save time by importing settings from an .ins file if the settings needed for the new package are similar to those of an existing package. After the settings have been imported, you can use the Customization wizard to refine them to fit your needs.

- **Component Download folder**—Use this box to specify the location for the components and setup files that you'll download. If you change this location, the AVS feature will not be able to determine whether you have the latest components available. You should change this folder only if you plan to retain the files that you downloaded the last time you ran the wizard for archiving, and you want to download a new set of components.

- **Language Selection**—Specify a target language so that your build can be placed in a localized subfolder for the appropriate platform and media type. You must run the Customization wizard for each language version that you plan to deploy. For strategies for doing this efficiently, see Chapter 17, "Time-Saving Strategies That Address Diverse User Needs."

Note You can install a language version of Internet Explorer that doesn't match your operating system, provided that you are not installing the Windows Desktop Update. If users attempt to install the browser with the Windows Desktop Update in a language different from that of the operating system, only the browser will be installed.

In addition, if you are a corporate administrator, and you import your security zones from a different language version of Internet Explorer, there may be some unrecognizable characters in the users' Security Zones user interface.

- **Media Selection**—Select the distribution methods you plan to use: download (for Internet or intranet download), compact disc, flat (for network download), multiple floppy disks (ISPs and ICPs only), single floppy disk (ISPs only), or single-disk branding. You will need additional disk space for each type of media that you select.

  You can use single-disk branding to customize the browser on computers where Internet Explorer 4.01 Service Pack 1 or higher is already installed. Single-disk branding enables you to customize Internet Explorer features, including Internet sign-up (if you're an ISP), without reinstalling Internet Explorer. This option, however, does not enable you to package and install custom components. It creates a Setup.exe file in the \BrndOnly folder of your build folder, which you can distribute on any media or on a server.

- **Feature Selection**—On this screen, select the features that you want to customize or clear the features that you don't want to see.

Stage 2: Specifying Setup Parameters

Windows Update Setup for Internet Explorer 5 and Internet Tools is a small, Web-based setup package that lets users install the latest Internet Explorer components directly from a Web site. When Windows Update Setup downloads Internet Explorer 5, it breaks it up into several small segments. This makes it possible, in the event of a failure or dropped connection, to restart an installation from where it was interrupted, instead of having to start over from the beginning.

The Stage 2 options are as follows:

- **Download Locations**—Select the Microsoft site from which you will download the browser and other Internet components you plan to deploy. It's recommended that you choose a location close to your region.

- **Automatic Version Synchronization**—Download or update Microsoft components used to build the package. You must download Internet Explorer to proceed with the wizard. You should also download any component that you plan to install or make available to users using Automatic Install. For more information about Automatic Install, see Chapter 16, "Customizing Setup."

- **Add Custom Components**—Enter information about the optional custom components that you want to include. This option can be helpful if you have custom programs or scripts that you want to distribute with Internet Explorer. For more information about creating custom components, see Chapter 12, "Preparing for the IEAK."

Stage 3: Customizing Setup

You can customize the setup program in several different ways. In addition to specifying screen options in the wizard, you can also use a setup batch file or command-line switches. For more information, see Chapter 16, "Customizing Setup."

The Stage 3 options are as follows:

- **CD-ROM Autorun Customizations**—If you are creating a CD-ROM package, specify an optional custom CD-ROM Autorun screen. The Autorun screen is a graphical interface that appears when users insert the CD-ROM for 32-bit versions of Internet Explorer. To create the screen, you'll need to provide a path to a bitmap and specify other graphical options. For more information about graphics requirements, see Chapter 12, "Preparing for the IEAK," and Appendix D, "Checklists for Preparing to Use the IEAK."

- **More CD Options**—For more information, provide a text file—such as a readme file—that appears as a link from the Autorun screen. Another option is to specify an HTML page that opens in the user's browser in Kiosk mode, without the toolbar showing.

Note To customize the CD Autorun screens, you must create a CD build of Internet Explorer. If you do not see the CD-ROM Autorun Customizations or the More CD Options screens, and you want to set CD-ROM custom options, click **Back** until you see the Media Selection screen. Then, select the **CD-ROM** option, and click **Next** until you see the CD-ROM screens.

- **Customize Setup**—Use this option to customize how the setup program appears to your users. You can change the title bar and the graphic that appears when users run the Windows Update Setup wizard. If you provide a group of customized components, you can assign a name to them. For more information about customizing the appearance of the setup program, see Chapter 12, "Preparing for the IEAK," Chapter 16, "Customizing Setup," and Appendix D, "Checklists for Preparing to Use the IEAK."

- **Silent Install (corporate administrators only)**—Depending on how you plan to install your custom packages, decide whether to provide your users with an interactive installation, a hands-free installation with prompts if errors occur, or an installation with no prompts.

Note In a silent install, you can specify only one installation option and one download site for your users.

The following settings determine how much interaction occurs between the setup program and the user:

- If you want to provide an interactive installation for your users, in which they make installation decisions, click **Interactive install**.

- If you want to provide a hands-free installation, in which users aren't prompted to make decisions, but are informed of the installation progress and errors, click **Hands-free install**.

- If you want your users to install the custom browser without receiving prompts, click **Completely silent install**. You should select this option when you want to control all setup options and suppress feedback to the user. If installation does not finish successfully, users will not see an error message.

- **Installation Options**—Specify up to 10 unique installation options. You can also determine which components are included with each option.

  Installation options can be helpful if your users have different needs. For example, if you're an ISP, you might want to create a setup option for customers who subscribe to a specific set of services. If you're a corporate administrator, you might want to specify setup options for different divisions of your company.

Note If you are installing Internet Explorer 5 on a computer that has never run Internet Explorer 4.0, and you want your users to have channels, add the Offline Browsing Pack to your installation.

- **Download Sites**—Specify at least one download site, using an HTTP or FTP server, from which your users can download your package. You can, however, specify up to 10 sites for downloads. You must place all the Microsoft components and custom components at each URL you specify.

- **Component Information**—Decide whether you'll have your users download additional components from Microsoft, or install components from your original media or download servers by using a custom add-on component page. The component page appears when users click the **Tools** menu, and then click **Windows Update** or click the **Add/Remove Programs** icon in Control Panel. For more information about setting up a custom component page, see Chapter 12, "Preparing for the IEAK."

- **Installation Directory**—Decide how to handle the installation directory. You can allow the user to choose the location for installing Internet Explorer, or you can specify the location. You can specify a folder in the Windows folder, the Program Files folder, or enter a complete custom path. If Internet Explorer is already installed on the user's computer, the new version is installed over the existing version. The customized browser, in that case, is not installed in the custom location you specify.

- **Corporate Install Options (corporate administrators only)**—Decide to what extent users can customize the setup program. You can specify whether they can run a custom installation to add or remove specific components, or select the Internet Explorer compatibility mode. You can also specify whether the uninstall information is saved or whether Internet Explorer is set as the default browser.

Note Less disk space is needed if the uninstall information is not saved on the user's hard disk. However, in that case, the user will not be able to remove Internet Explorer 5 by clicking the **Add/Remove Programs** icon in Control Panel, and some troubleshooting steps may be more difficult. For more information, see Chapter 11, "Setting Up and Administering a Pilot Program."

- **Advanced Installation Options**—Further customize the setup program by having it detect whether a component already exists on the user's computer and by fine-tuning which components users can add if they customize the setup process.

  If you want the setup program to detect whether the same version of a component is already installed on the user's computer, select the **Optimize for Web download** check box. If a version of the same component is already installed, and it will work with Internet Explorer 5, the setup program does not download it. This can save download time.

If your users can customize their installations, but you don't want them to customize specific components, clear the check boxes for the components that you do not want the users to be able to customize. **Force Install** appears in the right column beside the components that will be installed automatically with the browser.

- **Connection Manager Customization (ISPs and corporate administrators only)**—Use the Connection Manager Administration Kit (CMAK) to customize and manage how users connect to the Internet. With the CMAK, you can change the appearance and settings of the Connection Manager dialer. For more information about the Connection Manager Administration Kit, see Chapter 14, "Customizing Connection Management and Settings."

- **Windows Desktop Update (corporate administrators only)**—Decide whether to include the Windows Desktop Update. The Windows Desktop Update makes the desktop and folders look and work more like the Web. Although the Windows Desktop Update is not a part of Internet Explorer 5, you can include it with your custom package. If your users are running Windows 98, they already have the desktop features.

  If you choose to install the Windows Desktop Update, you can customize its settings in Stage 4 of the wizard if your build computer is running one of the following configurations:

  - Internet Explorer 5 upgraded from Internet Explorer 4.0 with the Windows Desktop Update installed

  - Internet Explorer 5 and Windows 98, which includes the new desktop

  This option can be helpful in configuring a corporate standard desktop.

- **Digital Signatures**—Determine whether to digitally sign files. If you have a publisher certificate from a certification authority or from Microsoft Certificate Server, you can have the Customization wizard sign your custom package. Digital signatures show where programs come from and verify that they haven't been altered. Signing custom files can be critical if users are downloading Internet Explorer from the Internet or an intranet that isn't specially configured, since security settings in the user's browser can prevent unsigned controls and programs from being downloaded.

  To prepare certificates for use by the IEAK, you can import them to your computer by using the Certificate Manager Import wizard. Then, in the Customization wizard, specify the paths to the software publishing certificates (.spc) and private key (.pvk) files, or click **Browse** to locate them. For more information about importing certificates, see Chapter 12, "Preparing for the IEAK."

Stage 4: Customizing the Browser

In this stage, you can customize the appearance and functionality of the browser. ISPs can also specify settings for Internet sign-up.

The Stage 4 options are as follows:

- **Browser Title**—Use this option to customize the text that appears in the title bar of the Internet Explorer Web browser and Outlook Express, if you include Outlook Express in your package. Type the string that you want to appear. It will be added after the text "Microsoft Internet Explorer Provided by" or "Outlook Express Provided by."

- **Browser Toolbar Buttons**—Use this option to customize the toolbar buttons in the user's browser. You can specify the script or program that the buttons launch, as well as their appearance. For more information about designing custom programs, see the MSDN Online Web site. For more information about designing toolbar icons, see Chapter 12, "Preparing for the IEAK."

- **Internet Explorer Logos**—Determine whether you want to customize the logo. The Internet Explorer logo in the upper-right corner of the browser appears in two states: animated when the browser is in use and static when no action is taking place. You can replace the logo bitmap with your own animated or static bitmap. For more information about preparing the logo files, see Chapter 12, "Preparing for the IEAK," and Appendix D, "Checklists for Preparing to Use the IEAK."

  If you use an animated bitmap, the first frame appears static when no action is taking place in the browser, and the remaining frames appear animated when the browser is in use. To use your own animated logo, you must provide two animated bitmaps; one should be 22-by-22 pixels and the other 38-by-38 pixels.

  If you use a static bitmap, it will appear static whether or not any action is taking place in the browser. To use your own static logo, you must provide two bitmaps; one should be 22-by-22 pixels and the other 38-by-38 pixels. Type the paths of the small and large custom static bitmaps in the boxes on this page.

- **Important URLs**—Determine whether you want to specify URLs for the home, search, and online support pages.

  The home page, sometimes known as a start page, appears when the user clicks the **Home** button. Internet Explorer can show a default home page, or you can specify a URL for your own page.

  The Search bar appears in the Explorer bar on the left side of the screen. This bar enables a user to see the search query and search results at the same time. The Search bar comes with the Search Assistant and multiple search engines. You can overwrite this page if you want.

In Internet Explorer, support information is available by clicking **Help**, and then clicking **Online Support**. It's recommended that you develop a support page and make it available to your users.

■ **Favorites and Links**—Customize the Favorites folder and Links bar by adding links. For example, you might want to add links related to your organization or services. You can add links to the default folders or add new folders. When a user clicks **Favorites**, the Favorites list appears on the left side of the window. The Links bar appears by default at the top of the user's screen, and it comes with a set of default links.

You can move Favorites to the top of the users' Favorites list, so they are easier for the user to find. If you are a corporate administrator, you can also delete items on the users' Favorites and Links lists. It is recommended that you use this setting with caution, however, because it removes the links and favorites that the users have set up for their own use.

▶ **To add a folder to the Favorites list or Links bar**

1. Click **Favorites**, **Links**, or a folder within **Favorites** or **Links**, and then click **Add Folder**.

2. Type the name of your folder in the **Name** box. This can be a friendly name that helps the user recognize what types of links are in the folder.

Note You can import a folder containing links by clicking **Import**, or you can click an existing folder to create a new subfolder.

▶ **To add a Web page to the Favorites list or Links bar**

1. Click **Favorites**, **Links**, or a folder within **Favorites** or **Links**, and then click **Add URL**.

2. Type a name for this Web page in the **Name** box. This can be a friendly name that helps the user recognize what the link refers to.

3. Type the path of your link in the **URL** box.

4. To specify a 16-by-16-pixel custom icon, type the name of the file in the **Icon** box.

5. To make this page available to users when they aren't connected to the Internet, select the **Make available offline** check box. This option is often helpful for users with laptop computers.

Note Do not use semicolons and slashes in the titles of Links or Links folders.

- **Channels**—Add a custom channel or channel category (folder), or import the channel settings from your computer. When you import channels, you can further customize them. For example, you could import your channel settings, but delete one of the channels you import.

  To add channels, you should already have information about your channel or channel category, such as the path to the images and the titles you want to use. You should also have a Channel Definition Format (.cdf) file for each channel.

  If you are a corporate administrator, you can delete existing channels on the user's computer. You can also set up the Channel bar on the user's desktop if you are setting up the Windows Desktop Update or installing Internet Explorer 5 on Windows 98 computers.

  For more information about channels and dimensions for these files, see Chapter 12, "Preparing for the IEAK," and Appendix D, "Checklists for Preparing to Use the IEAK."

- **Welcome page**—Determine whether to customize the welcome page, which Internet Explorer displays when the browser is first started. You can display the default Internet Explorer welcome page, or you can specify your own custom welcome page. The welcome page can be different than the home page, which is the page that opens when the user starts the browser after the first time or clicks the **Home** button.

- **Folder Webviews (corporate administrators only)**—Use this option to customize how My Computer and Control Panel appear on your company's computers by customizing the files that serve as templates for them. Then, if the user installs the Windows Desktop Update, My Computer and Control Panel can appear as Web pages. One reason to customize these folders is to provide instructions, a company logo, or links to support or corporate sites. To customize Folder Webviews, specify the path to the custom Mycomp.htt file for My Computer and Controlp.htt for Control Panel. For more information about preparing these files, see Chapter 12, "Preparing for the IEAK."

- **User Agent String**—Some companies track site statistics, such as how many times Web content is accessed and by which types of Web browsers. User agent strings help identify the browser type when compiling those statistics.

  You can append a custom string to the user-agent string for Internet Explorer. You do not need to customize the user-agent string, unless you want to track the usage of your custom browser and you gather browser statistics from other Internet sites.

  Your customized string will appear in any statistics that include the user-agent string. Because other companies that track statistics will see your customized string, avoid using a string that you don't want others to see.

  The following syntax shows a user-agent string to which a customized string has been added:

  Mozilla/4.0(compatible; MSIE 5.0; WindowsNT; *YourCustomString*)

- **Automatic Configuration (corporate administrators only)**—Assign URLs to files that will automatically configure the customized browsers. This feature is helpful if you want to control the settings of several users from one central location. For more information about automatic configuration, see Chapter 21, "Using Automatic Configuration and Automatic Proxy."

  You can configure options by using .ins files, which you can edit with the IEAK Profile Manager. You can include standard proxy settings in the .ins file. For 32-bit and 16-bit versions of the browser, you can also specify script files in JScript (.js), JavaScript (.jvs), or proxy automatic configuration (.pac) format that enable you to configure and maintain advanced proxy settings.

  If you specify URLs for both automatic configuration and automatic proxy, the automatic proxy URL will be incorporated into the .ins file. The correct form for the URL is http://share/test.ins.

  Network servers using Domain Name System (DNS) and Dynamic Host Configuration Protocol (DHCP) can automatically detect and configure a browser's proxy settings using proxy configuration keys.

  You can specify the interval in minutes for the automatic configuration feature. If you enter zero or don't enter a value, automatic configuration happens only when the user's computer is restarted.

- **Connection Settings**—Preset connection settings for your users by importing the connection settings from your computer. To import the settings on your computer, click **Import the current connection settings**. If the settings displayed are not the settings you want to use, you can change them. If you are a corporate administrator, you can clear the existing settings on your users' computers by clicking **Delete existing connection settings, if present**. For more information about connection settings, see Chapter 14, "Customizing Connection Management and Settings."

- **Desktop Toolbars (Corporate administrators only)**—Determine whether to support desktop toolbars. If users have the new desktop, they can add toolbars to the Windows taskbar. These toolbars make it easier for them to get to programs, files, folders, subscriptions, and favorite Web pages. They can also position toolbars on any part of your desktop and resize them. To specify desktop toolbars, you must include the Windows Desktop Update in your browser package, and run the desktop on your build computer. You can import your current settings by clicking **Import the current Desktop Toolbar settings**.

- **Active Desktop**—Determine whether to provide the Active Desktop. The Active Desktop enables users to put Web content, such as weather maps that update on a regular schedule, on their desktops. You can import the settings on your desktop as the corporate standard so that all users have the same desktop. In the next stage of the wizard, you can determine whether users can change those settings. You must include the Windows Desktop Update in your browser package and be running the desktop on your build computer. To use your current settings as the standard desktop for your company, click **Import the current Active Desktop components**.

- **Add a Root Certificate**—Add a root certificate to your custom package by typing the URL into the **New root certificate path** box. The root certificate provides a level of trust that certificates lower in the hierarchy can inherit. Each certificate is inspected for a parent certificate until it reaches the root certificate.

- **Sign-up Method (ISPs only)**—If you are an ISP, use this option to specify how users sign up with your service and connect to the Internet. You can create server solutions that exchange information with the screens of the Internet Connection wizard or with the browser in Kiosk mode, without toolbar buttons showing. You can also select a serverless sign-up method. This method doesn't require a sign-up server; it works locally on the user's computer instead. The server-based solutions provide a more dynamic way to interact with users and update information, but serverless sign-up enables you to sign users up for Internet services without a sign-up server. For more information about Internet sign-up, see Chapter 13, "Setting up Servers," and Chapter 20, "Implementing the Sign-up Process."

- **Sign-up Files (ISPs only)**—Use this option to include sign-up files. The Customization wizard checks for copies of the Internet sign-up files and prompts you to copy them to the build folder. After you copy them, you can modify the Internet sign-up (.isp) and Internet settings(.ins) files. If you choose to modify these files, additional screens of the wizard will be displayed so that you can change their settings.

  If you have entered these settings manually in the past, you may find the graphical method more intuitive. If you prefer to enter these settings manually, however, you can have the wizard check for these files and then copy them to the build folder.

- **Sign-up Server Information and Internet Settings Files (ISPs only)**—Use these options to specify sign-up options. On the Sign-up Server Information screen, you can configure your users' dial-up connections, so they can make a connection to your Internet server. On the Internet Settings Files screen, you provide settings that the Customization wizard uses to generate an .ins file. The .ins file can be posted on your server or incorporated into the custom package you are creating for serverless sign-up. For more information about Internet sign-up, see Chapter 13, "Setting up Servers," and Chapter 20, "Implementing the Sign-up Process." Note that some options may not be displayed, depending on the type of sign-up solution you are preparing.

Enter the dialing and connection information, and then click **Advanced Options** to configure the following:

- **Use static DNS address**— To ensure that all DNS servers will be searched in an attempt to map name and IP addresses, select this check box and type a primary and alternate address. DNS is a set of protocols and services for Transmission Control Protocol/Internet Protocol (TCP/IP) networks. DNS enables you to use "friendly names," such as www.microsoft.com, instead of numeric addresses.

- **Requires Logon**—Set this if you need to ensure that the client computer has Windows logon authentication turned on. Providing a Windows password enables access to the Windows password cache, where the ISP password is stored. This option is particularly useful if you assign long random strings as passwords. This option is valid for Windows 95 and Windows 98 clients only.

- **Negotiate TCP/IP**— Specifies whether to enable TCP/IP negotiation in establishing an Internet connection.

- **Disable LCP**— Indicates whether to use the Link Control Protocol (LCP) extensions in establishing a Point-to-Point protocol link. If the sign-up server cannot handle LCP extensions, then you should disable LCP on the client computer that will be connecting to your server. This value is valid for Windows NT 4.0 clients only.

- **Dial number as shown**—Use this option to prevent a default area code from being set. You might want to set this option if, for example, some users might be calling from an area code different from the default. If users aren't aware that the default area code differs from their current area code, they could unexpectedly incur long-distance charges.

- **Encrypt passwords**—Use to specify that only encrypted passwords can be sent to, or accepted by, your computer. This option is useful if you need additional security for a connection. The computer you are connecting to must support encrypted passwords for this option to take effect.

- **Use software compression**—Use to specify whether incoming or outgoing information is compressed before it is sent. This option is useful to speed up the transfer of information. Compression occurs only if both computers are using compatible compression.

- **Use IP header compression**—Determine whether to use TCP/IP header compression. This compression is designed to improve the efficiency of bandwidth use over low-speed serial links. It typically optimizes data transfer between computers. By reconstructing a smaller header that identifies the connection and indicates the fields that changed, fewer bytes can be transmitted. For compression to work, packets must arrive in order.

Compression may not always be desirable. For example, if you are using older equipment, you may not be able to use compression. For the sake of interoperability, serial-line IP drivers that allow header compression should include some sort of user-configurable flag to disable compression.

- **Use default remote gateway**—Use to specify whether IP traffic is routed to the wide area network (WAN) connection by default. A gateway is a connection or interchange point that connects two networks that otherwise would be incompatible.

- **Branding file information**—You can specify whether to apply branding information to or modify branding information in the Internet sign-up or Internet settings file that you create by using the Customization wizard.

- **Internet Connection wizard (ISPs only)**—You can specify the Internet Connection wizard (ICW) as the tool that customers use to sign up for Internet services. You can create server solutions that exchange information with the screens of the ICW. This feature is not available for the serverless sign-up method. For more information about Internet sign-up, see Chapter 13, "Setting up Servers," and Chapter 20, "Implementing the Sign-up Process." For more information about preparing graphics files for ICW sign-up, see Chapter 12, "Preparing for the IEAK," and Appendix D, "Checklists for Preparing to Use the IEAK."

You will need to include the Dynamic HTML Data Binding component with your browser package to ensure that the Internet Connection wizard can interact with your server. Data binding allows the wizard page to display the list of .isp files in Signup.txt. You can specify that this option does not appear as a custom installation choice, so that users cannot choose not to install it. To do this, on the Advanced Installation Options screen, clear the **Dynamic HTML Data Binding** check box; **Force Install** will appear in the right-hand column.

- **Security (corporate administrators only)**—Use certification authorities and Authenticode technology to help manage security. You can use certification authorities to control the sites where users can download certain content, such as ActiveX controls. Site authorities are a form of digital certificate for an Internet site.

Authenticode technology is used to show where programs come from and verify that they haven't been altered. You can import these settings from your computer. If you want to modify the settings that you will apply to your users' computers, click **Import current certification authorities**, and then click **Modify Settings**. You can then use Certificate Manager to view and manage your certification authorities information. Certificates can apply to network server authentication, network client authentication, secure e-mail authentication, and software publishing.

You can use Authenticode technology to designate software publishers and credentials agencies as trustworthy. You can also import these settings from your computer. If you want to modify the settings that you will apply to your users' computers, click **Import current Authenticode security information**, and then click **Modify Settings**.

- **Security Settings (corporate administrators only)**—Use this option to manage security zones and content ratings for your company. You can customize the settings for each security zone. Through content ratings, you can also prevent users from viewing content that may be considered offensive. If you want to modify the settings that will be installed on your users' computers, click **Import the current security zone settings** setting, and then click **Modify Settings**. In Stage 5, you can also specify whether users will be able to change their security settings.

Note that the following settings do not apply to UNIX and 16-bit versions of the browser:

Settings not available for

UNIX versions of the browser	16-bit versions of the browser
ActiveX controls and plugins	Active scripting
Font download	Font download
Software channel permissions	Software channel permissions
Launching applications and files	Launching applications and files from an IFRAME element
Installation of desktop items	Installation of desktop items
	User authentication

Internet Explorer 5 helps you control the types of content that your users' computers can access on the Internet. You can adjust the settings to reflect what you think is appropriate content in four areas: language, nudity, sex, and violence. If you want to modify the ratings that you will apply to your users' computers, click **Import the current content ratings settings**, and then click **Modify Settings**. You can then modify your settings by using Content Advisor.

Note Content Advisor uses very cautious ratings standards when you first enable it. You can adjust these settings to match your own preferences. Not all Internet content is rated. If you choose to allow others to view unrated sites, some of those sites could contain inappropriate material.

Stage 5: Customizing Components

In this stage, ISPs and corporate administrators can customize Outlook Express and Windows Address Book settings, if these components are included with their Internet Explorer package. For more information about Outlook Express, see Chapter 2, "Microsoft Internet Explorer 5 Components."

Corporate administrators who are distributing UNIX packages can also specify UNIX-specific file associations and default programs.

Corporate administrators, ISPs, and ICPs/developers can specify Internet settings. To see the current settings, click the **Tools** menu in **Internet Explorer**, and then click **Internet Options**. Corporate administrators can also determine whether users can change their settings.

The Stage 5 options are as follows:

- **Servers and Accounts**—Specify the e-mail and news servers and indicate whether you will require users to log on using Secure Password Authentication (SPA) to access a server. You can use also "lock down," or control, account settings for your users. When users set up their accounts, such as e-mail and news, those accounts will be configured using the restrictions you specify.

  You can specify the following server and account information:

  - **Choose mail server type**—Select the protocol that your e-mail servers are running. You can choose Post Office Protocol 3 (POP3), used by most Internet subscribers for e-mail, or Internet Mail Access protocol (IMAP), used mainly by corporate users who want to read their e-mail from a remote location. POP3 servers allow access to a single inbox, while IMAP servers provide access to multiple server-side folders.

  - **Incoming mail server**—Type the fully qualified server address in the text box—for example, pop01.microsoft.com. Then, click **Log on using SPA** (Secure Password Authentication) if your POP3 or IMAP server requires authentication from a Security Support Provider Interface (SSPI) provider such as NT LAN Manager (NTLM).

  - **Outgoing mail (SMTP) server**—Specify the SMTP server for outgoing e-mail. In some cases, the SMTP server may have the same name as your POP3 server—for example, smtp.microsoft.com. Type the fully qualified SMTP server address in the text box. Then, click **Log on using SPA** (Secure Password Authentication) if your SMTP server requires authentication from an SSPI provider such as NTLM.

- **Internet news server**—Specify the Internet news server by typing in an Network News Transfer Protocol (NNTP) address. NNTP is the protocol used to distribute network news messages to NNTP servers and to NNTP clients (news readers) on the Internet. Type the NNTP address in the text box—for example, nntp.microsoft.com. Then, click **Log on using SPA** (Secure Password Authentication) if your NNTP server requires authentication from an SSPI provider such as NTLM.

- **Make all preconfigured accounts read-only**—Select this option to create account settings that can be viewed, but not modified, by users.

- **Prevent deletion of all preconfigured accounts**—Select this option to prevent users from deleting accounts that you have preconfigured for them.

- **Prevent configuration of additional accounts for users with preconfigured accounts**—Select this option to prevent users from creating accounts in addition to the preconfigured accounts created for them. This option is recommended for corporate administrators only.

- **Outlook Express IMAP Settings**—Create default IMAP settings for your users. These settings are preconfigured for users when they create their IMAP accounts. The root folder path is the mailbox that contains all of the users' folders on the IMAP server. For Cyrus servers, all users' folders must be contained in the Inbox folder. For UNIX-based IMAP servers, e-mail is usually stored in its own folder in the user's home folder—for example, ~username/Mail. Do not end the root folder path with a hierarchy character. For example, ~username/Mail is a valid root folder path, but ~username/Mail/ is not. Some IMAP servers, such as Microsoft Exchange Server, do not require a root folder path.

  To specify that folders for the users' sent messages and in-progress messages should be created on the IMAP server, select **Store special folders on IMAP server**. You can also specify the path for the Sent Items folder and Draft folder. These paths will be used by all users who create IMAP accounts.

  To automatically poll all of an IMAP user's subscribed folders for changes in the number of messages, select **Check for new messages** under the **Check for new messages in subscribed folders** area. This polling happens when the user starts Outlook Express as well as at the user's regular e-mail-polling interval. If this option is not selected, Outlook Express checks for new messages only in the Inbox.

- **Outlook Express Custom Content**—Give Outlook Express a custom look and welcome new users with an e-mail message by using this option. The Outlook Express InfoPane is an area for content providers to place helpful information and links. You can customize this pane with support numbers, frequently asked questions (FAQs), and information about your company. This can be a URL to a file on a server or a local file.

The InfoPane appears as a 50-pixel high panel at the bottom of the Outlook Express main window. You can customize the InfoPane with an HTML file that is either a local file or an Internet address (URL). If you specify a local file, that file will be copied into your custom package and subsequently copied onto the user's computer during installation.

Note The InfoPane does not appear as part of the Outlook Express user interface, unless a URL or file is specified in the Customization wizard.

You can also provide a welcome message as the first item in each user's Inbox. The welcome message is an HTML file. You must also provide the sender's friendly name—for example, your company or organization name—and the recipient's e-mail address. The Customization wizard does not provide a way to add an image to the welcome message. However, if you edit the welcome message outside of the IEAK, you can add a link to an image from the Web.

- **Outlook Express Custom Settings**—Use this option to specify Outlook Express settings that will apply to all of your users. These include setting a default e-mail and news client. Also, you can provide information that users need to obtain additional e-mail accounts. Finally, you can provide a default message rules file for your users.

  If you want Outlook Express to start whenever a user clicks an e-mail link in Internet Explorer, select the **Make Outlook Express the default mail program** check box. If you want Outlook Express to start whenever a user clicks a news link in Internet Explorer, select the **Make Outlook Express the default news program** check box. The default e-mail client setting is also used by many programs when a user sends documents by e-mail. Note that this replaces any current default e-mail client that the user has specified.

  You can specify one or more newsgroups that you want your users to be subscribed to automatically. For example, your ISP or organization may have several newsgroups that provide assistance and information beneficial to your users.

  You can add a menu item that users can click to get an additional e-mail account from your ISP. This entry is added to the **New Account From** menu in Outlook Express. Type the name of your ISP in the **Service Name** box. Then, type a URL in the **Service URL** box. When the user chooses this service name from the menu, the Web page is opened. An account number, which can be specified in the .ins file, and a unique identifier for the user will be sent to the ISP when the Web page is opened.

■ **Outlook Express View Settings**—Customize views that determine which elements of Outlook Express are displayed and how they are displayed.

You can use the following basic settings to determine which elements of the Outlook Express interface are included in the default view for new users.

- ■ To include the Folder bar as a default for users, select the **Folder bar** check box.

- ■ To include a list of e-mail and news folders in the left column, select the **Folder list** check box.

- ■ To display a tip every time Outlook Express is started, select the **Tip of the Day** check box.

- ■ To display the status bar, which appears at the bottom of the Outlook Express window, select **Status Bar**.

- ■ To display the Outlook Bar, a horizontal bar that displays certain folders, such as the Inbox, select **Outlook Bar**.

You can choose whether you want users to see the toolbar and whether you want to include text on it. The toolbar appears at the top of the Outlook Express window. It contains buttons that correspond to common commands and can be configured by the user.

You have the option of including a message preview pane for your users' default view of e-mail and news messages. The preview pane can either be a horizontal pane located below the list of messages, or a vertical pane located beside and to the right of the list of messages. The preview pane includes a *preview pane header* area that can be used to display message header information, including the From, To, Cc, and Subject lines of the message.

■ **Outlook Express Compose Settings**—Use this setting to include a default signature, such as a corporate disclaimer, that will appear in Outlook Express newsgroup or e-mail messages. A disclaimer is often used to show that messages submitted by employees over the Internet do not represent official company policies. The maximum size of the signature is 1 KB. You can append signatures only to newsgroup messages, only to e-mail messages, or to both types of messages.

By default, e-mail messages are composed in HTML, and news postings are composed in plain text. You can choose to override these settings with the **HTML vs. plain text for mail and news messages** setting. For example, in an environment where bandwidth is limited or many users have simple e-mail programs that cannot understand HTML, changing the default to plain text might make sense.

- **Windows Address Book Directory Service**—Specify additional directory service options for the Windows Address Book. Directory services are powerful search tools that help your users find people and businesses around the world. The Windows Address Book supports LDAP (Lightweight Directory Access Protocol) for accessing directory services, and it comes with built-in access to several popular directory services.

You can specify the following Address Book Directory Service settings:

- **Service Name**—Type the friendly name of your LDAP service. This is the name that will be displayed to your users.

- **Server Name**—Type the name of the directory service you want to add, such as ldap.AcmeISP.com or ldap.switchboard.com. If you require authentication for an SSPI package, such as NTLM, for users who access these services, click the **Logon using SPA** check box. Basic authentication using a user name and password combination can be configured by using .ins files.

- **Service Web Site**—Use this setting to specify the service Web site. This is the directory service's home page that appears if the user clicks the **Start** button, points to **Find**, clicks **People**, and then clicks **Web Site**.

- **Search base**—Identify the search base, which is sometimes known as the root or scope. The search base, which is the hierarchical level that a given LDAP server uses to search, can be a country, organization, or other type of grouping. The Outlook Express default for the search base when none is specified is "c=us." To specify no search base, type **NULL**.

- **Service bitmap**—Specify a custom 134-by-38-pixel, 16-color .bmp file to identify the directory service. To ensure consistent color mapping, it is highly recommended that you use only the Windows 16-bit color palette when composing the bitmap. To locate the .bmp file on your computer, click **Browse**.

- **Search timeout**—Specify how long your users will wait before the browser times out a search request by using the slider to set a time value between 30 seconds and 5 minutes.

- **Maximum number of matches to return**—Control the maximum number of results that can be returned to your users by typing the number in this box.

- **Name resolution**—To have Outlook Express resolve names against the server when a user sends a message, select **Check names against this server when sending mail**. This setting instructs Outlook Express to look up e-mail addresses for names typed on the To, Cc, and Bcc lines of an e-mail message.

- **UNIX Mappings (corporate administrators only)**—If you are deploying a UNIX package, specify options for associating extensions and MIME (Multipurpose Internet Mail Extensions) types with a program so that the appropriate program starts when a user clicks a link. To create a new association, click **New**. To remove an association, click **Delete**.

Type the associations, description, extensions, and the MIME type to associate with each program. A MIME type enables a browser to differentiate between different file types using a type designation rather than a file extension.

Type the command line or program that you want to execute when a file is opened or a link of this type is clicked. If a script is placed into the bin folder of the installation directory, you do not need to include path information. You should include the program name, followed by a space, and %1 as shown in the following example:

```
component %1
```

- **UNIX Programs**—Use these settings to specify which programs will run when the user performs tasks related to e-mail, newsgroups, or printing, or when the user views the HTML source of a page.

Type the name of the program to use as a default e-mail client, or select the **Use Outlook Express as default e-mail client** check box. Type the name of the program to use for reading and posting (sending) newsgroup messages, the name of the program to use for printing tasks, and the name of the program to use when the user views the HTML source of Web pages.

Type the name of the folder that contains additional font caches you would like to install with this browser package. A font cache is a summary listing the characteristics of fonts that are available on a display. A font cache is used by Internet Explorer for UNIX to efficiently determine the best match for the fonts requested by each page of content. There is a different font cache for each combination of server release and font path. A number of prebuilt font caches are supplied with the product. They are installed into the following folder and listed in the readme file located there: /*path*/Common/Fontcache.

When Internet Explorer starts for the first time, the program checks the /*path*/Common/Fontcache folder for the appropriate font cache file. If Internet Explorer is started with an X server or font path that is not represented in the preinstalled set, the program creates a new font cache for that configuration.

The first time the user runs Internet Explorer, the browser starts more slowly if a prebuilt font cache is not available. After Internet Explorer is started again with the same configuration, it uses the same font cache. To reduce initial startup time, you can create font caches in advance for your most common configurations and add them to your custom package using the Customization wizard.

If you would like to add additional font caches to your browser package, carry out the following procedure.

▶ **To add a prebuilt UNIX font cache**

1. Install and run the browser using the configurations for which you want to create font caches.

2. For each configuration, identify the newest files in the Fontcache folder of the Common subfolder. This is the font cache that was built automatically for your current configuration.

3. After you create caches for your common configurations, move the caches to a place accessible from the Windows computer where you will be running the Internet Explorer Customization wizard.

4. On the UNIX Programs screen in the Customization wizard, type the location of the appropriate font caches in the **Font Directory** box. These font caches will then be built into your custom package and installed in the Fontcache folder during the setup process.

Note   To add font caches to existing installations, you can copy them into the Fontcache folders.

▪ **System Policies and Restrictions**—Use these settings to make desktop, shell, and security options consistent across your organization. Corporate administrators, ISPs, and ICPs/developers can specify default settings for their users.

Corporate administrators can customize and restrict numerous settings, ranging from whether users can delete printers to whether they can add items to their desktops. For more information, see Appendix E, "Setting System Policies and Restrictions."

The settings displayed in the wizard are contained in administration (.adm) files that come with the IEAK. If you are familiar with .adm files, you can use the wizard to import the policies and restrictions you have set up in your own .adm files by clicking **Import**.

▶ **To set system policies and restrictions**

1. Double-click each category to display the options.

2. Select or clear the check boxes you want.

   User settings that are stored in a central location can follow users as they log on from computer to computer. This feature can, for example, benefit users who need low security settings, but who use a computer that is typically operated by someone whose security settings are very restrictive.

CHAPTER 16

Customizing Setup

You can customize Microsoft Windows Update Setup for Internet Explorer and Internet Tools to fit the needs of your organization.

To customize Windows Update Setup, you can use the Microsoft Internet Explorer Administration Kit (IEAK), or you can use a batch file or command-line switches. The following information applies to anyone who wants to modify Windows Update Setup, including Internet service providers (ISPs), Internet content providers (ICPs), corporate administrators, developers, and independent software vendors (ISVs).

In This Chapter

See Also

- For more information about testing the deployment process before the final rollout, see Chapter 11, "Setting Up and Administering a Pilot Program."

- For more information about building custom packages for installation, see Chapter 15, "Running the Internet Explorer Customization Wizard."

- For more information about rolling out Microsoft Internet Explorer 5 to your users, see Chapter 19, "Deploying Microsoft Internet Explorer 5."

- For more information about batch files and command-line switches, see Appendix C, "Batch-Mode File Syntax and Command-Line Switches."

Overview

Windows Update Setup can be customized to fit the needs of your organization. You can include custom programs or installation scripts when you install Internet Explorer, or you can suppress prompts to users so that Windows Update Setup can integrate smoothly with your custom setup program. You can also determine how much control users have over the setup process.

Reasons to Customize Windows Update Setup

The goals you want to achieve during deployment affect how you customize Windows Update Setup. Through customization, you can benefit from these features:

- **Hands-free installation**—Perhaps you want to specify setup options for your users and install after hours. You can preset the options and suppress prompts that users receive during the setup process to make the installation hands-free.

- **Setup branding**—By customizing the title bar and graphics in the Internet Explorer Customization wizard, you can brand Windows Update Setup so that its appearance is unique to your organization.

- **Greater control over installation**—You might want to enable users to make some setup choices but control certain other choices. For example, you could require users to install some components, but allow them to choose additional components based on their needs.

- **Addition of custom components**—Perhaps you want users to receive custom components when they install Internet Explorer. For example, you might be an ISP with custom programs or installation scripts that you want to install when users sign up for your services. You can include up to 10 of these custom components with the Customization wizard.

- **Adaptation to user needs**—Various groups in an organization might have different setup needs. For example, one department might need only basic programs, while another department that authors international content for the Web might require more utilities and language tools.

- **Redistribution of Internet Explorer**—Perhaps you want to install Internet Explorer without the icons or browser interface. For example, you might plan to host Internet Explorer with a custom program.

- **Setup changes without rebuilding the IEAK package**—Perhaps you need to revise Internet Explorer settings in a particular way, and you don't want to rebuild your IEAK package. You can use a batch file to change settings you specified in the Customization wizard.

Ways to Customize Windows Update Setup

To customize Windows Update Setup, you can use the Microsoft Internet Explorer Customization wizard, which comes with the IEAK.

You can use the Customization wizard to change the appearance and control the user experience of Windows Update Setup. You can customize the graphics and title bar. In addition, you can add up to 10 custom components and create 10 different setup options.

You can create a batch file, and place it in the same installation location as the setup executable file (IE5Setup.exe), such as in the same download server directory or the same folder on the installation CD-ROM.

You can also use command-line switches. To avoid entering command-line switches at each user's computer, you would typically use the switches in connection with a program that bundles the Internet Explorer setup files and command-line switches, such as the IExpress wizard or your own custom program.

In addition, you can also use a combination of these methods. For example, you could use the IEAK to create custom setup settings, but also use a batch file or command-line switches later if you find that your needs change.

Files Needed to Customize Windows Update Setup

To customize Windows Update Setup with the IEAK, you specify custom program and graphics files using the Internet Explorer Customization wizard. If you are a corporate administrator, you can configure user settings after deployment by using the IEAK Profile Manager. Both the Customization wizard and the IEAK Profile Manager are installed when you set up the IEAK.

Before running the Customization wizard, you should make sure any custom program files that you want to include are ready. If you plan to customize the appearance of Windows Update Setup, you should prepare the graphics files before using the IEAK.

If you plan to distribute files over the Internet, you'll want to ensure that your custom files are digitally signed. Digital signatures show where programs come from and verify that they haven't been altered. If you already have a digital publisher's certificate, the Customization wizard can use it to sign your custom files automatically. For more information about preparing custom files, see Chapter 12, "Preparing for the IEAK." For more information about certificates, see Chapter 6, "Digital Certificates," and Chapter 12, "Preparing for the IEAK."

Customizing Windows Update Setup

You'll need to perform these basic tasks to customize Windows Update Setup by using the Internet Explorer Customization wizard:

- Download the components and tools that you want to install. If you plan to include custom programs, you should prepare them for installation.

- Choose different installation options for your users.

- Specify which setup options you want.

- Specify options for corporate installation.

- Customize the appearance and functionality of Windows Update Setup. If you are a corporate administrator, you can also determine how much control users have over the setup process.

These basic tasks are described in the following sections.

Downloading Components and Tools

When you run the Customization wizard, you'll be prompted to download setup files, known as cabinet (.cab) files, for Microsoft Internet Explorer and its components. You should download Internet Explorer and any components and tools you plan to install with Internet Explorer.

Internet Explorer 5 allows users to choose only the components that they want. For example, beginning users may not need some of the advanced components.

Note Depending on your situation, there are two components that you might need to include in your custom packages. If you want your users to use channels on a computer that has never run Internet Explorer 4.0, you should download the Offline Browsing Pack and include it with your packages. If you are an ISP, and you want your customers to use a customized version of the Internet Connection wizard to sign up for your services, you should include the Dynamic HTML Data Binding component.

You download components that you will include in your packages by using Automatic Version Synchronization (AVS), which enables you to manage component versions.

Keeping Components Synchronized

Keeping track of program versions and determining whether new components are available can be challenging. For example, if you are deploying a new version of one component, you may want to pick up newer versions of other components, so you can ensure that all your components are up-to-date. Or if you are creating a new package for only some of your users, you may want to keep the earlier versions of components so that all users have the same versions.

Automatic Version Synchronization will:

- Provide version information for all components of a specific language.
- Help you see which components you've already downloaded and determine whether you have the latest versions.

The following illustration shows how AVS works.

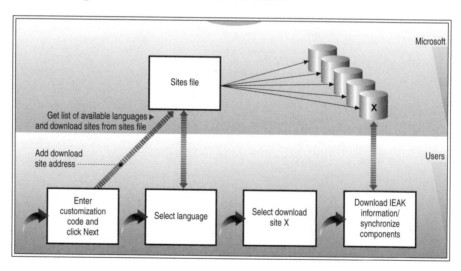

Illustration 16.1   How Automatic Version Synchronization Works

To use AVS, you must be connected to the Internet. In Stage 2 of the Customization wizard, you are prompted to choose a Microsoft site to download programs from, and then you must download the components that you plan to include in your custom package. The components are marked as follows:

- **White X in red circle**—Components that you haven't downloaded yet.
- **Exclamation point in yellow triangle**—Components for which an updated version is available.
- **Check mark in green circle**—Components that are the most recent versions.

You must download Internet Explorer at this point to continue with the Customization wizard.

The following illustration shows the AVS screen of the Customization wizard.

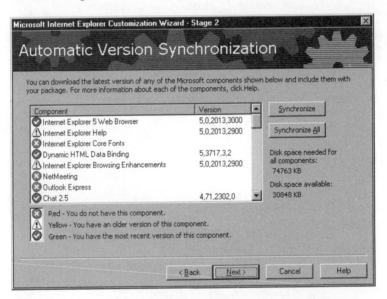

You must use AVS when you create your first Internet Explorer package. In most situations, you will want to use AVS when you build subsequent packages. However, you can choose not to use it if you don't plan to check for updated versions or to update any components. For example, you might choose not to use AVS if you're rebuilding a custom package using the same component versions while not connected to the Internet.

To specify that the Customization wizard will not use AVS to check for updated component versions, carry out the following procedure.

▶ **To specify that the Customization wizard will not use AVS**

1. On the File Locations screen in Stage 1 of the wizard, click **Advanced Options**.

2. Clear the check box labeled **Check for latest components via Automatic Version Synchronization**.

Installing Components Automatically

It can be difficult to anticipate future user needs. You may not want to include a component in every IEAK package, because you aren't sure that all users will need it and have hard-disk space for it. However, you may want to ensure that users can easily install that component if the need arises.

The Automatic Install feature enables users to install components easily after you deploy your custom packages. Automatic Install prompts users to install the appropriate component if they visit a Web page that uses it. For example, a user might be prompted to install the Dynamic HTML Data Binding component when visiting a Web page that contains a form using that feature. When the user accepts the prompt, the component will be installed.

The following procedure shows how to use Automatic Install.

▶ **To enable a component to be installed at a later date**

1. On the Automatic Version Synchronization screen in Stage 2 of the Customization wizard, download the component.

   The component becomes part of your IEAK package, but it won't be installed with Internet Explorer unless you include it with a setup option.

2. On the Components on Media screen in Stage 3 of the wizard, select the check box beside each component that you want to specify for Automatic Version Synchronization.

3. Make sure that the .cab file for each component is copied to the location from which users will install their components.

Note Automatic Install is not available for packages that you create for multiple floppy disks.

If you are a corporate administrator, and you do not want Automatic Install to be used, you can disable it on the System Policies and Restrictions screen in Stage 5 of the Customization wizard or though a system policy.

Adding Custom Components

You can specify up to 10 custom components to install with Internet Explorer. A custom component can be a program that adds Internet functionality or an installation script that runs immediately after Internet Explorer is installed.

On the Add Custom Components screen in Stage 3 of the Customization wizard, you can specify a self-extracting executable file that will automatically set itself up when it is run, or you can specify a .cab file. If you specify a .cab file, you should include a command to set up the .cab file. If you need to run a command-line switch with the command, you can also specify it.

For the UNIX platform, you must specify a .cab file that contains your component and your configuration scripts. For more information about working with UNIX components, see "Preparing Components for UNIX" later in this chapter.

Setting Up Component Download

When the user clicks **Tools** and then clicks **Windows Update** in 32-bit versions of the browser, the browser can update components from the Microsoft Windows Update site. This also happens when the user clicks **Add/Remove Programs** in Control Panel, clicks **Internet Explorer 5 and Internet Tools**, clicks **Add/Remove**, and then selects **Add a component**. Users can also update components from an Add-on Component URL that you specify.

Sample Add-on Components Web Pages

The IEAK Toolkit contains a sample Add-on Components Web page, Addon.htm, which you can customize. This page is located in the \Program Files\IEAK\ Toolkit\Addons\HTML folder. This page also links to the files Head.htm, Main.htm, and Info.htm.

The following is a description of the four sample files in the \Toolkit\Addons\HTML folder:

- **Addon.htm**—Frameset that references these two files:
  - **Head.htm**—Header frame for title
  - **Main.htm**—Main frame with install scripting and link to Info.htm
- **Info.htm**—Information about all of the available components

You'll be making most of your changes in Main.htm, which has three parts:

- Install scripting
- Table of check boxes, component names, and sizes
- Setup ActiveX control

Using the Sample Files

Copy all four sample files to your download location or to the location you specify, then edit them in a text editor or an HTML editor.

For the scripting to work properly, your files must be set up as follows:

- The IEcif.cab file should be on a Web server. In Main.htm, the L_cab_Address= entry in the <script LANGUAGE="VBScript"> section should point to the same folder location.

- The table in Main.htm should contain only the components you have downloaded from Microsoft and want to provide.

▶ To add new components

1. Make sure you have downloaded the components during Automatic Version Synchronization (AVS).

2. Look up the correct name of the component in IESetup.cif.

3. Add a check box with that name to Addon.htm.

If you are an expert Web-page author, you may choose not to use the template provided in the IEAK.

Information for Expert Web-Page Authors

Two scripting languages are used in Main.htm: Microsoft JScript and Visual Basic Scripting Edition (VBScript). The JScript code contains the function **Install()**. This function is called when the user clicks the **Install** button at the bottom of the page. It controls the flow of the install process. The **Install()** function makes calls to several VBScript subroutines.

The scripts use the **name** property (part of the INPUT tag) of the check boxes to read the IESetup.cif file. This file is contained in the IEcif.cab file and is opened by the Window_onLoad() subroutine.

Note   There may be different names for Windows and Windows NT components. This information can be found in IESetup.cif.

To find out whether a component is already installed, you can use the IsComponentInstalled() VBScript Edition subroutine. Use this syntax:

IsComponentInstalled(ComponentID)

Where ComponentID is the same as the check box name and the value in IESetup.cif.

Return:

- 0 = Component not installed
- 1 = Component already installed
- 2 = Component installed, but newer version available
- 3 = User security lockout: No status determined

When the first component is checked using this method, the ActiveX engine activates a security dialog box that requests permission to check the status of installed components on the use's computer. If the user chooses "No," then the return for all components is 3.

Removing Components by Using an Uninstall Program

You should also determine whether you'll want custom components to be easily uninstalled by the user. To make the component appear in the list when the user clicks **Add/Remove Programs** in Control Panel, you'll need to specify information for the **Uninstall** subkey in the following registry key:

HKEY_LOCAL_COMPUTER\Software\Microsoft\Windows\CurrentVersion\Uninstall*ApplicationName******UninstallString*

This is the information that you'll need to specify for **Uninstall**:

- *ApplicationName* = display name of your program
- *UninstallString* = path [switches]

Warning You should use caution when working with the registry. Deleting or changing information can make programs or your system inoperable.

Both *ApplicationName* and *UninstallString* must be supplied and be complete for your uninstall program to appear in Control Panel. The path you supply for *UninstallString* must be the complete command line used to carry out your uninstall program. The command line you supply should carry out the uninstall program directly rather than from a batch file or subprocess.

The Uninstall key field should match the *ApplicationName* value if you want this program to be uninstalled when Internet Explorer is uninstalled.

You can find a sample .inf file for uninstalling a component in the Inf folder of the IEAK Toolkit. For more information about working with .inf files, see Chapter 18, "Working with .inf Files," and Appendix H, "Structural Definition of .inf Files."

Preparing Components for UNIX

For the UNIX platform, you create a .cab file that contains your add-on components and installation scripts. Then you specify the name of the .cab file, the script name, and size information in the Internet Explorer Customization wizard. You can specify up to 10 components that will be installed with Internet Explorer.

The following procedure helps you create a script and a cabinet file so that you can prepare a UNIX component for your IEAK package.

▶ **To prepare a UNIX component for download**

1. Prepare or download the component you want to install.

   Compress the program if needed. You can use file formats such as .tar and .gz.

2. Create a script to install your program. For the IEAK, the script must begin with **#!/bin/sh**. The table of UNIX component script syntax later in this section shows how to specify the target location and decompress the executable file.

3. Test this script on the UNIX platform.

4. Move the script and the compressed component to the 32-bit operating system where you plan to run the Internet Explorer Customization wizard.

5. Create a .cab file consisting of your program and script.

6. Start the Customization wizard, and complete the steps for the UNIX platform until you reach the Add Custom Components screen in Stage 2 of the wizard.

7. Type information in the following boxes on the Add Custom Components screen:

   - **Component**—The friendly name of the component you plan to install.

   - **Location**—The location of the cabinet file on your build computer.

   - **Program**—The name of the installation script. No additional parameters can be specified.

8. Complete the steps in the Customization wizard. When you reach the UNIX Mapping screen in Stage 5 of the wizard, you may need to create an association for your component.

   When you install your customized IEAK package, it decompresses the cabinet file, runs the script, and installs your component before it customizes the browser. After the script has run, it is deleted automatically.

Note If you are familiar with writing setup programs, you can add setup functionality to your compiled program instead of writing a script.

Your installation script can use the following default parameters; no custom parameters can be specified:

- Argument 1 (**$1**), which specifies the location of the installation.
- Argument 2 (**$2**), which together with [*install_dir*]/[*target*], specifies the target destination of the component (the place where you want the .cab files to be located).
- Argument 3 (**$3**), which is an integer specifying whether silent mode is used [0=standard installation/1=silent installation]. It is not used in the example below, but you can include it in your setup script.

The current directory (default directory) when the script is run is the user's home directory. This is important because the files are extracted to the root directory of the installation.

A script must contain the characters **#!** and the path to the script interpreter on the first line. If Setup encounters **#!** on the first line of the script, it processes the file by using dos2unix, which converts line-terminating characters (from the Windows and Microsoft MS-DOS® platforms) to the UNIX equivalent. Without this conversion process, a script created on a personal computer will not be able to run.

You can use the following script syntax:

UNIX component script syntax	Code comments
#!/bin/sh	
cd $2	# Go to the location of the zip file.
Mkdir *<directory name>*	# Create an installation directory.
mv *<compressed component> <directory name>*	# Move the zip file into that directory.
cd *<directory name>*	# Switch to that directory.
Gunzip *<compressed component>*	# Unzip the component.
Chmod +x *<uncompressed component>*	# Assign "execute" or other needed permissions to this file, so it can be run as a program.
cd $1/bin	# Switch to the Internet Explorer bin directory.
ln -s *../<directory name>/<uncompressed component executable>*	# Create a link to the executable program.

Specifying Different Installation Options

Depending on how you plan to install your custom packages, you can provide your users with one of three installation options:

- **Interactive installation**—To provide an interactive installation in which your users make installation decisions, click **Interactive install**.

- **Hands-free installation**—To provide a hands-free installation in which users aren't prompted to make decisions but are informed of the installation progress and errors, click **Hands-free install**.

- **Silent installation**—To provide a silent installation, in which users install the customized browser without receiving prompts, click **Completely silent install**. You should select this option when you want to control all setup options and suppress feedback to the user or for installations deployed when the users aren't present.

  Note that this installation option is not interactive; users do not have control over the installation process. If installation does not finish successfully, users do not see an error message.

Either silent installation (**Hands-free install** or **Completely silent install**) does the following:

- Answers prompts that enable the setup program to continue.

- Accepts the license agreement.

- Specifies that Internet Explorer will be installed and not just downloaded.

- Carries out the type of installation that you specify (such as Standard or Custom). You set this option on a later screen in the Internet Explorer Customization wizard.

- Installs Internet Explorer in the location you specify, unless Internet Explorer is already installed. In that case, the new version of the browser is installed in the same location as the previous version.

- Connects to the first specified download site. You provide a list of download sites on a later screen in the Customization wizard.

You set silent installation options on the Silent Install screen of the Internet Explorer Customization wizard.

Note When you use a silent installation, you can specify only one setup option (such as Typical or Full) and one download site.

To fine-tune the installation, you can use Internet Explorer batch files and command-line switches. For more information, see "Customizing Setup with Batch Files and Switches" later in this chapter.

Specifying Setup Options

You can create up to 10 setup options. Common examples of setup options are typical, minimal, or full, but you can create options based on any criteria you want.

ISPs can create different setup options for different sets of customers. Corporate administrators can create setup options for different divisions or offices in different regions. For example, an international division might need multiple-language support that is not used by the domestic division.

The list of components you can add to each setup option includes the components you have downloaded and the custom components you have specified. You will be prompted to provide a name and description for each setup option. This text appears in the Windows Update Setup wizard that users will see.

Options for Corporate Installation

If you are a corporate administrator, you can determine to what extent, if any, your users can customize the setup process.

The following illustration shows the Corporation Install Options screen.

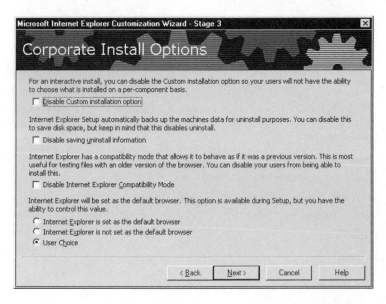

Users can add or remove components to further customize setup. To prevent users from adding or removing specific components, administrators can select the **Disable Custom Installation** option.

Windows Update Setup automatically saves uninstall information. To save disk space, you can disable this feature by selecting the **Disable saving uninstall information** check box. However, users will not then be able to remove Internet Explorer 5 by clicking the **Add/Remove Programs** icon in Control Panel. For more information, see Chapter 19, "Deploying Microsoft Internet Explorer 5."

With the Internet Explorer compatibility option, users can run Internet Explorer 4.0 on the same computer as Internet Explorer 5. This mode is designed for testing purposes—for example, when a Web author needs to view Web content in both versions of the browser. It is not recommended for a corporate roll-out configuration. To prevent users from selecting this option during Setup, select the **Disable Internet Explorer Compatibility mode** check box.

You can determine whether or not Internet Explorer is the default browser, and whether or not users can make this choice. The default browser runs when users open .htm, .html, and other associated file types. This option also determines whether Windows Media Player is the default program for playing multimedia files.

Note If you are using a silent installation or customizing Internet Explorer for Microsoft Office deployment by using the Office Custom Install wizard, corporate install options will not be available.

Customizing Setup Appearance and Functionality

You can use the IEAK to customize the appearance and functionality of Windows Setup Update. Adding custom titles and graphics changes its appearance, while specifying different installation and browser options changes its functionality.

Modifying the Appearance of Windows Update Setup

You can customize the appearance of Windows Update Setup by specifying title bar text and custom graphics when you run the Customization wizard.

To customize the wizard graphics for 32-bit versions of Internet Explorer, you need to prepare a 162-by-312 pixel bitmap for the left side of the first Windows Update Setup screen, and a 496-by-56 pixel bitmap for the top of the remaining Windows Update Setup screens.

To customize the setup wizard for the 16-bit platform, you need to prepare one 162-by-312 pixel bitmap. A 16-color bitmap is recommended.

For more information, see Chapter 12, "Preparing for the IEAK," and Appendix D, "Checklists for Preparing to Use the IEAK."

Note The Windows Update Setup wizard is not used on the UNIX platform.

Modifying the Functionality of Windows Update Setup

Corporate administrators, ISPs, and ICPs, and developers can use the following features to change the functionality of Windows Update Setup:

- **CD-ROM**—You can customize the Autorun screen that appears when users insert the CD-ROMs into their CD-ROM drives. This feature is not available for Windows 3.x packages. For more information about preparing files for the Autorun screen, see Chapter 12, "Preparing for the IEAK."

- **Optimize for Web download**—Windows Update Setup can detect whether the same version of a component is already installed on a user's computer. If a version of the same component is already installed, and it will work with Internet Explorer 5, Windows Update Setup will not download it. This feature can save download time.

- **Prevent users from customizing Setup for specific components**—If you allow users to customize their installations, but you don't want them to customize specific components, you can specify the components that you do not want users to customize. This feature can be used when you need to ensure that a component is installed with your package.

The following features are also available to corporate administrators:

- **Setup Location**—You can specify where you want Internet Explorer and other components to be installed, and determine whether the user can change the folder that you specify. If Internet Explorer is already installed on the user's computer, the new version is installed over the existing version.

- **Disable Custom Installation option**—Described earlier in this chapter.

- **Disable saving uninstall information**—Described earlier in this chapter.

- **Disable Internet Explorer Compatibility mode**—Described earlier in this chapter.

- **Default browser options**—You can determine whether Internet Explorer is the default browser and whether users can make this choice. The default browser runs when users open .htm, .html, and other associated file types.

Customizing Setup by Using Batch Files and Switches

The Internet Explorer Customization wizard enables you to control user experience during Windows Update Setup. You can further control the setup process by using a batch file. You can use this method whether Internet Explorer is installed alone or with Microsoft Office.

When installing Internet Explorer, you can further control the setup process by using command-line switches. This method is also supported in Internet Explorer 5, and some new switches are available. To include switches, you typically use the IExpress wizard or another program to package your setup files.

In most cases, the batch-file method gives you more control over the installation of individual components and involves fewer steps. The command-line switches are provided for backwards compatibility and to support custom solutions.

Using Batch Files

It's easy to create a batch file and integrate it with your custom package. You can also place the batch file in the same installation location as Windows Desktop Update (IE5Setup.exe), such as in the same download server folder or the same folder on the installation CD-ROM.

You can use a batch file in two ways:

- Add it to your custom package.
- Include it with your setup files when you distribute your custom package.

You create a batch file the same way for both methods.

▶ **To create a batch file**

- Use a text editor, such as Microsoft Notepad, and name the file IEBatch.txt.

Modifying Setup by Using a Batch File

To include the batch file as part of your IEAK package, place it in the \Iebin*<Language>*\Optional folder. *<Language>* represents the language of the version you are creating. For example, English language versions are created in the En folder.

If you distribute Internet Explorer over the Internet or an intranet, you can post the batch file to the site where users download Internet Explorer. If you distribute Internet Explorer on other media, such as a compact disc or floppy disk, you can add the batch file to the media. Place it in the same folder as the IE5Setup.exe file.

> **Caution** If you use a batch file to suppress restarting, you should make sure that your custom program restarts Internet Explorer after installation. Setup will not be complete until the computer has been restarted.

For information about batch-file syntax, see Appendix C, "Batch-Mode File Syntax and Command-Line Switches."

Using Command-Line Switches

You may want to control the way that the setup program is run. You can use command-line switches to choose the installation mode, specify a quiet mode (which removes or reduces the prompts the user receives), or control whether the computer is restarted after installation.

You can have users include command-line switches when they run Windows Update Setup, but a more typical scenario is packaging Internet Explorer with the switches by creating a custom setup program.

One tool for creating custom setup programs is the IExpress wizard (IExpress.exe), which is included with the IEAK. You can also use your own setup program.

A common use of command-line switches is to suppress user feedback and prompts from Internet Explorer if you are redistributing Internet Explorer as part of a custom program.

> **Caution** If you use command-line switches to suppress restarting, you should make sure that your custom program restarts Internet Explorer after installation. Setup will not be complete until the computer has been restarted.

Command-line switches take precedence over similar settings in batch files and IEAK packages. You can use this precedence to your advantage if you need to change the settings you specified in the IEAK temporarily without rebuilding your IEAK package.

Scenarios for Using Command-Line Switches

Here are some scenarios that illustrate the use of command-line switches:

- You could specify a silent, or quiet, installation and specify that the third option in the list of setup options is run. An example installation type is "typical," but it depends on which types you specify when you run the IEAK. You could also specify that the computer is not restarted after installation, providing your custom solution takes care of restarting the computer.

- You could specify that a batch file is run and include the name and location of the batch file.

- You could override the download sites that you specified in the IEAK and install Internet Explorer from a location you specify. This might be helpful, for example, if you need to change the download site temporarily for troubleshooting reasons without rebuilding your IEAK package.

Integrating Setup Solutions with Other Programs

You may want to integrate Setup into your custom program or solution.

If you are integrating Internet Explorer functionality into your custom program—for example, by using the WebBrowser control—you can suppress user feedback and prompts by using a batch file or command-line switches. For more information about developing programs and custom solutions with Internet Explorer, see the MSDN Online Web site and "How to Create Intranet Applications for Your Corporation," located on the CD-ROM included with the Resource Kit.

You can also deploy Internet Explorer by using Microsoft Systems Management Server (SMS). SMS can help you gather information before installing and produce a report after installation. For more information about SMS, see Chapter 5, "Understanding Related Tools and Programs."

If you are installing Internet Explorer with Office 2000, you can use the Custom Installation wizard (CIW) for Office, which enables you to customize how you install Office programs. To simplify the installation process, the IEAK is designed to work with the CIW.

You can work with the CIW in two ways:

- If you do not plan to customize Internet Explorer, you can install Internet Explorer components by using the CIW; you do not need to use the IEAK.
- If you plan to customize Internet Explorer, and you are deploying Office, specify in the CIW that you want to customize Internet Explorer. The Custom Installation wizard starts the IEAK.

When used with CIW, the Customization wizard runs in corporate administrator mode with the following settings:

- The distribution media is CD-ROM.
- Two installation options are available. You cannot change the names of these options, but you can specify which components will be installed with each installation option.

Note The CIW installs Microsoft NetMeeting and Microsoft Outlook Express with all installation options.

- All of the .cab files and custom components that are created by the IEAK are placed in the same directory.

For more information about working with Office 2000, see Chapter 5, "Understanding Related Tools and Programs."

Understanding Windows Update Setup

To better understand how to customize the setup process, it is helpful to learn how Windows Update Setup works.

Windows Update Setup is designed to minimize the download time and to recover by itself if it is interrupted—for example, if an Internet connection is broken. This can eliminate the need to run Setup multiple times, which reduces user frustration.

Windows Update Setup (IE5Setup.exe) is small. When the user clicks IE5setup.exe, it causes the .cab files for Internet Explorer and its components to start downloading from the sites specified in the IE5Sites.dat file.

The following is an illustration of how the setup process works.

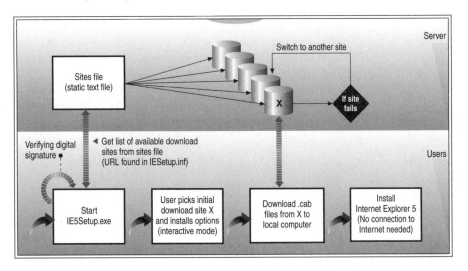

Illustration 16.2   How Windows Update Setup Works

Windows Update Setup is based on an ActiveX™ engine, which runs on the client computer. The process begins with a small setup package. This self-extracting file can be downloaded to the computer by using an existing browser, or it can be copied directly onto a computer with no existing browser. Because of its small file size, it downloads quickly or fits on a single floppy disk.

This small setup package also allows Windows Update Setup to collect information about the host computer before the download process begins. Windows Update Setup uses this information to intelligently manage the download of Internet Explorer .cab files and make installation as efficient and problem-free as possible.

While Windows Update Setup is running, log files are created. The Active Setup Log.txt file is a log of the entire setup process from the moment IE5Setup.exe is executed until the download of the last .cab file is complete. When IE5Setup.exe starts, Active Setup Log.txt is created in the C:*Operating System* folder. If an Active Setup Log.txt from a previous Windows Update Setup session exists, it is renamed to Active Setup Log.bak.

The log begins with the date and time the setup program was launched and ends with the date and time it successfully downloads the last .cab file. As the user runs Windows Update Setup, logging entries are continually written to this file. It is the most informative log file for determining what caused a download failure and when the failure occurred. Most entries logged in this file are also written to the registry.

For more information about Active Setup Log.txt, see Appendix B, "Troubleshooting."

C H A P T E R   1 7

Time-Saving Strategies That Address Diverse User Needs

If your users or customers have diverse needs—for example, your marketing department requires different Microsoft Internet Explorer settings than your finance department—there are ways that you can address those needs without repeating all customization steps.

This chapter will provide some strategies that corporate administrators and Internet service providers (ISPs) can use to efficiently address diverse user needs.

In This Chapter

See Also

- For more information about testing the deployment process before the final rollout, see Chapter 11, "Setting Up and Administering a Pilot Program."

- For more information about preparing for the IEAK, see Chapter 12, "Preparing for the IEAK."

- For more information about using the sample Internet sign-up files, see Chapter 13, "Setting Up Servers."

- For more information about building custom packages for installation, see Chapter 15, "Running the Internet Explorer Customization Wizard."

- For more information about customizing the set-up process, see Chapter 16, "Customizing Setup."

- For more information about rolling out Internet Explorer 5 to your users, see Chapter 19, "Deploying Microsoft Internet Explorer 5."

- For more information about automatic configuration, see Chapter 21, "Using Automatic Configuration and Automatic Proxy."

Overview

Addressing multiple user needs in an organization can be a challenge. By utilizing some Internet Explorer Administration Kit (IEAK) and Internet Explorer features, however, you can address the needs of different groups of users without repeating all of your customization steps. Consider the following scenarios and determine if one or more of these situations describes your needs:

- Corporate administrators can use automatic configuration to address specific needs for different sets of users. You do not need to create additional packages for those users.

- ISPs can create multiple Internet sign-up (.isp) files without rebuilding custom packages. The .isp files contain connection, gateway, server, and other information. You can use the Internet Explorer Customization wizard to produce multiple .isp files. However, if you prefer to enter the information yourself, you can also edit them manually.

- For multiple platforms, there are strategies that you can use to avoid repeating all your customization steps. For example, you can use an Internet settings (.ins) file from one platform to create an .ins file for another platform.

- When building multiple custom packages (also commonly known as IEAK packages), you can use certain strategies to avoid having to build a new package each time. Some key strategies are to use the Feature Information and Automatic Version Synchronization (AVS) features, and to import pre-existing .ins files.

- To change setup options without rebuilding a custom package, you can use a batch file. For example, use a batch file if you want to customize the setup program and you aren't building a custom package, or if you need to change some settings, but don't want to rebuild the custom package.

- If you need to customize the way Internet Explorer runs, without customizing the Internet Explorer program, you can start Internet Explorer by using command-line parameters. For example, you can start Internet Explorer in Kiosk or full-screen mode by using the **-k** command-line parameter.

Using Automatic Configuration in a Corporate Setting

Automatic configuration enables corporate administrators to change settings globally after deploying Internet Explorer. You can use automatic configuration with multiple IEAK profiles and change settings for specific groups of users.

You create IEAK profiles with the IEAK Profile Manager; the profiles consist of .ins files and any custom cabinet (.cab) files associated with your package. You can have more than one .ins file, such as a Mkting.ins file for your marketing department and a Finance.ins file for your finance department.

To use automatic configuration, you must set the users' browsers to point to the location of the .ins file. To use multiple .ins files, you would need to change the automatic-configuration path for different groups of users or automate a server solution.

Changing Automatic-Configuration Paths

To change the path for different user groups, you can rebuild similar custom packages, each with a different automatic-configuration path. Another option is to change the path for a group of users after deployment, either by changing the path manually or by using a script.

Automating Server Solutions

You also can use automated server solutions, which enable you to use multiple .ins files without rebuilding your packages. A sample Active Server Page (.asp) file is provided in the \Toolkit\Corp subfolder of your IEAK program folder.

If you are using a Web server that supports Active Server Pages, you can modify the sample solution to fit your organization's needs.

To use the sample, assign users to groups, based on their needs. Then, create an .ins file for each group, such as Mkting.ins or Finance.ins. You can create as many user groups as you need.

On your automatic-configuration server, create global groups that correspond to your .ins file name (without the extension)—for example, IE_*groupname*.

For example, the .ins file for the finance department might be Finance.ins, and the group name on your automatic-configuration server would be IE_finance.

Add the user names of your finance department to the global IE_finance group on your domain. Then, post your .asp files to the automatic-configuration server.

Procedures for working with the automatic-configuration sample are covered in the file Asphelp.htm, which is also in the Corp folder.

Another key feature of automatic configuration that you can enable is the automatic detection of browser settings. For more information about working with this feature, see Chapter 13, "Setting Up Servers." For more general information about automatic configuration, see Chapter 21, "Using Automatic Configuration and Automatic Proxy."

Creating Multiple .isp Files for Internet Services

If you are an ISP, you can create multiple .isp files without rebuilding your custom package. The .isp files contain connection, gateway, server, and other information. Use the Customization wizard to produce multiple .isp files or, if you prefer to enter the information yourself, you can edit them manually.

The following illustration shows the Sign-up Server Information screen in Stage 4 of the Customization wizard, which creates .isp files based on your settings. To change settings in your .isp files manually, use a text editor, such as Notepad. For reference information about .isp and .ins files, see the Insref.xls file, located in the IEAK Toolkit folder.

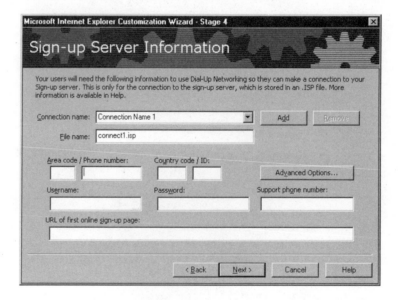

The IEAK Toolkit contains an Internet sign-up server sample for use with the Internet Connection wizard that is based on using multiple .isp files. The sample files are located in the \Toolkit\Isp\Server\Icw folder of your IEAK program folder. For more information about using the sample files, see Chapter 13, "Setting Up Servers."

Important   To use a sign-up server solution with multiple .isp files similar to the sample sign-up server solution, you must include the Dynamic HTML Data Binding component in your custom package.

Working with Multiple Platforms

If you create customized browsers for different platforms, and you want the browsers to share similar settings, you can avoid repeating all customization steps for each platform version. If you use automatic configuration, you can use the IEAK Profile Manager to efficiently create profiles for more than one platform.

For most multiple-platform scenarios, you would build the 32-bit custom package first. Then, you can use those settings when using the IEAK Profile Manager or the Customization wizard for other platforms.

Recreating an Automatic-Configuration Profile in a Corporate Setting

If you are a corporate administrator, and you use automatic configuration, you can recreate an .ins file based on a profile from a different platform. This method eliminates the need to specify all the settings for each platform again. Note, however, that some features differ slightly across platforms. For more details, see Chapter 4, "Working with Different Platforms."

To rebuild an .ins file for another platform by using the IEAK Profile Manager, carry out the following procedure.

▶ **To rebuild an .ins file by using the IEAK Profile Manager**

1. Open the .ins file that you want to use as a starting point in the IEAK Profile Manager (if it is not already open).

2. On the **Platform** menu, click the platform that you want, such as UNIX.

3. Set any additional platform-specific settings that you want.

4. Save the IEAK profile, and copy the profile to your automatic-configuration server.

   The profile consists of the .ins file and any .cab files associated with your package.

Rebuilding a Custom Package for Another Platform

All IEAK users can rebuild packages for another platform by building in the same folder. Corporate administrators can build 32-bit, 16-bit, and UNIX packages. Developers, Internet content providers, and Internet service providers can build 32-bit and 16-bit packages.

Typically, you would build the 32-bit package first. Then, specify the same build location for subsequent packages on the File Locations screen in Stage 1 of the wizard. You do not need to specify the same settings for subsequent packages that you set for the first package.

If you build a Windows 32-bit-package and then rebuild a Windows 16-bit-package in the same folder, the file names are automatically converted to eight-character names with three-character extensions (8.3 format). If you build a Windows 32-bit-package in the same location as an existing Windows 16-bit package, the file names will continue to be in 8.3 format.

If you need to build a Windows 32-bit-package after you have built a Windows 16-bit-package, it's recommended that you build it in a new location.

Rebuilding Custom Packages Efficiently

If you aren't using multiple .ins or .isp files, and you need to build multiple custom packages, you can use certain strategies to avoid downloading files again or resetting options on every page of the wizard.

Here are three ways to build multiple custom packages more efficiently using the Customization wizard:

- Clear the options on the Feature Selection screen for the settings you don't plan to change.
- Use AVS to keep track of components you've already downloaded. You only need to download components that have changed, if you want newer versions of them.
- Import settings from a pre-existing .ins file if your new package contains many of the same settings.

Using the Feature Selection Screen

If you create multiple packages with the Customization wizard, you can use the Feature Selection screen in Stage 1 of the wizard to select which wizard screens you want to view.

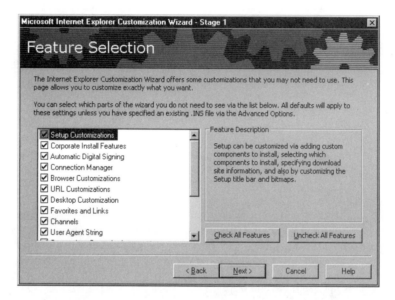

If you don't plan to change any settings associated with a feature, you can clear the check box for that feature. The screens associated with that feature will not be displayed. Note, however, that a few screens are displayed every time you run the wizard because they are necessary to create the package.

By displaying only the screens necessary for your additional custom package, you can possibly save time, because you won't need to view or specify options for settings that don't change.

Note If your packages include custom graphics, verify that the graphics are still available in the specified locations. If you have moved or changed the name of any graphics since you last built a custom package, you'll need to display the screen associated with the graphics, and change the path.

Using Automatic Version Synchronization

The IEAK can check on the Internet for the latest versions of components when you create your custom package. This feature can help you detect whether new versions have become available since the last time you ran the Internet Explorer Customization wizard. It can also help you avoid downloading components a second time.

To use AVS, you'll need to specify the same Component Download folder that you used for a previous package, and keep the components that you downloaded earlier on your computer.

You specify the Component Download folder on the File Locations screen in Stage 1 of the wizard. To set the location, click **Advanced Options**, and then enter the path you want in the **Component Download Folder** box. If you have already run the wizard and downloaded the components you want, you do not need to change this path if you want to reuse the components that you've already downloaded.

To see if new versions of components are available from Microsoft, view the Automatic Version Synchronization screen in Stage 2 of the wizard. If you have the latest version of a component, the icon will be green; if a newer version is available, the icon will be yellow; and if you've never downloaded the component (or if you have changed the path since you downloaded a component), the icon will be red.

It is not necessary to download the latest version of a component, although this is recommended for most scenarios. To retain version consistency across your organization, you may not want to deploy a newer version of a component if several members of your organization already have an earlier version.

If you haven't planned to deploy an updated version of a component, don't click **Synchronize** or **Synchronize All** on the Automatic Version Synchronization screen. However, if you download a newer version of a component using **Synchronize** or **Synchronize All**, you will be prompted if you already have some of the files associated with the component. That way, you won't have to download files that aren't necessary to update your component.

Importing a Pre-Existing .ins File

If you have created a custom package or worked with automatic configuration before, and you want to build a new package with many of the same settings, you can import your .ins file when you run the Customization wizard.

The settings from the .ins file can serve as a starting point for your new package. You won't have to reset the options that you want to retain; you'll only need to set options that you want to change and options that are new to this version of the Customization wizard.

When importing an .ins file, verify that the .ins file applies to the package type you are creating. For example, if you create a corporate administrator package, you would not want to import an .ins file from a package created for Internet service providers.

To import a pre-existing .ins file, use the following procedure.

▶ **To import settings from an .ins file with the Customization wizard**

1. In Stage 1 of the wizard, click **Next** until you see the File Locations screen.

2. Click **Advanced Options**.

3. Enter the path of your .ins file in the **Path of .ins file to import settings from** check box, or click **Browse** to locate the .ins file you want to import.

4. Continue to use the wizard, and specify any new settings that you need for your new package.

Using Batch Files to Customize the Setup Program

If you want to change setup options without creating or rebuilding a custom package, you can use a batch file.

A batch file can be helpful in the following scenarios:

- If you build a custom package and need to change a setup option later, you can use the batch file without rebuilding the package and rerunning the Customization wizard.

- If you temporarily need to change a setup option—for example, if your network servers aren't working and you're using an alternate download location for a short period of time—then you can use the batch file without impacting the settings in your custom package.

- If you want to address different setup needs without building multiple custom packages, you can use different batch files for different groups of users that have specific needs.

- If you want to customize the setup program without building a custom package, you can use a batch file.

For more information about working with batch files, see Chapter 16, "Customizing Setup," and Appendix C, "Batch-Mode File Syntax and Command-Line Switches."

Starting Internet Explorer by Using Command-Line Parameters

You can customize how Internet Explorer is run without customizing the browsing program. If you run Internet Explorer by using a command-line prompt and parameters, you can customize the way Internet Explorer starts or appears during the browsing session. To do this, you would not need to customize the program by using the IEAK.

You can either type the syntax into a command-line prompt or use a script to perform this process. If you need to always run Internet Explorer in a specific way, then you may want to explore the customization features that are available with the IEAK. The command-line syntax can be helpful, however, if you need to run Internet Explorer in a certain way for a specific session or if you use the parameters in connection with a script.

For a list of the command-line parameters for starting Internet Explorer, see Appendix C, "Batch-Mode File Syntax and Command-Line Switches."

C H A P T E R   1 8

Working with .inf Files

A setup information (.inf) file is a text file that you can use to extend the setup process. This chapter discusses ways to use .inf files to fine-tune the setup process using the setup engine built into the Microsoft Windows operating system.

In This Chapter

See Also

Customizing Installation by Using .inf Files

Although you can use the IEAK, batch files, command-line switches, and third-party programs to customize setup, you can also extend setup by using setup information (.inf) files.

Scripts based on .inf files take advantage of the setup engine built into Windows. The primary advantage of using the built-in setup engine is its smaller size. Such functions as copying files, adding registry entries, and creating shortcuts are already part of the Windows operating system. You need to ship only the .inf file and the program files you want to install. A separate script is required for each component that you want to install or uninstall.

Note that a Windows .inf file cannot prompt the user for a destination directory—the directory must be hard-coded in the .inf file.

You can use .inf files to perform these tasks:

- **Manipulate folders and files**—You can use .inf files to perform tasks such as creating folders and links in folders, creating and deleting long file names, setting attributes for files and folders, and copying files to the Program Files folder.

- **Extend Windows 32-bit setup**—You can extend Windows Update Setup for Internet Explorer 5 and Internet Tools by using the **Run** command (Rundll.exe or Rundll32.exe) to run .inf files from the command line. To do this, you would install optional Windows software components by using 32-bit program code, and then create an icon on the Windows desktop that the user can click to run an .inf file. For more information about these methods, see "Extending Setup" later in this chapter.

- **Provide uninstall functionality**—To provide uninstall functionality in your .inf files, you would add an installation section that removes the files, registry entries, and shortcuts for your program. The .inf file would also add your component to the list of programs that can be uninstalled from the **Add/Remove Programs** dialog box in Control Panel. An example is included in the Inf folder of the IEAK Toolkit.

- **Use RunOnce technology**—The **RunOnce** registry key enables you to run a program one time in Windows. You can specify how much interaction occurs between the program and the user.

For more information about .inf files, see Appendix H, "Structural Definition of .inf Files."

Manipulating Folders and Files by Using .inf Files

You can manipulate files and folders in several ways by using .inf files:

- Create folders and links in folders.
- Manage long file names.
- Set attributes for files and folders.
- Copy files to the Program Files folder.

Creating Folders and Links in Folders

After a component is installed, Windows creates a folder in the Program Files folder or creates links in a folder. The setup program looks in the Setup.ini file for a **[progman.groups]** section and then parses it to create folders and links in those folders.

If you are installing a component that requires a folder or links in the Program Files folder, you need to create an **[UpdateInis]** section in an .inf file that will create the proper entries in the Setup.ini file.

Use the following syntax in the Setup.ini file to create folders and links. Note that folders are relative to the **Start** menu:

[progman.groups]
  folder_1=Folder_1_Name
  folder_2=Folder_2_Name
  :
  folder_n=Folder_n_Name

[folder_1]
  link-name, .exe-name, icon-file-name, icon-index, profile

If you specify NULL as the profile, the link is always added to the folder.

If you specify NULL as the .exe name, the name will be deleted from the group if it exists there.

Note If a folder or link has a space in its description, you must use double quotation marks.

Managing Long File Names

To support backwards compatibility, the setup engine in Windows 32-bit versions of the browser is a 16-bit dynamic link library (.dll) file. Because of this, the Windows setup engine can only copy files that have 8.3 file names.

The setup engine runs a 32-bit program when it exits that manages files with long names. The 32-bit program gets its instructions from predefined paths in the registry.

The following is the path for rename operations in the registry:

HKEY_LOCAL_MACHINE\Software\Microsoft\Windows\CurrentVersion\ RenameFiles

The following is the path for delete operations in the registry:

HKEY_LOCAL_MACHINE\Software\Microsoft\Windows\CurrentVersion\ DeleteFiles

Each group of rename and delete operations is added to entries under each path. Each group of operations is limited to renaming or deleting files in a single folder. For each rename or delete operation, you must include a minimum of two entries in each subkey: the folder path for the files to be renamed or deleted, and the actual rename or delete operation.

The first element in each group of operations is the folder entry. Each rename operation in the folder entry has the following form:

"old_short_name"="new_long_name,[attrib_flag]"

You can use the optional *attrib_flag* to set file attributes during the rename operation. The flag is composed of the following values:

1 READONLY 2 HIDDEN 3 SYSTEM

To set multiple attributes for a file or folder, the flags are added together. For example, to set the READONLY and HIDDEN attributes, *attrib_flag* would be 3.

The following examples are from an **AddReg** section that sets the SYSTEM and HIDDEN attributes for the \Windows\System\Sample folder:

```
HKLM,Software\Microsoft\Windows\CurrentVersion\RenameFiles\Sys,,,%11%
```

```
HKLM,Software\Microsoft\Windows\CurrentVersion\RenameFiles\Sys,SAMPLE,,"
SAMPLE,6"
```

Each delete operation in the folder entry has the following form:

"arbitrary_key_name"="long_name_to_delete"

The following example shows an **AddReg** entry that performs these tasks:

- Renames the Oldname.txt file as the New Long Name.txt file in the C:\Samples folder.
- Renames the Myreadme.txt file to the My App Readme.txt file in the Windows folder.

```
[MyAppShort2Long]
HKLM,Software\Microsoft\Windows\CurrentVersion\RenameFiles\Samples,,,C:\
Samples
HKLM,Software\Microsoft\Windows\CurrentVersion\RenameFiles\
Samples,oldname.txt,,"New Long Name.txt"
HKLM,Software\Microsoft\Windows\CurrentVersion\RenameFiles\Win,,,%25%
HKLM,Software\Microsoft\Windows\CurrentVersion\RenameFiles\Win,myreadme.
txt,,"My App Readme.txt"
```

The following example shows an **AddReg** entry that performs these tasks:

- Deletes the New Long Name.txt file from the C:\Samples folder.
- Deletes the My App Readme.txt file from the Windows folder.

```
[MyAppDelLong]
HKLM,Software\Microsoft\Windows\CurrentVersion\DeleteFiles\Samples,,,C:\
Samples
HKLM,Software\Microsoft\Windows\CurrentVersion\DeleteFiles\Samples,oldna
me.txt,,"New Long Name.txt"

HKLM,Software\Microsoft\Windows\CurrentVersion\DeleteFiles\Win,,,%25%
HKLM,Software\Microsoft\Windows\CurrentVersion\DeleteFiles\Win,myreadme.
txt,,"My App Readme.txt"
```

After these rename and deletion operations have been processed, the entries are removed from the registry.

Note During the rename operation, the destination file is deleted before any files are renamed. If the same rename operation is queued twice, it could result in a loss of the file. For example, a bitmap that needs to be renamed from Picture.bmp to Windows Screen Picture.bmp might get deleted before the rename operation happens if Windows Screen Picture.bmp already exists from an earlier rename operation. The exception to this rule is when the existing destination file name is a folder.

Setting Attributes for Files and Folders

To set the attributes for a file or folder, you use the same convention as when you create long file names by using an optional flag. For more information, see "Managing Long File Names" earlier in this chapter.

Copying Files to the Program Files Folder

Because copying Windows files is a 16-bit operation, only short (8.3) file names can be used. Therefore, to access the Program Files folder, you need to use the 8.3 equivalent, "24,PROGRA~1", in the **[DestinationDirs]** section of an .inf file. Similarly, the short file name equivalent must be used to access any folders with long file names that are in the Program Files folder.

The following example copies three files to the \Program Files\Accessories folder and creates links to one of the files:

```
[WordPadInstall]
CopyFiles = WordPadCopyFiles
UpdateInis = WordPadInis

[DestinationDirs]
WordPadCopyFiles = 24,%PROGRAMF%\%ACCESSOR%

[WordPadCopyFiles]
mswd6_32.wpc
wordpad.exe
write32.wpc

[WordPadInis]
setup.ini, progman.groups,, "group4=%APPS_DESC%"
;creates Accessories folder (if not already there)
setup.ini, group4,, """%WORDPAD_LINK%""",
""%24%\%PROGRAMF%\%ACCESSOR%\WORDPAD.EXE"""
;creates link in Accessories folder

[Strings]
APPS_DESC = "Accessories"
WORDPAD_LINK = "WordPad"
; Folder names - note that the short versions must match the truncated
; 8-character names for the long versions, or there will be problems.
PROGRAMF = "Progra~1" ; first 6 chars of Program_Files, + "~1"
ACCESSOR = "Access~1" ; first 6 chars of Accessories, + "~1"
```

Limitations of .inf Files

The following are limitations of .inf files:

- You cannot delete a directory.

- You cannot move a file to a different location by using the **RenFiles** entry. (**RenFiles** only renames a file in place.)

- You cannot copy a file to another location on your hard disk by using the **CopyFiles** entry. (**CopyFiles** only copies files from the source disk to the destination directory.)

Extending Setup

You can extend Setup in three ways:

- Execute Windows .inf files from the command line by using the **Run** command (Rundll.exe or Rundll32.exe).

- Install optional Windows software components by using 32-bit program code instead of having the user install software from the **Add/Remove Programs** dialog box in Control Panel.

- Create an icon on the Windows desktop that the user can click to run an .inf file (this may eliminate the need to develop installation program code).

Executing .inf Files from the Command Line

You can use the **Run** command to execute an Install section in an .inf file. The syntax of the command line is as follows:

RunDll setupx.dll,InstallHinfSection *section reboot-mode inf-name*

This command assumes that the disk space required to install any files is available. It does not perform any disk-space checks.

The *section* argument specifies an Install section in the .inf file. The following example shows the command line that installs the optional Games component and, if Windows Update Setup determines that restarting the computer is necessary, prompts the user about whether to restart the computer immediately after the installation is complete.

```
RunDll setupx.dll,InstallHinfSection games 4 applets.inf
```

Using the Reboot Mode Argument

You can specify five reboot modes from the command line:

- define HOW_NEVER_REBOOT 0
- define HOW_ALWAYS_SILENT_REBOOT 1
- define HOW_ALWAYS_PROMPT_REBOOT 2
- define HOW_SILENT_REBOOT 3
- define HOW_PROMPT_REBOOT 4

Important The only recommended values for *reboot-mode* are 4 (if the .inf file is a 32-bit .inf file) or 132 (if the .inf file is provided by you). Using any of the other values in the preceding list may cause the computer to restart unnecessarily or cause the computer not to restart when it should.

NeverReboot

Set *reboot-mode* to 0 or 128. Whatever happens, the computer is not automatically restarted. It's up to the end user to determine whether the computer should be restarted. For Setup, this means that the C:\Windows\Wininit.ini file is not zero bytes in size.

AlwaysSilentReboot

Set *reboot-mode* to 1 or 129. The user does not see a prompt about whether to restart the computer, and the computer always restarts.

AlwaysPromptReboot

Set *reboot-mode* to 2 or 130. The user always sees a prompt about whether to restart the computer. Windows Update Setup does not try to determine whether restarting the computer is necessary.

SilentReboot

Set *reboot-mode* to 3 or 131. If Windows Update Setup determines that the computer needs to be restarted, there is no user interaction.

PromptReboot

Set *reboot-mode* to 4 or 132. If Windows Update Setup determines that the computer needs to be restarted, it prompts the user with a dialog box.

Using the .inf File Name

If *inf-name* specifies your .inf file instead of a Windows .inf file, add 128 to the values shown above. In the example described previously, the *reboot-mode* for the Games optional component is set to 4 because Applets.inf is a Windows .inf file. If you are installing an optional component that has its own .inf file, you should set *reboot-mode* to 132. If you add 128 to *reboot-mode*, all of the files that you are installing must be in the same folder location as your .inf file on the installation disk.

Installing Optional Components by Using 32-bit Programs

After Windows is installed on a computer, it may be necessary to add one or more of the Windows optional components (for example, Games). This type of installation, which occurs after Windows Update Setup initially installs Windows, is called maintenance-mode setup. Typically, you start maintenance-mode setup from Windows by clicking the **Add/Remove Programs** icon in Control Panel. However, if you are a vendor or a supplier of an optional software component, you can install the optional component by using a call to the **CreateProcess** function in a 32-bit program.

Note You can use the **CreateProcess** function to install an optional component only in 32-bit programs.

To install an optional component from a 32-bit program, use a combination of the following methods:

- Registry keys
- The **CreateProcess** function

Checking the Registry

Before starting the installation operation, determine whether the optional component is currently installed. You can do this by either checking in the registry or looking for the files. The registry path for information about all the currently installed optional components follows:

HKEY_LOCAL_MACHINE\SOFTWARE\Microsoft\Windows\ CurrentVersion\SETUP\OptionalComponents

Values under **OptionalComponents** point to subkeys, and each subkey contains information about the optional components installed, as well as information needed to install a new optional component. For example, to see whether Games are installed as an optional component, look for the following entry under **OptionalComponents**:

```
"Games"="Games"
```

Then, open the **Games** subkey under **OptionalComponents** to find the following information:

**HKEY_LOCAL_MACHINE\SOFTWARE\Microsoft\Windows\
CurrentVersion\SETUP\OptionalComponents\Games**

The following example shows that the Games optional component is not installed on this Windows computer, because the **Installed** entry is set to 0.

```
"INF"="applets.inf"
"Section"="games"
"Installed"="0"
```

Calling the CreateProcess Function

You can install an optional component, such as Games, by using the **INF** and **Section** values in the **Games** subkey (shown in the previous example) in a call to the **CreateProcess** function, which then runs Setupx.dll using Rundll.exe. The call to **CreateProcess** does exactly what the **Add/Remove Programs** dialog box in Control Panel does when it installs a component. The command-line string specified in the *lpCommandLine* parameter for **CreateProcess** has the following syntax:

RunDll setupx.dll,InstallHinfSection *section reboot-mode inf-name*

The values for *section* and *inf-name* are those found in the registry key described earlier. This example shows the command-line string used by **CreateProcess** to install the optional Games component and, if Windows Update Setup determines that restarting the computer is necessary, to prompt the user whether to restart immediately after the installation is complete.

```
RunDll setupx.dll,InstallHinfSection games 4 applets.inf
```

Note It is recommended that you have your installation program check for available disk space before it installs the component. When your program checks for available disk space, it should determine whether there is sufficient disk space for system swap files.

Your installation program must not have any code that executes after the call to **CreateProcess**, because once Setupx.dll has control, the additional code may cause the user's computer to restart. If your installation process requires other code to run after the call to **CreateProcess**, use the **RunOnce** entry in your .inf file.

Caution The **RunOnce** entry must not run the optional component that you are installing.

Running an .inf File by Right-Clicking the File Icon

Setup recognizes a special installation section name, **[DefaultInstall]**, in .inf files that install optional components. If you use that section in your .inf file, the user can right-click a file icon for the .inf file in the user interface of 32-bit Windows versions to run the **[DefaultInstall]** section. (After the user right-clicks the .inf file icon, a pop-up menu appears with installation options the user must select from to actually run the **[DefaultInstall]** section.

The **[DefaultInstall]** section in the .inf file provides a convenient method of installing optional components. It is particularly useful during the development of your installation program because it provides you with a method for installing your optional component before you write the installation program.

The following example shows typical entries in a **[DefaultInstall]** section:

```
[DefaultInstall]
CopyFiles=QCD.copy.prog, QCD.copy.hlp, QCD.copy.win, QCD.copy.sys,
QCD.copy.inf
UpdateInis=QCD.Links
AddReg=QCD.reg, QCD.run
Uninstall=FlexiCD_remove
```

Providing Uninstall Functionality in an .inf File

You can provide uninstall functionality in your .inf file by adding an installation section that removes the files, registry entries, and shortcuts and then adds your component to the list of programs that can be uninstalled from the **Add/Remove Programs** dialog box in Control Panel. An example is included in the Inf folder of the IEAK Toolkit.

To add your component to the **Add/Remove Programs** dialog box, add the following registry information:

```
HKLM,SOFTWARE\Microsoft\Windows\CurrentVersion\Uninstall\app-
name,"DisplayName",,"display description"
HKLM,SOFTWARE\Microsoft\Windows\CurrentVersion\Uninstall\app-
name,"UninstallString",,"command-line description"
```

display description

The description string is displayed in the list box in the **Add/Remove Programs** dialog box.

command-line

The command line is executed when the user selects the component from the list box in the **Add/Remove Programs** dialog box. To execute a section in an .inf file, you can use the **InstallHinfSection** entry-point function in Setupx.dll.

The following examples show how to use **AddReg** entries to add "My Test Application" to the list box in the **Add/Remove Programs** dialog box and execute the **[Remove_TestApp]** installation section in Test.inf:

```
HKLM,SOFTWARE\Microsoft\Windows\CurrentVersion\Uninstall\Test,
"DisplayName",,"My Test Application"

HKLM,SOFTWARE\Microsoft\Windows\CurrentVersion\Uninstall\Test,"Uninstall
String",,"RunDll setupx.dll,InstallHinfSection Remove_TestApp 4
test.inf"
```

Note Your installation code must copy the .inf file to the \Windows\Inf folder when your component is installed. This is the default location that is searched when the **InstallHinfSection** entry-point function is called.

Your code for uninstallation should remove the subkey that you created under the **Uninstall** registry key so that your optional component will no longer appear in the **Add/Remove Programs** list box after it has been uninstalled.

Using RunOnce Technology

Entries added to the **RunOnce** registry key run programs after the .inf file executes. If the .inf file specifies that the computer must be restarted, the **RunOnce** entries execute after the computer restarts.

The **RunOnce** registry key enables you to launch programs one time in Windows and to specify whether they should run "silently" (without prompts to the user) or as part of a list of programs or actions that the user sees. The reference to the program is then deleted so that the program will not be run again.

To run programs silently, add *description-string=command-line* entries under the following registry key:

HKEY_LOCAL_MACHINE\Software\Microsoft\Windows\CurrentVersion\RunOnce

To execute programs that run synchronously using **RunOnce**, add *description-string=command-line entries* under the following registry key:

HKEY_LOCAL_MACHINE\Software\Microsoft\Windows\CurrentVersion\RunOnce\Setup

P A R T   4

Installing

Chapter 19: Deploying Microsoft Internet Explorer 5

After extensive research, planning, testing, and analysis, the final step in the deployment process is rolling out the Microsoft Internet Explorer 5 installation to your users. This chapter describes the steps to follow when you are ready to deploy Internet Explorer.

Chapter 20: Implementing the Sign-up Process

Internet service providers (ISPs) can use the Microsoft Internet Explorer Customization wizard to create custom packages of Internet Explorer 5 that specify how new users sign up with their service and connect to the Internet. This chapter describes how to implement a sign-up process, with or without a server, for your custom Internet Explorer installation.

C H A P T E R   1 9

Deploying Microsoft Internet Explorer 5

19

After extensive research, planning, testing, and analysis, the final step in the deployment process is rolling out the Microsoft Internet Explorer 5 installation to your users. This chapter describes the steps to follow when you are ready to deploy Internet Explorer.

Important Although the processes described in this chapter are based on a corporate business model for deployment, it is recommended that Internet service providers and Internet content providers follow similar procedures when they roll out Internet Explorer to their users.

In This Chapter

See Also

- For more information about preparing the teams, tools, resources, and plans for deploying Internet Explorer, see Chapter 9, "Planning the Deployment."

- For more information about testing the deployment process before the final rollout, see Chapter 11, "Setting Up and Administering a Pilot Program."

- For more information about building custom packages for installation, see Chapter 15, "Running the Internet Explorer Customization Wizard."

Announcing the Deployment

Before the installation begins, inform the users about the process. You might want to announce the deployment through an e-mail memo or in face-to-face meetings. Either way, you will want to communicate the benefits of using Internet Explorer 5, the details of the overall plan, and the specific process to be followed by each group or department.

Next, distribute preliminary instructions, including the preparations users need to make. Users who are not familiar with Internet Explorer might require training sessions before Internet Explorer installation begins. For more information about user training, see "Providing User Training and Support" later in this chapter.

Preparing the Users' Computers

To prepare for the installation, upgrade the hardware on users' computers as needed. Make a backup copy of critical data and configuration files on the computers and defragment the hard disks. You need to ensure that each user's computer is working properly before proceeding with the installation.

There are several ways to do this:

- Your technicians can perform these tasks on each computer.

- The users can complete the tasks using instructions you provide.

- You can use system management software, such as Microsoft Systems Management Server, to perform the tasks from a central location.

Note To install Internet Explorer on computers with the Microsoft Windows NT operating system, you must enable administrative privileges. For more information about installing Internet Explorer on supported platforms, see Chapter 4, "Working with Different Platforms."

Providing User Training and Support

User training and user support are both critical to the success of deployment. Time and resources spent on training will decrease the demand for user support.

As final deployment approaches, the training and support teams should promote the benefits of this change. It is important to set expectations and build users' mastery of browser skills. Users need to understand the advantages of participating in the training program and the benefits of learning how to use the browser software. You can promote Internet Explorer by giving presentations and demonstrations and by providing users with tips and answers to frequently asked questions.

In general, you will train users before Internet Explorer is installed, and then provide user support during the rollout. Training and support teams typically carry out the user training and support according to the training and support plans, which were revised and improved following the pilot program. For more information about training and support during the pilot program, which precedes Internet Explorer deployment, see Chapter 11, "Setting Up and Administering a Pilot Program."

Building Custom Package Files

You can use the Internet Explorer Customization wizard to build custom packages of Internet Explorer that are tailored to meet the needs of your user groups. By specifying all user setup options and controlling most browser and Outlook Express features, you can ensure that users install Internet Explorer with the settings that are most appropriate for their use. For more information about using the Internet Explorer Customization wizard to build your custom packages, see Chapter 15, "Running the Internet Explorer Customization Wizard."

Signing Custom Package Files

Digital signatures identify the source of programs and guarantee that the code has not changed since it was signed. Depending on which operating systems users are running and how security levels are set, users might be prevented from or warned against downloading programs that are not digitally signed. If you are running a 32-bit version of Internet Explorer, you should digitally sign the cabinet (.cab) files created by the Internet Explorer Customization wizard, unless you specify in the wizard that the local intranet zone is to have a low security setting. You should also digitally sign any custom components you distribute with Internet Explorer for those Windows versions.

Note If you are running Internet Explorer on the Windows 16-bit or UNIX operating systems, you do not need to sign your programs or .cab files. These systems do not support Authenticode technology.

To digitally sign .cab files or custom programs, you need to carry out the following steps:

1. Obtain a digital certificate from a Certification Authority (CA), such as VeriSign or GTE.
2. Sign the code.

For more information about signing your files, see Chapter 12, "Preparing for the IEAK."

Preparing the Distribution Media

After you build and sign your custom package files, you should prepare the media that you will use to distribute Internet Explorer to your users. Choose one or more of the following types of distribution media:

- Download Web or FTP sites on the Internet or intranet
- Flat network share (all files in one directory)
- CD-ROMs
- Multiple floppy disks
- Single floppy disk (Internet service providers only)
- Single disk branding

Using Download Sites on the Internet or Intranet

The Internet Explorer Customization wizard places the setup file, IE5Setup.exe, in the location you entered at Stage 1 of the wizard. For example, you might have specified the following location:

```
C:\Webshare\WWWroot\CIE\Download\Win32\En\IE5Setup.exe
```

If you created the browser package on an Internet or intranet server, you need to set up your Web site so that users can download the files. For example, you might create a page where you post download information and provide a link to the setup file, IE5Setup.exe.

If you created the browser package on your hard disk or on a network drive, you need to move the following items to your Internet or intranet server:

- The folder that contains the language version you are posting. This folder is located within the destination folder you specify for each media type and platform. For example, if you specify your destination folder as C:\Inetpub\WWWroot\Cie\Dist, the English language version for Windows 32-bit versions would be created in the following folder: C:\Inetpub\WWWroot\Cie\Dist\Download\Win32\En

- The IE5Sites.dat file. This file points to the download site (or sites) you specified when you ran the wizard.

Using a Flat Network Share

If you build your custom packages on a local area network, or if you plan to distribute your packages from one, select the **Flat** media option during Stage 1 of the Internet Explorer Customization wizard. This option places all of the necessary files in one directory that you specify using the wizard. For example, you might specify the following directory:

```
C:\Cie\Lan
```

Using CD-ROMs or Floppy Disks

If you want to distribute the custom package to your users on CD-ROMs or 1.44 MB floppy disks, you can specify your preference during Stage 1 of the Internet Explorer Customization wizard. The wizard produces a custom package that is designated for the media you specify.

Using a Combination of Media Types

If you plan to build different media types, you only have to create a custom package once (assuming that you aren't changing other settings). For example, you can build a downloadable package and CD-ROM package at the same time. Because the packages are built in subfolders within your build folder, you just need to transfer the files (as necessary) to their distribution or imaging locations.

Illustration 19.1 shows a build folder that contains files for Internet download and for CD-ROM. The files for Internet download have been built in the target Web server location on the build computer. The location or locations where you post files for Internet download should correspond to the URLs that you specify on the Component Download Sites screen of the Internet Explorer Customization wizard.

The files in the CD folder should be copied or moved to a CD-ROM imaging program. If the media imaging program supports drag-and-drop, you can simply drag the CD folder to the CD-ROM imaging software interface. For more information about whether your program provides that option, see the imaging software documentation.

The following illustration shows how to set up files for distribution.

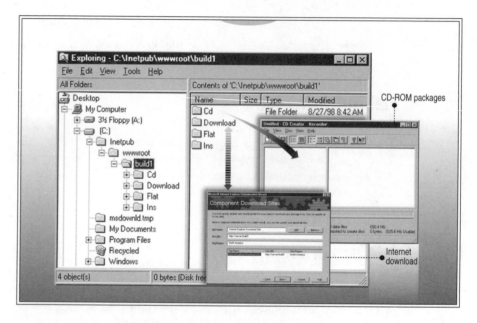

Illustration 19.1   How to Set Up Files for Distribution

Installing Microsoft Internet Explorer 5

Users install Internet Explorer by running Windows Update Setup for Internet Explorer 5 and Internet Tools, IE5Setup.exe. Be sure to provide written instructions to guide users through the installation process.

Running Setup from Download Sites on the Internet or Intranet

From download sites on the Internet or intranet, you can provide IE5Setup.exe directly to your users as an e-mail attachment, if your network can support sending multiple copies of the setup file. Or you can direct users to an Internet or intranet site from which they can choose to run IE5Setup.exe directly or download the file to their hard drive. This file is located in the Download folder within a unique subfolder for each language and platform version—for example, \Download\Win32\En or \Download\Unix\En.

Running Setup from a Flat Network Share

You should direct users to the designated directory on your local area network where IE5Setup.exe and the other setup files are located. Users can then run the setup program directly from this location.

Running Setup from CD-ROMs or Floppy Disks

If you distribute the custom package from CD-ROMs or floppy disks, IE5Setup.exe is included on the distribution media. Users install Internet Explorer by running IE5Setup.exe from the AutoRun splash screen of the CD-ROM or from Disk 1 of the floppy disk set. Windows Update Setup offers users the choice of installing the custom package or viewing more information. If the current version of Internet Explorer is already installed, the AutoRun program detects it.

> **Note** If you selected **Single disk branding** as your media option during Stage 1 of the Internet Explorer Customization wizard, the floppy disk that you create will customize an existing installation of Internet Explorer 4.01 Service Pack 1 (which is part of Windows 98) or higher. It does not install Internet Explorer 5, and you cannot include any custom components with this media type.

Running Windows Update Setup

When users run IE5Setup.exe, Windows Update Setup carries out the following steps to install the browser and any custom components you have designated:

- IE5Setup.exe extracts the setup files into a temporary directory.
- IESetup.inf checks the **[String]** section for the URL location of the IE5Sites.dat file.
- Windows Update Setup finds the IE5Sites.dat file, which points to the location of the download .cab files, and then displays the download options to the user.
- Windows Update Setup downloads the .cab files, which are placed in the specified directory—for example, C:\Program Files\Internet Explorer.
- Windows Update Setup extracts the .cab files.
- Windows Update Setup installs the browser and each component for the custom package.

After the browser is installed, Windows Update Setup prompts the user to restart the computer. After the computer restarts, Windows Update Setup configures the user's desktop and opens the Welcome splash screen to introduce the user to Internet Explorer 5.

Troubleshooting the Setup Process

To troubleshoot Windows Update Setup:

- Review the Internet Explorer Active Setup Log.txt file in the Windows folder. Each installation creates a log file, which collects information about that particular installation. If there is already an existing Internet Explorer Active Setup Log.txt file, Windows Update Setup renames the existing log as a .bak file and creates a new log file.

- Make sure that the download URLs that you specify during setup are the same as the URLs for the download server.

- See Appendix B, "Troubleshooting," which includes information about commonly reported problems and useful tools, such as Internet Explorer Repair, which helps you identify and resolve problems caused by out-of-date, deleted, or corrupted files.

Assisting Users During Installation

The support team should monitor the progress of the Internet Explorer installation and assist users as necessary. It is recommended that you create an online support Web site that provides users with help resources to solve common problems. You can integrate the online support site with your help desk and provide ways to refer unusual or difficult problems to user-support specialists.

As solutions are developed to solve users' problems during the deployment process, you can update the support Web site to provide that information.

C H A P T E R   2 0

Implementing the Sign-up Process

Internet service providers (ISPs) can use the Microsoft Internet Explorer Customization wizard to create custom packages of Internet Explorer 5 that specify how new users sign up with their service and connect to the Internet. You can select a server-based or serverless sign-up process, or disable the sign-up feature altogether (for distributing software updates to existing users). This chapter describes how to implement a sign-up process, with or without a server, for your custom Internet Explorer installation.

In This Chapter

See Also

- For more information about preparing custom sign-up files, see Chapter 12, "Preparing for the IEAK."

- For more information about setting up an Internet sign-up server, see Chapter 13, "Setting Up Servers."

- For more information about using the Internet Explorer Customization wizard to create custom browser packages, see Chapter 15, "Running the Internet Explorer Customization Wizard."

Implementing a Server-Based Sign-up Process

The server-based sign-up process automates the registration and set-up tasks for new and existing users. This process uses an Internet sign-up server (ISS) to collect information from each user. The sign-up server adds the data to your customer database and then sends a configuration packet back to the user's computer. This packet configures the browser for subsequent connections to your Internet services.

The following server-based sign-up methods are available to ISPs:

- **Internet Connection wizard**—Using the Internet Explorer Customization wizard, you can specify the Internet Connection wizard (ICW) as the tool that customers will use to sign up and configure their computers for Internet services. This is the recommended method because it uses a standard wizard interface that you can customize to fit the needs of your organization and its users. The ICW automatic-configuration feature also enables you to configure settings for users that already have Internet accounts.

  For more detailed information about how to develop an ICW sign-up process, including the files that you need to generate and install on your server for ICW sign-up, see Chapter 13, "Setting Up Servers."

- **Full-screen Kiosk mode**—Using the Internet Explorer Customization wizard, you can specify that the sign-up process screens you create are displayed in full-screen Kiosk mode.

Note If you are using single-disk branding and members of your user community have Internet Explorer 4.01 Service Pack 1 installed, it is recommended that you use the Kiosk-mode sign-up method. The ICW is not available through single-disk branding unless users are running version 5 of the ICW (the ICW version that accompanies Windows 98 is not enabled for the Internet Explorer ICW sign-up method).

Creating a Custom Package with a Server-Based Sign-up Method

To create a custom browser package that includes a server-based sign-up method, specify the following in Stage 4 of the Internet Explorer Customization wizard:

- Either **Server-based sign-up using the Internet Connection Wizard** or **Server-based sign-up using full-screen Kiosk mode** as your sign-up method.

- The path of the working folder that contains your custom sign-up files. These files enable users to configure their computers to connect to your sign-up server.

- The sign-up server information, including dial-up-networking parameters that enable users to establish a connection to your sign-up server and the URL of the first online sign-up page.

- The ICW customization information, including your title bar and custom images (if you selected **Server-based sign-up using the Internet Connection Wizard**).

To ensure that your package installs correctly, the folder that contains your custom sign-up files must include the following:

- **Signup.htm**—This HTML page provides information about your Internet services and must include a link to an appropriate HTML page on the sign-up server. You can customize the sample Signup.htm file, which is located in the IEAK \Reskit\ISP\Server\Client folder. For example, you can add technical support data or include links to Internet sign-up (.isp) files.

- **Signup.isp**—This Internet sign-up file is used to dial your sign-up server and is referenced in Signup.htm. This file should also contain a link to the URL of the server script that generates your Internet settings (.ins) files. Using the Internet Explorer Customization wizard, you can edit the parameters contained in this sign-up file. The Internet Explorer Customization wizard also generates other .isp files for the sign-up process.

- **All other sign-up files**—All related files, including .gif and .jpg graphics files, must be saved in the same folder with your custom sign-up files. For example, you may want to include your own customized versions of the Install.gif file.

For more information about building a browser package with custom sign-up files, see Chapter 12, "Preparing for the IEAK" and Chapter 15, "Running the Internet Explorer Customization Wizard."

Distributing a Custom Package with a Server-Based Sign-up Method

If you use a server-based sign-up method, the sign-up process for your custom browser package occurs in three steps:

1. The user's computer establishes a connection with the sign-up server.

2. The sign-up server collects information from the user, and adds the data to your customer database.

3. The sign-up server passes a configuration packet back to the user's computer, which is then configured with the appropriate browser settings.

Establishing a Connection with the Sign-up Server

The user opens the sign-up program, which starts Internet Explorer, dials the sign-up server, and posts an initial connection request. Then, the sign-up server does the following:

- Accepts the request from the user's computer (the HTTP client) and establishes an HTTP connection.

- Creates a local data store for accumulating the information that the user enters.

- Assigns a unique session handle that is embedded in all subsequent HTTP transactions with the client.

HTTP is a sessionless protocol; however, the sign-up server operates in a session-oriented mode and uses the session handle to identify all transactions associated with the sign-up process for a particular user. For example, the session handle could be an automatically generated number sequence assigned to this transaction by your database. For more information about sign-up server processing, see Chapter 13, "Setting Up Servers."

Collecting the User's Sign-up Information

The sign-up server collects user information from a sequence of HTML pages that walk the user through the sign-up process, much like a wizard in a Windows-based program. The sign-up server uploads the pages, on demand, to the user's computer. The sign-up process concludes when the user clicks the appropriate button on the final HTML page to either accept or decline the sign-up agreement.

You can choose your own content and format for the HTML pages. Typically, each HTML page includes the following:

- A form for the user to fill out.

- Navigation buttons that the user can click to move forward or backward between pages.

- A button that the user can click to cancel the sign-up session.

Each HTML form includes controls for collecting input text, navigating between pages, and identifying the session. The form gathers information from the user and passes it to the sign-up server when the user clicks a navigation button. Also, the sign-up server can validate the data and post an edit page to the user's computer if the data is not acceptable. For more information about setting up HTML forms on your sign-up server, see Chapter 13, "Setting Up Servers."

Note Make sure that you save the HTML file in the correct folder on the sign-up server; the Signup.isp file includes a link to server files for Windows 32-bit versions, and the Signup.htm file includes a link to server files for Windows 16-bit versions.

Passing a Configuration Packet Back to the User's Computer

If the user accepts the sign-up agreement, the sign-up server builds a configuration packet with an .ins file (generated by the Internet Explorer Customization wizard) that includes information about the user and your Internet services. The .ins file can contain only connection settings, or it can contain connection, browser, and mail settings that include graphics.

The sign-up server passes the configuration packet back to the user's computer by using the .ins file, which can be generated on the fly, or simply redirected to the client computer. Then, the user's computer can continue the process of installing the custom browser package. If the user declines or quits the sign-up agreement, the sign-up server redirects the user's computer to a file that cancels the sign-up process.

The configuration packet includes the following information:

- Data for configuring Internet connections
- Capabilities of the user's account (including e-mail and newsreaders)
- Branding information, which customizes the appearance of the sign-up pages for your organization
- The local phone number, so the user can access your Internet services

The first two types of data are created as part of the sign-up server. The Internet Explorer Customization wizard prepares the .ins file for branding. Some settings, such as Entry, User, Phone, Device, Server, and TCP/IP, cannot be specified in the wizard; you must assign these settings manually in the .ins file.

If you want to provide a variety of custom "private-branded" versions of Internet Explorer for different user groups, you can maintain multiple sets of branding information that the sign-up server downloads in the .ins file. For example, you may want to customize versions with different logos, title bars, favorites, search pages, start pages, special links, or locations for online assistance. All of the compact discs that you distribute to users will be the same, but they will be branded differently when the users sign up for Internet services.

Implementing a Serverless Sign-up Process

The serverless sign-up process enables ISPs that do not want to use a sign-up server to provide customized installations to their users. A serverless sign-up process avoids the creation of a sign-up server by manually giving account information to the users.

Creating a Custom Package with a Serverless Sign-up Method

To create a custom browser package that includes a serverless sign-up method, specify the following in Stage 4 of the Internet Explorer Customization wizard:

- **Serverless sign-up** as your sign-up method.
- The path of the folder that contains your custom sign-up files. These files enable users to configure their computers for Internet services.
- The dial-up networking parameters that enable users to establish a connection for Internet services.

To ensure that your package installs correctly, the folder that contains your custom sign-up files must include the following:

- **Signup.htm**—This HTML page provides information about your Internet service and must include a link to the .ins file, which contains the configuration settings for your custom browser package.
- **All other sign-up files**—All related files, including .gif and .jpg graphic files, must be saved in the same folder with your custom sign-up files. For example, you may want to include your own customized versions of the Install.gif and Logohere.gif files.

For more information about building a browser package with custom sign-up files, see Chapter 12, "Preparing for the IEAK" and Chapter 15, "Running the Internet Explorer Customization Wizard."

Distributing a Custom Package with a Serverless Sign-up Method

Your custom package includes a configuration file, named Install.ins, that contains the settings you specified for your custom browser. Unlike the Internet sign-up server method, this .ins file contains no user-specific configuration information. When the user starts the sign-up program, a link from the local HTML page starts the .ins file. The user provides the user name, password, and connection information. Then, the .ins file configures the user's account to connect to the Internet using the custom browser.

Note The serverless sign-up process also includes an advanced option, which uses an ActiveX control to generate the .ins file on the fly to incorporate the user's information.

PART 5

Maintaining and Supporting

Chapter 21: Using Automatic Configuration and Automatic Proxy

Automatic configuration and automatic proxy enable you to change settings globally after you deploy Internet Explorer. This can be useful if you expect the needs of your users or your organization to change.

Chapter 22: Keeping Programs Updated

This chapter describes the three primary tools you can use to keep Internet Explorer programs and settings updated: the Internet Explorer Administration Kit (IEAK) the Internet Explorer Profile Manager, the update-notification page, and software distribution channels.

Chapter 23: Implementing an Ongoing Training and Support Program

After your users install Microsoft Internet Explorer 5, you can implement an ongoing training and support program. Because learning how to use Internet Explorer is an ongoing process, basic training and support during deployment followed by an ongoing program customized for your organization's needs is the best means for getting the most out of your investment in Internet Explorer. This chapter describes ongoing training and support options.

C H A P T E R   2 1

Using Automatic Configuration and Automatic Proxy

Automatic configuration and automatic proxy enable you to change settings globally after you deploy Internet Explorer. Information in this chapter is useful if you expect the needs of your users or your organization to change.

In This Chapter

See Also

- For more information about customizing Internet Explorer, see Chapter 3, "Understanding Customization and Administration."

- For more information about building custom packages for installation, see Chapter 15, "Running the Internet Explorer Customization Wizard."

- For more information about keeping programs updated, see Chapter 22, "Keeping Programs Updated."

Understanding Automatic Configuration and Automatic Proxy

The automatic configuration and automatic proxy features enable you to change settings after you deploy Internet Explorer. By providing a pointer to configuration files on a server, you can change the settings globally without having to change each user's computer.

When deciding whether to use automatic configuration, you should estimate how often you anticipate changes to your users' settings. You would also need to set up a server that could host the necessary files.

A new feature in Internet Explorer 5 enables automatic configuration and automatic proxy to work when a user connects to a network for the first time. This can help reduce administrative overhead and potentially reduce help desk calls about browser settings.

This feature extends the functionality of automatic configuration and automatic proxy. With automatic detection, the browser can now automatically be configured when it is started, even if the browser was not first customized by the administrator. For example, if a user were to download a non-customized browser from the Internet, instead of installing a customized version from the corporate servers, automatic detection can automatically configure and customize the user's browser.

Using Automatic Configuration

To use automatic configuration, you must create an IEAK Profile by using the IEAK Profile Manager. The profile consists of an .ins file and any cabinet (.cab) files generated by the Profile Manager. The profile contains information that is used to configure users' browsers. After creating the profile, you place it on a server.

When you run the Internet Explorer Customization wizard, you type the server path for the .ins file. If you need to change user settings later, you just edit the .ins file. The next time your users start the browser, or on a schedule that you specify, the changes are reflected on each user's computer.

The following illustration shows how automatic configuration works.

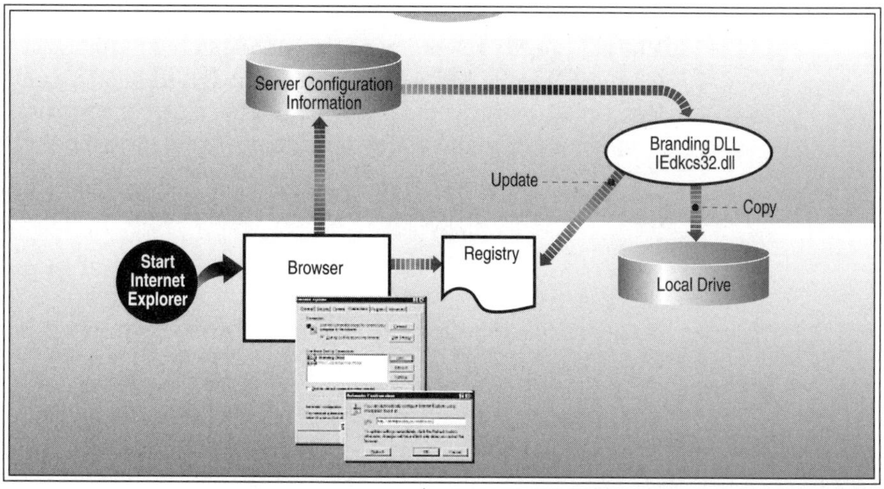

Illustration 21.1   Automatic Configuration

How Automatic Proxy Works

Proxy servers can be used with a firewall to create a barrier between your organization and the Internet, to cache frequently used content, and to balance server load.

Internet Explorer can make system administration easier by enabling you to configure proxy settings such as server addresses and bypass lists automatically. You can use the IEAK to configure proxy settings, or you can create an HTML file that specifies the settings in script files. The script files are executed whenever a network request is made.

You can configure multiple proxy servers for each protocol type, and Internet Explorer can automatically cycle through the different proxy servers to avoid overloading any particular server.

You can also specify script files in .js, .jvs, or .pac format that enable you to configure and maintain advanced proxy settings. If you specify URLs for both automatic configuration and automatic proxy (auto-proxy), the auto-proxy URL is incorporated into the .ins file. The correct form for the URL is http://share/test.ins.

Using Proxy Selection and Proxy Bypass Lists

As an administrator, you can use a proxy server to limit access to the Internet. You can specify the proxy server in the Internet Explorer Customization wizard, the IEAK Profile Manager (formerly the INS Editor), or through the browser. You can also restrict the users' ability to change the proxy settings by using the Restrictions page in the Customization wizard or in the Profile Manager.

Note The proxy bypass feature may eliminate the need for using JavaScript or JScript to select a proxy.

▶ **To configure the proxy selection and proxy bypass settings**

1. In Internet Explorer, click the **Tools** menu, and then click **Internet Options**.

2. Click the **Connections** tab, and then click **LAN Settings**.

3. In the Proxy Server area, select the **Use a proxy server** check box.

4. Click **Advanced**, and then fill in the proxy location and port number for each Internet protocol that is supported.

Note In most cases, only a single proxy server is used for all protocols. In those cases, enter the proxy location and port number for the HTTP setting, and then select the **Use the same proxy server for all protocols** check box.

JavaScript or JScript Auto-Proxy Examples

The following 10 scripts provide examples of how an auto-proxy configuration (.pac) file could be used to specify an auto-proxy URL. To use these functions, you must change the proxy names, port numbers, and IP addresses.

Note The **isInNet()**, **isResolvable()**, and **dnsResolve()** functions query a DNS server.

References to Object Model objects, properties, or methods cause the .pac file to fail silently. For example, the following references—window.open(...), alert(...), password(...)—all cause the .pac file to fail on Internet Explorer.

Example 1: Local hosts connect direct, all others connect through a proxy

The following function checks to see whether the hostname is a local host, and if it is, whether the connection is direct. If the hostname is not a local host, the connection is through the proxy.

```
function FindProxyForURL(url, host)
  {
    if (isPlainHostName(host))
      return "DIRECT";
    else
      return "PROXY proxy:80";
  }
```

The **isPlainHostName()** function checks to see if there are any dots in the hostname. If so, it returns false; otherwise, it returns true.

Example 2: Hosts inside the firewall connect direct, outside local servers connect through a proxy

The following function checks to see whether the host is either a "plain" hostname (meaning the domain name is not included) or part of a particular domain (.company.com), but the hostname is not either www or home.

```
function FindProxyForURL(url, host)
  {
    if ((isPlainHostName(host) ||
      dnsDomainIs(host, ".company.com")) &&
      !localHostOrDomainIs(host, "www.company.com") &&
      !localHostOrDomainIs(host, "home.company.com"))

      return "DIRECT";
    else
      return "PROXY proxy:80";
```

Note The **localHostOrDomainIs()** function is executed only for URLs in the local domain.

The **dnsDomainIs()** function returns true if the domain of the hostname matches the domain given.

Example 3: If host is resolvable, connect direct, else connect through a proxy

The following function asks the DNS server to try to resolve the hostname passed to it. If it can, a direct connection is made. If it cannot, the connection is made through aproxy. This is useful when an internal DNS server is used to resolve all internal hostnames.

```
function FindProxyForURL(url, host)
  {
    if (isResolvable(host))
      return "DIRECT";
    else
      return "PROXY proxy:80";
  }
```

See note on the **isResolvable()** function.

Example 4: If host is in specified subnet, connect direct, else connect through a proxy

The following function compares a given IP address pattern and mask with the hostname. This is useful if certain hosts in a subnet should be connected directly and others should be connected through a proxy.

```
function FindProxyForURL(url, host)
  {
    if (isInNet(host, "999.99.9.9", "255.0.255.0"))
      return "DIRECT";
    else
      return "PROXY proxy:80";
  }
```

See note on the **isInNet()** function.

The **isInNet**(host, pattern, mask) function returns true if the host IP address matches the specified pattern. The mask indicates which part of the IP address to match (255=match, 0=ignore).

Example 5: Determine connection type based on host domain

The following function specifies a direct connection if the host is local. If the host is not local, this function determines which proxy to use based on the host domain. This is useful if the host domain name is one of the criteria for proxy selection.

```
function FindProxyForURL(url, host)
  {
    if (isPlainHostName(host))
      return "DIRECT";
    else if (shExpMatch(host, "*.com"))
      return "PROXY comproxy:80";
    else if (shExpMatch(host, "*.edu"))
      return "PROXY eduproxy:80";
    else
      return "PROXY proxy";
  }
```

The **shExpMatch**(str, shexp) function returns true if str matches the shexp using shell expression patterns.

Example 6: Determine connection type based on protocol being used

The following function extracts the protocol being used and makes a proxy selection accordingly. If no match is made on the protocol, a direct connection is made. This is useful if the protocol being used is one of the criteria for proxy selection.

```
function FindProxyForURL(url, host)
  {
      if (url.substring(0, 5) == "http:") {
        return "PROXY proxy:80";
      }
      else if (url.substring(0, 4) == "ftp:") {
        return "PROXY fproxy:80";
      }
      else if (url.substring(0, 7) == "gopher:") {
        return "PROXY gproxy";
      }
      else if (url.substring(0, 6) == "https:") {
        return "PROXY secproxy:8080";
      }
      else {
        return "DIRECT";
      }
  }
```

The **substring**() function extracts the specified number of characters from a string.

Example 7: Determine proxy setting by checking to see if hostname matches IP address

The following function makes a proxy selection by translating the hostname into an IP address and comparing it to a specified string.

```
function FindProxyForURL(url, host)
  {
      if (dnsResolve(host) == "999.99.99.999") { // = http://secproxy
        return "PROXY secproxy:8080";
      }
      else {
        return "PROXY proxy:80";
      }
  }
```

See note on the **dnsResolve()** function.

Example 8: If host IP matches specified IP, connect through a proxy, else connect direct

The following function is another way to make a proxy selection based on specifying an IP address. This example, unlike Example 7, uses the function call to explicitly get the numeric IP address (Example 7 uses the **dnsResolve()** function to translate the hostname into the numeric IP address).

```
function FindProxyForURL(url, host)
  {
      if (myIpAddress() == "999.99.999.99") {
        return "PROXY proxy:80";
      }
      else {
        return "DIRECT";
      }
  }
```

The **myIpAddress()** function returns the IP address (in integer-dot format) of the host that the browser is running on.

Example 9: If there are any dots in the hostname, connect through a proxy, else connect direct

The following function checks to see how many dots are in the hostname. If there are any dots in the hostname, connection is made through a proxy. If there are no dots in the hostname, a direct connection is made. This is another way to determine connection types based on hostname characteristics.

```
function FindProxyForURL(url, host)
  {
      if (dnsDomainLevels(host) > 0) { // if number of dots in host > 0
        return "PROXY proxy:80";
      }
        return "DIRECT";
  }
```

The **dnsDomainLevels()** function returns an integer equal to the number of dots in the hostname.

Example 10: Specify days of the week to connect through a proxy, other days connect direct

The following function determines the connection type by specifying days of the week that are appropriate for a proxy. Days that do not fall between these parameters use a direct connection. This function could be useful in situations where you might want to use a proxy when traffic is heavy and allow a direct connection when traffic is light.

```
function FindProxyForURL(url, host)
  {
    if(weekdayRange("WED", "SAT", "GMT"))
      return "PROXY proxy:80";
    else
      return "DIRECT";
  }
```

The **weekdayRange(** <day1> [,<day2>] [,<GMT>]) function returns whether the current system time falls within the range specified by the parameters <day1>, <day2>, and <GMT>. Only the first parameter is necessary. The GMT parameter sets the times to be taken in GMT rather than in the local time zone.

Note   Where the function is called with <day1> == <day2>, previous versions of Internet Explorer would yield results different from Netscape Navigator. Specifically, previous versions of Internet Explorer would interpret this day range as an entire week, while Internet Explorer 5 and Netscape Navigator interpret the range as a single day. For example, if the current day is Monday, the call **weekdayRange**("TUE", "TUE") returns TRUE on previous versions of Internet Explorer and FALSE on Internet Explorer 5 and Netscape Navigator.

Working with Automatic Detection of Browser Settings

Automatic detection of browser settings, which is based on Web Proxy AutoDiscovery (WPAD), is supported by both Dynamic Host Configuration Protocol (DHCP) and Domain Name System (DNS). With the appropriate settings, DHCP and DNS servers can automatically detect and configure a browser's settings. Your DHCP server must support the DHCPINFORM message; otherwise, use DNS.

This feature builds on existing automatic configuration technologies, in which a browser can be configured from a central location by using an automatic configuration URL (.ins file) or a proxy configuration (js, .jvs, or .pac) file.

When setting up automatic detection of browser settings when using the IEAK, you should select **Automatically detect settings** on the Automatic Configuration screen of the Internet Explorer Customization wizard. This option can also be set in the Internet Options dialog box of the Internet Explorer browser.

For details about setting up a DHCP or DNS server for automatic detection of browser settings, see Chapter 13, "Setting up Servers."

CHAPTER 22

Keeping Programs Updated

This chapter describes the three primary tools you can use to keep Internet Explorer programs and settings updated:

- **IEAK Profile Manager**—Use the IEAK Profile Manager to create and modify auto-configuration files, which are used to update the browser configurations on users' computers.

- **Update notification page**—Set the update notification page to notify users automatically about new versions of Internet Explorer. You can customize or disable this page.

- **Software distribution channels**—Use software distribution channels to provide future software updates over the Internet or intranet to channel subscribers.

In This Chapter

See Also

- For more information about Internet Explorer Customization wizard settings, see Chapter 15, "Running the Internet Explorer Customization Wizard."

- For more information about system policies and restrictions, see Appendix E, "Setting System Policies and Restrictions."

IEAK Profile Manager

Before Internet Explorer is installed, you can use the Internet Explorer Customization wizard to preconfigure your custom packages to include automatic browser configuration and Automatic Detection. With these features, the users' computers can automatically locate the auto-configuration .ins file (which is maintained on your server) and use it to update browser configuration settings at a specified interval.

After Internet Explorer is installed, you can use the IEAK Profile Manager to maintain browser configuration settings on your users' computers. With the IEAK Profile Manager, you can open any auto-configuration .ins file and change settings, such as digital signature and security zone options.

You can also use the IEAK Profile Manager to enable automatic browser configuration if you didn't preconfigure this feature before installation. The Automatic Detection feature (if enabled) will locate the updated auto-configuration .ins file, or you can set the automatic browser configuration manually on client computers.

For more information about setting up automatic browser configuration and Automatic Detection, see Chapter 21, "Using Automatic Configuration and Automatic Proxy." For more information about setting up your servers for automatic browser configuration and auto-discovery, see Chapter 13, "Setting Up Servers."

Updating Browser Configuration Settings

The Internet Explorer Customization wizard creates an auto-configuration .ins file for each custom package you build. By default, this file is named Install.ins, but you can rename the file for each custom package.

After you install the browser, you can use the IEAK Profile Manager to update configuration settings by opening the auto-configuration .ins file, changing settings, and then saving the file. The IEAK Profile Manager also keeps the companion files current each time you save the auto-configuration .ins file.

You can change two types of configuration settings:

- **Wizard settings**—These settings correspond to browser and component options that you initially configured in Stages 2 through 5 of the Internet Explorer Customization wizard.

- **Policies and restrictions**—These settings correspond to options that you initially configured on the **System Policies and Restrictions** screen in Stage 5 of the Internet Explorer Customization wizard.

▶ **To change configuration settings by using the IEAK Profile Manager**

1. On the **Start** menu, point to **Programs**, point to **Microsoft IEAK**, and then click **IEAK Profile Manager**.

2. On the **File** menu, click **Open**, and then open the auto-configuration .ins file for your custom package.

3. On the **Platform** menu, click the operating system for your custom package.

4. On the left side of the window, click **Wizard Settings** or **Policies and Restrictions**.

   The following illustration shows the Wizard Settings screen.

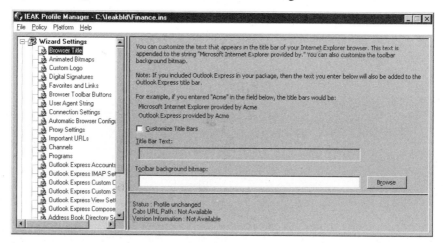

5. On the left side of the window, click each category you want to change, and then on the right side, change the options you want.

6. On the **File** menu, click **Save as**. Type a name for the file, keeping its .ins extension.

The default location for saving the auto-configuration .ins file is the *build directory*\Ins*operating system**language* folder. For example, an English version of the .ins file that was created for the Windows 32-bit platform might be saved in the \Build1\Ins\Win32\En folder.

Before updating the configuration settings on your users' computers, you should copy the auto-configuration .ins file and the companion .cab files generated by the IEAK Profile Manager to a working directory and test the configuration. After you validate your changes, copy the new auto-configuration .ins file to your production server. The automatic browser configuration feature then updates the configuration settings on the users' computers.

Files Generated by the IEAK Profile Manager

When you update and save your configuration settings, the IEAK Profile Manager generates the following files:

- **Auto-configuration .ins file**—This file contains the browser and component settings that Internet Explorer uses to update the browser configuration on users' computers. You can specify these settings in the Wizard Settings section of the IEAK Profile Manager.

- **Cabinet (.cab) files**—These files are used to organize the installation files that are downloaded to the users' computers. You should digitally sign the .cab files created by the IEAK Profile Manager. For more information about signing your .cab files, see Chapter 12, "Preparing for the IEAK."

  The auto-configuration .cab files also contain information (.inf) files.

- **Information (.inf) files**—These files contain the system policies and restrictions that the operating system uses to update the system configuration on users' computers. You can specify these settings in the Policies and Restrictions section of the IEAK Profile Manager.

  Each .inf file also contains version information. When you change configuration settings, the IEAK Profile Manager updates the affected .inf files and their version information and repackages the companion .cab files.

Internet Explorer downloads and processes the contents of the auto-configuration .ins file and makes the necessary configuration changes on the users' computers. Internet Explorer also downloads and unpacks the companion .cab files for the operating system to process. If the version number of the auto-configuration .ins file does not change, new .cab files are not downloaded. The version number consists of the date the .ins file was modified and the number of times the file has been revised.

Creating Unique Configurations for Different Groups of Users

If you have users with different needs or if you want to change some users' configuration settings independently of others, you can create multiple auto-configuration .ins files. You can use the IEAK Profile Manager to specify different configuration settings for each group and save them as individual *usergroup*.ins files, where *usergroup* is a unique name for each user group. The IEAK Profile Manager automatically generates the companion .cab files. For example, you could specify a unique configuration for the Finance Department and save the configuration as Finance.ins. The IEAK Profile Manager would then generate the necessary companion .cab files.

Note If you create multiple auto-configuration .ins files, make sure that your custom packages are configured to use the correct file. You can also use an automated server solution, which enables you to use multiple .ins files without rebuilding your custom packages. For more information about using an automated server solution, see Chapter 17, "Time-Saving Strategies That Address Diverse User Needs."

Using Custom Policy Templates

The IEAK Profile Manager uses a default set of Windows policy template, or administration (.adm), files to define the rules for system policies and restrictions. The .adm files and system policies and restrictions are standard features of Windows 32-bit and Windows 16-bit platforms. If you are familiar with .adm files, you can create your own templates to define additional restrictions. For more information, see your Windows documentation.

Using the IEAK Profile Manager, you can import your own custom .adm files and include them with your updated configuration settings. The IEAK Profile Manager generates an associated .inf file, using the file prefix for the custom .adm file that you import. For example, if you import a file named Custom.adm, a Custom.inf file is generated and added to the companion .cab files. For more information about using custom .adm files, see Appendix E, "Setting System Policies and Restrictions."

Changing the Location of an Auto-Configuration .ins File

If you need to move the auto-configuration .ins file to a different production server, you can use the IEAK Profile Manager to update the URL for automatic browser configuration. If you set the auto-configuration .ins file to update at a specified interval, you must allow for two intervals after you update the URL for automatic browser configuration before the change takes effect.

▶ **To update the URL for automatic browser configuration**

1. On the **Start** menu, point to **Programs**, point to **Microsoft IEAK**, and then click **IEAK Profile Manager**.

2. On the **File** menu, click **Open**, and then open the auto-configuration .ins file from your custom package.

3. On the left side of the window under Wizard Settings, click **Automatic Browser Configuration**.

The following illustration shows the Automatic Browser Configuration options.

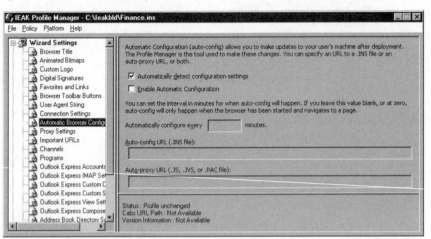

4. On the right side of the window, type the new server path in the **Auto-config URL (.INS File)** box.

5. On the **File** menu, click **Save as**. Type a name for the file, keeping its .ins extension.

6. Type the new server location for your .ins file to match the URL that you entered, the URL to your .cab files, and the names of your .cab files.

   You must copy any .cab files that are created in the build folder to the same folder that contains your .ins file.

When the user starts the browser and the configuration settings are scheduled to be updated, the pointer to the URL for automatic browser configuration is then updated on the user's computer. At this point, the browser is still using the settings from the original auto-configuration .ins file (for example, http://*existing path*/Default.ins).

When the user starts the browser a second time and the configuration settings are scheduled to be updated again, the browser reads the new auto-configuration .ins file (for example, http://*new path*/Default.ins). When you are sure that the settings on all users' computers have been updated, you can remove the copy of the auto-configuration .ins file from its original location.

Update Notification Page

Internet Explorer automatically notifies your users when a new version of the browser is available. At a specified interval, the Internet Explorer home, or start, page is temporarily replaced by an update notification page when the user starts the browser. The default update notification page is the Microsoft Windows Update page. From this page, users can download a newer version of the browser, add the update notification page to their Favorites list, or cancel the browser update.

The update notification page compares the browser update version against the version of the browser on the users' computers. If the browser update version is newer, users are given the option to install it. If no update is available at the specified interval, the update notification page is automatically redirected to the user's home page.

At the specified interval, the update notification page appears once when the user starts the browser. The update notification page does not force the user to install the browser update. If the user closes the browser without selecting the update or the update is not completed, the user does not see the page again until the next interval. If you want to force the update to install a new program or update on your users' computers, you can use other system management tools, such as Microsoft System Management Server (SMS). For more information about using SMS, see Chapter 5, "Understanding Related Tools and Programs."

Specifying a Different Update Notification Page and Update Interval

You can use the Internet Explorer Customization wizard or the IEAK Profile Manager to replace the URL for the default update notification page with a URL for your own custom Web page or another Web site. You can also change the update interval, which specifies how often the update notification page is displayed.

You might want to customize the update notification page for the following reasons:

- If your users' computers do not have Internet access (which is needed to access Internet Explorer updates from Microsoft distribution sites), you must change the URL to a location on your local intranet.

- You might want to redirect users to your custom Addon.htm file rather than to the Windows Update page. For more information about Addon.htm, see Chapter 16, "Customizing Setup."

- You might want to provide other information, news, or software updates at a regular interval. For software updates of programs other than Internet Explorer, the browser prompts the user to install the update without comparing the update version with the version on the users' computers.

- You might want to redirect the update notification page temporarily to an executable (.exe) file for a program that you want to install on your users' computers. When the users start the browser, the .exe file begins to install the program automatically, and the update notification page does not appear.

For more information about specifying a different URL and update interval for the update notification page when you build your custom packages of Internet Explorer, see Chapter 15, "Running the Internet Explorer Customization Wizard."

After you deploy Internet Explorer, you can use the IEAK Profile Manager to change the settings for the update notification page.

▶ **To change the settings for the update notification page by using the IEAK Profile Manager**

1. On the **Start** menu, point to **Programs**, point to **Microsoft IEAK**, and then click **IEAK Profile Manager**.

2. On the **File** menu, click **Open**, and then open the auto-configuration .ins file from your custom package.

3. On the left side of the window under Policies and Restrictions, click **Internet Settings**, and then click **Component Updates**.

   The following illustration shows the Component Updates options.

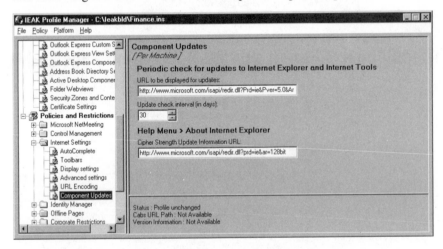

4. On the right side of the window in the **URL to be displayed for updates** box, type the URL for your custom update notification page.

5. In the **Update check interval (in days)** box, type the number of days for the update interval.

6. On the **File** menu, click **Save as**. Type a name for the file, keeping its .ins extension.

For more information about using the IEAK Profile Manager, see "IEAK Profile Manager" earlier in this chapter.

Disabling the Update Notification Page

When you use the Internet Explorer Customization wizard to build your custom packages of Internet Explorer, you can disable the update notification page. For more information, see Chapter 15, "Running the Internet Explorer Customization Wizard."

You can also disable the update notification page after you deploy Internet Explorer by using the IEAK Profile Manager.

▶ **To disable the update notification page by using the IEAK Profile Manager**

1. On the **Start** menu, point to **Programs**, point to **Microsoft IEAK**, and then click **IEAK Profile Manager**.

2. On the **File** menu, click **Open**, and then open the auto-configuration .ins file from your custom package.

3. On the left side of the window under Policies and Restrictions, click **Corporate Restrictions**, and then click **Software Updates**.

   The following illustration shows the Software Updates options.

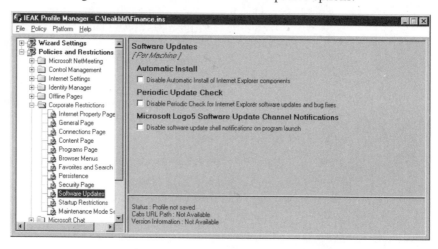

4. On the right side of the window, select the **Disable Periodic Check for Internet Explorer software updates and bug fixes** check box.

5. On the **File** menu, click **Save as**. Type a name for the file, keeping its .ins extension.

> **Note** After you disable the update notification page, users can still turn on the page in the browser. To disable the page completely so that users cannot enable it in the browser, set the **Update check interval** to a value of 0. For more information about setting the update check interval, see "Specifying a Different Update Notification Page and Update Interval" earlier in this chapter.

For more information about using the IEAK Profile Manager, see "IEAK Profile Manager" earlier in this chapter.

Software Distribution Channels

After Internet Explorer is installed, you can provide future software updates over the Internet or intranet by using software distribution channels, which are Web sites dedicated to software distribution. You can make a software update, such as a new custom package of Internet Explorer, available on your Internet or intranet server and then use a software distribution channel to distribute the update to channel subscribers. By default, Internet Explorer also notifies users when new browser releases and updates are available. You can use software distribution channels to control how often Internet Explorer checks for this updated information.

A Channel Definition Format (.cdf) file contains the software distribution channel settings, including the files to be updated and the daily, weekly, or monthly schedule for updating them on subscribers' computers. Each time the channel is updated, the latest version of the .cdf file is downloaded to subscribers' computers.

When the Open Software Distribution (OSD) section of the .cdf file indicates that a new version of the software is available, subscribers' computers can be instructed to do the following:

- Install the updates automatically and notify users that the updates were made.
- Download the installation files to users' hard disks, notify users, and provide instructions and links so that users can run the installation program manually.
- Automatically notify users by e-mail when new software updates are available. Provide instructions and links so that users can download the software manually.

Configuring Software Distribution Channels

To configure software distribution channels, you must complete the following tasks:

- Create the Web content to support the channels.
- Create the .cdf files.
- Create the software distribution packages.
- Configure the Web servers to support the channels.

After you configure software distribution channels on your computer, you can import them into your custom browser packages by using the Internet Explorer Customization wizard. For more information about using the Internet Explorer Customization wizard to import channels, see Chapter 15, "Running the Internet Explorer Customization Wizard."

If automatic browser configuration is enabled on your users' computers, you can use the IEAK Profile Manager to add or delete software distribution channels after you distribute your custom packages.

Creating Web Content

You can create the following Web content, which is included with each .cdf file:

- **Notification Web pages**—A notification Web page is used to describe the software updates and typically provides users with links to the individual notification Web pages for more details. This summary page can be an HTML file or an Active Server Page (.asp) file.

  The notification page is specified in the .cdf file for the CHANNEL element HREF attribute—for example, HREF="http://*Web server/filename*.htm," where *filename* is the name of the summary page. When users select the channel on the Channel bar or on the Favorites menu, the summary page appears on the right side of the browser window. If USAGE VALUE="E-mail" is specified, a notification page is sent by e-mail to users who have e-mail notification enabled.

- **Optional Channel bar graphic images**—You can create two optional graphic images in either .gif or .jpg format for the desktop Channel bar logo and the browser Channel bar logo. You can also create an optional .ico image, which appears to the left of each item in the Channel bar hierarchy.

The following list describes the specifications for these images:

- **Desktop Channel bar logo**—32 pixels high by 80 pixels wide with a black background.

  .cdf file entry: <LOGO HREF="*filename*.gif" STYLE="Image">

- **Browser Channel bar logo**—32 pixels high by 194 pixels wide with a color background.

  .cdf file entry: <LOGO HREF="*filename*.gif" STYLE="Image-Wide">

- **Browser Channel bar icon**—16 pixels high by 16 pixels wide, with different images, colors, or shapes to indicate whether an item is a container for other items or is actual content.

  .cdf file entry: <LOGO HREF="*filename*.ico" STYLE="Icon">

You can use the Channel bar logo for the browser window logo, and the extra area will be filled in with the same color as the rightmost top pixel. Animated .gif files are not supported. Images are displayed with a fixed 256-color palette regardless of the monitor color depth. Therefore, you should use the Windows halftone palette.

Note The Channel bar provides users with a 14-pixel-high by 14-pixel-wide red gleam to indicate when channel content has been updated. The gleam is a triangular overlay applied to the upper-left corner of the Channel bar logos. When you create Channel bar logos, do not place critical text or visual elements in this area. A 7-pixel-high by 7-pixel-wide gleam is also applied to the upper-left corner of icons to indicate when item content has been updated.

Creating the .cdf Files

Create a .cdf file for each software distribution channel that will be installed on users' computers. When you deploy custom packages of Internet Explorer to your users' computers, you should have enough preconfigured software distribution channels to meet your organization's needs.

Your .cdf file should include the schedule for updates. Using the SCHEDULE element in the .cdf file, you can specify daily, weekly, or monthly update frequencies as well as the time of day and the interval during which updates can occur. Assigning user groups to different schedules, such as alternating days or weeks, can help distribute network load.

You should schedule software downloads for times of low network traffic, especially for large software packages. To avoid a heavy load on your Web servers when all subscribers update the software distribution channel, you should specify that Internet Explorer updates the channel at random times.

Creating Software Distribution Packages

Create the software distribution packages you need to support your software distribution channels. Software distribution packages contain files that are compressed by using the .cab compression format. Each .cab file contains an .inf file that specifies how the .cab file should be installed. To locate the .cab files for the update, Setup reads the information in the IE5Sites.dat file.

Important You should digitally sign your .cab and .exe files before distributing software updates to users' computers. Digital signatures identify the source of programs and guarantee that the code hasn't changed since it was signed. Depending on how users' browser security levels are configured, users could be prevented from downloading .cab and .exe files that aren't signed. For more information about signing your files, see Chapter 12, "Preparing for the IEAK."

Configuring Web Servers

You should configure enough Web servers to support your software distribution channels, as well as the volume of software you distribute. You can include multiple channels on each Web server.

To configure Web servers to support your distribution channels, complete the following tasks:

1. Install Web server software, such as Microsoft Internet Information Server (IIS).

2. Configure file systems for each software distribution channel.

3. Copy the notification pages, graphics files, and software distribution packages to your Web servers.

For more information about configuring Web servers, see your Web server documentation.

C H A P T E R   2 3

Implementing an Ongoing Training and Support Program

After your users install Microsoft Internet Explorer 5, you can begin implementing an ongoing training and support program. Because learning how to use Internet Explorer is an ongoing process, basic training and support during deployment, followed by an ongoing program customized for your organization's needs, is the best means for getting the most out of your investment in Internet Explorer. This chapter describes ongoing training and support options.

In This Chapter

See Also

- For more information about developing your training and support plans, see Chapter 9, "Planning the Deployment."

- For more information about testing your training and support plans before deploying Internet Explorer, see Chapter 11, "Setting Up and Administering a Pilot Program."

- For more information about implementing training and support plans during the Internet Explorer rollout, see Chapter 19, "Deploying Microsoft Internet Explorer 5."

Overview

Your ongoing training and support program can increase productivity by promoting, expanding, and enhancing your users' Internet Explorer knowledge and skills. If you are using an internal training and support staff, they can effectively implement the program using their experience from the pilot program and Internet Explorer deployment.

Ongoing Training Options

Consider the following options for ongoing user training:

- **Offer follow-up training sessions for continuing education**—Based on the content of your deployment training and feedback from your users, you might want to offer additional formal or informal training sessions. These sessions can cover some skills in more detail or provide training for different features and functionality based on the changing needs of your organization and users. You might also want to repeat training sessions as new users join your organization.

- **Provide a Web page on the Internet or intranet for ongoing training**—You can develop a training Web page on the Internet or corporate intranet and then use an e-mail message or memo to tell your users about the page and point them to the URL. To make the Web page most useful, you should update it frequently with new tips, hints, and answers to frequently asked questions. Also, users can review Internet Explorer information on the Microsoft Web site for ongoing education about features, benefits, and enhancements.

- **Periodically distribute a newsletter or other written communication about Internet Explorer features and functionality**—You can produce and distribute an Internet Explorer memo, e-mail message, newsletter, or other written communication on a regular basis to all of your users. The communication can announce news relevant to your ongoing training efforts, including tips about new browser features and dates for additional training sessions. You can ask users to contribute articles that contain helpful advice and convey information that they have learned.

- **Supply users with additional Internet Explorer publications and training materials**—As part of your ongoing training and support program, you can supply users with additional publications and training materials, such as Microsoft Press books, for more detailed information about browser features and functions. For more information about Internet Explorer publications that are available from Microsoft Press, visit the Microsoft Press Web site. Microsoft Press books are available in stores that sell computer books.

- **Employ Microsoft training services**—Microsoft offers a variety of training services for educating computer professionals about Microsoft products. As part of your ongoing training program, you may want to offer these training services to your users. The following section describes Microsoft training services in greater detail.

Microsoft Training Services

Different training services are offered by Microsoft to help users become experts in Microsoft product solutions. These services include the Microsoft Certified Professional Program and Microsoft Technical Training courses.

Microsoft Certified Professional Program

The Microsoft Certified Professional Program offers an excellent way to gain the knowledge and skills necessary to build, implement, and support effective solutions with Microsoft products. To become a Microsoft Certified Professional, users must pass a series of rigorous, standardized certification exams. Users who become Microsoft Certified Professionals receive many benefits, including access to technical information, use of the Microsoft Certified Professional logo, and special invitations to Microsoft conferences and technical events. For more information about the Microsoft Certified Professional program, visit the Microsoft Training and Certification Web site.

Microsoft Technical Training

Microsoft technical training courses provide computer professionals with the knowledge to expertly install and support Microsoft solutions. Courses have been developed in close cooperation with the Microsoft product and technical support groups. They include in-depth, accurate information and hands-on lab exercises based on real-world experience. Microsoft technical training courses are designed to help users prepare effectively for Microsoft Certified Professional exams.

The Microsoft technical training curriculum is available in three forms:

- **Classroom instruction**—Instructor-led classes are given by Microsoft Certified Professional trainers at Microsoft Authorized Certified Education Centers (CTECs). As members of the Certified Solution Provider program, the CTECs are independent businesses qualified to teach the official Microsoft curriculum.

- **Online training**—For a more flexible alternative to instructor-led classes, users can turn to online training. They can learn at their own pace and on their own schedule in a virtual classroom, often with easy access to an online instructor. Without ever leaving their desk, users can gain the expertise they need. Because it's training on demand, users can access learning resources 24 hours a day.

- **Self-paced training**—Microsoft's self-paced curriculum enables users to learn at their own convenience. For motivated learners who are ready for the challenge, self-paced training is the most flexible, cost-effective way to increase knowledge and skills. There is a wide variety of comprehensive training kits, books, online resources, and CD-ROM-based multimedia—all developed or approved by Microsoft.

For more information about Microsoft technical training courses, visit the Microsoft Training and Certification Web site.

Ongoing Support Options

Consider the following options for ongoing user support:

- **Use the built-in product support**—Help files included with Internet Explorer provide users with a comprehensive set of topics, which they can view from within the browser. To view Help topics, on the **Help** menu, click **Contents and Index**. Also, users can find updates and technical information in the Readme.txt files that come with Internet Explorer.
- **Provide help desk services for ongoing user support**—Depending on resources, an organization can staff a help desk or use existing help desk services to support Internet Explorer users. Help desk support of this type, however, needs to be available on an ongoing basis. Users should be encouraged to call the help desk when they have questions. The staff at the help desk should monitor the types of questions that users ask and assess how well the staff provides accurate, timely answers.
- **Provide a Web page on the Internet or intranet for ongoing support**—Internet Explorer provides an **Online Support** option on the **Help** menu. By default, when users click **Online Support**, the Microsoft Technical Support Web page is displayed in the browser window. From this page, users can gain access to the Microsoft Technical Support problem-solving tools and technical information, including the Knowledge Base, troubleshooting wizards, and download sites.

An organization can also create its own Web page to provide online technical support tailored to the needs of users. When the organization creates custom packages of Internet Explorer, the URL for this support page can replace the default link used by the **Online Support** menu option.

- **Employ Microsoft support services**—In addition to the extensive online help and user support available from the Microsoft Technical Support Web page, Microsoft offers a variety of other support services for Internet Explorer. The following section describes these Microsoft support services in greater detail.

Microsoft Support Services

Microsoft support services are available to users by telephone and through various online services.

Note For a complete listing of support services, including telephone numbers, pricing, terms, and conditions, visit the Microsoft Technical Support Web site.

Standard No-Charge Support

Internet Explorer users who cannot find the answers they need using online help and other resources can contact Microsoft Technical Support directly. No payment or purchase is required to obtain 90 days of telephone and Web Response support from the first reported incident.

In the United States, no-charge support is available from Microsoft support engineers through a toll call between 6:00 A.M. and 6:00 P.M. Pacific time, Monday through Friday, excluding holidays. In Canada, no-charge support is available through a toll call between 8:00 A.M. and 8:00 P.M. Eastern time, Monday through Friday, excluding holidays. Outside the United States and Canada, users can contact Microsoft Product Support Services at the Microsoft subsidiary office that serves their area.

Users who call Microsoft Product Support Services should be at the computer and have the appropriate product documentation in hand. The following information is required:

- Version number of the Microsoft product in use
- Type of hardware in use
- Exact wording of any messages that appear on the screen
- Description of what happened and what was being done when the problem occurred
- Description of what was tried to solve the problem

Pay-Per-Incident Support

Microsoft Product Support Services offers priority telephone access to Microsoft support engineers in the United States 24 hours a day, 7 days a week, excluding holidays. In Canada, priority support is available from 6:00 A.M. to 12:00 A.M. Eastern time, 7 days a week, excluding holidays. Microsoft charges a fixed rate per incident, which appears on the user's telephone bill (not available in Canada) or is billed to the user's VISA, MasterCard, or American Express card.

Priority Plus and Priority Annual Support

Microsoft Product Support Services offers annual fee-based support plans. These plans are designed for businesses that require priority access to support engineers for business-critical needs 24 hours a day, 7 days a week. These businesses anticipate a high volume of calls or require access to specialized information.

Premier Support

Microsoft Technical Support offers a complete program of professional support services for business enterprise customers called Premier Support. These support services are designed to help large enterprises successfully develop, deploy, and manage mission-critical business systems that are built with Microsoft technologies. Premier Support provides access to the professional services and technical expertise that large enterprises need to maximize use of their business systems and minimize their total costs.

Each Premier Support customer is assigned a Technical Account Manager (TAM) who works directly with enterprise staff to help resolve problems and make sure that Premier Support services meet the unique needs of the organization. Premier Support customers have priority access, 24 hours a day, to experienced Microsoft support engineers for personalized support services and fast resolution of technical issues. In addition, the Premier Service Desk provides access to a secure Web site with support-related information for enterprise customers.

Other Microsoft Support Resources

Microsoft offers a variety of other support resources to meet the unique needs of organizations and their users.

Microsoft Authorized Support Centers

Microsoft Authorized Support Centers (ASCs) are a select group of strategic support providers who offer high-quality, customized support services for each phase of system development, including planning, implementing, and maintaining multi-vendor environments.

Services available from ASCs include:

- On-site support
- Integration and implementation services
- Help desk services
- Hardware support
- Development resources

An ASC vendor can provide comprehensive technical support and service. ASC services can supplement an in-house help desk or Microsoft support service option that's most appropriate for in-house needs. For more information about Microsoft Authorized Support Centers, visit the Microsoft in the Enterprise Web site.

Microsoft Certified Solution Providers

Microsoft Certified Solution Providers (MCSPs) are independent organizations that provide consulting, integration, development, training, technical support, and other services for Microsoft products. The MCSP program supplies Certified Solution Providers with information, business development assistance, and tools that help create additional value for Microsoft-based software technology. For more information about the program, visit the MCSP Public Web site.

MSDN Online

The Microsoft Developer Network (MSDN) is the official source for comprehensive programming information, development toolkits, and testing platforms. A subscription to MSDN includes quarterly updates of information and technology. For more information about subscribing to this development resource, visit the MSDN Online Web site.

Microsoft Seminar Online

Microsoft Seminar Online delivers valuable seminar content from industry experts directly to users' desktops over the Internet. Users are in control of their learning experience. They have instant access to the hottest technical topics, which are tailored to their interests and available at a time that fits their schedule. To learn about featured seminars or to review a list of seminars by date, subject, or title, visit the Microsoft Seminar Online Web site.

Microsoft TechNet

Microsoft TechNet is the comprehensive CD-ROM information resource for evaluating, implementing, and supporting Microsoft business products. A one-year subscription to Microsoft TechNet includes two CD-ROMs every month with over 150,000 pages of up-to-date technical information. The first CD-ROM contains current technical notes, reviewers' guides, background papers, Microsoft product resource kits, the entire Microsoft Knowledge Base, and much more. The second CD-ROM contains the Microsoft Software Library with the latest drivers and service packs for Microsoft products. For more information about subscribing, visit the Microsoft TechNet Web site.

P A R T   6

Appendixes

Appendix A: What's on the Resource Kit CD-ROM?

The *Microsoft Internet Explorer 5 Resource Kit*, which is distributed on a
CD-ROM, contains comprehensive technical information, software tools,
and sample files for deploying and supporting Internet Explorer 5. You can
browse the contents of the CD-ROM, copy files, or install software. This
appendix provides a complete list of the CD-ROM contents.

Appendix B: Troubleshooting

This appendix provides detailed information for troubleshooting Microsoft
Internet Explorer 5, including an effective troubleshooting strategy and a
description of the most commonly reported problems. For easy troubleshooting,
problems are categorized into several broad areas.

Appendix C: Batch-Mode File Syntax and Command-Line Switches

This appendix describes how you use batch files and command-line switches to
customize setup, and command-line parameters to start Internet Explorer with
specific settings.

Appendix D: Checklists for Preparing to Use the IEAK

When preparing to use the Microsoft Internet Explorer Administration Kit
(IEAK), you may find checklists helpful. This chapter contains checklists for
the files you will need to prepare and information you will need to gather before
using the IEAK.

Appendix E: Setting System Policies and Restrictions

This appendix describes how you can use system policies and restrictions to control user and computer access to Microsoft Internet Explorer 5 features and functions. Using the Internet Explorer Customization wizard or IEAK Profile Manager, you can predefine Internet Explorer options and customize the Internet Explorer environment for different groups of users.

Appendix F: Country/Region and Language Codes

If you are an Internet service provider, you may find this list of country/region and language codes to be helpful.

Appendix G: Microsoft Internet Explorer 5 File Types

This appendix provides an overview of the common types of files that are used as part of Microsoft Windows Update Setup for Internet Explorer 5 and Internet Tools. Learning about the purposes of these files and how they work together can make it easier to troubleshoot potential setup issues.

Appendix H: Structural Definition of .inf Files

Although the IEAK wizard, Internet Explorer batch files, and third-party programs can customize the setup program, you can also use setup information (.inf) files to develop a customized setup solution. This appendix describes the sections of an .inf file and provides a sample.

Appendix I: Microsoft Internet Explorer 5 Resource Directory

This appendix contains lists of product resources and Web sites. These lists provide sources for additional information about Microsoft Internet Explorer 5 and its components, and information about related Microsoft products.

APPENDIX A

What's on the Resource Kit CD-ROM?

The Microsoft Internet Explorer 5 Resource Kit CD-ROM contains comprehensive technical information, software tools, and sample files for deploying and supporting Internet Explorer 5. You can browse the contents of the CD-ROM, copy files, or install software. This appendix provides a complete list of the CD-ROM contents.

In This Appendix

See Also

- For general information about this Resource Kit and its contents, see the "Welcome" chapter at the beginning of this book.

- For a list of additional resources that provide information about the browser and its components and about related Microsoft products, see Appendix I, "Microsoft Internet Explorer 5 Resource Directory."

Internet Explorer 5

The Internet Explorer 5 Web browser is included, along with the following browser components:

- Offline Browsing Pack
- Internet Explorer Help
- Microsoft Virtual Machine
- Microsoft Internet Connection wizard
- Internet Explorer core fonts
- Dynamic HTML data binding
- Internet Explorer browsing enhancements
- Microsoft NetMeeting 2.11
- Microsoft Outlook Express 5
- Microsoft Chat 2.5
- Microsoft Windows Media Player
- Microsoft Windows Media Player codecs
- Microsoft Media Player RealNetwork support
- Microsoft DirectAnimation
- Vector Graphics Rendering
- AOL Art Image Format support
- Macromedia Shockwave Director
- Macromedia Flash

- Microsoft FrontPage Express
- Microsoft Web Publishing wizard
- Web folders
- Visual Basic scripting support
- Additional Web fonts
- Microsoft Wallet 3.0
- Language auto-selection
- Japanese text display support
- Japanese text input support
- Korean text display support
- Korean text input support
- Pan-European text display support
- Chinese (traditional) text display support
- Chinese (traditional) text input support
- Chinese (simplified) text display support
- Chinese (simplified) text input support
- Vietnamese text display support
- Hebrew text display support
- Arabic text display support
- Thai text display support

Microsoft Windows NT 4.0 Service Pack 4

Windows NT 4.0 Service Pack 4 includes advanced management and security features, as well as Year 2000 and euro currency changes. Internet Explorer 5 requires Service Pack 3 or higher for installation on Windows NT 4.0 workstations.

Internet Explorer 5 Resource Kit

This comprehensive guide for deploying, administering, and maintaining Internet Explorer is a technical supplement to other browser product documentation. The entire text of the printed Resource Kit book is presented in Help format, with Contents and Search to help you locate topics quickly and easily.

Internet Explorer Administration Kit 5

You can use this administration tool to create, distribute, and update customized installations of the Internet Explorer browser. The Internet Explorer Administration Kit 5 includes the following:

- **Internet Explorer Customization wizard**—The wizard enables you to customize and lock down all key features of Internet Explorer. You can create custom browser packages that you can distribute to users from a Web site, CD-ROM, local area network (LAN) share, or floppy disk.
- **Microsoft Connection Manager Administration Kit (CMAK)**—You can use the CMAK to centrally configure the dial-up remote access interface, including an automated logon process for dial-up access to Internet services.
- **IEAK Profile Manager**—If you're an administrator, you can use the Profile Manager to maintain browser settings, policies, and options from a central location. Also, you can use it to administer Windows desktop settings and system policies.

Corporate Applications Kit

The Corporate Applications Kit includes sample coding, applications, and templates to help you build Web-enabled programs. Blend the networked capabilities of the Web with traditional desktop Windows programs using HTML, dynamic HTML, and other Web-based technologies.

Internet Explorer 5 Deployment Guide

The Internet Explorer 5 Deployment Guide provides detailed instructions, checklists, and examples that help corporate administrators step through the process of planning, deploying, and maintaining Internet Explorer. This guide addresses the specific needs of corporate customers by highlighting methods, functions, and features that can enhance and simplify Internet Explorer deployment in an organization.

Additional Resources

The Additional Resources page contains lists of product resources and Web sites that may be useful to Internet service providers, corporate administrators, and Internet content providers. These lists provide sources of additional information about Internet Explorer 5 and its components, as well as about related Microsoft products.

APPENDIX B

Troubleshooting

This appendix provides detailed information for troubleshooting Microsoft Internet Explorer 5, including an effective troubleshooting strategy and a description of the most commonly reported problems. For easy troubleshooting, problems are categorized into several broad areas.

In This Appendix

See Also

- For more information about setting up a pilot program, which enables you to troubleshoot potential Internet Explorer issues before deployment, see Chapter 11, "Setting Up and Administering a Pilot Program."

- For more information about installing Internet Explorer and assisting users with setup issues, see Chapter 19, "Deploying Microsoft Internet Explorer 5."

Overview: Troubleshooting Strategy

To troubleshoot problems with Internet Explorer, follow these basic steps:

1. Identify and analyze the problem.
2. Check to see whether the problem is a common one by reviewing this appendix, Internet Explorer Help, and the Readme file included with this product.
3. Isolate and test the error conditions.
4. If you cannot resolve the problem, consult online troubleshooting and support options.

Identifying and Analyzing the Problem

Start troubleshooting by analyzing symptoms to determine a strategy for resolving the problem. Consider the following questions:

- Are there any error messages?
- When does the problem occur?
- Is the problem reproducible or random?
- Is the problem specific to an Internet Explorer feature, such as Windows Desktop Update or Web Folders?
- Does the problem occur in any or all other applications?
- Have you changed any applications, programs, or settings on your computer, such as adding or removing programs or adding new hardware?
- Has Internet Explorer worked previously? If so, what has changed?
- Does the problem occur on only one computer, only one operating system, or on only one Web site, or does it occur on many?
- Does your computer meet the necessary hardware and software requirements for running Internet Explorer 5? (For a list of requirements, see Chapter 9, "Planning the Deployment.")

Checking for Common Problems

Check to see whether the problem is a commonly reported one described in this appendix, in Internet Explorer Help, or in the Internet Explorer Readme file. Internet Explorer Help includes topics that can help you solve problems related to Internet Explorer features and components.

▶ **To use Internet Explorer Help**

1. On the Internet Explorer **Help** menu, click **Contents and Index**.
2. Click the **Contents**, **Index**, or **Search** tab, and then select the topic you want.

Isolating and Testing Error Conditions

You can resolve a problem more quickly by systematically isolating and testing error conditions. Use the following methods for isolating your error conditions:

- Eliminating variables helps to determine a problem's cause. For example, consider closing all other programs except Internet Explorer to eliminate the other programs as the potential cause of your problem.

- You can isolate the cause by changing a specific value and then testing to see whether the problem is corrected or altered. For example, if you are unable to play videos or animations, changing the Multimedia options in the Internet Options dialog box might resolve the issue.

- If a component doesn't work properly after you upgrade to new hardware or software, replace the new version with the original item and then retest it. For example, if you install a new sound card driver and lose audio capability, you can replace the new driver with the original version and retest it to see whether the problem still occurs.

Test each modification individually to see whether the change resolves your problem. Make note of all modifications and their effect on symptoms. If you contact product support personnel, this information helps them troubleshoot your problem. Also, the information provides an excellent reference for future troubleshooting.

Consulting Online Troubleshooting and Support Options

When possible, check the appropriate online forum. Other users might have discovered, reported, and found workarounds for your problem. Suggestions from others could save you time in tracking down the source of the problem and might give you ideas that can help with troubleshooting.

▶ **To get online support**

- On the Internet Explorer **Help** menu, click **Online Support**.

  The Microsoft Technical Support page on the Web is displayed. From this page, you can choose from several topics, including Knowledge Base articles, Frequently Asked Questions, Troubleshooting wizards, newsgroups, and other support options.

Installation and Uninstallation

This section describes some of the problems you may encounter during and after installation and uninstallation of Internet Explorer. Troubleshooting topics include:

- Problems occur due to out-of-date, deleted, or corrupted files.
- The Internet Explorer setup process fails.
- All the components in the installation checklist fail.
- The download server connection times out.
- You cannot install Internet Explorer after download.
- Problems occur when you are reinstalling Windows 95 with Internet Explorer.
- An invalid page fault occurs when you are installing additional components.
- The Internet Explorer uninstall process fails.
- You cannot uninstall Internet Explorer by using **Add/Remove Programs** in **Control Panel**.

Problems occur due to out-of-date, deleted, or corrupted files

Internet Explorer 5 includes a Repair tool, which you can use to diagnose and possibly fix problems with Internet Explorer. You can use this tool to do the following:

- Identify problems with Internet Explorer caused by files that are out of date.
- Fix problems caused by the incorrect or incomplete registration of Internet Explorer files.
- Restore or repair the desktop or **Start** menu shortcuts for Internet Explorer that have been deleted or do not function properly.

The result of the repair process is logged in the Fix IE Log.txt file in the Windows folder. The Repair tool uses slightly different error checking depending on the operating system you are using. To start the Internet Explorer Repair tool, use either of the methods described below.

▶ **To use the Internet Explorer Repair tool**

Method 1

- On the Internet Explorer **Help** menu, click **Repair**.

Method 2

1. Click **Start**, point to **Settings**, and then click **Control Panel**.
2. Double-click the **Add/Remove Programs** icon.
3. On the **Install/Uninstall** tab, click **Internet Explorer 5 and Internet Tools**, and then click **Add/Remove**.
4. Click **Repair Internet Explorer**.

If the Repair tool detects an error, it may generate the following error message or one similar to it:

Internet Explorer 5 cannot be repaired. Please reinstall Internet Explorer 5.

If you receive this error message, it is recommended that you reinstall Internet Explorer 5. To read a description of the problem, click **Details**. For example, you may receive the following types of explanations:

- **Internet Explorer 5 cannot be repaired due to the following errors: File *<file name>* is missing.**

- **Internet Explorer 5 cannot be repaired due to the following errors: Version 4.72.3110.0 of file *<file name>* exists but needs to be greater than 5.0.20x.xxxx.**

For the File Verification procedure, the version number listed is the minimum version of the file required by Internet Explorer 5. If no version number is associated with a file, then the existence of the file, but not its version, is verified.

The Internet Explorer setup process fails

If the Internet Explorer setup process fails, you can troubleshoot setup errors by using the Active Setup Log.txt file. This file contains a log of the entire setup process from the moment IE5Setup.exe is executed until the last .cab file is downloaded. When IE5Setup.exe is executed, Active Setup Log.txt is created in the folder where Windows is installed (typically, the C:\Windows folder). If an Active Setup Log.txt file from a previous Internet Explorer setup session exists, it is renamed to Active Setup Log.bak.

The log begins with the date and time Windows Update Setup for Internet Explorer and Internet Tools was launched and ends with the date and time it successfully downloads the last .cab file. As you go through the Windows Update Setup wizard, logging entries are continually written to this file. It is the most informative log file for determining what caused a download failure and when the failure occurred. Most entries logged in this file are also written to the registry; this data is recorded to assist with safe recovery.

The following HResult error codes identify the download phases when errors occur. This information can help you determine what Windows Update Setup was doing when it failed and also help you determine the cause of the failure.

HResult error code	Download phase
0	Initializing (making a Temp folder, checking disk space)
1	Dependency (checking for all dependencies)
2	Downloading (server to download folder)
3	Copying (download folder to Temp installation folder)
4	Retrying (restarting download due to timeout or some other download error)
5	Checking trust
6	Extracting
7	Running (.inf or .exe)
8	Finished (installation complete)
9	Download finished (downloading complete)

The following list identifies other common error codes:

- **80100003**—During install, one or more files are missing from the download folder.
- **800b*xxxx***—Any error starting with 800b indicates a trust failure.
- **800C*xxxx***—Any error starting with 800C indicates a Urlmon failure (for example, 800C005—file or server not found, or 800C00B—connection timeout).
- **8004004**—The user canceled setup.

All the components in the installation checklist fail

When you install Internet Explorer, all the components in the installation checklist may quickly fail. If this failure occurs during the file download, it is typically caused by the existing trust-checking mechanism on the computer. You can review the Active Setup Log.txt to determine whether the trust-checking mechanism is the cause of the problem. For more information about Active Setup Log.txt, see "The Internet Explorer setup process fails" earlier in this chapter.

To resolve this problem, you can do the following:

- Rerun Windows Update Setup. After you repeat Windows Update Setup three times, the trust-checking mechanism is automatically disabled.
- Try to fix the existing trust-checking mechanism by installing the Authenticode 2 update.
- Bypass trust checking by using one or more of the following methods:
  - Rename Wintrust.dll before running IE5Setup.exe again.
  - Add the following key to the registry:

    HKEY_LOCAL_MACHINE\Software\Microsoft\Active Setup\"DisableCheckTrust"="y"
  - Rename Digsig.dll.

If the problem occurs during installation rather than during the file download, the problem may be caused by a corrupted cabinet (.cab) file. You should review the Active Setup Log.txt file to identify the file that failed. Then, you can manually delete the corrupted file and rerun Windows Update Setup.

Typically, the .cab file fails to self-extract, rather than failing the trust check. If the trust check fails during installation, Windows Update Setup replaces the file automatically rather than causing a failure. However, in some cases, the trust check may fail incorrectly rather than replacing the file.

The download server connection times out

Windows Update Setup has the ability to switch servers during an installation to maintain maximum throughput or recover from a distribution site that is not responding. Switching servers occurs when Windows Update Setup detects no throughput or less than one byte in two minutes.

If a connection times out, Windows Update Setup will try to connect to the next download site in the list and continue the setup process at the beginning of the partially downloaded .cab file.

If a connection times out and Windows Update Setup does not switch servers, Windows Update Setup tries to reconnect to the download site and continue the setup process at the point where it left off. If a connection to the download site cannot be established, Windows Update Setup asks whether you want to cancel the installation or try again.

You cannot install Internet Explorer after download

When you download Internet Explorer, Windows Update Setup determines the version of the operating system that is currently running on your computer and automatically downloads the appropriate files. Because these files are unique to the operating system, you cannot download the Internet Explorer installation files by using one operating system and then install Internet Explorer on a different operating system.

If you try to install Internet Explorer from files that were downloaded by using a different operating system than the one you are currently running, the following error message may appear:

The Internet Explorer files on your computer are not the correct files for your operating system. To continue, you must download the correct files from the Internet. Do you want to continue?

To quit Windows Update Setup, click **No**. To continue Windows Update Setup and try to download the appropriate files from the Internet, click **Yes**.

Note   You must be connected to the Internet for the download to continue.

To resolve this installation issue, you can do one of the following:

- Download the installation files using the same operating system on which you intend to install Internet Explorer; you can choose the correct operating system during the setup process.
- Download the installation files for both operating systems in one session (by selecting **Custom** setup, clicking the **Advanced** button, and then selecting **Download only**).

Problems occur when you are reinstalling Windows 95 with Internet Explorer

Before you reinstall any version of Windows 95, you should uninstall Internet Explorer. If you do not uninstall Internet Explorer before reinstalling Windows 95, you may be unable to start Windows or run Internet Explorer or related components. To avoid these problems, uninstall Internet Explorer, reinstall Windows 95, and then reinstall Internet Explorer.

Note   If you install Windows 98 on a computer that has Internet Explorer 5 already installed, the browser, related components, and settings are preserved by default. For more information, see the Microsoft Windows 98 Resource Kit.

If you already reinstalled Windows 95 without first uninstalling Internet Explorer and are having problems, review the following sections and select the appropriate recovery method.

Determining Your Windows 95 Version

To select the correct method for recovery, you must determine the version of Windows 95 that you are running.

▶ **To determine the version of Windows 95 that you are running**

1. Click **Start**, point to **Settings**, and then click **Control Panel**.

2. Double-click the **System** icon.

3. On the **General** tab, under the System heading, locate the version number, and then match that number to the version of Windows 95 in the following table:

Version number	Version of Windows 95
40.950	Windows 95
40.950A	Windows 95 plus the Service Pack 1 Update or OEM Service Release 1
40.950B	OEM Service Release 2 (OSR2) or Release 2.1 (OSR2.1)
40.950C	OEM Service Release 2.5 (OSR2.5)

Note The 40.950B version number indicates that you may be running OSR2 or OSR2.1. To determine whether you are running OSR 2.1, do one of the following:

- In **Control Panel**, click **Add/Remove Programs**, then check the list of installed programs for "USB Supplement to OSR2."

- In the Windows\System\Vmm32 folder, check for the Ntkern.vxd file, version 43.1212.

Identifying an OEM Installation of Windows 95

Windows 95 may have been preinstalled on your computer. These installations are referred to as original equipment manufacturer (OEM) installations.

▶ **To determine whether you have an OEM installation of Windows 95**

1. Click **Start**, point to **Settings**, and then click **Control Panel**.

2. Double-click the **System** icon.

3. On the **General** tab, under the Registered to heading, locate the Product ID number. This number typically contains 20 digits. If digits 7, 8, and 9 contain the letters "OEM," you have an OEM installation of Windows 95.

For example:

```
12345-OEM-6789098-76543
```

If you are using an OEM installation of Windows 95, you should contact your computer's manufacturer for Windows 95 support.

Choosing a Recovery Method

The methods outlined below are specific to the version of Windows 95 you are running and whether you selected **Yes** or **No** in all Version Conflict dialog boxes that appeared while you reinstalled Windows 95.

Version of Windows 95	Response to version conflicts	Use this method
Windows 95 or A	Yes	1
Windows 95 or A	No	2
Windows 95B	Yes	3
Windows 95B	No	4
Windows 95C	Yes	3
Windows 95C	No	4

Method 1

You do not need to make any changes to your current configuration. Reinstalling Windows 95 with Internet Explorer installed and answering **Yes** to all file version conflicts does not cause any problems.

Method 2

Windows 95 works properly, but you may need to reinstall Internet Explorer to resolve browser problems. Reinstalling Internet Explorer should resolve any file version conflicts resulting from reinstalling Windows 95.

Method 3

Windows 95 works properly, but you may experience problems running Internet Explorer 5 because Windows 95 reinstalls a previous version of Internet Explorer. To resolve this problem, reinstall Internet Explorer 5.

Method 4

If you installed the Windows Desktop Update, the following error messages may appear:

- When you start your computer:

  Error loading Explorer.Exe. You must reinstall Windows.

- When you click **OK**:

  Error Starting program: The Explorer.Exe File is Linked to Missing Export SHLWAPI.DLL:ShopenRegstreamA

In addition, the following problems may occur:

- Your computer stops responding (hangs) or shuts down.
- If you did not have the Windows Desktop Update installed, you may be able to start Windows 95, but you cannot run Internet Explorer. Also, your desktop icons cannot be moved.

▶   **To resolve these issues**

1. Restart your computer. When the "Starting Windows 95" message appears, press the F8 key; then choose **Command Prompt Only** on the **Startup** menu.
2. Type the following line, and then press ENTER to change to the Uninstall folder:

   cd *uninstall folder*

   The ***uninstall folder*** is the location of the uninstall folder for Internet Explorer (for example: cd C:\Progra~1\Intern~1\Uninst~1).
3. Type the following line, and then press ENTER to view the hidden files:

   attrib -s -h -r *.*
4. Type the following lines to restore the files necessary to start Windows 95:

   iextract integr~1.dat
5. Type the following lines to place the files in their proper folders:

   copy explorer.exe c:\windows

   copy shell32.dll c:\windows\system
6. Restart the computer.
7. Uninstall Internet Explorer, and then reinstall it.

An invalid page fault occurs when you are installing additional components

When you try to install additional components from the Internet Explorer Components Download page, an invalid page fault may occur in Kernel32.dll. As a result, you may not be able to restart your computer successfully. This problem can occur if a component installation fails, resources were not available, or you do not have enough free hard disk space to install the selected components. To correct this problem, run the setup process again. Also you may want to free up some hard disk space, and then try to install the additional components again.

Note The Components Download page does not indicate the amount of hard disk space that you need to install the selected components. Instead, the Web page lists the total size of the components.

The Internet Explorer uninstall process fails

When the uninstall process fails, your most important troubleshooting tool is the uninstall log, IE5 Uninstall Log.txt, which is located in the Windows folder. This log covers the entire uninstallation process, including every file addition or removal; every registry addition, change, or removal; and any dialog boxes shown to the user.

The log is divided into Passes, which denote the different phases of an uninstallation. Entries in the log also have an Object number that corresponds to the line entry in Setup.stf. Lines without an Object number result from custom actions specific to Internet Explorer 5 and are contained in the IE5.inf file or in an .inf file from an external component uninstallation.

You cannot uninstall Internet Explorer by using Add/Remove Programs in Control Panel

If you cannot uninstall Internet Explorer by using **Add/Remove Programs** in **Control Panel**, most likely the uninstall information was deleted. The necessary files for uninstallation are IE5bak.dat, IE5bak.ini, Integrated Browser.dat, and Integrated Browser.ini.

The Internet Explorer Advanced Uninstall dialog box offers the option to uninstall this backup information, but doing so will prevent you from uninstalling Internet Explorer in the future. If you try to reinstall Internet Explorer after deleting these files, the following message will appear:

You are upgrading a version of Internet Explorer 5 in which the uninstall feature has been disabled. If you choose to continue, Setup will update your PC with the newer version, but the uninstall feature will remain disabled.

Browser Features and Functions

This section describes some of the problems you may encounter when you use browser features and functions. Troubleshooting topics include:

- Problems occur when you use a proxy server and Novell NetWare.
- You are unable to remove an ActiveX control.
- You cannot enable or disable style sheets in Internet Explorer.
- Errors occur when a Java program is run.
- An ActiveX control doesn't run properly.
- You cannot connect to the Internet—the proxy server configuration is not working.

Problems occur when you use a proxy server and Novell NetWare

When you use Internet Explorer with a proxy server and Novell NetWare 32-bit client software to browse the Internet, you may experience the following:

- Slow connections
- Inconsistent downloads
- An inability to view non-Microsoft sites

First, verify that you are using the Novell NetWare 32-bit client and that you are connecting to the Internet by using a proxy server.

▶ **To verify that you are using the Novell client**

1. On the **Start** menu, point to **Settings**, and then click **Control Panel**.

2. Double-click the **Network** icon.

3. On the **Configuration** tab, verify that **Novell 32** appears on the list of network connections.

▶ **To verify that you are connecting to the Internet by using a proxy server**

1. On the Internet Explorer **Tools** menu, click **Internet Options**, and then click the **Connection** tab.

2. Click **LAN Settings**.

3. Verify that the **Use a Proxy Server** check box is selected and that the Address box contains entries. This indicates that Internet Explorer is set up to connect to the Internet through a proxy server.

If you are using the Novell NetWare 32-bit client and are connecting to the Internet by using a proxy server, you will need to add to the Internet settings registry key to resolve the connection and download problems.

Warning This section contains information about editing the registry. Before you edit the registry, you should first make a backup copy of the registry files (System.dat and User.dat). Both are hidden files in the Windows\System folder. Using Registry Editor incorrectly can cause serious problems that may require you to reinstall your operating system. Microsoft cannot guarantee that problems resulting from the incorrect use of Registry Editor can be solved. Use Registry Editor at your own risk.

▶ **To add to the Internet settings registry key**

1. Open Windows Registry Editor and locate the following registry key:

   **HKEY_CURRENT_USER\Software\Microsoft\Windows\
   CurrentVersion\Internet Settings**

2. In this key, create a new binary value named:

   DontUseDNSLoadBalancing

3. Set the value of the new registry key to:

   01 00 00 00

4. Restart your computer.

Note   The Novell NetWare 32-bit client is not manufactured by Microsoft. Microsoft makes no warranty, implied or otherwise, regarding this product's performance or reliability.

You are unable to remove an ActiveX control

Internet Explorer includes the Occache.dll file, which is used to enumerate, update, and safely uninstall ActiveX controls by using a shell folder. Internet Explorer supports multiple Occache folders. The list of Occache folders is located in the following registry key:

**HKEY_LOCAL_MACHINE\SOFTWARE\Microsoft\Windows\
CurrentVersion\Internet Settings\ActiveX Cache**

By default, Internet Explorer stores ActiveX controls in the Windows\Downloaded Program Files or Winnt\Downloaded Program Files folder. If you upgraded from Internet Explorer 3.x, both an Occache and Downloaded Program Files folder may exist. In this case, all new ActiveX controls are installed in the Downloaded Program Files folder, but previously installed ActiveX controls still work in the Occache folder.

Restoring the Ability to Easily Uninstall ActiveX Controls

The Downloaded Program Files folder contains functionality that enables you to easily uninstall ActiveX controls. When this folder is deleted, a new Downloaded Program Files folder is created the next time Internet Explorer downloads new program files. However, the newly created folder does not contain the functionality to easily uninstall ActiveX controls. You can restore this ability to the Downloaded Program Files folder by using the Internet Explorer Repair tool. For more information about the Repair tool, see "Problems occur due to out-of-date, deleted, or corrupted files" earlier in this chapter.

Errors When Removing an ActiveX Control

When you try to remove an ActiveX control by using **Add/Remove Programs** in **Control Panel**, you may receive an error message for the following reasons:

Share Violations

The following message appears:

These program files are currently being used by one or more programs. Please close some programs, and try again. You may need to restart Windows.

This message occurs if the ActiveX control you are trying to remove is currently loaded in memory by Internet Explorer or an Internet Explorer desktop component.

▶ **To resolve this share violation**

1. Close all open Internet Explorer windows.

2. Disable the Internet Explorer desktop.

   To do so, right-click an empty area on the desktop, point to **Active Desktop**, and then click **View As Web Page** to clear the check mark.

3. Restart Windows.

4. To remove the ActiveX control, click the **Add/Remove Programs** icon in Control Panel.

Note The following ActiveX controls are used by Internet Explorer and should not be removed:

- DirectAnimation Java Classes
- Internet Explorer Classes for Java
- Microsoft XML Parser for Java
- Win32 Classes

Component Removal

The following message appears:

About to remove a Windows system DLL: (<*path\filename*>). Okay to delete?

This error occurs if the ActiveX control installed files into a folder other than a registered Occache folder (for example, Windows\System or Winnt\System32), and Occache cannot determine whether those files are shared by other programs.

If you are certain the file listed in the message is not being used by Windows or another program, click **Yes**. Otherwise, click **No**.

You cannot enable or disable style sheets in Internet Explorer

When you use Internet Explorer, you may experience the following symptoms:

- You disabled the use of style sheets in Internet Explorer 3.x, but after you upgrade to Internet Explorer 5 or Windows 98, you cannot re-enable them.

- You cannot disable the use of style sheets in Internet Explorer 5.

This problem can occur because the ability to disable style sheets was removed from Internet properties. You can resolve this problem by setting registry values to disable or re-enable the use of style sheets.

Warning This section contains information about editing the registry. Before you edit the registry, you should first make a backup copy of the registry files (System.dat and User.dat). Both are hidden files in the Windows\System folder. Using Registry Editor incorrectly can cause serious problems that may require you to reinstall your operating system. Microsoft cannot guarantee that problems resulting from the incorrect use of Registry Editor can be solved. Use Registry Editor at your own risk.

▶ **To disable or re-enable the use of style sheets**

1. Open Windows Registry Editor and locate the following registry key:

   HKEY_CURRENT_USER\Software\Microsoft\Internet Explorer\Main

2. To disable the use of style sheets, set the string value of **Use StyleSheets** to **no**.

   To enable the use of style sheets, set the string value of **Use StyleSheets** to **yes**.

Note When you disable the use of style sheets, it may affect the appearance of Web sites or the Internet Explorer desktop.

Errors occur when a Java program is run

If a problem occurs when you run a Java program, a summary of Java error messages might be displayed in the status bar in Internet Explorer. However, if the Java program cannot be loaded, it may not write Java error messages to the status bar.

When a Java program is run and an error occurs, Internet Explorer also creates a Javalog.txt file in the Windows\Java folder. The Javalog.txt file provides information about the Java error and the classes affected.

In order for Internet Explorer to create the Javalog.txt file, you must enable Java logging.

▶   **To enable Java logging**

1.   Click **Start**, point to **Settings**, and then click **Control Panel**.

2.   Double-click the **Internet Options** icon, and then click the **Advanced** tab.

3.   Click the **Java logging enabled** check box.

An ActiveX control doesn't run properly

If a Web page is not displayed properly, an ActiveX control may not have loaded or may be out-of-date. The following procedure helps you determine whether an ActiveX control is the cause of the problem.

▶   **To determine whether an ActiveX control may not have loaded or may be out-of-date**

1.   On the Internet Explorer **View** menu, click **Source**.

2.   Look for source code similar to the following:

    <OBJECT ID=NewsBrowser WIDTH=92 HEIGHT=244 BORDER=0 STANDBY="Click here for help installing MSNBC News Menu" CLASSID=CLSID:2FF18E10-DE11-11d1-8161-00A0C90DD90C CODEBASE=/download/nm0713.cab#Version=3,0,0713,0>

    This source code indicates that the MSNBC NewsBrowser is an ActiveX control by listing the CLASSID (CLSID) where it is stored in the registry under HKCR\CLSID. It also lists the CODEBASE, which indicates where to retrieve the .cab file for installing the control and the version that it currently needs.

    The control is loaded from the Downloaded Program Items folder. This process is not visible to the user. If the control cannot be loaded from this folder, Internet Explorer tries to download the control from the CODEBASE. If the control is corrupted, it may not load and won't display the proper control needed to view the Web page properly.

After you check the source code to determine whether an ActiveX control may not have loaded or may be out-of-date, update the control, if necessary.

▶   **To update the ActiveX control**

1.   On the **Tools** menu, click **Internet Options**.

2.   In the Temporary Internet Files area, click **Settings**.

3.   To view the ActiveX control installed on the computer, click **View Objects**.

4.   Right-click the ActiveX control, and then click **Update**.

> **Note** If you are not sure which control in the Downloaded Program Files folder is associated with the control identified in the source code, you can check the registry under HKCR\CLSID\<*clsid number that is listed in the source*>. Click the number, and it will list the name of the control at that registry key.

5. Try to view the Web page.

6. If the Web page is still not being displayed correctly, repeat steps 1 through 3, right-click the ActiveX control, and then click **Remove**.

7. Try to view the Web page again. The control should automatically be reinstalled based on the CODEBASE information.

You cannot connect to the Internet—the proxy server configuration is not working

Your organization might use a proxy server on a local area network (LAN) to connect to the Internet. A proxy server acts as a gateway for the computers on the network to access the Internet. A proxy server does not prevent other people on the Internet from accessing your network—a firewall can serve this purpose.

To successfully connect to the Internet, you must correctly configure Internet Explorer to use your proxy server. If Internet Explorer is configured for your proxy server, you should consider the following:

- If you configured the settings for the proxy server manually within the browser, you should verify the proxy server address.

  ▶ **To verify your proxy server address**

  1. On the **Tools** menu, click **Internet Options**, and then click the **Connections** tab.

  2. Click **Settings**, or click **LAN Settings**.

  3. In the Proxy Server area, verify the address.

- If you are using automatic detection and automatic configuration, the DHCP and DNS servers should automatically detect and configure the browser's proxy settings on a per-connection basis. You should verify that automatic detection and automatic configuration are enabled within the browser. Your DHCP server must support the DHCPINFORM message; otherwise, use DNS.

▶ **To verify that automatic detection and automatic configuration are enabled**

1. On the **Tools** menu, click **Internet Options**, and then click the **Connections** tab.

2. Click **Settings**, or click **LAN Settings**.

3. In the Automatic Configuration area, verify that the **Automatically detect settings** check box is selected.

Note that automatic detection is enabled by default for LAN connections and disabled by default for RAS connections. For more information about automatic detection and automatic configuration, see Chapter 21, "Using Automatic Configuration and Automatic Proxy." For more information about setting up DHCP and DNS servers for automatic detection and automatic configuration, see Chapter 13, "Setting Up Servers."

- If automatic detection and automatic configuration are configured correctly and proxy server detection still fails, you can click **Detect my network settings** on the error dialog box to try proxy-server detection again.

- If you are using an auto-proxy URL, you should verify that the browser is configured with the correct URL address.

▶ **To verify that the browser is configured with the correct auto-proxy URL address**

1. On the **Tools** menu, click **Internet Options**, and then click the **Connections** tab.

2. Click **Settings**, or click **LAN Settings**.

3. In the Automatic Configuration area, verify that the **Use automatic configuration script** check box is selected and that the address is correct for your auto-proxy URL.

Windows Desktop Update

This section describes some of the problems you may encounter when you use the Internet Explorer desktop. Troubleshooting topics include:

- Pointing to desktop icons causes text to disappear.

- Images copied to the desktop are saved as desktop items.

- Desktop items stop working.

- Desktop items stop working when Internet Explorer is offline.

- System Properties do not show that Microsoft Plus! is installed.

- Internet Explorer cannot find the desktop.

Pointing to desktop icons causes text to disappear

If your computer is running Internet Explorer and the Windows Desktop Update and you point to an icon on the desktop, the text under the icon may disappear. This occurs when the selected items and the desktop are configured to use the same color in the Display Properties dialog box. To resolve this problem, configure Windows 95 so that the selected items and the desktop use different colors.

▶ **To configure Windows 95 so that the selected items and the desktop use different colors**

1. On the **Start** menu, point to **Settings**, and then click **Control Panel**.

2. Double-click the **Display** icon, and then click the **Appearance** tab.

3. In the Item list, click **Selected Items** or **Desktop**.

4. In the Color list, select a different color.

Images copied to the desktop are saved as desktop items

When you have the Windows Desktop Update installed and try to save an image file to the desktop by dragging the image from a Web page to the desktop, you may receive the following prompt:

Security Alert
Do you want to add a desktop item to your Active Desktop?

When you click **Yes**, the Subscription wizard starts to set up a subscription for updating the image. When the wizard is finished, the image appears as a desktop item instead of as a file icon. This change occurs only when you drag Web-based content to the desktop. You can drag items from My Computer or Windows Explorer to the desktop, and the file is copied normally.

To avoid changing an image to a desktop item, you can manually save the image.

▶ **To manually save an image**

1. Right-click the image you want to copy to your desktop, and then click **Save Picture As**.

2. Double-click your Desktop folder, and then click **Save**.

   By default, the Desktop folder for Windows 95 is C:\Windows\Desktop. The Desktop folder for Windows NT is C:\Winnt\Profiles*name*\Desktop.

You can also avoid this problem by uninstalling the Windows Desktop Update component.

Desktop items stop working

If you use a Web page as your desktop wallpaper and it contains frames, some desktop items may stop working. For example, you may find that the Channel bar is removed from the desktop. The Internet Explorer desktop cannot display wallpaper with frames. These pages are actually several separate pages tied together with links. If a frame set is copied to a computer, it is not usable as wallpaper, even if all related pages are copied. To resolve this problem, choose a different wallpaper for your desktop.

Desktop items stop working when Internet Explorer is offline

Desktop items that host Java programs may stop working when Internet Explorer is offline. This problem can occur if the Java program is removed from the Temporary Internet Files folder. Also, if the Java program is not packaged into a .cab, .zip, or .jar file, it may not get cached at all.

Desktop items are retrieved from the cache when Internet Explorer 5 is offline. If the cache reaches its maximum size, Java programs may be removed from the cache automatically to make room for current downloads. If a desktop item hosts a Java program that has been removed from the cache and Internet Explorer is offline, the Desktop item stops working.

To resolve this problem, you can either empty the Temporary Internet Files folder or increase the amount of hard disk space it uses.

▶ **To empty the Temporary Internet Files folder**

1. On the Internet Explorer **Tools** menu, click **Internet Options**.

2. On the **General** tab, in the Temporary Internet Files area, click **Delete Files**.

▶ **To increase the amount of hard disk space used for the Temporary Internet Files folder**

1. On the Internet Explorer **Tools** menu, click **Internet Options**.

2. On the **General** tab, in the Temporary Internet Files area, click **Settings**.

3. Move the slider to the right.

System Properties do not show that Microsoft Plus! is installed

If you install Microsoft Plus! and then install Internet Explorer, the **System Properties** dialog box may indicate that Microsoft Plus! is not installed. The information line no longer displays:

Microsoft Plus! for Windows 95

Instead, this line reads:

IE 5 *7-digit build number*

The opposite behavior can also occur. If you install Microsoft Plus! after installing Internet Explorer 5, the **System Properties** dialog box line no longer shows:

IE 5 *7-digit build number*

Instead, this line reads:

Microsoft Plus! for Windows 95

This behavior does not affect your ability to run installed Microsoft Plus! or Internet Explorer.

Internet Explorer cannot find the desktop

When you make changes to the Internet Explorer desktop, the following error message might appear:

Internet Explorer cannot find the Active Desktop HTML file. This file is needed for your Active Desktop. Click OK to turn off Active Desktop.

This error message appears when the Windows\Web folder has been moved or renamed, because Internet Explorer needs to write to certain files stored within that folder.

To resolve the problem, you can do one of the following:

- Use Windows Explorer to create a new Windows\Web folder.
- Remove and reinstall Internet Explorer to recreate the folder.

Outlook Express

This section describes some of the problems you may encounter when you use Microsoft Outlook™ Express. Troubleshooting topics include:

- You cannot import an address book in Outlook Express.
- The preview pane does not display news messages.
- You receive the following error message:

  The command failed to execute.
- Windows Address Book files are changed.

You cannot import an address book in Outlook Express

When you try to import an address book in Outlook Express, the address book may not be imported, and you may not see an error message. This problem occurs when the Wabmig.exe file is missing or damaged.

If the Wabmig.exe file is damaged, rename the file, and then reinstall Outlook Express.

▶ **To rename the Wabmig.exe file**

1. On the **Start** menu, point to **Find**, and then click **Files or Folders**.
2. In the Named box, type **Wabmig.exe**, and then click **Find Now**.
3. Right-click the file, and then click **Rename**.
4. Rename the file to **Wabmig.*xxx***.
5. Reinstall Outlook Express.

The preview pane does not display news messages

While you are reading news messages in Outlook Express, you may receive the following message in the preview pane:

Press <Space> to display the selected message. You can also choose to automatically show messages in the preview pane from the Options command.

To redisplay the message, press the SPACEBAR. If you double-click the news message to open it, you receive the following error message:

There was an error opening the message.

This problem occurs when there is not enough free space on your hard disk to open the news message. To resolve this problem, increase the amount of free space on your hard disk by using one or more of the following methods:

- Remove any unnecessary files from the hard disk.

- Empty the Recycle Bin.

- Delete unnecessary files from the Internet Explorer 5 Setup folder. Deleting this entire folder is not recommended. While it does not affect the performance of Internet Explorer, you will not be able to reinstall or uninstall Internet Explorer or its components from the hard disk; you would have to download another copy from the Microsoft Web site.

Warning The Setup folder contains important backup files that are necessary for reinstalling and uninstalling Internet Explorer. The following files are critical: IE5bak.dat, IE5bak.ini, and, if Windows Desktop Update is installed, Integrated Browser.dat and Integrated Browser.ini. It is recommended that you not delete these files. If you need to free up more disk space, it is recommended that you delete other files in the folder.

You receive the following error message:
The command failed to execute

When you try to save a mail attachment to your hard disk in Outlook Express, you may receive the following error message:

The command failed to execute.

This problem occurs when there is not enough free disk space on your hard disk to save the attachment. To resolve this problem, increase the amount of free space on your hard disk by using one or more of the following methods:

- Remove any unnecessary files from the hard disk.

- Empty the Recycle Bin.

- Delete unnecessary files from the Internet Explorer 5 Setup folder. Deleting this entire folder is not recommended. While it does not affect the performance of Internet Explorer, you will not be able to reinstall or uninstall Internet Explorer or its components from the hard disk; you would have to download another copy from the Microsoft Web site.

> **Warning** The Setup folder contains important backup files that are necessary for reinstalling and uninstalling Internet Explorer. The following files are critical: IE5bak.dat, IE5bak.ini and, if Windows Desktop Update is installed, Integrated Browser.dat and Integrated Browser.ini. It is recommended that you not delete these files. If you need to free up more disk space, it is recommended that you delete other files in the folder.

After you free up some hard disk space, try to save the attachment again.

Windows Address Book files are changed

When you install the Windows Address Book, files used by earlier versions are backed up and removed, and new versions of the files are installed. Note that Windows Address Book files are shared with other applications in addition to Outlook Express.

The following table identifies the files, previously located in the Windows\System or Winnt\System32 folder and their new directory locations.

File name	New location
Wab32.dll	Program Files\Common Files\System
Wabfind.dll	Program Files\Outlook Express
Wabimp.dll	Program Files\Outlook Express

The following table identifies the files, previously in the Windows folder, and their new directory locations.

File name	New location
Wab.exe	Program Files\Outlook Express
Wabmig.exe	Program Files\Outlook Express

HTML Authoring

This section describes some of the problems related to Microsoft Internet Explorer HTML authoring. Troubleshooting topics include:

- Text does not wrap in text boxes.
- Background images are not displayed.
- Internet Explorer is not automatically redirected.
- Frames are not displayed in Web pages.
- Permission is denied when scripting across frames.
- Errors occur when you use Web Folders.

Text does not wrap in text boxes

When you enter text in a text box created by using the <TEXTAREA> tag on a Hypertext Markup Language (HTML) page, the text may not wrap correctly. In this case, the text continues to flow to the right side of the text box without breaking or wrapping. This problem occurs because the HTML page does not contain the parameters that activate text wrapping in a text box.

To wrap text in a text box, use one of the following methods:

- Use the WRAP attribute of the <TEXTAREA> tag with either the Physical or Virtual value to enable word wrapping.

  For example, you might type the following <TEXTAREA> tag:

  ```
  <TEXTAREA NAME="Name" ROW99S=6 COL99S=40>
  </TEXTAREA>
  ```

- Insert WRAP=Physical as part of the <TEXTAREA> tag.

  For example, you might type the following <TEXTAREA> tag:

  ```
  <TEXTAREA NAME="Name" ROW99S=6 COL99S=40 WRAP=Physical>
  </TEXTAREA>
  ```

Note When you are typing in the text box, press ENTER to manually insert line breaks, which forces the text to wrap.

Background images are not displayed

Pages created by using the Data Form Wizard by Microsoft Visual InterDev™ may not display background images in Internet Explorer. This problem occurs because cascading style sheet (CSS) tags take precedence over HTML tags. Pages created by using the Data Form Wizard reference a CSS; the CSS has a tag for the background image of Transparent, which overrides any value in the body tag of the Active Server Page (.asp) file.

▶ **To display background images**

- Delete the **background: transparent** line from the BODY property of the CSS.

Internet Explorer browser is not automatically redirected

When you load a Web page that contains the <meta http-equiv="refresh"...> HTML tag, the browser may not automatically be redirected to another Web page. This problem may occur for one of the following reasons:

- The author of the page did not place the <meta http-equiv="refresh"...> tag in the <HEAD> section of the HTML source code.
- The syntax of the <meta http-equiv="refresh"...> HTML tag is incorrect.

To resolve this problem, update the Web page by using the appropriate method:

- **If the <META> tag is not located in the <HEAD> section**

  Modify the HTML source code to place the <META> tag in the <HEAD> section of the Web page. This may require adding the <HEAD> and </HEAD> tags to the Web page.

- **If the syntax of the <META> tag is incorrect**

  Modify the HTML source code to correct the syntax of the <META> tag. For example, a <META> tag might look like this:

```
<meta http-equiv="refresh" content="n;url=http://www.domain.com/
    pagename.htm">
```

The *n* is the number of seconds the browser program pauses before loading the new Web page.

Frames are not displayed in Web pages

When you are using Internet Explorer to view a Web page, a blank page may appear instead of a defined set of frames. If you right-click an empty area of the Web page and then click **View Source**, the following message may appear:

This document might not display properly because there is a <FRAMESET> within the <BODY> of the document.

This behavior is by design and occurs when the Web author puts the <FRAMESET> tag after the <BODY> tag in the main or "framing" HTML document. All <FRAMESET> tags and underlying instructions should precede any <BODY> tags.

▶ **To display frames on the blank page**

1. Remove the <BODY> tag.
2. Remove any additional HTML code between the <HEAD> of the document and the <FRAMESET>.

The framing HTML document defines the frame regions that appear in the browser and the documents or objects that initially appear in the frames.

Permission is denied when scripting across frames

If your script code tries to access a script or an object in a different frame, you may see the following script error message:

Permission denied: 'Parent.RemoteFrame.RemoteObject'

Internet Explorer implements cross-frame security. A script or an object in one frame is not allowed to access scripts or objects in another frame when the documents referenced by the frames' SRC attribute specify Web servers in different second-level domains. This corresponds to the *domain-name.xxx* portion of the full server-name syntax *server.domain-name.xxx*.

The Internet Explorer Dynamic HTML object model allows a certain subset of safe actions to be scripted. For example, the window.location property of a remote server's frame can be set to allow navigation, but it cannot be scripted to prevent one frame from accessing the contents of another frame. For example, it is valid for a document retrieved from http://test.microsoft.com to manipulate another document retrieved from http://test.microsoft.com. It is not valid for a document retrieved from http://server1.some-domain-name.org to manipulate a document retrieved from http://server2 or http://server3.microsoft.com.

The intention of cross-frame security is to prevent a Web page author from accessing or misusing the trusted objects authored by another Web page author. Only pages hosted in the same domain can be trusted to safely script the contents of a particular page. Cross-frame security should also prevent unwanted communication between documents on opposite sides of a corporate firewall. For more information, visit the MSDN Online Web site.

In order for two documents hosted on the same second-level domain to interact, both documents must set the document.domain property to their shared second-level domain. For example, one document on http://example.microsoft.com could script and access another document on http://test.microsoft.com if both documents used the following line of script code:

```
<SCRIPT LANGUAGE="VBScript">
document.domain = "microsoft.com"
</SCRIPT>
```

Given the following FRAMESET:

```
<FRAMESET COLS="50%, *" FRAMEBORDER=1>
<FRAME SRC="http://server1/server1.html" ID="Server1Frame">
<FRAME SRC="http://server2/server2.html" ID="Server2Frame">
</FRAMESET>
```

Script in the "Server1Frame" frame is not permitted to access script or objects in the "Server2Frame" frame, and vice versa.

The following sample script code in server1.html causes the "Permission Denied" error, given that **RemoteTextBox** is an object created on the server2.html document:

```
<!-- From server1.html -->
<SCRIPT LANGUAGE="VBScript">
Sub CommandButtonLocal_Click()
Parent.Server2Frame.RemoteTextBox.Text = "Changed Text"
'Server2Frame has SRC on different server
end sub
</SCRIPT>
```

Errors occur when using Web folders

Web Folders enable you to manage files on a Web Distributed Authoring and Versioning (WebDAV) or Web Extender Client (WEC) server by using the familiar Windows Explorer or My Computer interface. WebDAV is an extension of the Hypertext Transfer Protocol (HTTP) that defines how basic file functions—such as copy, move, delete, and create—are performed by using HTTP. WEC is a Microsoft FrontPage protocol that is used for Web publishing.

The following sections describe errors that may occur when you use Web Folders with Internet Explorer.

The site is not available or not publishable

If you add a Web Folder for a site that is not available or not publishable (for example, FrontPage Extensions is installed but Authoring is disabled), you receive the following error message:

Cannot connect to the Web server http://<*server*>/<*folder*>. The server could not be located, or may be too busy to respond. Please check your typing or check to make sure the Web server is available. For details, see c:\<windows>\TEMP\wecerr.txt.

To resolve this problem, use Internet Explorer to verify that the server is available. If you can open the server in Internet Explorer, contact the server administrator to request that publishing be enabled.

You do not have rights to view or modify files

If you add a Web Folder for a site that is publishable (for example, FrontPage Server Extensions are present and authoring is enabled) but you do not have rights to view or modify files, you are prompted for your user name and password and you receive the following error message:

You do not have permission to access this Web Folder location.

To resolve this problem, contact your server administrator to grant you the necessary permissions.

You specified a non-HTTP URL

If you specify a non-HTTP Internet address (URL) when you add a Web Folder by using the Add Web Folder wizard, you receive the following error message:

The location you have entered is not an HTTP URL. Web Folder locations must be HTTP URL's which point to a folder on a Web server.

To resolve this problem, specify a valid HTTP URL (for example, http://*server/folder*). Note that you can specify *server/folder,* and Web Folders automatically tries to open http://*server/folder*. But specifying a non-HTTP URL (for example, ftp://*server/folder*) results in the above error message.

You specified a folder that does not exist or a protocol that is not supported

If any non-specific error occurs when you try to open a Web Folder, you receive the following prompt to browse to the URL:

Internet Explorer could not open http://*<server>/<folder>* as a Web Folder. Would you like to see its default view instead?

To cancel the operation, click **No**. If you click **Yes**, Internet Explorer tries to open the Web site. If Internet Explorer is unable to open the Web site, you may have specified a folder on a publishable server that does not exist. If Internet Explorer is able to open the Web site, you may have specified a protocol that is not supported by Web Folders. For example, if you are trying to open a Web Folder by clicking **Open** on the Internet Explorer **File** menu and you specify a protocol that is not supported (for example ftp:// or file://), you receive this error message.

APPENDIX C

Batch-Mode File Syntax and Command-Line Switches

This appendix describes how you use batch files and command-line switches to customize Windows Update Setup, as well as command-line parameters for starting Internet Explorer.

In This Appendix

See Also

- For more information about using batch files and command-line switches to customize the setup program, see Chapter 16, "Customizing Setup."

Using Internet Explorer Batch-Mode Setup

The Internet Explorer Customization wizard enables you to control functionality and user experience during setup. You can further control the setup process by using a batch file. You can use this method whether Internet Explorer is installed alone or with Microsoft Office.

When installing Internet Explorer 4.0, you can further control the setup process with command-line switches. This method is also supported in Internet Explorer 5, and some new switches are available. To use command-line switches, you typically use the IExpress wizard or another program to package your setup files.

You can also use a combination of the batch file and the command-line switches.

In most cases, the batch-file method gives you more control over the installation of individual components and involves fewer steps. The command-line switches are provided for backward compatibility and to support custom solutions.

Creating a Batch File

To create a batch file, use a text editor such as Microsoft Notepad, and name the file IEBatch.txt.

You can use a batch file in two ways:

- Include it with the setup program. You can use it with or without creating a custom Internet Explorer Administration Kit (IEAK) package.
- Include it in your IEAK package.

You create the batch file the same way for both methods.

Using a Batch File to Modify the Setup Program

After you create the batch file, you can use it in two ways to modify the setup process.

- To include the batch file as part of your IEAK package, place it in the \Iebin\<Language>\Optional folder. <Language> represents the language of the version you create; for example, English-language versions are created in the En folder.
- If you distribute Internet Explorer over the Internet or an intranet, you can post the batch file to the site where users download Internet Explorer. If you distribute Internet Explorer on other media, such as a compact disc or floppy disk, you can add the batch file to the disk. Place it in the same folder as the IE5Setup.exe file.

Batch-File Syntax

The following table shows the sections and entries for the batch file.

Batch file entry	Description
[Options]	
SaveUninstallInfo=[0,1]	Determines whether or not information about removing components is stored.
	0 specifies that information is not stored. If you use this switch, you will not be able to uninstall Internet Explorer from Control Panel.
	1 (default) specifies that information is stored.
ExtraSection=	Runs the sections specified in the IESetup.inf file. Separate sections with commas; for example, *section1,section2,section3*.
Quiet=[A,C,U]	Represents quiet mode, in which the installation runs with little or no input from the user.
	A specifies administrative mode, in which the setup program does not appear to the user and error checking is not performed.
	C suppresses the **Cancel** button on the progress page.
	U specifies that the setup program does not appear to the user unless required input (such as the download location) is not available.
ShowErrors=[0,1]	Determines whether or not setup errors are displayed to the user.
	0 specifies that the setup program carries out the default action for each message with no user input.
	1 (default) specifies that setup errors are displayed to the user.
[Welcome]	
Display=[0,1]	Determines whether or not the initial setup screen is displayed on the user's computer.
	0 specifies that the initial setup screen is not displayed to the user.
	1 (default) specifies that the initial setup screen is displayed to the user.

Batch file entry	Description
[SetupChoice]	
Display=[0,1]	Determines whether the screen on which users can choose to customize the setup program is displayed on the user's computer.
	0 specifies that the setup-type screen is not displayed to the user.
	1 (default) specifies that the setup-type screen is displayed to the user.
SetupChoice=[0,1]	Determines which setup option is chosen.
	0 (default) specifies **Install now - Typical Setup of Components**.
	1 specifies **Custom Setup**.
[Custom]	
Display=[0,1]	Determines whether or not the Component Options screen, in which users can select components and click **Advanced** to specify more options, is displayed on the user's computer.
	0 specifies that the Component Options screen is not displayed to the user.
	1 (default) specifies that the Component Options screen is displayed to the user.
InstallDir=foldername	Specifies the folder for installing files. If you do not include this setting, the setup program uses the current settings in the IESetup.inf file. If you have installed an earlier version of Internet Explorer, the setup program installs into the same directory as the earlier version.
InstallDirRO=[0,1]	Specifies whether or not the user can change the installation folder.
	0 (default) specifies that the user can change the installation folder.
	1 specifies that the user cannot change the installation folder.
UseInfInstallDir=[0,1]	Specifies the folder into which Internet Explorer is installed.
	0 (default) specifies that the setup program uses the default installation folder or the same folder in which an earlier version of Internet Explorer is already installed.
	1 specifies that the installation folder is the folder specified in the IESetup.inf file.

Batch file entry	Description
SetupMode=[0,1,2]	Specifies what kind of installation will be performed.
	0 specifies a Minimal installation.
	1 (default) specifies a Typical installation.
	2 specifies a Full installation.
SetupModeRO=[0,1]	Determines whether or not the user can change the setup type.
	0 specifies that the user can change the setup type.
	1 (default) specifies that the user cannot change the setup type.
Component=[Comma-separated list of component IDs]	Specifies that only the components specified in the Component= setting will be installed. The ComponentID is a string that uniquely identifies a component; you can find the corresponding string in the component sections of the IESetup.cif file.
ComponentListRO=[0,1]	Determines whether or not the user can specify which components are installed (in addition to the components in the setup type).
	0 (default) specifies that the user can change the list of components.
	1 specifies that the user cannot change the list of components.
DownloadOnly=[0,1]	Determines whether or not Internet Explorer is just downloaded, or downloaded and installed.
	0 (default) specifies that the files are downloaded and then installed.
	1 specifies that the files are downloaded but not installed.
DownloadOnlyRO=[0,1]	Determines whether or not the user can specify that files are downloaded or downloaded and installed.
	0 (default) specifies that the user can change this setting.
	1 specifies that the user cannot change this setting.
IECompat=[0,1]	Determines whether or not Internet Explorer 5 is installed on the same computer as Internet Explorer 4.0, so that functionality from both programs is available.
	0 specifies that Internet Explorer 5 cannot be installed side-by-side with Internet Explorer 4.0.
	1 (default) specifies that Internet Explorer 5 can be installed so that it works with Internet Explorer 4.0.

Batch file entry	Description
IECompatRO=[0,1]	Determines whether or not the user can specify if Internet Explorer 5 will be installed with Internet Explorer 4.0.
	0 (default) specifies that the user can change this setting.
	1 specifies that the user cannot change this setting.
IECompatShow=[0,1]	Determines whether or not the **Compatibility** check box, which enables users to run Internet Explorer side-by-side with Internet Explorer 4.0, is displayed.
	0 specifies that the check box is not displayed in the wizard.
	1 (default) specifies that the check box is displayed in the wizard.
ShowAdvanced=[0,1]	Determines whether or not the **Advanced** button is displayed on the Component Options screen in the Windows Update Setup wizard. Clicking the **Advanced** button displays the **Download only**, **Compatibility**, and **Don't associate file types** options.
	0 specifies that the **Advanced** button is not displayed in the wizard.
	1 (default) specifies that the **Advanced** button is displayed in the wizard.
IEDefault=[0,1]	Determines whether or not Internet Explorer is the default browser.
	0 specifies that Internet Explorer is not the default browser.
	1 (default) specifies that Internet Explorer is the default browser.
IEDefaultRO=[0,1]	Specifies whether or not users can determine if Internet Explorer is their default browser.
	0 specifies that users can determine whether Internet Explorer is their default browser.
	1 (default) specifies that users cannot determine whether Internet Explorer is their default browser.
[Download]	
Display=[0,1]	Determines whether or not the option to download or install files is displayed on the user's computer.
	0 specifies that the option to download or install files is not displayed to the user.
	1 (default) specifies that the option to download or install files is displayed to the user.

Batch file entry	Description
DownloadDir=*foldername*	Specifies the folder for downloading files. If you do not include this setting, the setup program creates a folder named Windows Update Setup Files on the drive that has the most disk space.
DownloadDirRO=[0,1]	Specifies whether or not users can change the folder where their files are downloaded.
	0 (default) specifies that users can change the download folder
	1 specifies that users cannot change the download folder.
DownloadOS=[0,1,2,3]	Specifies that files for a specific operating system are downloaded; this setting is valid only if you are downloading but not installing files (DownloadOnly=1).
	0 (default) specifies the current operating system.
	1 specifies Windows NT and Windows 95/Windows 98.
	2 specifies Windows 95/Windows 98 only.
	3 specifies Window NT only.
DownloadOSRO=[0,1]	Determines whether or not users can specify the operating system of the files that are downloaded to their computer.
	0 (default) specifies that users can change this setting.
	1 specifies that users cannot change this setting.
[DownloadSite]	
Display=[0,1]	Determines whether or not the download sites are displayed to the user.
	0 specifies that the download sites are not displayed to the user.
	1 (default) specifies that the download sites are displayed to the user.
DownloadLocation=*URL*	Specifies the address of the Web site that users download cabinet (.cab) files from, if you are distributing from the Web. If you used Display=0 for this section, or any switch that would result in this page not being displayed, you should enter a download site.
DownloadSiteList=*URL*	Specifies the location for the list of download sites; by default, this list is the IE5Sites.dat file. If you do not include this setting, the setup program uses the current settings in the IESetup.inf file.

Batch file entry	Description
[PrepareSetup]	
Display=[0,1]	Determines whether or not the Preparing Setup screen is displayed on the user's computer.
	0 specifies that the Preparing Setup screen is not displayed to the user.
	1 (default) specifies that the Preparing Setup screen is displayed to the user.
[Diskspace]	
Display=[0,1]	Specifies whether or not to display the amount of disk space needed on the user's computer.
	0 specifies that the amount of disk space needed is not displayed on the user's computer. If the user does not have enough disk space, the setup program will close.
	1 (default) specifies that the amount of disk space needed is displayed on the user's computer.
[Progress]	
Display=[0,1]	Specifies whether or not to display the installation progress to the user.
	0 specifies that the installation progress is not displayed to the user.
	1 (default) specifies that the download progress is displayed to the user.
[RebootPartial]	
Display=[0,1]	Determines whether or not the Installation Incomplete screen appears if a component fails to install.
	0 specifies that the Installation Incomplete screen does not appear if a component fails to install.
	1 (default) specifies that the Installation Incomplete screen appears if a component fails to install.
[Finish]	
Display=[0,1]	Specifies whether or not to display the message that the computer is restarting after setup is complete.
	0 specifies not to display the message that the computer is restarting after the setup is complete. If you plan to turn off restarting after installation, use 0.
	1 (default) specifies to display the message that the computer is restarting after the setup is complete.

Batch file entry	Description
[Reboot]	
Reboot=[0,1]	Specifies whether or not to restart the computer after the setup is complete.
	0 specifies that you do not want to restart the computer after the setup is complete. If you turn off restarting, your program should take care of restarting the computer. Internet Explorer will not be configured correctly until the computer is restarted.
	1 (default) specifies that you do want to restart the computer after the setup is complete.
[Upgrade]	
ReinstallAll=[0,1]	Specifies whether or not to reinstall all components if the setup program is run a second time.
	0 (default) specifies not to run the setup program again if all components are already installed.
	1 specifies to reinstall all components.

Sample Batch File

The following is an sample batch file that shows installation directory choices, performs the first listed installation option, and automatically restarts the computer.

```
[Welcome]
Display=0

[SetupChoice]
Display=0

[Custom]
Display=0
Mode=0
InstallDir=c:\ie\en\

[Download]
Display=0
DownloadDir=c:\iedown\
[Finish]
Display=0
[Reboot]
Reboot=1
```

Using Command-Line Switches

You may want to control the way that the setup program is run. You can use command-line switches to choose the installation mode, specify a quiet mode (which removes or reduces the prompts the user receives), or control whether the computer is restarted after installation.

You can have users include these switches when they run the setup program, but a more typical scenario is packaging Internet Explorer with another program for a batch installation.

You can use the following Internet Explorer switches:

- **/B:***iebatch.txt*—Specifies the batch file to use.
- **/Q**—Specifies a quiet "hands-free" mode. The user is prompted for information that isn't specified.
- **/Q:A**—Specifies a quiet mode with no user prompts.
- **/Q:C**—Specifies a quiet mode with the **Cancel** button not displayed, so the user cannot cancel the setup program. The Internet Explorer Customization wizard uses this switch if you select the **Install package silently** option when you are installing as a corporate administrator.
- **/M:[0|1|2|3...]**—Specifies the installation mode. For customized IEAK packages, 0 refers to the first installation choice, 1 refers to the second choice, and so on (for example, 0=minimal, 1=typical (default), 2=full).
- **/E:ComponentID,ComponentID**—Specifies extra components to be installed regardless of the installation mode. Use this switch to specify components that aren't a part of the installation type you specified in the Customization wizard. This switch also overrides settings in the batch file, if used. The ComponentID is a string that uniquely identifies a component; you can find the corresponding string in the component sections of the IESetup.cif file.
- **/S:""""#e""""**—Designates the source path of IE5Setup.exe. The ""#e"" refers to the full path and name of the executable (.exe) file. Note that the path must be surrounded by two pairs of double quotation marks.
- **/R:N**—Suppresses restarting the computer after installation. If you suppress restarting, your program should take care of restarting the computer. Internet Explorer is not configured correctly until the computer is restarted.
- **/D**—Specifies that you want to download only the files for the current operating system.
- **/D:1**—Specifies that you want to download files for Microsoft Windows and Windows NT operating systems.
- **/G:**—Runs specified installation sections in IESetup.inf. Separate sections with commas.

- **/X**—Installs Internet Explorer without the shell, icons, or links. This option is useful for hosting browser controls in your own application.

- **/X:1**—Installs Internet Explorer with the shell, icons, or links, but does not take over default browser or HTTP protocol associations.

- **/P**—Reports the required component and disk-space cost for an installation. It enables you to see how much disk space will be used based on the installation options selected.

- **/F -(Fix)**—Reinstalls all items on the user's computer that are the same version or newer. Using the /F switch ensures that no component is replaced with an earlier version.

IExpress Switches

The following switches are frequently used IExpress switches that control the extraction process during the setup. They are not specific to Internet Explorer.

- **/Q**—Specifies quiet mode.

- **/QU**—Specifies user-quiet mode, which presents some dialog boxes to the user.

- **/QA**—Specifies administrator-quiet mode, which does not present any dialog boxes to the user.

- **/C:<>**—Specifies the path and name of the Setup.inf or .exe file.

- **/R:N**—Never restarts the computer after installation.

- **/R:A**—Always restarts the computer after installation.

- **/R:S**—Restarts the computer after installation without prompting the user.

- **/T:<*directory path*>**—Specifies the target folder for extracting files.

Examples of Switches

Here are some example scenarios:

- The following expression runs the third installation option:

```
IE5Setup.exe /C:"ie5wzd /S:""#e"" /M:2"
```

- The following expression performs a quiet installation. It does not prompt the user, and the computer is not restarted after installation:

```
IE5Setup.exe /C:"ie5wzd /S:""#e"" /Q /R:N"
```

Command-Line Parameters for Starting Internet Explorer

In addition to using command-line switches to customize Setup, you can use command-line parameters to customize how Internet Explorer is started.

For example, you can start Internet Explorer in Kiosk or full-screen mode by adding a parameter to the Internet Explorer executable file name by using the following syntax:

```
/path/Iexplore.exe -k
```

The following is a list of parameters you can use for starting Internet Explorer:

- **-new**—Launches the browser window in a new browsing process.
- **-remote**—Starts a remote instance of Internet Explorer on UNIX platforms only.
- **-k**—Starts the browser in Kiosk or full-screen mode.
- **-nohome**—Starts Internet Explorer without its home page.
- **-embedding**—Starts the Web browser control (no home page is displayed).
- **-channelband**—Displays the channels folder.
- **-e**—Starts Internet Explorer Help on UNIX platforms only.
- **-v** (also **-version**)—Can be used to specify the version on UNIX platforms only.

APPENDIX D

Checklists for Preparing to Use the IEAK

When preparing to use the Microsoft Internet Explorer Administration Kit (IEAK), you may find checklists helpful. This chapter contains checklists for the files you will need to prepare and information you will need to gather before using the IEAK.

In This Appendix

See Also

- For more information about preparing for the IEAK, see Chapter 12, "Preparing for the IEAK."

- For more information about using the Internet Explorer Customization wizard, see Chapter 15, "Running the Internet Explorer Customization Wizard."

Files and Information to Gather Before Running the IEAK

You can use the following checklists to prepare to run the Internet Explorer Customization wizard.

Tasks for Corporate Administrators

Write title bar text	Notes
CD Autorun screen title bar text	The CD Autorun screen appears when the user inserts the CD-ROM into the drive, unless the user has disabled this feature.
Setup wizard title bar text	The custom text that you provide appears after **Windows Update Setup Provided by** in the title bar.
Browser title bar text	The custom text that you provide appears after **Microsoft Internet Explorer Provided by** in the title bar.
Outlook Express title bar text (Internet service providers and corporate administrators)	The custom text that you provide appears after **Microsoft Outlook Express Provided by** in the title bar.

Collect files	Notes
Setup wizard top banner	For more information about all graphics files, see "Specifications for IEAK Graphics" later in this chapter.
Setup wizard left bitmap	For more information about all graphics files, see "Specifications for IEAK Graphics" later in this chapter.
Browser toolbar background bitmap	For more information about all graphics files, see "Specifications for IEAK Graphics" later in this chapter.
Animated browser logo (large)	For more information, see "Creating an Animated Logo" in Chapter 12, "Preparing for the IEAK."
Animated browser logo (small)	For more information, see "Creating an Animated Logo" in Chapter 12, "Preparing for the IEAK."
Static browser logo (large)	For more information, see "Creating an Animated Logo" in Chapter 12, "Preparing for the IEAK."

Collect files	Notes
Static browser logo (small)	For more information, see "Creating an Animated Logo" in Chapter 12, "Preparing for the IEAK."
CD Autorun custom bitmap path	This is used for CD-ROM packages.
CD Autorun "More Information" text file	This is the first screen that users of CD-ROM packages see.
CD Autorun Kiosk mode startup HTML file	This is the first screen that users of CD-ROM packages see.
Icon for custom browser toolbar button	For more information, see "Designing Browser Toolbar Icons for Internet Explorer 5" in Chapter 12, "Preparing for the IEAK."
Connection Manager custom profile	You can also create the profile while you are using the Customization wizard.
Graphics for icons in the Favorites list	For more information about all graphics files, see "Specifications for IEAK Graphics" later in this chapter.
Outlook Express files	For a complete listing, see the Outlook Express section of this checklist.
Channel files	For a complete listing, see the Channels section of this checklist.
Custom My Computer and Control Panel files	These files are used only if you are a corporate administrator and are installing the desktop component with Internet Explorer 5.
Custom components	This includes the name, path, and additional information related to any custom components you plan to include. For more information, see Chapter 16, "Customizing Setup."

Collect URLs	Notes
Home page URL	This is the page that appears when the user clicks the **Home** button in the browser.
Search page URL	This is the page that appears when the user clicks the **Search** button in the browser.
Online support page URL	This is the page that appears when the user clicks **Online Support** on the **Help** menu in the browser.
Custom welcome page	This is the first page that appears when the user starts the browser.

Collect URLs	Notes
Automatic configuration URL	This is used only by corporate administrators.
Automatic detection of browser settings URL	This is used only by corporate administrators.
Automatic proxy URL	This is used only by corporate administrators.
Favorite URLs	You can also import favorite URLs from your computer.
Product update page	This page is used if you plan to notify users when new products are available or update users periodically for other reasons.
Component update page	This is used if you plan to customize the page from which users will download additional components.

Gather information for Outlook Express settings and files	Notes
Incoming mail server address	This is the POP3 or IMAP server address.
Outgoing mail server address	This is the SMTP server address.
News server address	This is the NNTP server address.
InfoPane URL path	This URL is needed if the .htm file used to customize the InfoPane is on an intranet or the Internet.
InfoPane local file path	This path is needed if you include a local .htm file to customize the InfoPane with your custom package.
Local file image path	This path is needed if you include an image file to customize the InfoPane with your custom package.
HTML path for custom welcome message	For more information about specifying Outlook Express information in the Internet Explorer Customization wizard, see Chapter 15, "Running the Internet Explorer Customization Wizard." For general information about Outlook Express, see Chapter 2, "Microsoft Internet Explorer 5 Components."

Gather information for Outlook Express settings and files	Notes
Sender address for custom welcome message	For more information about specifying Outlook Express information in the Internet Explorer Customization wizard, see Chapter 15, "Running the Internet Explorer Customization Wizard." For general information about Outlook Express, see Chapter 2, "Microsoft Internet Explorer 5 Components."
Reply-to address for custom welcome message	For more information about specifying Outlook Express information in the Internet Explorer Customization wizard, see Chapter 15, "Running the Internet Explorer Customization Wizard." For general information about Outlook Express, see Chapter 2, "Microsoft Internet Explorer 5 Components."
Subscribed newsgroups	This is needed if you want to specify some newsgroups that your users will already be subscribed to.
Service for additional e-mail accounts (service name)	For more information about specifying Outlook Express information in the Internet Explorer Customization wizard, see Chapter 15, "Running the Internet Explorer Customization Wizard." For general information about Outlook Express, see Chapter 2, "Microsoft Internet Explorer 5 Components."
Service for additional accounts (URL)	For more information about specifying Outlook Express information in the Internet Explorer Customization wizard, see Chapter 15, "Running the Internet Explorer Customization Wizard." For general information about Outlook Express, see Chapter 2, "Microsoft Internet Explorer 5 Components."
Default signature text for e-mail messages	This text appears on outgoing e-mail messages. The maximum size is 1 KB.
Default signature text for newsgroup messages	This text appears on outgoing news messages. The maximum size is 1 KB.

Specify LDAP address server settings	Notes
Service name	For more information about specifying Outlook Express and LDAP information in the Internet Explorer Customization wizard, see Chapter 15, "Running the Internet Explorer Customization Wizard." For general information about Outlook Express and directory services, see Chapter 2, "Microsoft Internet Explorer 5 Components."
Server name	For more information about specifying Outlook Express and LDAP information in the Internet Explorer Customization wizard, see Chapter 15, "Running the Internet Explorer Customization Wizard." For general information about Outlook Express and directory services, see Chapter 2, "Microsoft Internet Explorer 5 Components."
Service Web site	For more information about specifying Outlook Express and LDAP information in the Internet Explorer Customization wizard, see Chapter 15, "Running the Internet Explorer Customization Wizard." For general information about Outlook Express and directory services, see Chapter 2, "Microsoft Internet Explorer 5 Components."
Search base	For more information about specifying Outlook Express and LDAP information in the Internet Explorer Customization wizard, see Chapter 15, "Running the Internet Explorer Customization Wizard." For general information about Outlook Express and directory services, see Chapter 2, "Microsoft Internet Explorer 5 Components."
Service bitmap path	For more information about all graphics files, see "Specifications for IEAK Graphics" later in this chapter.

Gather information for digital signatures	Notes
Company name on certificate	Digital signatures are needed if you plan to distribute files over the Internet or, in some cases, an intranet.
Software publishing certificates file	This is a file with an .spc extension.
Private key file	This is a file with a .pvk extension.
Description text	This is the text that appears when the user is prompted with the certificate information.
More information URL	This is the URL that the user can click for more information about your certificate.

Gather information for channels	Notes
Channel title	This is needed if you plan to include a channel or channel category in your custom package.
URL of Channel definition format (.cdf) file on Web server	This is the URL where your .cdf file will be posted on the Internet or an intranet. The .cdf file provides information about when and how to update your content.
Channel definition file	You must provide the .cdf file associated with the channel you want to add.
Narrow channel image path	This is the path to the image or logo that represents your channel.
Channel icon path	For more information about all graphics files, see "Specifications for IEAK Graphics" later in this chapter.
Category title	This is the title of your channel category. It will appear in the user's Favorites list.
Category HTML page	This is the HTML page for your channel category.
Narrow category image path	This is the path to the image that represents your channel category.
Category icon path	For more information about all graphics files, see "Specifications for IEAK Graphics" later in this chapter.

Specify custom identifiers	Notes
User agent string	This string is used to identify the user's browser type. You can add a custom string to the custom browsers you create.

Tasks for Internet Service Providers

Write title bar text	Notes
CD Autorun screen title bar text	The CD Autorun screen appears when the user inserts the CD-ROM into the drive, unless the user has disabled this feature.
Setup wizard title bar text	The custom text that you provide appears after **Windows Update Setup Provided by** in the title bar.
Browser title bar text	The custom text that you provide appears after **Microsoft Internet Explorer Provided by** in the title bar.
Outlook Express title bar text (Internet service providers and corporate administrators)	The custom text that you provide appears after **Microsoft Outlook Provided by** in the title bar.

Collect files	Notes
Setup wizard top banner	For more information about all graphics files, see "Specifications for IEAK Graphics" later in this chapter.
Setup wizard left bitmap	For more information about all graphics files, see "Specifications for IEAK Graphics" later in this chapter.
Browser toolbar background bitmap	For more information about all graphics files, see "Specifications for IEAK Graphics" later in this chapter.
Animated browser logo (large)	For more information, see "Creating an Animated Logo" in Chapter 12, "Preparing for the IEAK."
Animated browser logo (small)	For more information, see "Creating an Animated Logo" in Chapter 12, "Preparing for the IEAK."
Static browser logo (large)	For more information, see "Creating an Animated Logo" in Chapter 12, "Preparing for the IEAK."
Static browser logo (small)	For more information, see "Creating an Animated Logo" in Chapter 12, "Preparing for the IEAK."
CD Autorun custom bitmap path	This is used for CD-ROM packages.
CD Autorun "More Information" text file	This is the first screen that users of CD-ROM packages see.
CD Autorun Kiosk mode startup HTML file	This is the first screen that users of CD-ROM packages see.

Collect files	Notes
Icon for custom browser toolbar button	For more information, see "Designing Browser Toolbar Icons for Internet Explorer 5" in Chapter 12, "Preparing for the IEAK."
Sign-up files	These files are used only if you are an ISP. For more information, see the sign-up files section of this checklist.
Internet Connection wizard image (large)	This image is used only if you are an ISP implementing a server-based sign-up. This image appears on the first page of the wizard.
Internet Connection wizard image (small)	This image is used only if you are an ISP implementing a server-based sign-up. This image appears on the top of all but the first wizard page.
Connection Manager custom profile	You can also create the profile while you are using the Customization wizard.
Graphics for icons in the Favorites list	For more information about all graphics files, see "Specifications for IEAK Graphics" later in this chapter.
Outlook Express files	For a complete listing, see the Outlook Express section of this checklist.
Channel files	For a complete listing, see the Channels section of this checklist.
Custom components	This includes the name, path, and additional information related to any custom components you plan to include. For more information, see Chapter 16, "Customizing Setup."

Collect URLs	Notes
Home page URL	This is the page that appears when the user clicks the **Home** button in the browser.
Search page URL	This is the page that appears when the user clicks the **Search** button in the browser.
Online support page URL	This is the page that appears when the user clicks **Online Support** on the **Help** menu in the browser.
Custom welcome page	This is the first page that appears when the user starts the browser.
Favorite URLs	You can also import favorite URLs from your computer.

Collect URLs	Notes
Product update page	This page is used if you plan to notify users when new products are available or update users periodically for other reasons.
Component update page	This is used if you plan to customize the page from which users will download additional components.

Gather information for Outlook Express settings and files	Notes
Incoming mail server address	This is the POP3 or IMAP server address.
Outgoing mail server address	This is the SMTP server address.
News server address	This is the NNTP server address.
InfoPane URL path	This URL is needed if the .htm file used to customize the InfoPane is on an intranet or the Internet.
InfoPane local file path	This path is needed if you include a local .htm file to customize the InfoPane with your custom package.
Local file image path	This path is needed if you include an image file to customize the InfoPane with your custom package.
HTML path for custom welcome message	For more information about specifying Outlook Express information in the Internet Explorer Customization wizard, see Chapter 15, "Running the Internet Explorer Customization Wizard." For general information about Outlook Express, see Chapter 2, "Microsoft Internet Explorer 5 Components."
Sender address for custom welcome message	For more information about specifying Outlook Express information in the Internet Explorer Customization wizard, see Chapter 15, "Running the Internet Explorer Customization Wizard." For general information about Outlook Express, see Chapter 2, "Microsoft Internet Explorer 5 Components."

Gather information for Outlook Express settings and files	Notes
Reply-to address for custom welcome message	For more information about specifying Outlook Express information in the Internet Explorer Customization wizard, see Chapter 15, "Running the Internet Explorer Customization Wizard." For general information about Outlook Express, see Chapter 2, "Microsoft Internet Explorer 5 Components."
Subscribed newsgroups	This is needed if you want to specify some newsgroups that your users will already be subscribed to.
Service for additional e-mail accounts (service name)	For more information about specifying Outlook Express information in the Internet Explorer Customization wizard, see Chapter 15, "Running the Internet Explorer Customization Wizard." For general information about Outlook Express, see Chapter 2, "Microsoft Internet Explorer 5 Components."
Service for additional accounts (URL)	For more information about specifying Outlook Express information in the Internet Explorer Customization wizard, see Chapter 15, "Running the Internet Explorer Customization Wizard." For general information about Outlook Express, see Chapter 2, "Microsoft Internet Explorer 5 Components."
Default signature text for mail messages	This text appears on outgoing mail messages. The maximum size is 1 KB.
Default signature text for newsgroup messages	This text appears on outgoing news messages. The maximum size is 1 KB.

Specify LDAP address server settings	Notes
Service name	For more information about specifying Outlook Express and LDAP files in the Internet Explorer Customization wizard, see Chapter 15, "Running the Internet Explorer Customization Wizard." For general information about Outlook Express and directory services, see Chapter 2, "Microsoft Internet Explorer 5 Components."
Server name	For more information about specifying Outlook Express and LDAP files in the Internet Explorer Customization wizard, see Chapter 15, "Running the Internet Explorer Customization Wizard." For general information about Outlook Express and directory services, see Chapter 2, "Microsoft Internet Explorer 5 Components."
Service Web site	For more information about specifying Outlook Express and LDAP files in the Internet Explorer Customization wizard, see Chapter 15, "Running the Internet Explorer Customization Wizard." For general information about Outlook Express and directory services, see Chapter 2, "Microsoft Internet Explorer 5 Components."
Search base	For more information about specifying Outlook Express and LDAP files in the Internet Explorer Customization wizard, see Chapter 15, "Running the Internet Explorer Customization Wizard." For general information about Outlook Express and directory services, see Chapter 2, "Microsoft Internet Explorer 5 Components."
Service bitmap path	For more information about all graphics files, see "Specifications for IEAK Graphics" later in this chapter.

Gather information for digital signatures	Notes
Company name on certificate	Digital signatures are needed if you plan to distribute files over the Internet or, in some cases, an intranet.
Software publishing certificates file	This is a file with an .spc extension.
Private key file	This is a file with a .pvk extension.
Description text	This is the text that appears when the user is prompted with the certificate information.
More information URL	This is the URL that the user can click for more information about your certificate.
New root certificate path	This information is needed only if you are an ISP.

Gather information for channels	Notes
Channel title	This is needed if you plan to include a channel or channel category in your custom package.
URL of Channel definition format (.cdf) file on Web server	This is the URL where your .cdf file will be posted. The .cdf file provides information about when and how to update your content.
Channel definition file	You must provide the .cdf file associated with the channel you want to add.
Narrow channel image path	This is the path to the image or logo that represents your channel.
Channel icon path	For more information about all graphics files, see "Specifications for IEAK Graphics" later in this chapter.
Category title	This is the title of your channel category. It will appear in the user's Favorites list.
Category HTML page	This is the HTML page for your channel category.
Narrow category image path	This is the path to the image that represents your channel category.
Category icon path	For more information about all graphics files, see "Specifications for IEAK Graphics" later in this chapter.

Specify custom identifiers	Notes
User agent string	This string is used to identify the user's browser type. You can add a custom string to the custom browsers you create.

Create sign-up files	Notes
Signup.htm	For server-based sign-up, the signup.htm file should contain a pointer to sign-up files on your Web server.
	For examples of all sign-up files, see the \IEAK\Toolkit\ISP folder.
Signup.isp	In serverless sign-up, this file enables your sign-up server to be dialed.
Internet Connection wizard (ICW) files	These files are needed if you use the ICW for Internet sign-up. For more information, see Chapter 13, "Setting Up Servers," and Chapter 20, "Implementing the Sign-up Process."
.ins and .isp file(s)	These files contain Internet settings. You can edit them yourself, or have the Internet Explorer Customization wizard create these files for you. You can also create scripts, such as Active Server Page scripts, to generate the .ins files for you.
	You will want to create a Cancel.ins file, which is a simple .ins file that cancels the user's sign-up process.

Tasks for Internet Content Providers

Write title bar text	Notes
CD Autorun screen title bar text	The CD Autorun screen appears when the user inserts the CD-ROM into the drive, unless the user has disabled this feature.
Setup wizard title bar text	The custom text that you provide appears after **Windows Update Setup Provided by** in the title bar.
Browser title bar text	The custom text that you provide appears after **Microsoft Internet Explorer Provided by** in the title bar.

Collect files	Notes
Setup wizard top banner	For more information about all graphics files, see "Specifications for IEAK Graphics" later in this chapter.
Setup wizard left bitmap	For more information about all graphics files, see "Specifications for IEAK Graphics" later in this chapter.
Browser toolbar background bitmap	For more information about all graphics files, see "Specifications for IEAK Graphics" later in this chapter.
Animated browser logo (large)	For more information, see "Creating an Animated Logo" in Chapter 12, "Preparing for the IEAK."
Animated browser logo (small)	For more information, see "Creating an Animated Logo" in Chapter 12, "Preparing for the IEAK."
Static browser logo (large)	For more information, see "Creating an Animated Logo" in Chapter 12, "Preparing for the IEAK."
Static browser logo (small)	For more information, see "Creating an Animated Logo" in Chapter 12, "Preparing for the IEAK."
CD Autorun custom bitmap path	This is used for CD-ROM packages.
CD Autorun "More Information" text file	This is the first screen that users of CD-ROM packages see.
CD Autorun Kiosk mode startup HTML file	This is the first screen that users of CD-ROM packages see.

Collect files	Notes
Icon for custom browser toolbar button	For more information, see "Designing Browser Toolbar Icons for Internet Explorer 5" in Chapter 12, "Preparing for the IEAK."
Graphics for icons in the Favorites list	For more information about all graphics files, see "Specifications for IEAK Graphics" later in this chapter.
Channel files	For a complete listing, see the Channels section of this checklist.
Custom components	This includes the name, path, and additional information related to any custom components you plan to include. For more information, see Chapter 16, "Customizing Setup."

Collect URLs	Notes
Home page URL	This is the page that appears when the user clicks the **Home** button in the browser.
Search page URL	This is the page that appears when the user clicks the **Search** button in the browser.
Online support page URL	This is the page that appears when the user clicks **Online Support** on the **Help** menu in the browser.
Custom welcome page	This is the first page that appears when the user starts the browser.
Favorite URLs	You can also import favorite URLs from your computer.
Product update page	This page is used if you plan to notify users when new products are available or update users periodically for other reasons.
Component update page	This is used if you plan to customize the page from which users will download additional components.

Gather information for digital signatures	Notes
Company name on certificate	Digital signatures are needed if you plan to distribute files over the Internet or, in some cases, an intranet.
Software publishing certificates file	This is a file with an .spc extension.
Private key file	This is a file with a .pvk extension.

Gather information for digital signatures	Notes
Description text	This is the text that appears when the user is prompted with the certificate information.
More information URL	This is the URL that the user can click for more information about your certificate.

Gather information for channels	Notes
Channel title	This is needed if you plan to include a channel or channel category in your custom package.
URL of Channel definition format (.cdf) file on Web server	This is the URL where your .cdf file will be posted on the Internet or an intranet. The .cdf file provides information about when and how to update your content.
Channel definition file	You must provide the .cdf file associated with the channel you want to add.
Narrow channel image path	This is the path to the image or logo that represents your channel.
Channel icon path	For more information about all graphics files, see "Specifications for IEAK Graphics" later in this chapter.
Category title	This is the title of your channel category. It will appear in the user's Favorites list.
Category HTML page	This is the HTML page for your channel category.
Narrow category image path	This is the path to the image that represents your channel category.
Category icon path	For more information about all graphics files, see "Specifications for IEAK Graphics" later in this chapter.

Specify custom identifiers	Notes
User agent string	This string is used to identify the user's browser type. You can add a custom string to the custom browsers you create.

Specifications for IEAK Graphics

The following table contains information about dimensions, resolutions, and other requirements for the graphics that you can customize by using the IEAK.

Graphic name	What it's used for	Dimension and resolution	Preparation
Static logo	To brand the Internet Explorer browser with your static logo	38-by-38-pixel and 22-by-22-pixel .bmp files using 256 colors	Create two bitmaps in the specified dimensions and resolution. Save the files in the custom bitmap folder (\CIE\Bitmaps). When the browser isn't active, the first frame of the animated logo will be used as the static logo.
Animated logo	To brand the Internet Explorer browser with your animated logo	38-by-38-pixel and 22-by-22-pixel .bmp files using 256 colors	Create two bitmaps in the specified dimensions and resolution. The bitmaps must contain a vertical stack of animation cell images that follow Internet Explorer animation rules (see the following section). Save the files in the custom bitmap folder (\CIE\Bitmaps). When the browser isn't active, the first frame of the animated logo will be used as the static logo.
Setup bitmaps (for Microsoft Windows versions only)	Windows Update Setup wizard	**For 32-bit Internet Explorer versions:** Left vertical: 162-by-312-pixel, 256-color .bmp file (on the first Setup wizard page) Top horizontal: 496-by-56-pixel, 256-color .bmp file (on all but first page) **For 16-bit Internet Explorer versions:** 162-by-312-pixel, 16-color .bmp file with few or no background colors and patterns (recommended format)	For 32-bit versions, the top horizontal banner needs to be light, like a "watermark," to allow text in the user interface to be readable.
Toolbar background	A "watermark" behind the browser toolbar	No specific dimensions or resolutions	The background should be the size of the toolbar and be light enough to show black text.

Graphic name	What it's used for	Dimension and resolution	Preparation
Autorun splash screen (Windows 95 and Windows NT 4.0 only)	To display a splash screen when the user inserts the CD-ROM	If you distribute your custom browser on a CD-ROM, you need to create bitmaps for the Autorun splash screen that appears when the user inserts the CD-ROM.	Before you create the splash screen, you need to convert any 24-bit images to the 256-color Windows identity palette.
Channels	Channels, which the user can access from the Favorites folder (and the desktop if the user has Windows 98 or the Windows Desktop Update).	For each channel: 32-by-32-pixel .bmp file for the icon, 80-by-32-pixel graphic file in .bmp, .gif, or .jpeg format for the channel category, and 194-by-32-pixel graphic file in .bmp, .gif, or .jpeg format for the channel pane.	No special steps are required.
Internet Connection wizard	To customize the Internet Connection wizard when used for Internet sign-up	Banner image: 49-by-49-pixel .bmp file that appears on the upper-right corner of the Internet Connection wizard. Watermark image: Type the path to the 164-by-458-pixel .bmp file that appears on the left side of the Internet Connection wizard.	Internet Connection wizard sign-up is not available for serverless sign-up.
Lightweight Directory Access Protocol (LDAP) service bitmap	This bitmap identifies a custom directory service, where users look up reference information, such as addresses or phone numbers.	134-by-38-pixel, 16-color .bmp file	No special steps are required.

Note Internet Explorer animation rules are as follows:

Cells 1 through 4 are lead-in cells, which are played when Internet Explorer begins to browse.

Cells 5 through X, where X is the total number of cells, loop until the browse operation is complete.

APPENDIX E

Setting System Policies and Restrictions

This appendix describes how you can use system policies and restrictions to control user and computer access to Microsoft Internet Explorer 5 features and functions. Using the Internet Explorer Customization wizard or Internet Explorer Administration Kit (IEAK) Profile Manager, you can predefine Internet Explorer options and customize the Internet Explorer environment for different groups of users.

Note You can also use the System Policy Editor in Windows 95, Windows 98, and Windows NT 4.0 to set system policies and restrictions. For specific instructions about how to install and use the System Policy Editor, see the Microsoft Windows 95 Resource Kit, the Microsoft Windows 98 Resource Kit, or the Microsoft Windows NT Workstation 4.0 Resource Kit.

In This Appendix

See Also

- For more information about planning your system policy choices, see Chapter 9, "Planning the Deployment."

- For more information about implementing system policies and restrictions as part of your custom browser packages, see Chapter 15, "Running the Internet Explorer Customization Wizard."

Overview

System policies and restrictions for Internet Explorer are a powerful mechanism for improving the control and manageability of computers. System policies and restrictions, which are defined in a policy file, control user and computer access privileges by overriding default registry values when the user logs on.

You can use the Internet Explorer Customization wizard to predefine system policies and restrictions and to create a standard Internet Explorer configuration as part of your custom browser package. After the Internet Explorer installation, you can use the IEAK Profile Manager to centrally manage and update system policies and restrictions on your users' desktops. Also, if different groups of users have unique needs, you can use the IEAK Profile Manager to create separate policy files for each group.

For example, you might want to implement system policies and restrictions to do the following:

- Determine the features that users can change, such as the Active Desktop and Internet Explorer toolbars.
- Manage bandwidth, and control the behavior and appearance of Internet Explorer.
- Specify server lists for components, such as Microsoft Chat and Microsoft NetMeeting.
- Determine which programs are used for electronic mail and for placing Internet calls.
- Specify the users' connection settings.

Benefits of Using System Policies and Restrictions

Organizations can realize the following benefits from implementing system policies and restrictions:

- System policies and restrictions enable you to implement a standard Internet Explorer configuration. You can create a custom browser package for your users that includes common settings for browser features and functions.
- You can restrict the features that users can access within Internet Explorer by using system policies and restrictions. For example, you can preset the NetMeeting options to control audio and video access. Also, you have the option to lock down features and functions, so they either don't appear or appear dimmed on users' desktops.
- Setting system policies and restrictions enables you to change default registry values. You can use the settings in a policy file to change registry values on multiple computers, eliminating the need to specify settings individually on each user's computer.

Issues to Consider Before Setting System Policies and Restrictions

Before implementing system policies and restrictions, you should consider the following issues:

- What types of system policies and restrictions would you like to define and manage centrally? For example, do you want to limit access to NetMeeting or Chat features?

- Do you want to use one set of standard system policies and restrictions for all users and computers, or do you want to create multiple policy files for groups of users? Different groups of users may have unique needs.

- What types of security settings do you want to implement? You can choose to lock down all the settings, to control the settings but make them available for roaming users to download, or to customize the settings while allowing users to modify them.

  You should consider the impact of these settings, especially if you have roaming users who share computers with other people. For example, what are the implications of removing icons from the desktop or not allowing users to change their security settings? Make sure that your users understand which features they can access.

- Do you want to store the policy files in a central location or on users' computers? You may want to store the file on a server so that roaming users can access the settings from computer to computer. This capability could be useful, for example, for a user who needs low security settings but who uses a computer that is operated by another person whose security settings are higher.

Setting System Policies and Restrictions

On the System Policies and Restrictions screen, you can select a category and change the corresponding system policies and restrictions. A default set of policy templates, or administration (.adm) files, define the rules for the wide range of settings that appear on the System Policies and Restrictions screen. These same settings appear in both the Internet Explorer Customization wizard (Stage 5) and the IEAK Profile Manager. The first time that the wizard is run, the .adm files are created in the C:\Program Files\Ieak\Policies directory.

▶ **To set system policies and restrictions**

1. To display the system policies and restrictions that you can define for a category, double-click the category name that appears in bold type.

   The following Internet Explorer Customization wizard screen shows the System Policies and Restrictions categories.

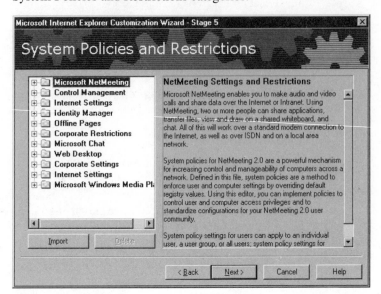

Note The system policies and restrictions that you can set depend on the title that you select as your role in Stage 1 of the Internet Explorer Customization wizard—either Content Provider/Developer, Service Provider, or Corporate Administrator. For example, a content provider or developer can set system policies and restrictions for Internet Options and Chat, while a service provider can also implement system policies and restrictions for NetMeeting.

2. Select or clear the check boxes. For example, you can expand the **Web Desktop** category and select the **Desktop** object to specify Desktop options, such as **Disable Active Desktop**.

The following table briefly describes each of the categories for which you can specify system policies and restrictions.

Area	Description
Microsoft NetMeeting	Specifies settings that restrict access privileges to NetMeeting. You can use these settings to control bandwidth, server access, and the appearance of NetMeeting components.
Control Management	Selects the approved set of controls for data binding, MSN online service, and Internet Explorer components. All other controls will be locked down and will not run on users' computers.
Internet Settings	Specifies a variety of Internet settings for users, including options for printing, searching, multimedia, and security. Most of these settings apply to default values in the Internet Control Panel.
Identity Manager	Prevents users from creating multiple identities within a Windows logon profile using the Microsoft Identity Manager.
Offline Pages	Controls the amount of information downloaded by disabling or limiting access to offline functions, such as the number of offline pages that users can download and the maximum number of minutes between scheduled updates. These settings improve server load by restricting bandwidth usage.
Corporate Restrictions	Specifies and locks down Internet Options settings and other browser options, such as search customization and software updates. These settings can lock out features of Internet Explorer that may be unnecessary or undesirable for users, and prevent modifications to settings made during setup or automatic configuration.
Microsoft Chat	Restricts access to Chat features and functions by using predefined values for the default chat server, character, and chat room.
Web Desktop	Restricts users' ability to add, access, modify, or delete various portions of the desktop. These settings control how users manage files, use printers, and accomplish other everyday tasks.
Corporate Settings	Specifies and locks down settings for Temporary Internet files, code download, browsing errors, and Microsoft Office file types. For example, you can choose which error messages the browser will suppress.
Microsoft Windows Media Player	Customizes the Windows Media Player, Internet Explorer Radio, and network settings, and also prevents the installation of Windows Media Player favorites.

Using Custom Policy Templates

If you are familiar with Windows administration (.adm) files, you can create your own policy templates with custom settings that you can distribute to users.

Important Be sure that you thoroughly test your templates before using them to make changes to users' systems.

▶ **To import your custom .adm file**

- If you are using the Internet Explorer Customization wizard, click **Import** on the System Policies and Restrictions screen.

  –or–

  If you are using the IEAK Profile Manager, on the **Policy** menu, click **Import**.

Note On the IEAK Profile Manager **Policy** menu, you can click **Check Duplicate Keys** to check for duplicate registry keys in the templates.

When you use custom policy templates, an information (.inf) file is generated using the file name of the imported custom template. For example, if you import custom.adm, a custom.inf file will be generated and added to the companion cabinet (.cab) files. When unpacked, the .inf files are used to change policies and restrictions on users' systems. The following illustration shows this process.

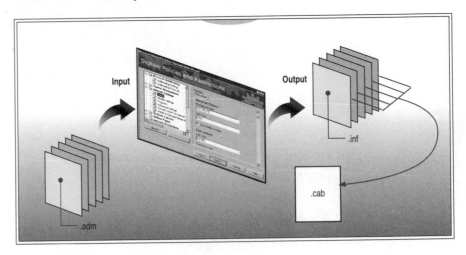

Illustration E.1   System Policies and Restrictions

Updating System Policies and Restrictions After Installation

After the system policies and restrictions are set and the browser is distributed, you can use the IEAK Profile Manager to manage these settings. The Profile Manager enables you to open the .ins file and make changes to system policies and restrictions. By storing an .ins file on the server and downloading it with each logon, you can adjust system policies and restrictions on an ongoing basis. Tying into existing logon scripts enables you to manage and regularly update these settings from a centralized server.

Note   You must reboot the computer in order for some system policies and restrictions to take effect.

For more information about using the Profile Manager to update system policies and restrictions, see Chapter 22, "Keeping Programs Updated."

APPENDIX F

Country/Region and Language Codes

If you are an Internet service provider, you may find this list of country/region and language codes to be helpful.

Note Because this information about country/region and language codes is subject to change, consult periodically the most recent telephone reference materials for updates to these codes.

In This Appendix

See Also

- For general information about creating sign-up solutions, see Chapter 20, "Implementing the Sign-up Process."

Country/Region Codes

Use the country/region identifier and code where required in your Internet sign-up files.

Country/Region	Identifier (unique)	Code (as dialed)
Afghanistan	93	93
Albania	355	355
Algeria	213	213
American Samoa	684	684
Andorra	376	376
Angola	244	244
Anguilla	101	264
Antarctica	—	672
Antigua	102	268
Argentina	54	54
Armenia	374	374
Aruba	297	297
Ascension Island	247	247
Australia	61	61
Australian Antarctic Territory	6721	672
Austria	43	43
Azerbaijan	994	994
Bahamas, The	103	242
Bahrain	973	973
Bangladesh	880	880
Barbados	104	246
Barbuda	120	1
Belarus	375	375
Belgium	32	32
Belize	501	501
Benin	229	229
Bermuda	105	441
Bhutan	975	975
Bolivia	591	591
Bosnia and Herzegovina	387	387
Botswana	267	267

Country/Region	Identifier (unique)	Code (as dialed)
Brazil	55	55
British Virgin Islands	106	284
Brunei	673	673
Bulgaria	359	359
Burkina Faso	226	226
Burundi	257	257
Cambodia	855	855
Cameroon	237	237
Canada	107	1
Cape Verde	238	238
Cayman Islands	108	345
Central African Republic	236	236
Chad	235	235
Chile	56	56
China	86	86
Christmas Island	672	61
Cocos-Keeling Islands	6191	61
Colombia	57	57
Comoros	2691	269
Congo	242	242
Congo (DRC)	243	243
Cook Islands	682	682
Costa Rica	506	506
Cote d'Ivoire	—	225
Croatia	385	385
Cuba	53	53
Cyprus	357	357
Czech Republic	42	42
Denmark	45	45
Diego Garcia	246	246
Djibouti	253	253
Dominica	109	767
Dominican Republic	110	809
Ecuador	593	593
Egypt	20	20

Country/Region	Identifier (unique)	Code (as dialed)
El Salvador	503	503
Equatorial Guinea	240	240
Eritrea	291	291
Estonia	372	372
Ethiopia	251	251
F.Y.R.O.M. (Former Yugoslav Republic of Macedonia)	389	389
Faroe Islands	298	298
Falkland Islands (Islas Malvinas)	500	500
Fiji Islands	679	679
Finland	358	358
France	33	33
French Antilles	5901	590
French Guiana	594	594
French Polynesia	689	689
Gabon	241	241
Gambia, The	220	220
Georgia	995	995
Germany	49	49
Ghana	233	233
Gibraltar	350	350
Greece	30	30
Greenland	299	299
Grenada	111	473
Guadeloupe	590	590
Guam	671	671
Guantanamo Bay	5399	5399
Guatemala	502	502
Guinea	224	224
Guinea-Bissau	245	245
Guyana	592	592
Haiti	509	509
Honduras	504	504
Hong Kong S.A.R.	852	852
Hungary	36	36

Country/Region	Identifier (unique)	Code (as dialed)
Iceland	354	354
India	91	91
Indonesia	62	62
INMARSAT (Atlantic-East) [Marisat (Atlantic)]	871	871
INMARSAT (Atlantic-West) [Marisat (Atlantic West)]	874	874
INMARSAT (Indian) [Marisat (Indian)]	873	873
INMARSAT (Pacific) [Marisat (Pacific)]	872	872
Iran	98	98
Iraq	964	964
Ireland	353	353
Israel	972	972
Italy	39	39
Ivory Coast	225	225
Jamaica	112	1
Japan	81	81
Jordan	962	962
Kazakhstan	705	7
Kenya	254	254
Kiribati	686	686
Korea, North	850	850
Korea	82	82
Kuwait	965	965
Kyrgyzstan	706	7
Laos	856	856
Latvia	371	371
Lebanon	961	961
Lesotho	266	266
Liberia	231	231
Libya	218	218
Liechtenstein	4101	41
Lithuania	370	370
Luxembourg	352	352
Macao	853	853

Country/Region	Identifier (unique)	Code (as dialed)
Madagascar	261	261
Malawi	265	265
Malaysia	60	60
Maldives	960	960
Mali	223	223
Malta	356	356
Marshall Islands	692	692
Martinique	596	596
Mauritania	222	222
Mauritius	230	230
Mayotte	269	269
Mexico	52	52
Micronesia, Federated States of	691	691
Moldova	373	373
Monaco	3302	33
Mongolia	976	976
Montserrat	113	1
Morocco	212	212
Mozambique	258	258
Myanmar	95	95
Namibia	264	264
Nauru	674	674
Nepal	977	977
Netherlands	31	31
Netherlands Antilles	599	599
Nevis (St. Kitts and Nevis)	114	1
New Caledonia	687	687
New Zealand	64	64
Nicaragua	505	505
Niger	227	227
Nigeria	234	234
Niue	683	683
Norfolk Island	6722	672
Norway	47	47
Oman	968	968

Country/Region	Identifier (unique)	Code (as dialed)
Pakistan	92	92
Palau	680	680
Panama	507	507
Papua New Guinea	675	675
Paraguay	595	595
Peru	51	51
Philippines	63	63
Poland	48	48
Portugal	351	351
Puerto Rico	121	1
Qatar	974	974
Reunion Island	262	262
Romania	40	40
Rota Island	6701	670
Russia	7	7
Rwanda	250	250
St. Lucia	122	758
Saipan	670	670
San Marino	378	378
Sao Tome and Principe	239	239
Samoa	685	685
Saudi Arabia	966	966
Senegal	221	221
Seychelles	248	248
Sierra Leone	232	232
Singapore	65	65
Slovakia	4201	42
Slovenia	386	386
Solomon Islands	677	677
Somalia	252	252
South Africa	27	27
Spain	34	34
Sri Lanka	94	94
St. Helena	290	290
St. Kitts	115	869

Country/Region	Identifier (unique)	Code (as dialed)
St. Pierre and Miquelon	508	508
St. Vincent and the Grenadines	116	809
Sudan	249	249
Suriname	597	597
Swaziland	268	268
Sweden	46	46
Switzerland	41	41
Syria	963	963
Taiwan	886	886
Tajikistan	708	7
Tanzania	255	255
Thailand	66	66
Tinian Island	6702	670
Togo	228	228
Tokelau	690	690
Tonga	676	676
Trinidad and Tobago	117	868
Tunisia	216	216
Turkey	90	90
Turkmenistan	709	993

Country/Region	Identifier (unique)	Code (as dialed)
Turks and Caicos Islands	118	649
Tuvalu	688	688
Uganda	256	256
Ukraine	380	380
United Arab Emirates	971	971
United Kingdom	44	44
United States of America	1	1
United States Virgin Islands	123	340
Uruguay	598	598
Uzbekistan	711	7
Vanuatu	678	678
Vatican City	379	39
Venezuela	58	58
Vietnam	84	84
Wallis and Futuna Islands	681	681
Yemen	967	967
Yugoslavia	381	381
Zambia	260	260
Zimbabwe	263	263

Language Codes

Language	Identifier
Afrikaans	1078
Albanian	1052
Arabic (Saudi Arabia)	1025
Arabic (Iraq)	2049
Arabic (Egypt)	3073
Arabic (Libya)	4097
Arabic (Algeria)	5121
Arabic (Morocco)	6145
Arabic (Tunisia)	7169
Arabic (Oman)	8193
Arabic (Yemen)	9217
Arabic (Syria)	10241
Arabic (Jordan)	11265
Arabic (Lebanon)	12289
Arabic (Kuwait)	13313
Arabic (U.A.E.)	14337
Arabic (Bahrain)	15361
Arabic (Qatar)	16385
Basque	1069
Byelorussian	1059
Bulgarian	1026
Catalan	1027
Chinese (Taiwan)	1028
Chinese (PRC)	2052
Chinese (Hong Kong S.A.R.)	3076
Chinese (Singapore)	4100
Croatian	1050
Czech	1029
Danish	1030
Dutch (Standard)	1043
Dutch (Belgium)	2067
English (US)	1033
English (UK)	2057
English (Canada)	4105

Language	Identifier
English (New Zealand)	5129
English (Australia)	3081
English (Ireland)	6153
English (South Africa)	7177
Estonian	1061
Faroese	1080
Farsi	1065
Finnish	1035
French (Standard)	1036
French (Belgium)	2060
French (Switzerland)	4108
French (Canada)	3084
French (Luxembourg)	5132
German (Standard)	1031
German (Switzerland)	2055
German (Austria)	3079
German (Luxembourg)	4103
German (Liechtenstein)	5127
Greek	1032
Hebrew	1037
Hungarian	1038
Icelandic	1039
Indonesian	1057
Italian	1040
Italian (Switzerland)	2064
Japanese	1041
Korean	1042
Korean (Johab)	2066
Latvian	1062
Lithuanian	1063
Norwegian (Bokmål)	1044
Norwegian (Nynorsk)	2068
Polish	1045
Portuguese (Standard)	2070
Portuguese (Brazil)	1046

Language	Identifier
Romanian	1048
Russian	1049
Serbian (Latin)	0
Slovak	1051
Slovenian	1060
Spanish (Mexico)	2058
Spanish (Traditional Sort)	1034
Spanish (Modern Sort)	3082
Swedish	1053
Thai	1054
Turkish	1055
Ukrainian	1058

APPENDIX G

Microsoft Internet Explorer 5 File Types

This appendix provides an overview of the common types of files that are used as part of the Microsoft Windows Update Setup for Internet Explorer 5 and Internet Tools. Learning about the purposes of these files and how they work together can make it easier to troubleshoot potential setup issues.

In This Appendix

See Also

- For more information about the setup process, see Chapter 19, "Deploying Microsoft Internet Explorer 5."

- For more information about Internet Explorer system policy files, see Appendix E, "Setting System Policies and Restrictions."

Common Setup Files

The following table describes the common file types that are used as part of the Windows Update Setup. For a complete list of files that are downloaded to your computer during the setup process, see the Microsoft Internet Explorer Support Web site and the Internet Explorer Knowledge Base.

File type	Description
.adm	An administration (.adm) file defines the system policies and restrictions for the desktop, shell, and security. You can customize and restrict the settings in an .adm file by using the Internet Explorer Administration Kit (IEAK) or the Windows System Policy Editor. For a list of system policies and restrictions that you can set in the .adm file, see Appendix E, "Setting System Policies and Restrictions."
	You can maintain .adm files on the users' desktops or from a central location. After Internet Explorer is installed, you can use the IEAK Profile Manager to update the .adm file settings on your users' desktops. For more information about using the IEAK Profile Manager, see Chapter 22, "Keeping Programs Updated."
.asp	If you distribute Internet Explorer from a Web server, you can include Active Server Page (.asp) files in your custom browser package. By using .asp files, you can embed script within your HTML pages to create dynamic, interactive Web content. For example, you can create sign-up pages that enable users to download the browser and register for Internet services. You can point to .asp files in the Internet Explorer Customization wizard or the IEAK Profile Manager. The Resource Kit CD-ROM includes sample .asp files.
.bmp, .gif, .jpeg, .jpg	Internet Explorer can include static and animated graphics that use .bmp, .gif, .jpeg, or .jpg file formats. In addition to using graphics files supplied with the IEAK, you can create your own and include them with your custom browser package. For example, you can replace the Internet Explorer logo or AutoRun splash screen with your own static or animated graphic files. The IEAK includes two tools to help you create customized animated graphics. For more information about the requirements for graphics that you customize, see Appendix D, "Checklists for Preparing to Use the IEAK."
.cab	Cabinet (.cab) files organize and store compressed installation files that are copied to the user's computer. Windows Update Setup (IE5Setup.exe) downloads the .cab files necessary for Internet Explorer installation to the user's computer. These .cab files can contain both browser and custom components. After the files are downloaded successfully, Windows Update Setup is complete. The IEAK contains a set of tools that can help you build .cab files for custom components.

File type	Description
.cdf	A channel definition format (.cdf) file enables you to use channels to distribute Web content or software updates to your users. The .cdf file provides an index of resources available in a channel and a recommended schedule for updating the channel on users' computers. A subscription to a channel updates the local cache on the user's computer with new information according to what the publisher specifies in the .cdf file.
.cif	A component information (.cif) file named IESetup.cif identifies the components that you can install with Internet Explorer, including any new components or component updates. In the .cif file, each component has an associated ComponentID. Windows Update Setup reads the .cif file to determine whether a component with a specific ComponentID has already been installed and whether a newer version is available for installation.
.exe	An executable (.exe) file named IE5Setup.exe is the installation program that controls the setup process. This .exe file downloads the .cab files that install your custom browser package on users' computers. Those .cab files can, in turn, include additional self-extracting .exe files for browser and custom components.
.htt	The HTML template (.htt) files provide customizable templates for My Computer (Mycomp.htt), Control Panel (Controlp.htt), Printers (Printers.htt), and the default Web view for folders (Folder.htt). Using a text or HTML editor, you can customize these files with special instructions, logos, or links to Web sites. You can include Mycomp.htt and Controlp.htt in your custom browser package. You need to customize the Printers.htt and Folder.htt templates directly on your users' computers.
.inf	Typically, each Internet Explorer .cab file contains an associated information (.inf) file, which provides further installation information. The .inf file can reference files in the .cab file, as well as files at other URLs.
.ins	Windows Update Setup contains an Internet settings (.ins) file, which configures the browser and its components. You can create multiple versions of your browser package by customizing copies of this .ins file. For more information about this process, see Chapter 17, "Time-Saving Strategies That Address Diverse User Needs." The IEAK Profile Manager also enables you to create, save, and load .ins files for updating Internet Explorer configuration settings.

File type	Description
.isp	If you are implementing a sign-up process with your custom browser package, an Internet sign-up (.isp) file named Signup.isp provides dial-up information for your Internet services. Using the Internet Explorer Customization wizard, you can edit the parameters contained in the Internet sign-up file. For a server-based sign-up method, this sign-up file also contains a link to the URL of the server script that generates your .ins configuration file.
.js, .jvs, .pac	You can use a text editor to create an auto-proxy script file for your custom browser package. An auto-proxy script file can be a JScript (.js), JavaScript (.jvs), or proxy auto-configuration (.pac) file. When an auto-proxy script file is specified, Internet Explorer uses the script to determine dynamically whether it should connect directly to a host or use a proxy server. In Stage 4 of the Internet Explorer Customization wizard, you can specify an auto-proxy URL for configuring and maintaining advanced proxy settings.
.pdf	If you use Microsoft Systems Management Server to distribute Internet Explorer, your custom browser package consists of a folder of installation files and a package definition file (.pdf) file. This file, named IE5.pdf, contains a setup program, installation options, and command-line syntax for automatically installing Internet Explorer on your server or users' computers. This .pdf file enables the installation to occur without administrative or user intervention.

APPENDIX H

Structural Definition of .inf Files

Although the IEAK wizard, Internet Explorer batch files, and third-party programs can customize Setup, you can also use setup information files (.inf) files to develop a customized setup solution. This appendix describes the sections of an .inf file and provides a sample.

In This Appendix

See Also

- For more information about how to use .inf files, see Chapter 18, "Working with .inf Files."

Sections of an .inf File

A basic information (.inf) file contains the following sections (more complex .inf files may have additional sections). Section names in bold are reserved keywords. Section names in italic are arbitrary names created by the .inf author.

Section	Description
[Version]	Provides basic version information for validating the .inf file.
[DefaultInstall]	Contains pointers to other sections specifying files to copy and delete, registry updates, .ini file updates, and so on. This section is executed by default.
[OtherInstall]	Uses the same format as the **[DefaultInstall]** section, but must explicitly be called. This section is useful for defining how a component should be uninstalled.
[DestinationDirs]	Specifies the location on the hard disk where a section's files will be copied, deleted, or renamed (for example, Windows or Windows\System).
[FileCopy/Delete/RenameSection(s)]	Lists files to be copied, deleted, or renamed.
[RegistryUpdateSection(s)]	Specifies registry additions or deletions.
[IniFileUpdateSection(s)]	Specifies updates to .ini files. Links are created in this section.
[SourceDisksNames]	Lists disks that contain the files.
[SourceDisksFiles]	Lists the specific disk that each file is on.
[Strings]	Lists localizable strings.
[Optional Components]	Lists Install selections that are displayed when the user clicks the **Add/Remove Programs** icon in Control Panel, clicks the **Windows Setup** tab, and then clicks the **Have Disk** button. For situations in which this section is ignored, see the description for this section later in the appendix.

For more information about .inf files, see the Windows 95 Resource Kit and the Windows 98 Resource Kit.

Version Section

[Version]

Signature="*$Chicago$*"

LayoutFile=filename.inf

This section defines the standard header for all Microsoft Windows .inf files. Note that if the signature is not $Chicago$, Windows does not accept the .inf file as belonging to any of the classes of devices recognized by Windows.

Note that signature string recognition is not case sensitive, so, for example, you can use either $Chicago$ or $CHICAGO$.

filename.inf

.inf file containing the layout information (source disks and files) required to install the component. This line is optional. If not provided elsewhere, the **[SourceDisksNames]** and **[SourceDisksFiles]** sections must be listed in this .inf file.

The following example shows a typical **[Version]** section:

```
[Version]
Signature="$CHICAGO$"
```

Install Sections (DefaultInstall and OtherInstall)

The Install sections, **[DefaultInstall]** and [*OtherInstall*], use the same format. They can contain the following entries:

- **CopyFiles=***file-list-section*[,*file-list-section*]
- **RenFiles=***file-list-section*[,*file-list-section*]
- **DelFiles=***file-list-section*[,*file-list-section*]
- **UpdateInis=***update-ini-section*[,*update-ini-section*]
- **UpdateIniFields=***update-inifields-section*[,*update-inifields-section*]
- **AddReg=***add-registry-section*[,*add-registry-section*]
- **DelReg=***del-registry-section*[,*del-registry-section*]
- **Ini2Reg=***ini-to-registry-section*[,*ini-to-registry-section*]
- **UpdateCfgSys=***update-config-section*
- **UpdateAutoBat=***update-autoexec-section*

The Install sections identify the additional sections in the .inf file that contain installation information for the component.

Not all the entries shown in the preceding syntax are needed or required in an Install section. If an entry is used, it must specify the name of a section in the .inf file. (An exception to this is the **CopyFiles** entry, which can use the @ character along with a file name to copy a single file without specifying a section name.) The section name must consist of printable characters.

Only one of each type of entry can be used in any one Install section. More than one section name can be listed in an entry, but each additional name must be preceded by a comma.

install-section-name

Name of the Install section, which can be **DefaultInstall** or *OtherInstall* (a name that you specify).

If you name the Install section **[DefaultInstall]**, it will execute when you right-click the .inf file and then select **Install**. This section will also execute when you select an .inf file as the setup option by using the Cabpack wizard.

The following example shows a typical Install section. It contains **Copyfiles** and **AddReg** entries that identify the sections containing information about which files to install.

```
[MyApplication]
Copyfiles=MyAppWinFiles, MyAppSysFiles, @SRSutil.exe
AddReg=MyAppRegEntries
```

Note that if you rename the **[MyApplication]** section in this example to **[DefaultInstall]**, the Install section will execute when you right-click the .inf file and then select **Install**.

The **CopyFiles** entry provides a special notation that allows a single file to be copied directly from the command line. You can copy an individual file by prefixing the file name with an @ symbol. The destination for any file that you copy using this notation is the *DefaultDestDir* entry, as defined in the **[DestinationDirs]** section later in this appendix. The following example shows how to copy individual files:

```
CopyFiles=FileSection1,@myfile.txt,@anotherfile.txt,LastSectionName
```

Copy Files Sections (CopyFiles)

[*CopyFiles-section-name*]

destination-file-name[, *source-file-name*][,*temporary-file-name*][,*flag*]

[*destination-file-name*[,*source-file-name*][, *temporary-file-name*]][,*flag*]

This section lists the names of files to be copied from a source disk to a destination directory. The source disk and destination directory associated with each file are specified in other sections of the .inf file. The *file-list-section* name must appear in the **CopyFiles** item of an Install section.

Note that you can specify the copying of a single file in the **CopyFiles** entry of the Install section itself without creating a **[CopyFiles]** section. To do this, you specify the *file-list-section* name in the **CopyFiles** entry of the Install section and use the @ character to force a single file copy. For an example of the @ character in a **CopyFiles** entry, see the previous section. Copying a single file in this way imposes limitations because the source and destination file names must be the same in this case, and you cannot use a temporary file.

destination-file-name

Name of the destination file. If no source file name is given, the name also specifies the source file.

source-file-name

Name of the source file. If the source and destination file names for the file copy operation are the same, the source file name is not required.

temporary-file-name

Name of a temporary file for the file copy operation. The installer copies the source file, but gives it the temporary file name. The next time the operating system starts, it renames the temporary file to the destination file name. This is useful for copying files to a destination that is currently open or in use by Windows.

flag

Optional flag used to perform special actions during the installation process. Multiple flags can be used by adding the values to create the combined flag. The following valid flags can be used.

Value	Meaning
1	For **CopyFiles**: Warn if user tries to skip the file.
1	For **DelFiles**: If the file is in use, queue up a delayed delete operation in Wininit.ini. Otherwise, a file that is currently in use won't be deleted.
2	Setup-critical: Don't allow the user to skip the file.
4	Ignore version checking and always copy the file. This action will overwrite a newer file.
8	Force a rename. The setup program treats a file as if it's in use. This happens only if the file already exists on the user's computer.
16	If the file already exists on the target computer, don't copy.
32	Suppress the version conflict dialog box, and don't overwrite newer files.

The following example copies three files:

```
[CopyTheseFilesSec]
file11; copies file11
file21, file22, file23 ; copies file22, temporarily naming it file23
file31, file32 ; copies file32 to file31
```

All of the source file names used in this example must be defined in a **[SourceDisksFiles]** section, and the logical disk numbers that appear in that section must have been defined in a **[SourceDisksNames]** section. For an alternate solution, you can use a Layout.inf file to supply this information.

Rename Files Sections (RenFiles)

[*rename-files-section-name*]

new-file-name, old-file-name

This section lists the names of files to be renamed. The name of the section must appear in a **RenFiles** entry in an Install section of the .inf file.

new-file-name

New name of the file.

old-file-name

Old name of the file.

The following example renames file42 to file41, file52 to file51, and file62 to file61:

```
[RenameOldFilesSec]
file41, file42
file51, file52
file61, file62
```

All the old file names used in this example (file42, file52, and file62) must be defined in a **[SourceDisksFiles]** section, and the logical disk numbers that appear in that section must have been defined in a **[SourceDisksNames]** section.

Delete Files Sections (DelFiles)

[*file-list-section*]

file-name[,,,flag]

This section lists the names of files to be deleted. The *file-list-section* name must appear in the **Delfiles** entry of an Install section.

file-name

File to be deleted.

flag

Optional flag used to force Windows to delete the file named in the item if it is in use during the installation process. To instruct Windows to queue the file deletion operation until the computer has restarted, set the flag value to 1. If a file marked with the flag=1 setting cannot be deleted because it is in use, the computer will restart after the device installation is complete.

If you do not use the flag value equal to 1 together with *file-name*, the file will not be deleted from the computer if it is in use when the **[DelFiles]** section executes.

The following example deletes three files:

```
[DeleteOldFilesSec]
file1
file2
file3
```

Update .ini File Sections (UpdateInis)

[update-ini-section-name]

ini-file, ini-section, [old-ini-entry], [new-ini-entry], [flags]

This section replaces, deletes, or adds complete entries in the given .ini file. The section name, *update-ini-section-name*, must appear in the **UpdateInis** entry in the Install section of the .inf file.

ini-file

Name of the .ini file containing the entry to change.

ini-section

Name of the section containing the entry to change.

old-ini-entry

Optional. Entry that usually has the form *Key=Value*.

new-ini-entry

Optional. Entry that usually has the form *Key=Value*. Either the key or value may specify replaceable strings. For example, either the key or value specified in *new-ini-entry* may be %String1%, where the string that replaces %String1% is defined in the **[Strings]** section of the .inf file.

flags

Optional action flag. It can be one of the following values:

Value	Meaning
0	Default. If *old-ini-entry* is present in an .ini file entry, that entry is replaced with *new-ini-entry*. Note that only the keys of *old-ini-entry* and the .inf file entry must match; the value of each entry is ignored.
	To add *new-ini-entry* to the .ini file unconditionally, set *old-ini-entry* to NULL. To delete *old-ini-entry* from the .ini file unconditionally, set *new-ini-entry* to NULL.
1	If both key and value of *old-ini-entry* exist in an .ini file entry, that entry is replaced with *new-ini-entry*. Note that *old-ini-entry* and the .inf file entry must match for both the key and value for the replacement to be made. This is in contrast to using an action flag value of 0, where only the keys must match for the replacement to be made.
2	If the key in *old-ini-entry* does not exist in the .ini file, no operation is performed on the .ini file.
	If the key in *old-ini-entry* exists in an .ini file entry and the key in *new-ini-entry* exists in an .ini file entry, the .ini file entry that matches the key in *new-ini-entry* is deleted. Also, the key of the .ini file entry that matches *old-ini-entry* is replaced with the key in *new-ini-entry*.
	If the key in *old-ini-entry* exists in an .ini file entry and the key in *new-ini-entry* does not exist in an .ini file entry, an entry is added to the .ini file made up of the key in *new-ini-entry* and the old value.
	Note that the match of *old-ini-entry* and an .ini file entry is based on key alone, not key and value.
3	Same as a flag parameter value of 2, except matching of *old-ini-entry* and an entry in the .inf file is based on both key and value, not just the key.

You can use the asterisk (*) wildcard character when specifying the key and value, and it will be interpreted correctly.

The *ini-file* name can be a string or a strings key. A strings key has the form %strkey%, where strkey is defined in the **[Strings]** section in the .inf file. In either case, the name must be a valid file name.

The name should include the name of the directory containing the file, but the directory name should be given as a logical directory identifier (LDID) rather than an actual name. The installer replaces an LDID with an actual name during installation.

An LDID has the form %ldid%, where ldid is one of the predefined identifiers or an identifier defined in the **[DestinationDirs]** section. Note that when the constants LDID_BOOT and LDID_BOOTHOST are replaced, the backslash is included in the path. For example, LDID_BOOT can be replaced with C:\. However, in your .inf file, you can either use the backslash character or not. For example, you can use either "%30%boot.ini" and "%30%\boot.ini" to reference Boot.ini in the root of the boot drive.

The following examples illustrate individual entries in an **[UpdateInis]** section of an .inf file:

```
%11%\sample.ini, Section1,, Value1=2 ; adds new entry
%11%\sample.ini, Section2, Value3=*, ; deletes old entry
%11%\sample.ini, Section4, Value5=1, Value5=4 ; replaces old entry
```

The following set of entries in an **[UpdateInis]** section of an .inf file work together to operate on the **[Boot]** section of System.ini. The conditionality built into flags of the .inf file entries is used to add the entry "comm.drv=comm.drv" to the **[Boot]** section, unless the entries "comm.drv=*vcoscomm.drv" or "comm.drv=*r0dmdcom.drv" exist in the **[Boot]** section, in which case the existing entry is preserved and the entry "comm.drv=comm.drv" is not added to the .ini file. In other words, after the four following .inf file entries are executed, there will be one "comm.drv=" entry in the **[Boot]** section of the .ini file: "comm.drv=*vcoscomm.drv", "comm.drv=*r0dmdcom.drv", or "comm.drv=comm.drv."

```
system.ini, boot, "comm.drv=*vcoscomm.drv","~CommDrvTemp~=*", 3
system.ini, boot, "comm.drv=*r0dmdcom.drv","~CommDrvTemp~=*", 3
system.ini, boot,,"comm.drv=comm.drv"
system.ini, boot, "~CommDrvTemp~=*","comm.drv=*", 3
```

Update .ini Fields Sections (UpdateIniFields)

[*update-inifields-section-name*]

ini-file, ini-section, profile-name, [old-field], [new-field],[flags]

This section replaces, adds, and deletes fields in the value of a given .ini entry. Unlike the **[UpdateIniFile]** section, this type of section replaces, adds, or deletes portions of a value in an .ini file entry rather than the whole value. The section name, *update-inifields-section-name*, must appear in the **UpdateIniFields** entry in the Install section of the .inf file.

ini-file

Name of the .ini file containing the entry to change. For more information about specifying the .ini file name, see the previous section.

ini-section

Name of the .ini file section containing the entry to change.

profile-name

Name of the entry to change.

old-field

Field value to delete.

new-field

Field value to add, if not already there.

flags

Flag specifying whether to treat old-field and new-field as if they have a wildcard character and to indicate what separator character to use when appending a new field to an .ini file entry. It can be any of these values:

Value	Meaning
0	Default. Treat the * character literally when matching fields and not as a wildcard character. Use a space as a separator when adding a new field to an entry.
1	Treat the * character as a wildcard character when matching fields. Use a space as a separator when adding a new field to an entry.
2	Treat the * character literally when matching fields and not as a wildcard character. Use a comma as a separator when adding a new field to an entry.
3	Treat the * character as a wildcard character when matching fields. Use a comma as a separator when adding a new field to an entry. Any comments in the .ini file line are removed, because they might not be applicable after changes. When fields in this line of the .ini file are processed, spaces, tabs, and commas are used as field delimiters. However, a space is used as the separator when the new field is appended to the line.

Add Registry Sections (AddReg)

[*add-registry-section*]

reg-root-string, [*subkey*], [*value-name*], [*flag*], [*value*]

[*reg-root-string,* [*subkey*], [*value-name*], [*flag*], [*value*]]

This section adds subkeys or value names to the registry, optionally setting the value. The *add-registry-section* name must appear in an **AddReg** entry in an Install section.

reg-root-string

Registry root name. It can be one of the following values:

- HKCR—Same as **HKEY_CLASSES_ROOT**
- HKCU—Same as **HKEY_CURRENT_USER**
- HKLM—Same as **HKEY_LOCAL_MACHINE**
- HKU—Same as **HKEY_USERS**
- HKR—Relative key used by the class installer. HKR is typically used by device drivers.

subkey

Optional. Subkey to set. This subkey, which has the form key1\key2\key3..., can be expressed as a replaceable string. For example, you could use %Subkey1%, where the string to replace %Subkey1% is defined in the **[Strings]** section of the .inf file.

value-name

Optional. Value name for the subkey. For a string type, if *value-name* is left empty, the value of the subkey specified in *subkey* is set to a NULL string. Note that *value-name* can be expressed as a replaceable string. For example, you could use %Valname1%, where the string to replace %Valname1% is defined in the **[Strings]** section of the .inf file.

flag

Optional. Flag that determines the value type and specifies whether the registry key is replaced if it already exists.

Value	Meaning
0	Default. The value is an ANSI string. Replace the key if it exists.
1	The value is a hexadecimal number. Replace the key if it exists.
2	The value is an ANSI string. Do not replace the key if it exists.
3	The value is a hexadecimal number. Do not replace the key if it exists.

value

Optional. Value to set. This value can be either an ANSI string or a number in hexadecimal notation and Intel format. Any item containing a binary value can be extended beyond the 128-byte line maximum by using a backslash (\) character. A string key of the form %strkey% can also be given. Note that *strkey* must be defined in the **[Strings]** section of the .inf file. To use a % character in the line, use %%.

At least two fields are required; however, one can be null (empty). Therefore, at least one comma is required when using this form.

The two entries in the following example add two value names to the registry. Note that %25% will be expanded to the computer's Windows directory.

```
[MyAppRegEntries]
HKLM,Software\MyApp,ProgramName,,"My Application"
HKLM,Software\MyApp,"Program Location",,"%25%\MyApp.exe"
```

Delete Registry Sections (DelReg)

[*del-registry-section*]

reg-root-string, subkey, [*value-name*]

[*reg-root-string, subkey,* [*value-name*]]

This section deletes a subkey or value name from the registry. The *del-registry-section* name must appear in a **DelReg** entry in an Install section.

reg-root-string

Registry root name. It can be one of the following values:

- HKCR—Same as **HKEY_CLASSES_ROOT**
- HKCU—Same as **HKEY_CURRENT_USER**
- HKLM—Same as **HKEY_LOCAL_MACHINE**
- HKU—Same as **HKEY_USERS**
- HKR—Means relative from the key passed into GenInstallEx

subkey

Subkey to delete. The subkey, which has the form key1\key2\key3..., can be expressed as a replaceable string. For example, you could use %Subkey1%, where the string to replace %Subkey1% is defined in the **[Strings]** section of the .inf file.

value-name

Optional. Value name for the subkey. Note that *value-name* can be expressed as a replaceable string. For example, you could use %Valname1%, where the string to replace %Valname1% is defined in the **[Strings]** section of the .inf file.

This type of section can contain any number of items. Each item deletes one subkey or value name from the registry.

.ini File to Registry Sections (Ini2Reg)

[*ini-to-registry-section*]

ini-file, ini-section, [ini-key], reg-root-string, subkey[,flags]

This section moves lines or sections from an .ini file to the registry, creating or replacing a registry entry under the given key in the registry. The section name *ini-to-registry-section* must appear in an **Ini2Reg** entry in the Install section of the .inf file.

ini-file

Name of the .ini file containing the key to copy. For more information about specifying the .ini file name, see "Update .ini File Sections (UpdateInis)" earlier in this appendix.

ini-section

Name of the section in the .ini file containing the key to copy.

ini-key

Name of the key in the .ini file to copy to the registry. If *ini-key* is empty, the whole section is transferred to the specified registry key.

reg-root-string

Registry root name. This parameter can be one of the following values:

- HKCR—Same as **HKEY_CLASSES_ROOT**
- HKCU—Same as **HKEY_CURRENT_USER**
- HKLM—Same as **HKEY_LOCAL_MACHINE**
- HKU—Same as **HKEY_USERS**
- HKR—Relative key for use by the class installer. This key is typically used by device drivers.

subkey

Subkey to receive the value. This subkey has the form key1\key2\key3...

flags

Flag that indicates whether to delete the .ini key after transfer to the registry and whether to overwrite the value in the registry if the registry key already exists. The flag can be one of the following values:

Value	Meaning
0	(Default) Do not delete the .ini entry from the .ini file after moving the information in the entry to the registry. If the registry subkey already exists, do not replace its current value.
1	Delete the .ini entry from the .ini file after moving the information in the entry to the registry. If the registry subkey already exists, do not replace its current value.
2	Do not delete the .ini entry from the .ini file after moving the information in the entry to the registry. If the registry subkey already exists, replace its current value with the value from the .ini file entry.
3	Delete the .ini entry from the .ini file after moving the information in the entry to the registry. If the registry subkey already exists, replace its current value with the value from the .ini file entry.

For example, the following example shows the **[Windows]** section in the Win.ini file:

```
[Windows]
CursorBlinkRate=15
```

If a **CursorBlinkRate** subkey does not exist under **\Control Panel\Desktop**, the following item in an **[Ini2Reg]** section creates the subkey, sets the value of the subkey to 15, and leaves the original line in Win.ini unchanged:

```
win.ini,Windows,CursorBlinkRate,HKCU,"Control Panel\Desktop"
```

If the subkey already exists, the .inf file item sets the value of the subkey to 15 and leaves the original line in Win.ini unchanged.

Update Config.sys Sections (UpdateCfgSys)

[*update-config-section*]

Buffers=*legal-dos-buffer-value*

DelKey=*key*

DevAddDev=*driver-name,configkeyword*[*,flag*][*,param-string*]

DevDelete=*device-driver-name*

DevRename=*current-dev-name,new-dev-name*

Files=*legal-dos-files-value*

PrefixPath=*ldid*[,*ldid*]

RemKey=*key*

Stacks=*dos-stacks-values*

This section provides entries to add, delete, or rename commands in the Config.sys file. The section name, *update-config-section* must appear in the **UpdateConfigSys** entry in an Install section of the .inf file.

Not all entries shown in the preceding syntax are needed or required. An update configuration section can contain as many **DevRename**, **DevDelete**, **DevAddDev**, **DelKey**, and **RemKey** entries as needed, but the **Buffers**, **Files**, and **Stacks** entries can be used only once in a section. When processing the section, the installer processes all **DevRename** entries first, all **DevDelete** entries second, and all **DevAddDev** entries last.

Buffers Entry

Buffers=legal-dos-buffer-value

This entry sets the number of file buffers. As it does with the **Stacks** entry, the installer compares the existing value with the proposed value and always sets the file buffers to the larger of the two values.

legal-dos-buffers-value

Legal MS-DOS buffers value.

DelKey Entry

DelKey=key

This entry causes the Config.sys command with the specified key to be remarked out in the Config.sys file. For example, the following .inf file entry would cause a Break=on command to be remarked out in the Config.sys file:

```
DelKey=Break
```

The **DelKey** entry has the same effect as the **RemKey** entry. There can be multiple **DelKey** and/or **RemKey** entries in a section of the .inf file.

key

Key of the Config.sys command to be remarked out.

DevAddDev Entry

DevAddDev=driver-name,configkeyword[,flag][,param-string]

This entry adds a device or install command to the Config.sys file.

driver-name

Name of the driver or executable file to add. The installer validates the file name extension, ensuring that it is .sys or .exe.

configkeyword

Command name. It can be device or install.

flag

Optional placement flag. If 0, the command is placed at the bottom of the file. If 1, it is placed at the top. If a flag is not specified, 0 is used by default.

param-string

Optional command strings. These strings must be valid for the given device driver or executable file.

DevDelete Entry

DevDelete=device-driver-name

This entry deletes any line containing the specified file name from the Config.sys file.

device-driver-name

Name of a file or device driver. The installer searches the Config.sys file for the name and deletes any line containing it. Because Microsoft MS-DOS does not permit implicit file name extensions in Config.sys, each device-driver-name must explicitly specify the file name extension.

In the following example, the **DevDelete** entry in an update configuration section deletes lines 1 and 3, but not line 2 of the example Config.sys file:

```
DevDelete=Filename.sys
;; lines in Config.sys
Device=Filename.sys;; line #1
Install=Filename.exe;; line #2
Device=Filename.sys /d:b800 /I:3 ;; line #3
```

DevRename Entry

DevRename=current-dev-name,new-dev-name

This entry renames a device driver in the Config.sys file.

current-dev-name

Name of the device driver or executable file to rename. The installer looks for the name on the right side of a device or install command in the Config.sys file.

new-dev-name

New name for driver or executable file.

Files Entry

Files=legal-dos-files-value

This entry sets the maximum number of open files in the Config.sys file. As it does with the **Stacks** entry, the installer compares the existing value with the proposed value and always sets the maximum number of open files to the larger of the two values.

legal-dos-files-value

Legal MS-DOS files value.

PrefixPath Entry

PrefixPath=ldid[,ldid]...

This entry appends the path associated with the given LDID to the path command.

ldid

Identifier that can be any of the predefined LDID values or a new value defined in the .inf file. For a definition of all the predefined LDID values, see the "DestinationDirs Section" later in this appendix.

RemKey Entry

RemKey=key

This entry causes the Config.sys command with the specified key to be remarked out in the Config.sys file. For example, the following .inf file entry would cause a Break=on command to be remarked out in the Config.sys file:

```
RemKey=Break
```

The **RemKey** entry has the same effect as the **DelKey** entry. There can be multiple **RemKey** and/or **DelKey** entries in a section of the .inf file.

key

Key of the Config.sys command to be remarked out.

Stacks Entry

Stacks=dos-stacks-values

This entry sets the number and size of stacks in the Config.sys file. The installer compares the existing value with the proposed value and always sets the stacks to the larger of the two values.

dos-stacks-value

Legal MS-DOS stacks value.

Update Autoexec.bat Sections (UpdateAutoBat)

[*update-autoexec-section*]

CmdAdd=*command-name*[*,command-parameters*]

CmdDelete=*command-name*

PrefixPath=*ldid*[*,ldid*]

RemOldPath=*ldid*[*,ldid*]

TmpDir=*ldid*[*,subdir*]

UnSet=*env-var-name*

This section provides commands to manipulate lines in the Autoexec.bat file. The section name, *update-autoexec-section* must appear in the **UpdateAutoBat** entry in an Install section of the .inf file.

Not all entry types shown in the preceding syntax are needed or required in an Update Autoexec.bat section. The section can contain as many **CmdAdd**, **CmdDelete**, and **UnSet** entries as needed, but only one **PrefixPath**, **RemOldPath**, and **TmpDir** item can be used in an .inf file.

The installer processes all **CmdDelete** entries before any **CmdAdd** entries.

CmdAdd Entry

CmdAdd =command-name[*,"command-parameters"*]

This entry adds the given command and optional command parameters to the Autoexec.bat file at the end of the file.

command-name

Name of an executable file with, or without, an extension. If the file name is also defined in the **[SourceDisksFiles]** and **[DestinationDirs]** sections of the .inf file, the installer adds the appropriate path to the file name before writing it to the Autoexec.bat file.

command-parameters

String enclosed in double quotation marks or a replaceable string such as %String1% or %Myparam%, where the strings that replace %String1% and %Myparam% are defined in the **[Strings]** section of the .inf file. The installer appends the string to the command-name before appending the line to the end of the Autoexec.bat file. The format of this line is dependent on the *command=line* requirements of the given executable file.

CmdDelete Entry

CmdDelete=command-name

This entry deletes any lines from Autoexec.bat that include the given command name. The installer searches for and deletes any occurrence of the given name that has a file name extension of .exe, .com, and .bat.

command-name

Name of an executable file without an extension.

PrefixPath Entry

PrefixPath=ldid[,ldid]...

This entry appends the path associated with the given LDID to the path command.

ldid

Identifier that can be any of the predefined LDID values or a new value defined in the .inf file. For a definition of all the predefined LDID values, see the **[DestinationDirs]** section later in this appendix.

RemOldPath Entry

RemOldPath=ldid[,ldid]

This entry removes the path associated with the given LDID from the path command. For example, if the user installs the new version of Windows into C:\Newwin and has an old copy of Windows in C:\Windows, the following .inf file item removes C:\Windows from the path environmental variable:

```
RemOldPath=10
```

ldid

Identifier that can be any of the predefined LDID values or a new value defined in the .inf file. For a definition of all the predefined LDID values, see the **[DestinationDirs]** section later in this appendix.

TmpDir Entry

TmpDir=ldid[,subdir]

This entry creates a temporary directory within the directory given by the LDID if it does not already exist.

ldid

Identifier that can be any of the predefined LDID values or a new value defined in the .inf file. For a definition of all the predefined LDID values, see the **[DestinationDirs]** section later in this appendix.

subdir

Path name. If the Ldid\Subdir directory does not already exist, it is created.

UnSet Entry

UnSet=env-var-name

This entry removes any set command from the Autoexec.bat file that includes the given environment variable name.

env-var-name

Name of an environment variable.

DestinationDirs Section

[DestinationDirs]

file-list-section =ldid[, subdir]

[DefaultDestDir=ldid[, subdir]]

The **[DestinationDirs]** section defines the destination directories for the operations specified in file-list sections, which are either **CopyFiles**, **RenFiles**, or **DelFiles** entries. Optionally, a default destination directory can be specified for any **CopyFiles**, **RenFiles**, or **DelFiles** entries in the .inf file that are not explicitly named in the **[DestinationDirs]** section.

file-list-section

Name of a **CopyFiles**, **RenFiles**, or **DelFiles** entry. This name must be referred to in a **Copyfiles**, **RenFiles**, or **DelFiles** entry in an Install section.

Ldid

Logical disk identifier (LDID). This identifier can be one of the following values:

Value	Meaning
00	Null LDID - can be used to create a new LDID
01	Source *Drive:\pathname*
10	Computer directory (maps to the Windows directory on a server-based setup)
11	System directory
12	IOSubsys directory
13	Command directory
17	Inf directory
18	Help directory
20	Fonts
21	Viewers
22	VMM32
23	Color directory
24	Root of drive containing the Windows directory
25	Windows directory
26	Guaranteed boot device for Windows (Winboot)
28	Host Winboot
30	Root directory of the boot drive
31	Root directory for host drive of a virtual boot drive

subdir

Name of the directory within the directory named by LDID to be the destination directory.

The optional *DefaultDestDir* entry provides a default destination for any **CopyFiles** entries that use the direct copy (@file name) notation or any **CopyFiles**, **RenFiles**, or **DelFiles** entries not specified in the **[DestinationDirs]** section. If a *DefaultDestDir* entry is not used in a **[DestinationDirs]** section, the default directory is set to LDID_WIN.

The following example sets the destination directory for the **MoveMiniPort** entry to Windows\Iosybsys and sets the default directory for other sections to be the Bin folder on the boot drive:

```
[DestinationDirs]
MoveMiniPort=12 ; Destination for MoveMiniPort section is
; windows\iosubsys

DefaultDestDirs=30,bin ; Direct copies go to boot:\bin
```

SourceDisksNames Section

[SourceDisksNames]

disk-ordinal="disk-description",disk-label,disk-serial-number

Disk(s) that contain the source files for file copy and rename operations.

disk-ordinal

Unique number that identifies a source disk. If there is more than one source disk, each must have a unique ordinal.

disk-description

String or strings key describing the contents or purpose of the disk. The installer displays this string to the user to identify the disk. The description is enclosed in double quotation marks.

disk-label

Volume label of the source disk that is set when the source disk is formatted.

disk-serial-number

Unused. The value must be 0.

This example identifies one source disk. The disk description is given as a strings key:

```
[SourceDisksNames]
55 = %ID1%, Instd1, 0
[Strings]
ID1="My Application Installation Disk 1"
```

SourceDisksFiles Section

[SourceDisksFiles]

file name=disk-number[,subdir] [,file-size]

This section specifies source files used during installation and source disks that contain the files.

File name

Name of the file on the source disk.

disk-number

Ordinal of the source disk that contains the file. This ordinal must be defined in the **[SourceDisksNames]** section, and must have a value greater than or equal to 1 (zero is not a valid disk-number parameter value).

subdir

Optional. Subdirectory on the source disk where the file resides. If *subdir* is not specified, the source disk root directory is the default.

file-size

Optional. Size of the file, in bytes.

The following example shows a **[SourceDisksFiles]** section that identifies a single source file, SRS01.386, on the disk having ordinal 1:

```
[SourceDisksFiles]
SRS01.386 = 1
```

Strings Section

[Strings]

strings-key=value

This section defines one or more strings keys. A strings key is a name that represents a string of printable characters. Although the **[Strings]** section is generally the last section in the .inf file, a strings key defined in this section can be used anywhere in the .inf file that the corresponding string would be used. The installer expands the strings key to the given string and uses it for further processing. You must enclose a strings key in percent signs (%).

strings-key

Unique name consisting of letters and digits.

value

String consisting of letters, digits, or other printable characters. It should be enclosed in double quotation marks if the corresponding strings key is used in a type of item that requires double quotation marks.

The **[Strings]** section makes translation of strings for international markets easier by placing all strings that can be displayed in the user interface when the .inf file is used in a single section of the .inf file. Strings keys should be used whenever possible.

The following example shows the strings section for a sample .inf file:

```
[Strings]
String0="My Application"
String1="My Application Readme File"
String2="CX2590 SCSI Adapter"
```

Optional Components Section

[Optional Components]

install-section-name

[*install-section-name*]

This section lists Install sections that are displayed when the user clicks the **Add/Remove Programs** icon in Control Panel, clicks the **Windows Setup** tab, and then clicks the **Have Disk** button. The Install sections show up as check boxes in the list.

Note that the Optional Components section is ignored when you right-click an .inf file and then select **Install** to execute the file. When you use an .inf file in this way, the **[DefaultInstall]** section executes. The **[Optional Components]** section is also ignored if the .inf file is being executed through the Setupx.dll **InstallHinfSection** entry-point function. When executing an .inf file by using the Setupx.dll entry point function, the Install section specified in the parameter of the entry point is executed.

The Install sections follow the same format as described previously, and the following additional keys can be added to the Install section to create the interface in the Have Disk dialog box:

OptionDesc=*option-description*

Tip=*tip-description*

InstallDefault=*0 | 1 ; Whether to install this component by default. 0=No, 1=Yes.*

IconIndex=*icon-index*

Parent=*install-section-name*

Needs=*install-section-name, [install-section-name]*

Include=*inf-file, [inf-file]*

option-description

String value that is used as the component name in the list box. The value can be %String1%, where the string that replaces %String1% is defined in the Strings section of the .inf file.

tip-description

String value that is displayed in the description box when the component is selected in the list box. The value, which has a 255-character limit, can be %String1%, where the string that replaces %String1% is defined in the **[Strings]** section of the .inf file.

icon-index

Numeric value that determines the mini-icon that is displayed next to the component name. The following values are valid:

Value	Icon
0	Machine (base and display)
1	Integrated circuit chip
2	Display
3	Network wires
4	Windows flag
5	Mouse
6	Keyboard (3 keys)
7	Phone
8	Speaker
9	Hard disks
10	Comm connector
11	Diamond (default value)
12	Checked box
13	Unchecked box
14	Printer
15	Net card
16	Same as 0
17	Same as 0 with a sharing hand underneath
18	Unknown (question mark)
19	At work
20	Grayed check box
21	Dial-up networking
22	Direct cable connection
23	Briefcase
24	Exchange
25	Partial check
26	Accessories group

Value	Icon
27	Multimedia group
28	QuickView
29	MSN
30	Calculator
31	Defrag
32	Generic document
33	DriveSpace®
34	Solitaire
35	HyperTerminal
36	Object Packager
37	Paint
38	Screen saver
39	WordPad
40	Clipboard Viewer
41	Accessibility
42	Backup
43	Bitmap document
44	Character map
45	Mouse pointers
46	Net Watcher
47	Phone Dialer
48	System Monitor
49	Help book
50	Globe (international settings)
51	Audio compression
52	CD player
53	Media Player
54	Sound scheme
55	Video clip
56	Video compression
57	Volume control
58	Musica sound scheme
59	Jungle sound scheme
60	Robotz sound scheme
61	Utopia sound scheme

install-section-name (Parent)

The list box displayed in the optional components interface can contain sublevels. If the optional component is a child, the section name for the Parent key defines the Install section that is the parent.

install-section-name (Needs)

If this component has dependencies on other components, the section name defines Install sections that are required by this component. If the component is selected, the user will be warned that the component requires the component(s) described in the Install section(s) listed for the Needs key.

Note that the Install sections listed for the Needs key must be in the same .inf file. However, if dependent components from other .inf files are listed for Needs, the .inf files must be specified for the Include key.

inf-file

The file name specifies .inf files that the setup program must also load into memory when it loads your .inf file, because these .inf files contain sections that must be run in addition to the Install sections in your .inf file. The section names for the Needs key specify the names of the sections you intend to run in the included .inf file(s).

Sample .inf File

The following example shows an .inf file that performs a number of different actions:

```
; - Copies files to the Windows, System, Inf, and Help folders.
; - Makes a number of registry entries (including entries that
;   will rename the copied files to long file names).
; - Creates a link on the Help menu.
; - Has an uninstall section that registers the uninstall
;   action in the Add/Remove Programs dialog box in Control Panel.
; - Uses replaceable strings to make localization easy.

[Version]
Signature=$CHICAGO$

[DestinationDirs]
SampleCopy = 24,%PROGRAMF%\Sample
SampleDel = 24,%PROGRAMF%\Sample
SampleWinCopy = 25
SampleSysCopy = 11
SampleINFCopy = 17
sampleHLPCopy = 18
```

```
[DefaultInstall]
CopyFiles = SampleCopy, SampleWinCopy, SampleSysCopy, SampleINFCopy,
SampleHLPCopy
AddReg = SampleRegisterApp, SampleRegUninstall, SampleRenameFiles
UpdateInis = SampleAddLinks

[RemoveSample]
DelFiles = SampleWinCopy, SampleSysCopy, SampleINFCopy, SampleHLPCopy
DelReg = SampleUnRegisterApp, SampleRegUninstall
AddReg = SampleRemoveLFNs
UpdateInis = SampleRemoveLinks

[SampleCopy]
sample.bmp

[SampleWinCopy]
sample.exe

[SampleSysCopy]
sample.dll

[SampleINFCopy]
sample.inf

[SampleHLPCopy]
sample.hlp

[SampleRegisterApp]
;Makes an arbitrary registry entry (for private use of Sample.exe):
HKLM,Software\Sample,Installed,,"1"

[SampleUnRegisterApp]
;Deletes the registry entry (note that this deletes the entire key):
HKLM,Software\Sample

[SampleRegUninstall]
;Adds entry to the Add/Remove Programs dialog box in Control Panel
;to uninstall the program:
HKLM,SOFTWARE\Microsoft\Windows\CurrentVersion\Uninstall\Sample,"Display
Name",,"Sample Application"
HKLM,SOFTWARE\Microsoft\Windows\CurrentVersion\Uninstall\Sample,"Uninsta
llString",,"RunDll setupx.dll,InstallHinfSection RemoveSample 4
sample.inf"

[SampleRenameFiles]
;Renames 8.3 file names to long file names:
HKLM,Software\Microsoft\Windows\CurrentVersion\RenameFiles\Sample,,,"%24
%\%PROGRAMF%\Sample"
HKLM,Software\Microsoft\Windows\CurrentVersion\RenameFiles\Sample,sample
.bmp,,"Sample Bitmap.bmp"
```

```
[SampleRemoveLFNs]
;Deletes files with long file names during uninstall:
HKLM,Software\Microsoft\Windows\CurrentVersion\DeleteFiles\Sample,,,"%24
%\%PROGRAMF%\Sample"
HKLM,Software\Microsoft\Windows\CurrentVersion\DeleteFiles\Sample,sample
.bmp,,"Sample Bitmap.bmp"

[SampleAddLinks]
;Adds shortcut to Sample.exe on the Start menu:
setup.ini, progman.groups,, "Sample=%SampleFolder%" ;creates folder
setup.ini, Sample,, """%SampleDesc%""", %25%\SAMPLE.EXE" ;creates link

[SampleRemoveLinks]
;Removes shortcut to Sample.exe on the Start menu during uninstall:
setup.ini, progman.groups,, "Sample=%SampleFolder%" ;creates folder
setup.ini, Sample,, """%SampleDesc%""" ;deletes link

[SourceDisksNames]
99 = %DiskName%,Sample,0

[SourceDisksFiles]
sample.exe = 1,,13456
sample.dll = 1,,20987
sample.bmp = 1,,64098
sample.hlp = 1,,55441
sample.inf = 1,,5687

[Strings]
PROGRAMF = "PROGRA~1"
SampleFolder = "Samples"
SampleDesc = "Sample Application"
DiskName = "Sample Application Installation Disk"
```

APPENDIX I

Microsoft Internet Explorer 5 Resource Directory

This appendix contains lists of product resources and Web sites. These lists provide sources of additional information about Microsoft Internet Explorer 5 and its components and about related Microsoft products.

In This Appendix

See Also

- For general information about this Resource Kit and its contents, see the "Welcome" chapter at the beginning of this book.

- For a list of the contents on the Microsoft Internet Explorer 5 Resource Kit CD-ROM, see Appendix A, "What's on the Resource Kit CD-ROM?"

Product Resources

Numerous resources exist to help you administer Internet Explorer and related products. These resources are available on the Web or from Microsoft Press.

Internet Explorer Administration Kit 5

The Internet Explorer Administration Kit 5 (IEAK) is an indispensable tool for Internet service providers, corporate administrators, and Internet content providers. Find out how to customize, distribute, and maintain Internet Explorer across multiple computer platforms quickly and easily.

Internet Explorer Small Business Kit

The Internet Explorer Small Business Kit includes Internet Explorer 5, as well as special offers and other resources to help you conduct business more effectively on the Web. Read the power tips and shortcuts, and explore the interactive tutorial, which demonstrates how small businesses can get maximum performance from Internet Explorer. The Small Business Kit also includes interactive wizards and utilities for migrating to Internet Explorer.

Microsoft Connection Manager Administration Kit

The Microsoft Connection Manager Administration Kit (CMAK) contains a wizard for creating a customized dialer for easy log-on to Internet access services. As part of the IEAK, the CMAK provides a fully customized logon-to-logoff solution with many value-added services for corporate and consumer clients.

Internet Explorer 5 Deployment Guide

The Deployment Guide is the one-stop resource for corporate administrators who want to successfully deploy Internet Explorer in their organizations. The Deployment Guide features the following information:

- Complete step-by-step instructions for using the Internet Explorer Customization wizard.

- A custom build checklist to help you assemble everything you need to create custom browser packages.

- Answers to frequently asked questions and troubleshooting information from Microsoft Technical Support.

- Examples of best practices for easily deploying Internet Explorer on corporate intranets.

Microsoft Office 2000 Resource Kit

This Resource Kit contains valuable information and guidelines for implementing and upgrading to Office 2000. Learn how to use the Custom Installation wizard (CIW) to customize Internet Explorer as part of your Office 2000 installation.

Microsoft Chat Software Development Kit

The Microsoft Chat Software Development Kit provides the tools and information you need to add Internet chat functionality to your programs and Web pages. Insert Microsoft Chat Controls or Script Chat into your Web pages and instantly create a place where people can meet and chat. Check out the samples that demonstrate how to moderate chat rooms and celebrity chat events.

Microsoft NetMeeting Resource Kit

This Resource Kit contains tools to help you deploy and administer NetMeeting. Use the NetMeeting Resource Kit wizard to create a customized version of NetMeeting with pre-configured installation settings. Also, review the tips about hosting and participating in online meetings found on the sample Web pages, and read the documentation, which describes NetMeeting features, customization options, and troubleshooting.

Microsoft NetMeeting Software Development Kit

The Microsoft NetMeeting Software Development Kit gives authors and developers a set of standard application programming interfaces (APIs) for integrating multimedia conferencing capabilities into their applications using C, C++, or Visual Basic. Read about how the NetMeeting ActiveX Control enables Web site creators to integrate conferencing directly into their Web pages with other ActiveX scripting solutions, such as JScript and Visual Basic Scripting Edition.

Microsoft Windows NT 4.0 Server Resource Kit

This Resource Kit provides valuable information and tools for deploying and supporting Windows NT Server in an organization. The Resource Kit includes many special utilities that add features, enhance functionality, and streamline support for Windows NT Server.

Microsoft Internet Information Server Resource Kit

This Resource Kit contains comprehensive technical information and tools for rolling out and supporting Microsoft Internet Information Server (IIS). Learn how to create, deploy, and test the content of Web pages, build a secure Web site, and develop Web applications that make the most of Internet technologies and server-side scripting. The Resource Kit CD contains more than 40 utilities, ISAPI filters, and components for customizing and deploying IIS.

Microsoft BackOffice Resource Kit

This Resource Kit provides dozens of tools for BackOffice professionals, as well as comprehensive resource information about deploying and administering Microsoft Windows NT Server, Microsoft Systems Management Server, Microsoft SQL Server, Microsoft Exchange Server, and Microsoft SNA Server.

Web Sites

Visit the following Web sites for up-to-date information about Internet Explorer and about related products.

Internet Explorer

The Microsoft Windows Technologies Internet Explorer Web site contains a wealth of information about the product, including access to the Internet Explorer Knowledge Base, technical support information, and answers to frequently asked questions. From this site, you can download the IEAK and access additional information and tools for Internet Explorer components, including Outlook Express, Chat, and FrontPage Express.

Microsoft Support Online

The Microsoft Support Online Web site enables you to search the entire Microsoft Knowledge Base, troubleshooting wizards, and downloadable files to find answers to your questions. From this site, you can also view popular Knowledge Base topics, access product newsgroups, and contact Microsoft Technical Support engineers.

Microsoft Windows

The Microsoft Windows Web site is the source for all the latest news and information about the Windows family of products, including the Windows 16-bit and Windows 32-bit versions. Download product add-ons, updates, service packs, and accessories. Also, learn more about these platforms through product demonstrations and partner resources.

Microsoft NetMeeting

The Microsoft NetMeeting Web site features video demonstrations and tutorials that demonstrate the product's multimedia conferencing capabilities. Read detailed case studies and find out how other companies are using NetMeeting to enhance their business practices. Also, this Web site provides links to the Microsoft NetMeeting Resource Kit and the Microsoft NetMeeting Software Development Kit.

Microsoft Windows Media Player

The Microsoft Windows Media Player Web site provides information about product features and benefits and supplies answers to frequently asked questions. Read the Windows Media Guide and Windows Media Showcase to learn more about Windows Media Player.

Microsoft Office

The Microsoft Office Web site is the definitive source for information about Office programs, enhancements, and product support. Also, this site provides a link to the Microsoft Office 2000 Resource Kit.

MSDN Online

The MSDN Online Web site features product and technology information for developers using Microsoft tools and applications. Find out how to bring state-of-the-art Web technology to Internet and intranet sites and learn how to author for different versions and platforms.

Microsoft Visual InterDev

The Microsoft Visual InterDev Web site provides the latest product information and tools for the Visual InterDev development environment. Find out how to build database-driven Web applications for Web platform products, Internet Explorer, and IIS.

Microsoft BackOffice

The Microsoft BackOffice Web site showcases the BackOffice family of servers, including Microsoft Internet Information Server, Index Server, and Windows Terminal Server. From this Web site, review product information about a specific BackOffice server, or visit the site's Solutions Base for comprehensive information about intranet, collaboration, and commerce solutions.

Microsoft Intranet Solutions Center

The Microsoft Intranet Solutions Center Web site contains many intranet applications, tools, and resources to help IT professionals build and manage corporate intranets. Microsoft updates this site regularly with new featured items, such as highlight articles, white papers, and case studies. This Intranet Solutions Center is also part of Microsoft TechNet, a Web site focused on the information needs of the IT community.

Microsoft Internet Services Network

The Microsoft Internet Services Network (ISN) Web site contains all the latest news and information about Microsoft Internet technologies. This Web site is a valuable resource for companies that provide Internet access, Web-hosting, and network services.

Microsoft TechNet

The Microsoft TechNet Web site is a centralized source of information for the IT community. Read about important industry topics and events, and access helpful IT resources, including an online bookstore and TechNet Reference Highlights.

Microsoft Press

The Microsoft Press Web site is the official online bookstore for Microsoft publications. Select from a comprehensive list of Internet Explorer titles, including *Microsoft Internet Explorer Technical Support Training Kit, Official Microsoft Internet Explorer Site Builder Toolkit, Microsoft Internet Explorer Step by Step,* and *Official Microsoft Internet Explorer Book.*

Glossary

address   In reference to the Internet, the name of a site that users can connect to, such as www.microsoft.com, or the address of an e-mail recipient, such as name@company.com. A typical address starts with a protocol name (such as ftp:// or http://) followed by the name of the organization that maintains the site. The suffix identifies the kind of organization. For example, commercial site addresses often end with .com.

Authenticode   A technology that makes it possible to identify who has published a piece of software and verify that it has not changed since publication.

automatic configuration   A process that enables corporate administrators to manage and update user settings for Microsoft Internet Explorer from a central location. A pointer to an automatic-configuration file can be set in the browser or by using the IEAK.

cache   An area on the hard disk that is reserved for storing images, text, and other files that have been viewed on the Internet.

CMAK (Connection Manager Administration Kit)   A tool that is used to customize the appearance and functionality of the Connection Manager, which is a client dialer.

Connection Manager   A versatile client dialer for the Internet that you can customize by using the CMAK.

corporate administrator   An individual whose responsibility is to oversee, maintain, and support computers and applications across a corporation.

DHCP (Dynamic Host Configuration Protocol)   An industry-standard TCP/IP protocol that assigns IP configurations to computers. The DHCP-server computer makes the assignments, and the client computer calls the server computer to obtain the address.

DNS (Domain Name System)   A set of guidelines and rules developed by the Internet community at large, which allows the use of words instead of complex strings of numbers to navigate the Internet.

DNS address   An address that typically contains four sets of numbers separated by dots and is different from the IP address. *Compare* IP address.

DNS server   A computer maintained by an ISP that matches IP addresses to host names. Some ISPs provide a specific DNS address.

Domain name   Name used by DNS. A domain name is the part of an e-mail address after the "@" sign.

Dynamic HTML   A collection of features that extends the capabilities of traditional HTML, giving Web authors more flexibility, design options, and creative control over the appearance and behavior of Web pages.

encryption   A method for making data indecipherable to protect it from unauthorized viewing or use.

Explorer bar   The left side of the browser where the Search, History, and Favorites lists appear when the user clicks the corresponding buttons on the toolbar. The user can also create a custom Explorer bar, as well as a custom toolbar button to open it.

gateway   A computer connected to multiple physical networks, capable of routing or delivering packets between them.

home page   The main page of a Web site. The home page usually contains a main menu or table of contents containing links to other pages within the site. For Macintosh users, the home page is also the first page they see when they start Internet Explorer (Windows users see the "start page").

HTML (Hypertext Markup Language)   The language used to create and design Web pages. HTML is a set of tags that Web authors use to create page layout, format text, insert graphics and multimedia, and more.

HTTP (Hypertext Transfer Protocol)   A protocol that makes hypertext information such as Web pages available over the Internet when a browser is connected to an appropriate server.

ICP (Internet content provider)   An organization that prepares content for posting on the Web.

IEAK (Internet Explorer Administration Kit)   A set of tools that enables corporate administrators, ISPs, and ICPs to customize and deploy Internet Explorer. It contains the Internet Explorer Customization wizard, the CMAK, the IEAK Profile Manager, and the IEAK Toolkit.

IETF (Internet Engineering Task Force)   IETF is a consortium that monitors the adoption of new technology for the Internet. IETF specifications are released in Requests for Comments.

IMAP (Internet Message Access Protocol)   A popular protocol for receiving e-mail messages. It allows an e-mail client to access and manipulate a remote e-mail file without downloading it to the local computer. It is used mainly by corporate users who want to read their e-mail from a remote location. *Compare* POP3.

IMAP server   A server that uses IMAP to provide access to multiple server-side folders. *Compare* POP3 server.

.inf file (information file)   A file that provides Windows Update Setup for Internet Explorer 5 and Internet Tools with the information required to set up a device or program. The file includes a list of valid configurations, the name of driver files associated with the device or program, and so on.

IP address (Internet Protocol address)   The numeric address of a computer. Some ISPs provide users with the IP address of their server. Users who are not sure about whether they need to enter an IP address should contact their provider. *Compare* DNS address.

ISDN (Integrated Services Digital Networking)   A worldwide digital-communication networking system, which is available from most telephone companies. ISDN is used for high-speed communication with the Internet, commercial online services, or corporate networks.

ISP (Internet service provider)   An organization that maintains a server directly connected to the Internet. Users who are not directly connected to the Internet typically connect through a service provider. To acquire these connections, users call the provider and set up an account.

LDAP (Lightweight Directory Access Protocol)   An open standard for storing and retrieving people's names, e-mail addresses, phone numbers, and other information.

MIME (Multipurpose Internet Mail Extensions)   A standard that extends SMTP to allow the transmission of such data as video, sound, and binary files across the Internet without translating it into ASCII format.

name resolution   The process used on the network for resolving a computer address as a computer name. Name resolution enables computers to find and connect to other computers on the network.

NNTP (Network News Transfer Protocol)   The protocol used to distribute network news messages to associated servers and clients (news readers) on the Internet.

PICS (Parental Internet Content Selection)   Rules that enable Web content providers to use meta tags to voluntarily rate their content according to agreed-upon PICS criteria. Browsers can then block user access to Web sites based on the values of the tags.

POP3 (Post Office Protocol 3)   A popular protocol used for receiving e-mail messages. This protocol is often used by ISPs. POP3 servers allow access to a single Inbox in contrast to IMAP servers, which provide access to multiple server-side folders. *Compare* IMAP.

POP3 server   A server that provides access to a single Inbox. *Compare* IMAP server.

proxy server   A server that works as a barrier between an internal network (intranet) and the Internet. Proxy servers can work with firewalls, which help keep other people on the Internet from gaining access to confidential information on the intranet. A proxy server also allows the caching of Web pages for quicker retrieval.

registry   The database repository for information about a computer's configuration. The registry supersedes the use of initialization (.ini) files for those systems that store and retrieve values in the registry.

registry key   An identifier for a record or group of records in the registry.

RAS (Remote Access Service)   A service that provides remote networking for telecommuters, mobile workers, and system administrators who monitor and manage servers.

search page   The page that users see when they click the **Search** button on the Internet Explorer toolbar. The search programs that can be used for the page vary depending on the selected ISP. A search page provides an organized way to find and go to other Internet sites. Many search pages provide different searching capabilities, such as the ability to search by topic or by keyword. Search pages can also have well-organized lists of links to other selected Internet sites.

SSL (Secure Sockets Layer)   A protocol that supplies secure data communication through data encryption and decryption. This protocol enables communications privacy over networks through a combination of public-key cryptography and bulk data encryption.

security zone   In Internet Explorer, a segment of the Internet or intranet assigned a particular level of security.

SMTP (Simple Mail Transfer Protocol)   A protocol used for transferring or sending e-mail messages between servers. Another protocol (such as POP3) is used to retrieve the messages.

system policies   Settings that allow an administrator to override local registry values for user or computer settings.

TCP/IP (Transmission Control Protocol/Internet Protocol)   A suite of communication protocols that allow computers to talk to each other.

WINS (Windows Internet Name Service)   A name resolution service that resolves Windows networking computer names to IP addresses in a routed environment. A server using this service handles name registrations, queries and releases.

Index

B

X

Microsoft Press Resource Kits— powerhouse resources to minimize costs while maximizing performance

Microsoft® Windows NT® Server 4.0 Resource Kit
ISBN   1-57231-344-7
U.S.A. $149.95
U.K.   £140.99 [V.A.T. included]
Canada $199.95

Microsoft Windows NT Workstation 4.0 Resource Kit
ISBN   1-57231-343-9
U.S.A. $69.95
U.K.   £64.99 [V.A.T. included]
Canada $94.95

Microsoft Internet Information Server Resource Kit
ISBN   1-57231-638-1
U.S.A. $49.99
U.K.   £46.99 [V.A.T. included]
Canada $71.99

Microsoft Windows® 98 Resource Kit
ISBN   1-57231-644-6
U.S.A. $69.99
U.K.   £64.99 [V.A.T. included]
Canada $100.99

Microsoft Internet Explorer Resource Kit
ISBN   1-57231-842-2
U.S.A. $49.99
U.K.   £46.99 [V.A.T. included]
Canada $71.99

Microsoft BackOffice® Resource Kit, Second Edition
ISBN   1-57231-632-2
U.S.A. $199.99
U.K.   £187.99 [V.A.T. included]
Canada $289.99

Direct from the Microsoft product groups, the resources packed into these bestselling kits meet the demand for hardcore use-now tools and information for the IT professional. Each kit contains precise technical reference, essential utilities, installation and rollout tactics, planning guides, and upgrade strategies. Use them to save time, reduce cost of ownership, and maximize your organization's technology investment.

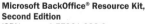

mspress.microsoft.com

Microsoft Press® products are available worldwide wherever quality computer books are sold. For more information, contact your book or computer retailer, software reseller, or local Microsoft Sales Office, or visit our Web site at mspress.microsoft.com. To locate your nearest source for Microsoft Press products, or to order directly, call 1-800-MSPRESS in the U.S. (in Canada, call 1-800-268-2222).

Prices and availability dates are subject to change.

http://mspress.microsoft.com/reslink/

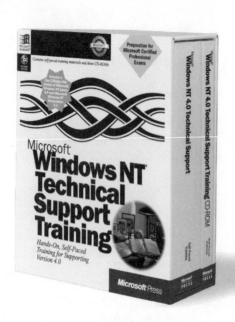

ResourceLink—your online IT library!

Access the full line of Microsoft Press® Resource Kits for the Windows® and BackOffice® families, along with MCSE Training Kits and other IT-specific resources at mspress.microsoft.com/reslink/. Microsoft Press ResourceLink is the essential online information service for IT professionals. Get the latest technical updates, support alerts, insider tips, and downloadable utilities—direct from Microsoft. If you evaluate, deploy, or support Microsoft® technologies and products, the information you need to optimize their performance—and your own—is online and ready for work at ResourceLink.

For a complimentary 30-day trial CD packed with Microsoft Press
IT products, order through our Web site: mspress.microsoft.com/reslink/

mspress.microsoft.com

MICROSOFT LICENSE AGREEMENT

Book Companion CD

IMPORTANT—READ CAREFULLY: This Microsoft End-User License Agreement ("EULA") is a legal agreement between you (either an individual or an entity) and Microsoft Corporation for the Microsoft product identified above, which includes computer software and may include associated media, printed materials, and "on-line" or electronic documentation ("SOFTWARE PRODUCT"). Any component included within the SOFTWARE PRODUCT that is accompanied by a separate End-User License Agreement shall be governed by such agreement and not the terms set forth below. By installing, copying, or otherwise using the SOFTWARE PRODUCT, you agree to be bound by the terms of this EULA. If you do not agree to the terms of this EULA, you are not authorized to install, copy, or otherwise use the SOFTWARE PRODUCT; you may, however, return the SOFTWARE PRODUCT, along with all printed materials and other items that form a part of the Microsoft product that includes the SOFTWARE PRODUCT, to the place you obtained them for a full refund.

SOFTWARE PRODUCT LICENSE

The SOFTWARE PRODUCT is protected by United States copyright laws and international copyright treaties, as well as other intellectual property laws and treaties. The SOFTWARE PRODUCT is licensed, not sold.

1. **GRANT OF LICENSE.** This EULA grants you the following rights:
    a. **Software Product.** You may install and use one copy of the SOFTWARE PRODUCT on a single computer. The primary user of the computer on which the SOFTWARE PRODUCT is installed may make a second copy for his or her exclusive use on a portable computer.
    b. **Storage/Network Use.** You may also store or install a copy of the SOFTWARE PRODUCT on a storage device, such as a network server, used only to install or run the SOFTWARE PRODUCT on your other computers over an internal network; however, you must acquire and dedicate a license for each separate computer on which the SOFTWARE PRODUCT is installed or run from the storage device. A license for the SOFTWARE PRODUCT may not be shared or used concurrently on different computers.
    c. **License Pak.** If you have acquired this EULA in a Microsoft License Pak, you may make the number of additional copies of the computer software portion of the SOFTWARE PRODUCT authorized on the printed copy of this EULA, and you may use each copy in the manner specified above. You are also entitled to make a corresponding number of secondary copies for portable computer use as specified above.
    d. **Sample Code.** Solely with respect to portions, if any, of the SOFTWARE PRODUCT that are identified within the SOFTWARE PRODUCT as sample code (the "SAMPLE CODE"):
        i. **Use and Modification.** Microsoft grants you the right to use and modify the source code version of the SAMPLE CODE, *provided* you comply with subsection (d)(iii) below. You may not distribute the SAMPLE CODE, or any modified version of the SAMPLE CODE, in source code form.
        ii. **Redistributable Files.** Provided you comply with subsection (d)(iii) below, Microsoft grants you a nonexclusive, royalty-free right to reproduce and distribute the object code version of the SAMPLE CODE and of any modified SAMPLE CODE, other than SAMPLE CODE (or any modified version thereof) designated as not redistributable in the Readme file that forms a part of the SOFTWARE PRODUCT (the "Non-Redistributable Sample Code"). All SAMPLE CODE other than the Non-Redistributable Sample Code is collectively referred to as the "REDISTRIBUTABLES."
        iii. **Redistribution Requirements.** If you redistribute the REDISTRIBUTABLES, you agree to: (i) distribute the REDISTRIBUTABLES in object code form only in conjunction with and as a part of your software application product; (ii) not use Microsoft's name, logo, or trademarks to market your software application product; (iii) include a valid copyright notice on your software application product; (iv) indemnify, hold harmless, and defend Microsoft from and against any claims or lawsuits, including attorney's fees, that arise or result from the use or distribution of your software application product; and (v) not permit further distribution of the REDISTRIBUTABLES by your end user. Contact Microsoft for the applicable royalties due and other licensing terms for all other uses and/or distribution of the REDISTRIBUTABLES.

2. **DESCRIPTION OF OTHER RIGHTS AND LIMITATIONS.**
    - **Limitations on Reverse Engineering, Decompilation, and Disassembly.** You may not reverse engineer, decompile, or disassemble the SOFTWARE PRODUCT, except and only to the extent that such activity is expressly permitted by applicable law notwithstanding this limitation.
    - **Separation of Components.** The SOFTWARE PRODUCT is licensed as a single product. Its component parts may not be separated for use on more than one computer.
    - **Rental.** You may not rent, lease, or lend the SOFTWARE PRODUCT.
    - **Support Services.** Microsoft may, but is not obligated to, provide you with support services related to the SOFTWARE PRODUCT ("Support Services"). Use of Support Services is governed by the Microsoft policies and programs described in the user manual, in "on-line" documentation, and/or in other Microsoft-provided materials. Any supplemental software code provided to you as part of the Support Services shall be considered part of the SOFTWARE PRODUCT and subject to the terms and conditions of this EULA. With respect to technical information you provide to Microsoft as part of the Support Services, Microsoft may use such information for its business purposes, including for product support and development. Microsoft will not utilize such technical information in a form that personally identifies you.
    - **Software Transfer.** You may permanently transfer all of your rights under this EULA, provided you retain no copies, you transfer all of the SOFTWARE PRODUCT (including all component parts, the media and printed materials, any upgrades, this EULA, and, if applicable, the Certificate of Authenticity), **and** the recipient agrees to the terms of this EULA.

- **Termination.** Without prejudice to any other rights, Microsoft may terminate this EULA if you fail to comply with the terms and conditions of this EULA. In such event, you must destroy all copies of the SOFTWARE PRODUCT and all of its component parts.

3. **COPYRIGHT.** All title and copyrights in and to the SOFTWARE PRODUCT (including but not limited to any images, photographs, animations, video, audio, music, text, SAMPLE CODE, REDISTRIBUTABLES, and "applets" incorporated into the SOFTWARE PRODUCT) and any copies of the SOFTWARE PRODUCT are owned by Microsoft or its suppliers. The SOFTWARE PRODUCT is protected by copyright laws and international treaty provisions. Therefore, you must treat the SOFTWARE PRODUCT like any other copyrighted material **except** that you may install the SOFTWARE PRODUCT on a single computer provided you keep the original solely for backup or archival purposes. You may not copy the printed materials accompanying the SOFTWARE PRODUCT.

4. **U.S. GOVERNMENT RESTRICTED RIGHTS.** The SOFTWARE PRODUCT and documentation are provided with RE-STRICTED RIGHTS. Use, duplication, or disclosure by the Government is subject to restrictions as set forth in subparagraph (c)(1)(ii) of the Rights in Technical Data and Computer Software clause at DFARS 252.227-7013 or subparagraphs (c)(1) and (2) of the Commercial Computer Software—Restricted Rights at 48 CFR 52.227-19, as applicable. Manufacturer is Microsoft Corporation/One Microsoft Way/Redmond, WA 98052-6399.

5. **EXPORT RESTRICTIONS.** You agree that you will not export or re-export the SOFTWARE PRODUCT, any part thereof, or any process or service that is the direct product of the SOFTWARE PRODUCT (the foregoing collectively referred to as the "Restricted Components"), to any country, person, entity, or end user subject to U.S. export restrictions. You specifically agree not to export or re-export any of the Restricted Components (i) to any country to which the U.S. has embargoed or restricted the export of goods or services, which currently include, but are not necessarily limited to, Cuba, Iran, Iraq, Libya, North Korea, Sudan, and Syria, or to any national of any such country, wherever located, who intends to transmit or transport the Restricted Components back to such country; (ii) to any end user who you know or have reason to know will utilize the Restricted Components in the design, development, or production of nuclear, chemical, or biological weapons; or (iii) to any end user who has been prohibited from participating in U.S. export transactions by any federal agency of the U.S. government. You warrant and represent that neither the BXA nor any other U.S. federal agency has suspended, revoked, or denied your export privileges.

6. **NOTE ON JAVA SUPPORT.** THE SOFTWARE PRODUCT MAY CONTAIN SUPPORT FOR PROGRAMS WRITTEN IN JAVA. JAVA TECHNOLOGY IS NOT FAULT TOLERANT AND IS NOT DESIGNED, MANUFACTURED, OR INTENDED FOR USE OR RESALE AS ON-LINE CONTROL EQUIPMENT IN HAZARDOUS ENVIRONMENTS REQUIRING FAIL-SAFE PERFOR-MANCE, SUCH AS IN THE OPERATION OF NUCLEAR FACILITIES, AIRCRAFT NAVIGATION OR COMMUNICATION SYSTEMS, AIR TRAFFIC CONTROL, DIRECT LIFE SUPPORT MACHINES, OR WEAPONS SYSTEMS, IN WHICH THE FAILURE OF JAVA TECHNOLOGY COULD LEAD DIRECTLY TO DEATH, PERSONAL INJURY, OR SEVERE PHYSICAL OR ENVIRONMENTAL DAMAGE. SUN MICROSYSTEMS, INC. HAS CONTRACTUALLY OBLIGATED MICROSOFT TO MAKE THIS DISCLAIMER.

DISCLAIMER OF WARRANTY

NO WARRANTIES OR CONDITIONS. MICROSOFT EXPRESSLY DISCLAIMS ANY WARRANTY OR CONDITION FOR THE SOFTWARE PRODUCT. THE SOFTWARE PRODUCT AND ANY RELATED DOCUMENTATION IS PROVIDED "AS IS" WITHOUT WARRANTY OR CONDITION OF ANY KIND, EITHER EXPRESS OR IMPLIED, INCLUDING, WITHOUT LIMITATION, THE IMPLIED WARRANTIES OF MERCHANTABILITY, FITNESS FOR A PARTICULAR PURPOSE, OR NONINFRINGEMENT. THE ENTIRE RISK ARISING OUT OF USE OR PERFORMANCE OF THE SOFTWARE PRODUCT REMAINS WITH YOU.

LIMITATION OF LIABILITY. TO THE MAXIMUM EXTENT PERMITTED BY APPLICABLE LAW, IN NO EVENT SHALL MICROSOFT OR ITS SUPPLIERS BE LIABLE FOR ANY SPECIAL, INCIDENTAL, INDIRECT, OR CONSEQUENTIAL DAMAGES WHATSOEVER (INCLUDING, WITHOUT LIMITATION, DAMAGES FOR LOSS OF BUSINESS PROFITS, BUSINESS INTERRUP-TION, LOSS OF BUSINESS INFORMATION, OR ANY OTHER PECUNIARY LOSS) ARISING OUT OF THE USE OF OR INABILITY TO USE THE SOFTWARE PRODUCT OR THE PROVISION OF OR FAILURE TO PROVIDE SUPPORT SERVICES, EVEN IF MICROSOFT HAS BEEN ADVISED OF THE POSSIBILITY OF SUCH DAMAGES. IN ANY CASE, MICROSOFT'S ENTIRE LIABIL-ITY UNDER ANY PROVISION OF THIS EULA SHALL BE LIMITED TO THE GREATER OF THE AMOUNT ACTUALLY PAID BY YOU FOR THE SOFTWARE PRODUCT OR US$5.00; PROVIDED, HOWEVER, IF YOU HAVE ENTERED INTO A MICROSOFT SUPPORT SERVICES AGREEMENT, MICROSOFT'S ENTIRE LIABILITY REGARDING SUPPORT SERVICES SHALL BE GOV-ERNED BY THE TERMS OF THAT AGREEMENT. BECAUSE SOME STATES AND JURISDICTIONS DO NOT ALLOW THE EXCLUSION OR LIMITATION OF LIABILITY, THE ABOVE LIMITATION MAY NOT APPLY TO YOU.

MISCELLANEOUS

This EULA is governed by the laws of the State of Washington USA, except and only to the extent that applicable law mandates governing law of a different jurisdiction.

Should you have any questions concerning this EULA, or if you desire to contact Microsoft for any reason, please contact the Microsoft subsidiary serving your country, or write: Microsoft Sales Information Center/One Microsoft Way/Redmond, WA 98052-6399.

Register Today!

Return this
Microsoft® Windows® Internet Explorer 5 Resource Kit
registration card today

Microsoft Press
mspress.microsoft.com

OWNER REGISTRATION CARD   0-7356-0587-4

Microsoft® Windows® Internet Explorer 5 Resource Kit

FIRST NAME   MIDDLE INITIAL   LAST NAME

INSTITUTION OR COMPANY NAME

ADDRESS

CITY   STATE   ZIP

                                                    (   )
E-MAIL ADDRESS   PHONE NUMBER

U.S. and Canada addresses only. Fill in information above and mail postage-free.
Please mail only the bottom half of this page.

For information about Microsoft Press®
products, visit our Web site at
mspress.microsoft.com

Microsoft Press